D0871908

Broken Landscape

Broken Landscape

Indians, Indian Tribes, and the Constitution

FRANK POMMERSHEIM

OXFORD
UNIVERSITY PRESS
2009

OXFORD
UNIVERSITY PRESS

Oxford University Press, Inc., publishes works that further
Oxford University's objective of excellence
in research, scholarship, and education.

Oxford   New York
Auckland   Cape Town   Dar es Salaam   Hong Kong   Karachi
Kuala Lumpur   Madrid   Melbourne   Mexico City   Nairobi
New Delhi   Shanghai   Taipei   Toronto

With offices in
Argentina   Austria   Brazil   Chile   Czech Republic   France   Greece
Guatemala   Hungary   Italy   Japan   Poland   Portugal   Singapore
South Korea   Switzerland   Thailand   Turkey   Ukraine   Vietnam

Copyright © 2009 by Frank Pommersheim

Published by Oxford University Press, Inc.
198 Madison Avenue, New York, New York 10016

www.oup.com

Oxford is a registered trademark of Oxford University Press

Library of Congress Cataloging-in-Publication Data
Pommersheim, Frank.
Broken landscape: Indians, Indian tribes, and the constitution /
Frank Pommersheim.
    p.   cm.
Includes index.
ISBN 978-0-19-537306-6
1. Indians of North America—Legal status, laws, etc.—History.
2. Constitutional history—United States.   3. United States. Supreme Court—
History.   4. Indians of North America—Government relations.   5. Indians of
North America—Politics and government.   6. Indians of North America—
Civil rights—History.   7. Tribal government—United States.   8. Sovereignty.   I. Title.
KF8205.P636 2009
342.7308'72—dc22   2008046841

9 8 7 6 5 4 3 2 1

Printed in the United States of America
on acid-free paper

for Vine (1933–2005) and Sam Deloria
Commitment, Challenge, Humor

But I'm not going to let you know how scared I sometimes
get of history and its ways. I'm a strong man, and I know that
silence is the best way of dealing with white folks.
Sherman Alexie, *What You Pawn I Will Redeem*

"That past is a long way off, Mamma."
"It's there, though."
"So is the future there. And that is ours."
William Trevor, *At Olivehill*

Indian people have often felt we have had no part in history—
American history in general and U.S. history in particular.
Because Indians were alienated from history. Because Indians
didn't matter. That was the feeling. We felt pushed away.
Purposely. Intentionally. Deliberately.
Simon J. Ortiz, *Sand Creek*

Acknowledgments

A SPECIAL, SPECIAL THANKS TO MY LONG-TERM SECRETARY, TERESA CARLISLE, who typed the entire manuscript from beginning to end from my *handwritten* draft. Way out west, we work hard and stick to our neo-Luddite roots. And of course, abiding gratitude to my research assistants, Kaci Schroeder, Leonika Charging, Jeff Fransen, Jeff Connolly, Blair Lawhon, Melissa Bates, and Alex Hagen, for their indefatigable efforts to tame many wild and elusive footnotes. Finally, a nod to the support of a steadfast dean, Barry Vickrey, and continuing grants from the University of South Dakota Law School Foundation.

This work of scholarship is also significantly indebted, beyond conventional acknowledgment, to the generosity and friendship of many colleagues within the field of Indian law and tribal justice systems throughout Indian country for the past quarter century. It has been fifteen years since *Braid of Feathers*, and while there has been much advance, many challenges remain. *Broken Landscape* seeks to explain what has happened and to propose a potential course for the future. And also, my family—Anne Dunham and our children, Nicholas, Kate, and Hannah (all adults now!); without them, nothing is possible.

Contents

Part One: The Early Encounter

1. Introduction: A New Challenge to Old Assumptions, 3

2. Early Contact: From Colonial Encounters to the Articles
   of Confederation, 9

3. Second Opportunity: The Structure and Architecture
   of the Constitution, 33

4. The Marshall Trilogy: Foundational but Not
   Fully Constitutional?, 87

5. *Lone Wolf v. Hitchcock*: The Birth of Plenary Power, Incorporation,
   and an Extraconstitutional Regime, 125

Part Two: Individual Indians and the Constitution

6. *Elk v. Wilkins*: Exclusion, Inclusion, and the Ambiguities
   of Citizenship, 155

7. Indians and the First Amendment: The Illusion of Religious
   Freedom?, 183

Part Three: The Modern Encounter

8. Indian Law Jurisprudence in the Modern Era: A Common
   Law Approach without Constitutional Principle, 211

9. International Law Perspective: A New Model of Indigenous
Nation Sovereignty?, 259

10. Conclusion: Imagination, Translation, and Constitutional
Convergence, 295

Notes, 313
Index, 407

PART I

The Early Encounter

I

Introduction

A New Challenge to Old Assumptions

THE INDIAN NATIONS[1] WERE HERE FIRST. THEN MUCH LATER CAME FOREIGN settlers from a continent across the ocean. The primary objectives of the settlers were trade and land acquisition. The principal means of interaction between the Colonies and Indian tribes were diplomacy and war. Diplomacy most often manifested itself in the signing of treaties as (binding) agreements between sovereigns. After the Revolutionary War, the United States became the successor nation to the European colonialist states. In 1787, the young United States adopted its constitution and formalized its relationship with Indian tribes and Indian people through treaty making, the Indian Commerce Clause, and the provision to exclude "Indians not taxed" from citizenship and enumeration in determining the number of representatives each state was entitled to receive.[2] The continuing diplomatic encounter resulted in the signing of more than 350 treaties—many of which were subsequently broken or disregarded. The wars, too, were many and varied. These experiences of diplomacy (manifested most often in matters of commerce and land acquisition) and war were the prime result of "contact" between these quite different societies. These encounters were transacted through governmental interaction, which itself was refracted through the lens of cultural difference.

These various and multiple encounters are best analyzed through the lenses of four primary themes, namely, commerce and land acquisition, diplomacy and war, cultural difference, and physical separation. These themes, in ways both obvious and not so obvious, possess a constitutional pedigree and resonance that provide the primary angle of vision for the ensuing exploration and analysis. In this same context, there will be a sustained inquiry into the role of history in Indian law and affairs, with a particular concern for how this checkered and uneven past might illuminate the present in a new way. This history is reconsidered to advance dignity and inclusion and a possibility for progressive change, rather than disrespect, exclusion, and indifference.

In response to these early interactions, Congress (and the Executive Branch) increasingly enacted a regime of law relative to trade and settlement. This further governed relations between the federal government and the tribes, and necessarily affected relationships between the tribes and states, as well as the relationships of all three governments—federal, state, and tribal—to individual Indians. Presumably, the Supreme Court reviewed all of these efforts to ensure that they were constitutionally permissible and within the legitimate authority of Congress and the Executive Branch. This expectation of careful review—especially vaunted in our constitutional democracy—was largely unattended to and unfulfilled in the field of Indian law. The Supreme Court, without sustained rigor, routinely upheld this regime and made much of its own law to deal with matters not directly taken up by Congress or the Executive Branch. It consistently approved actions that were not constitutionally authorized, with the net effect of recklessly extending federal power in Indian affairs and impairing tribal sovereignty to a considerable degree.

Despite the fact that the Constitution explicitly recognizes tribal sovereignty in the Indian Commerce Clause and implicitly in the treaty-making power, there has been almost no in-depth constitutional exegesis that elucidates how these provisions either protect tribal sovereignty or set boundaries for federal authority in Indian affairs. Instead, these constitutional provisions have proved mostly illusory and ineffective in protecting tribal sovereignty and constraining federal power in Indian affairs. This is the regime created by the extraconstitutional plenary power doctrine that was established in the 1903 case of *Lone Wolf v. Hitchcock*.[3]

From one perspective, none of this is truly unexpected. Indian tribes were not key players as participating sovereigns in the deliberations that led to the adoption of the U.S. Constitution. Those deliberations focused almost solely on forming a national government, developing its relationship to the states, and apportioning its enumerated powers within the three branches of the federal government. The creation of a national government and an accompanying federal-state structure was the central enterprise of the Constitution's architecture. Yet the tribes were "there," if not as genuine participants, then certainly as a constitutional shadow that could not be completely ignored. In the end, tribal sovereignty was (partially) recognized within the Constitution, but without sufficient national commitment, understanding, or adequate safeguard to vouchsafe it against the tides of national expansion and exploitation.

What is truly unexpected is that in the course of the ensuing 200-plus years, there has been very little scholarly or sustained political attention to this constitutional drift. As tribal citizens have developed higher and higher expectations of their own tribal governments, a review of constitutional expectations with regard to the performance of the national government in Indian affairs has also become necessary. Tribes (and tribal people), originally outside and on the margins of the new republic, were increasingly absorbed geographically, socially, politically, and "legally" (but without their consent) into the republic without the slightest constitutional ripple. This *is* remarkable. If it took constitutional amendments to bring African Americans and women fully into the domain of dignity and equity within the Constitution,[4] isn't an equivalent effort needed to guarantee enduring tribal sovereignty and full equality to Native people and tribal nations?

This book hopes to demonstrate that the answer is yes—a *yes* fully developed and calibrated through an in-depth examination of the historical development of tribal sovereignty and well-being that has been repeatedly eclipsed and negated by the blunt force of the extraconstitutional actions of Congress and the Supreme Court. This trajectory is not without its historical moments of honor and decency, but unfortunately such moments are the exception and not the rule. Currently, tribes are most often stymied in their attempts to effectuate meaningful self-determination by the lack of adequate constitutional recognition and protection.

In examining the trajectory of tribal sovereignty within our constitutional democracy, this book includes a review of early contact during the colonial period and adoption of the Articles of Confederation, the structure and architecture of the Constitution in regard to both a federal-state federalism and a federal-tribal federalism, the foundational Indian law cases of the early Supreme Court led by John Marshall, the development of the plenary power doctrine in *Lone Wolf v. Hitchcock*,[5] and Supreme Court Indian law jurisprudence in the modern era. Along the way, I identify and discuss the various models that have described the nature of tribal sovereignty and federal power in Indian law. These models were (and are) seldom well developed and often were (and are) more political and "pragmatic" than doctrinal or constitutional. They include the foundational principles of the Marshall trilogy, the congressional plenary power doctrine, Felix Cohen's retained sovereignty model, the current Supreme Court's judicial plenary power approach, and the forward-looking idea of treaty-based federalism.

In this book, I also discuss developing benchmarks of sovereignty and respect for indigenous people and societies from the international law perspective. In addition, this text tracks the history and status of native people as individuals within this republic in the context of federal and state citizenship, as well as in continuing the struggle to secure full protection of the freedom of religion guaranteed in the First Amendment. It concludes with a discussion of the substance, process, and potential for constitutional revision and amendment.

The *yes* to constitutional reform and amendment is not a *yes* of assimilative condescension or residual colonialism, but a *yes* that builds on the treaty diplomacy of the past, a *yes* that seeks to change the landscape of (dominant) history, and a *yes* that seeks to translate the promises of the past into permanent guarantees for the future. This *yes* is grounded in partnership, dignity, and respect— not an easy *yes* but the *yes* of hard work and dialogue—and a *yes* that brings (constitutional) sunlight where there has only been shadow. A *yes* whose very contours will (hopefully) emerge from sustained discussion and engagement. A *yes* that also realizes the need for much doctrinal change and political reform as a necessary prelude to any constitutional revision concerning the status of tribal sovereignty. And finally, it is a *yes* committed to developing a constitutional architecture that is fully inclusive yet respectful of differences within the weave of historical and cultural pluralism.

This book is intended for all readers, including people far and wide, in and out of Indian country, law students, dear (and inspiring) colleagues and practitioners in the Indian law community, and also interested and dedicated scholars in fields outside Indian law, such as constitutional law and federal courts, who have largely ignored the concerns raised here.[6] Without enhanced Indian law literacy and sustained and wider engagement with its challenges, the goal of respect and constitutional dignity and inclusion will continue to remain fugitive for those who were here first. The book, then, is also meant to confront this most unfortunate legacy of ignorance and exclusion.

Although this book is clearly meant to stand on its own as an independent endeavor, it is, in many ways, a natural companion to my earlier book *Braid of Feathers*.[7] *Braid of Feathers* focused on presenting an inside-out, reservation-based view of Indian law with a particular emphasis on tribal institutions and aspirations. The focus here is more on an outside-in complementary view that strives to demonstrate how so much has gone wrong within the field of Indian law at the national level because of Congress and the Supreme Court's continuing failure to identify a satisfactory constitutional basis from which to proceed. Finally, there is an optimism that this constitutional failure might yet be corrected with the development of a new constitutional mooring that constrains excessive federal (and state) authority in Indian affairs, while guaranteeing a meaningful and enduring tribal sovereignty.

Such an effort is particularly necessary at this moment in time because tribes are more actively committed to *actualizing* their sovereignty than ever before in the modern era. They are engaging in significant economic development, enacting laws and developing tribal legal institutions, protecting their cultural heritage, and increasingly engaging in legal encounters with the states and federal government. These wide-ranging efforts are unlikely to flourish in the dependent and depleted doctrinal soil that currently covers the field of Indian law. Much of this effort is at risk unless there is sure constitutional grounding for Indian nations. The federal government and the states consistently rely on a constitutional assurance that underpins and guides their activities. Tribes require and deserve a similar constitutional assurance.

All of this is unexpectedly yoked to larger efforts and findings in other disciplines, including archaeology, anthropology, ecology, and history, that have identified a larger, wider, and more significant Native presence in the Americas prior to 1491 than heretofore thought[8] and a more significant Native historical impact on the early American history that led up to the formation of the United States and the adoption and implementation of the U.S. Constitution.[9] If, as a noted biography of the Constitution indicates, "The story of America cannot be told apart from the landmass itself,"[10] it can hardly be told without reference to the first inhabitants of that "landmass." There is both a moral imperative and a historical obligation to trace the nature, effect, and reverberations of those encounters not only within the physical landscape but also within the constitutional landscape.

2

Early Contact

From Colonial Encounters to the Articles of Confederation

Colonial Encounters

The history of the united states predates the revolutionary war and the adoption of the Constitution. It is firmly rooted in the initial contact of European merchants and settlers (and their nation-states) with indigenous people and their nations. This contact was obviously unexpected in that, before the accidental meeting initiated by the exploration mishaps of Columbus and others in their search for the "Indies," neither side knew of the existence of the other.

This historically unexpected set of encounters is not very accurately described by the conventional notion of the "discovery of a new world" and is more fully captured through the use of the less charged term *contact*. More precise than notions of discovery is the acute observation that " 'Columbus did not discover a new world; he established contact between two worlds, both already old.' The word *contact* properly suggests the reciprocity of discovery that followed upon European initiatives of exploration; as surely as Europeans discovered Indians, Indians discovered Europeans."[1]

These early Indian-colonial encounters were largely related to four separate but overlapping streams of engagement: trade and land acquisition, diplomacy and war, governance, and cultural attitudes. The primary activities of commerce and land acquisition were most often mediated by diplomacy (and war) and carried out through governmental interaction. All three activities were in turn refracted through the lens of culture. All of these encounters played a role in establishing the foundation and early development of Indian law,

including its constitutional content. No adequate understanding of the dilem-
mas of contemporary Indian law is possible without some examination of these
early encounters.

The initial inquiry requires some inspection of the motivation and legal
authority that authorized and brought settlers and traders to North America in
the first place. The general legal and policy rationales that established the *formal* (as opposed to legitimate and moral) authority were fivefold: papal edict,
first *discovery*, sustained possession, voluntary self-subjection of native people,
and armed conquest.[2] Of course, these principles were transparent and self-
justifying, built on the use of force and notions of the prerogatives of *civilization* and "Christianity."[3] These various claims were nevertheless central in
developing a doctrinal footing within the Western rule of law tradition.[4]

The purpose of a colony was to extend the influence of and, more important, to generate wealth for the home country. The method that was most often
used—especially in the British context—was the process of "chartered expansion." This process generally consisted of three steps: (1) A head of state laid
claim to territory previously outside the reach of the state's government, (2) the
head of state authorized a person or an organized group by charter to conquer
the claimed territory, and (3) if the conquest was successful, the conquering
lord (whether personal or collective) became the possessor and governor of the
territory subject to the laws of the charter and acknowledged the sovereignty of
the charter issuer.[5] Such charters were thus the legal engine that brought most
of the first colonists, especially the British, to the "New World." Yet these charters, despite their legal formality, did not (and could not) describe the thick
human and cultural encounter that ensued.

The reality of any colony vis-à-vis its indigenous inhabitants was often
quite tenuous and marginal, to say the least. At first, "successful conquest"
often meant no more than survival.[6] The abstractions and rhetoric of the colonial experience that have come down to us often have had their own tyranniz-
ing effect, transforming a ramshackle past and bare survival to something
glorious and foreordained. Thus there is a need for caution and sensitivity in
discussing the dynamic and nuance of early encounter in order to avoid notions
of God's plan or manifest destiny. The colonial experience for both colonists
and Indians was fraught with change, yet it was not always clear what the role
or direction of the change was. In most instances, the trajectory went from
colonial dependence to mutual interdependence to Indian dependence. As part
of this dynamic, there also needs to be a sense of nuance about the many shades
of dependence and interdependence along the continuum of interaction, rather
than the more blatant either-or sense of independence or subjection. And as
part of this series of multicultural encounters, there were *choices* made on both

sides of the equation—choices that profoundly affected the direction, degree, and rate of change. The most significant variables in these encounters were economic, ecological, and epidemiological in nature. Their combined effect on the Native-colonist relationship was profound and completely redefined and restructured the political and legal relationships between Natives, colonists, and the land. These encounters encompassed much more than two centuries in their manifold variations.

Commerce

Commerce in the Western tradition is directed to increasing wealth and profit. Such was the purpose of establishing colonies in America pursuant to the colonial charters granted by England and other European countries. Early colonies such as Jamestown and Plymouth, for example, were funded by English merchants. The pursuit of wealth and profit was more than a private endeavor to establish personal and corporate fortune; it was also entwined with the pursuit of political dominance within the European family of nations.

Such economic growth had obvious moral consequences for the individual, but it also had moral consequences for society as a whole. This was the core of the theories that Adam Smith expounded in his classics *The Wealth of Nations* and *Moral Sentiments of Economic Growth*.[7] These works and others made the argument that such economic growth provided not only economic progress but also positive moral advance to European societies. In this Enlightenment thinking, commerce not only increased wealth but also reduced the need for war and advanced democracy, tolerance, and openness.[8]

This school of thought had both secular and religious roots, and they often formed a powerful convergence about notions of secular progress and religious deliverance. As noted by Benjamin Friedman:

> While the English Puritans and their spiritual descendants saw
> secular progress as inevitable, at the same time human effort directed
> toward bringing that progress about was a moral imperative.
> Moreover, as Max Weber famously emphasized, these early
> Reformed Protestants saw both material prosperity and the religious
> and moral higher state that they sought as desirable, and even tended
> to conflate the two. The Puritan "saints," as they called themselves,
> took it as their collective duty to reform society and thereby create the
> new Christian Commonwealth. And they also strived individually to
> achieve material prosperity.[9]

In this view, "economic prosperity was an outward sign of inward grace."[10]

Other thinkers—primarily the Romantics—did not take such a positive view of these changes. For writers such as Jean-Jacques Rousseau and Denis Diderot, Indians and their way of life were exemplary counterpoint:

> Rousseau admired what he saw as the remarkable individual
> freedom the Indians enjoyed, as well as the extraordinary degree of
> equality among a people with few material possessions and little
> formal hierarchy for governance. He therefore concluded that the
> peak of human social development had occurred shortly after the
> emergence of semipermanent settlements but before the advent of
> sustained agriculture, and therefore before the evolution of private
> property and the legal and institutional structures that notion
> entails.[11]

The experience of European monarchy, both as politically oppressive and corrupted by luxury, confirmed for Diderot and others that economic progress hindered moral development and that Indian societies were nearer to where human society began and thus were morally superior.[12] Needless to say, most Enlightenment writers failed to see that such commercial encounters with indigenous people would often have a vicious and exploitative underside and would lead to colonialism and brutal dispossession.

Throughout the period of pre-Independence America, most of eastern North America was neither English, nor French, nor Spanish territory. "It was, clearly, Indian country, and Europeans most often used the term *American* to describe descendants of the original inhabitants."[13] This change in perspective—facing east from Indian country as it were, not facing west from colonial America—provides an illuminating shift in the angle of vision, which offers an increased sense of nuance, complexity, and usable insight.

This "thickening" removes the cloak of manifest inevitability embedded in the dominant western expansion and colonizing narrative, and it suggests, rather, that human and cultural contact be viewed in such a way that "Native Americans appear in the foreground and Europeans enter from distant shores. North America becomes the 'old world' and Western Europe the 'new.'"[14] In this view,

> The continent becomes a place where diverse peoples had long
> struggled against and sometimes worked with one another, where
> societies and political systems had risen and fallen, and where these
> ancient trends continued right through the period of colonization.
> The process by which one particular group composed of newcomers

from Europe and their descendants—themselves a diverse and contentious lot—came to dominate the others becomes a much more complicated, much more interesting, much more revealing, if no less tragic, tale.[15]

Trade was the core of this encounter. It took place on several different levels and had multiple effects. Although these effects culminated in drawing Native Americans into a global economy that eventually placed most tribes in a position of growing dependence, other things happened as well. The nature of the commerce itself took many forms. Initially, many of the items from Europe that entered the stream of Native commerce were not valued as finished products but rather as raw materials to be reprocessed into recognized cultural goods. For example, iron goods such as axes were reworked into needles and awls, and copper from kettles into ornaments and jewelry.[16] Such transfers reveal Native agency and choice, not simple consumer passivity.

Yet, as such commerce expanded in volume and the range of available goods grew, many trade items

> ceased to be treated as raw materials and instead became direct replacements for traditional Native items: brass kettles for ceramic pots, iron axes for stone celts, woolen blankets for animal skins. The new things were always in some practical way superior to the old—lighter, sharper, more durable—but they were used in very familiar contexts.[17]

There were also aesthetic advances made possible by the new availability of glass beads, fine needles and thread, colorful cloth, and more intricate carving tools such as chisels and awls. Much of this new artistic potential was directed to the spiritual realm to make masks, ceremonial pipes, and sacred wampum beads.[18] Other items, such as alcohol and firearms, had more deleterious and well-known effects.

All went well while the primary trade in furs flourished, but when it declined, it had very asymmetrical effects. When European demand for furs decreased and its economic interests diversified, Europeans came to depend less and less on the fur trade, and this shift also adversely affected the political balance of power between Indian tribes and the colonies.[19] As their economic status slipped because of the change in international market forces, Indians and their tribes began to find themselves increasingly politically disadvantaged in dealing with the colonists and their colonies.

Indian participation in the fur trade was largely voluntary. They desired the available goods and probably perceived advantages in such trade. Yet despite the very real (initial) advantages, Indians were being brought into the web of developing worldwide mercantile markets that eventually created more, rather than less, dependence on commercial forces extrinsic to the face-to-face encounters that tribes relied on. The autonomy and reliability of such personal interaction was increasingly lost to impersonal market forces.[20]

Advancing trade had other effects as well. It often caused conflict among tribes as they jostled to attract the commercial favor of Europeans. "These efforts to reach out to people of alien and dangerous ways are more striking than the fact that, in the end, enmity won out over friendship."[21] Yet the multicultural changes that resulted from such efforts "to reach out" did not substantially change basic tribal values with their "emphasis on reciprocity and redistribution of goods."[22] These forces of economic change unleashed by European colonization interacted with Native American practices in such a way as to produce a "new world" that neither side envisioned nor fully understood.[23] This was a new world that created a growing Indian economic dependence on products and markets beyond their control.

These economic forces in turn produced other unforeseen changes that were largely ecological and epidemiological in nature. The fur trade, for example, caused the near extinction of many fur-bearing animals, such as beaver and kit fox. Yet the resulting ecological change was often quite intricate. With fewer or no beavers in a region, there were fewer beaver-made dams, which increased water flow and created expansive meadows. In turn, the smaller number of beaver-felled trees reduced the forage for deer, moose, and bear.[24] These changes provided beneficial haying and pasture for Europeans but reduced much of the important wildlife stock for Indian communities.

These ecological changes were especially significant because they tended to intensify the differences that already existed in how the land was used by the two different communities. In both communities, the basic concept of ownership of land was well understood, but the key difference was in the *meaning* of ownership. As the historian Daniel Richter has pointed out, the pivotal distinction was between land as a "resource" and land as a "commodity." As a resource, land could not really be owned. Instead, what was owned was the right to use the land for a particular purpose—farm, hunt, fish, gather—that was not necessarily exclusive or permanent. As a commodity, ownership included permanent and exclusive rights of usage, including nonusage.[25] Such a commodity-driven view of land was also an essential element of a nascent capitalism with its primary commitment to land as a vehicle for yielding profit.

Indian usage was also flexible and mobile. European usage—especially with domestic livestock—was more rigid and fixed and inclined to a keen sense of boundedness and boundaries.[26] This often produced a counterintuitive result, where fewer Indians needed more land than a similar number of colonists, and led to a colonial view of Indian "waste" of natural resources. In this stereotypical configuration, Indians were often seen as part of nature but not part of history, and non-Indians were seen as part of history but not part of nature. These perceptions were (and are) both inaccurate and demeaning. Nature itself is part of history. As noted by the historian William Cronon, "Our project must be to locate a nature which is within rather than without history, for only by so doing can we find human communities which are inside rather than outside nature."[27]

In early America, in Francis Jennings's telling phrase, the land was less virgin than it was widowed.[28] Indians had lived on the continent for thousands of years and had, to a significant extent, modified its environment for their purposes. The destruction of Indian communities thus brought some of the most important ecological changes that followed the European arrival in America. The choice was not between two landscapes, one with and one without a human influence; it was between two human ways of belonging to an ecosystem. In the context of "contact" between Indians and non-Indians, there were both their relationships to nature and their relationships to each other.[29] This is the historical whole. Part of this whole is also the ecological link to economic activity generally, and to capitalism in particular.

The transition to capitalism alienated the products of the land as much as the products of human labor, and so it transformed natural communities as profoundly as it did human ones. The desire to obtain nonessential goods increased the need for profit and placed increased demands on the land—which often produced adverse ecological consequences. By integrating New England ecosystems into an ultimately global capitalist economy, colonists and Indians together began an unstable process of ecological changes that continued well past 1800.[30] In the West, for example, the mid-nineteenth-century slaughter of buffalo by non-Indians bleakly paralleled this economic exploitation, transforming the natural landscape and disrupting tribal culture and economic well-being in catastrophic ways.[31] "We live with their legacy today. When the geographer Carl Sauer wrote in the twentieth century that Americans had 'not yet learned the difference between yield and loot,' he was describing one of the longest standing tendencies of their way of life. Ecological abundance and economic prodigality went hand in hand: the people of plenty were a people of waste."[32]

Indian country was also subject to the powerful material alterations caused by disease. Although the numbers cited often vary significantly, there is widespread scholarly agreement that Europeans brought to North America much disease for which Native people often had no immunity. These diseases, including smallpox, measles, and influenza, to which Europeans had already developed immunities, were most often carried by domestic livestock—cows, sheep, and pigs. Native people had not developed such immunities because they had no prior experience with domestic livestock as the colonists had.[33]

The sixteenth- and seventeenth-century swath of microbes decimated many eastern native communities, who were driven to their utmost to survive and reconstitute themselves. These losses from disease often fueled non-Indian perceptions about too much land and too few Indians. In many instances, however, such losses resulted in increased intertribal strife and the development of new cultural patterns to combat such losses. One example was that of the "mourning war" that

> required young men to raid their enemies for war captives who would be adopted, enslaved, or ritually killed to replace the loss and ease the grief of those who mourned the death of loved ones. Mourning-war raids were, on a fundamental level, an extension of the grieving process, an integral part of protracted funeral rites by which the loss of loved ones was redressed and the balance of spiritual and material forces was symbolically restored.[34]

In light of the variegated impact of those economic, ecological, and epidemiological forces, the early settlement and colonization of North America can be seen as much less inevitable and noble and rather more deeply illustrative of the ability of Native communities to resist and to survive such a powerful onslaught.

Land Acquisition

There is no doubt that as trade was exhausted and receded in importance, land acquisition came more and more to the fore. In the narrow sense, Indians were the producers of raw materials—furs and hides—that were processed into the finished products of hats and leather goods in Europe, where most of the profit was reaped. And when the demand for such finished products declined and prices plummeted, the economic and political clout of the Native producers of raw materials also declined.[35] With this decline in trade, there was a concomitant economic shift by colonists toward agriculture and increased land acquisition.

The growing colonial consensus held that economic prosperity was to be found less and less in international trade and more and more in capitalist agriculture, whether on small farms or on plantations supported by African American slave labor. This shift brought more and more immigrants to Indian country and greatly increased the pressure to acquire Indian land. To put it bluntly, trade required intercultural accommodation, but capitalist agriculture did not—and thus the pattern of accommodation began to shift more and more to enmity and hostility that focused on the acquisition of Indian land.[36]

As colonial-Indian economics shifted from trade to land acquisition, law became more visible and prominent. Although colonial-Indian commerce often proceeded with a relative absence of express law, real property transfer did not. Pressure on Indian land was not new; it was there from the beginning, especially in regard to the English colonies that formed the backbone of what would become the original states of the Union. It simply expanded and became exacerbated with the demise of the fur trade, and law became the central institution to mediate and facilitate this shift.

Despite these changes, during almost all of the colonial period, Indians and European settlers lived as "neighbors" up and down most of the Atlantic states. They adjusted to each other and for the most part lived in separate communities subject to different sovereigns. This state of affairs, however, was without lasting stability. The colonial commitment to continuous territorial expansion was a radical destabilizing force—radically destabilizing not only politically and economically but also legally. Individual property rights are creatures of a particular sovereign's law. Consequently, individual property transfers across sovereigns require some mutual understanding and (if necessary) the cross-enforcement of rights. This did *not* occur in the colonial context. Property rights were connected to jurisdiction, and without understanding or respecting the jurisdiction of the competing tribal sovereign, individual non-Indian property rights were not so reliable or safely guaranteed. In fact, this was one of the critical issues in the seminal 1823 Indian property rights case of *Johnson v. McIntosh*, which involved the issue of the legal capability of Indian tribes to transfer land to private, non-Indian purchasers without the approval of the federal government.[37]

Regardless of these problems, land transfers did occur in English colonies, but not without contradictory rationales. In one view (self-serving to be sure), property rights came in two vintages: natural and civil. According to John Winthrop, a leading colonial thinker, a "[n]atural right to the soil had existed 'when men held the earth in common with every man sowing and feeding where he pleased.'"[38] Yet this natural right could be trumped by a civil right that matured and came into being with the enclosure of land for individual crop raising and the keeping of domestic animals. Not surprisingly, Native landholding was seen as the former, not the latter, and this often meant Indian land was deemed a *vacuum domicilium* waiting to be claimed by a more productive people. If the raw power to enforce it existed, such a theory of property law became a conduit for appropriation.[39]

Yet there occasionally were non-Native voices to the contrary, especially when those non-Natives had "purchased" land directly from natives and their property rights were being challenged by other non-Natives. For example, Roger Williams of Massachusetts claimed title by direct purchase from the Indians, as opposed to the necessity of purchase directly from the English Crown with regard to the Salem settlement.[40]

More important, though almost completely ignored, was the question of how Indians understood property rights. Although there was significant variance across Indian tribes, it is reasonable to conclude that the Indian conception of property focused more on the collective (tribal) stewardship or "ownership" of property, with a system of rights for individual families (and other collectivities) to use the land for particular purposes and for particular periods of time. Such activities might include, for example, in the context of New England tribes, the right to hunt, trap, forage, and grow crops.[41]

Although such a system of property rights was similar to the notion of usufructuary rights that existed in England in earlier times, it was no longer much practiced, understood, or respected by invading Europeans. Europeans were not interested in Indian conceptions of property, only in identifying individuals with the real (or apparent) right to transfer property that would then be protected and interpreted under English (or other European) law.

As the historian William Cronon has demonstrated in his examination of early Indian land transfers in colonial New England, the Indians understood land transfers (often through "deeds") as essentially political in nature and involving the sharing of an ecological cornucopia. The English, on the other hand, understood land transactions as essentially economic in nature, involving the transfer of a valuable commodity known as land through a process identified as the right to alienate land. The legal frame of reference for interpreting the transaction was solely colonial-English law. Indian law or custom (i.e., sovereignty) was not recognized.[42]

Such land transfers reflected a paradox, if not an outright contradiction. There was interaction between two sovereigns, but the transfer was understood (at least operationally) on the colonial side in wholly instrumental terms consisting of the recognition of the authority of Indians to transfer what was wanted, but no coordinate authority to condition or to explain the transfer. There was Indian ownership but no sovereignty. On the Indian side, the concept of nonexclusive use rights did not prevent more than one transfer of individual rights by the chief or sachem. This reality set up the colonial problem of dealing with multiple transfers of the same commodity (rather than a transfer of a use right) that was never intended as such by the Indians themselves.[43]

In addition, there was the competing factor of colonial claims to ownership of land in New England based not on "purchase" from Indians but on grants from the English Crown. These transfers were rooted in the fiction of "discovery," and as the power dynamic continued to shift in favor of Europeans, most colonies relied more and more on a "title" deriving from a chartered grant from the home nation rather than on purchase from Indian occupants.[44]

This tension and developing hostility was further exacerbated with the conclusion of the French and Indian Wars, which culminated in British victory in the Seven Years' War and French withdrawal from most of eastern North America (except Canada).[45] The 1763 Treaty of Paris thus marked another turning point in Indian-colonial relations in that it greatly accelerated the demise of intercultural political alliances. The multicultural plurality of different tribes and different European peoples arranged in different cooperative and antagonistic relationships began to rapidly disappear. What had once been a complicated landscape of shifting alliances was redefined in accordance with the perception that "a far simpler, racially defined frontier line [had] popped into view."[46] The opportunity for Indians and non-Indians to continue to live parallel lives was rapidly evaporating into a historical mist that itself would soon be forgotten. The landscape of this new political reality was indeed the physical landscape itself, the relentless pursuit of land transfer.

The law of land transfer in colonial America and even early postrevolutionary America did not develop in any uniform manner. It was more or less a hodgepodge of legal and illegal approaches, all of which sought to obtain Indian land but were contingent, to a degree, on establishing the exact nature of Native property rights, the Native legal ability to transfer such rights, and to whom they might transfer such rights. Some of these manifold variations involved the rights of Indians to make sales to private individuals, to make sales directly to the colonies (and early states), and to make sales and transfers directly to the Crown (and the federal government). All of these sale or transfer possibilities hinged on legal recognition of what, if anything, Native people had the right to transfer and which sovereign had the authority to regulate and enforce the transfer.

In colonial America no uniform legal regime emerged. Private individuals—including land speculation syndicates—"purchased" and recorded land transfers directly from Indians, including groups of Indians and tribes. Many colonies claimed title to Indian land through their charters from the Crown and thus asserted sole authority to deal with Indians and their land. Sometimes the Crown itself claimed these prerogatives and took the position that the colonies had no authority over or ownership of Indian land except as *expressly* delegated by the Crown. The doctrine of "discovery" hovered everywhere in the background. Indian conceptions of their property rights were even further in the shadows. All of this was even more complicated by the problem of determining which Indian transfers were voluntary, which were involuntary, and what difference (if any) it made.

The first major Crown attempt to bring some order to this chaos was the Royal Proclamation of 1763. After the French and Indian Wars concluded with the Treaty of Paris of the same year, land speculation by private syndicates came to the fore, and the British Crown—temporarily free of war with France and most Indians—decided to end it. The Proclamation of 1763 was one of the major events of British imperial history:

> It included important changes in colonial policy in several areas related only tangentially to Indian land purchasing: It established governments for the various territories newly conquered from France; it authorized colonial governors to grant free land to all the soldiers who had fought in the war; and it set up a uniform system of licensing for the Indian trade. But the most fundamental of the changes instituted in 1763 was the complete overhaul of the process of acquiring Indian land.[47]

In the area of land transfers, the proclamation drew a line down the middle of the continent and prohibited new land grants and settlement west of the line. This was largely to achieve peace with Indians, who increasingly felt like prey being hunted and driven from their homeland by non-Indians. The net effect of the proclamation was the complete reorganization of Indian land purchasing:

> Before 1763, land was often purchased in private, far to the west of any English town, by individual English buyers, from individual Indian sellers. After 1763, land could be lawfully purchased only out in the open, only by English units of government, only from Indian units of government, and only east of the mountains, closer to English towns. The Proclamation of 1763 was a genuine effort by the imperial government, in the wake of recurring wars against Indian tribes north and south, to remove the major cause of Indian dissatisfaction with English settlement.[48]

This general practice was continued by individual states after the Revolutionary War and was one of the first laws enacted by Congress in 1790. As part of the Non-Intercourse Act, it was established that the federal government possessed the exclusive right to purchase land from Indians and to approve the purchase of Indian lands by others, including the states. These developments moved the purchase of Indian land away from the notion of contract, involving essentially private transactions, to one of treaty, involving transactions overseen by sovereigns.[49]

These new laws did not exactly halt all private land transactions with Indians. Some thought the proclamation was of no legal effect and certainly not binding on the United States as the successor to the Crown. Others were not sure of the validity of any of the early patchwork legal regime created before and immediately after the formation of the United States. None of this would ultimately be resolved until the U.S. Supreme Court decided the seminal Indian law property case of *Johnson v. McIntosh* in 1823.[50]

The Revolutionary War itself provided the final opportunity for many eastern tribes to make an alliance by choosing allegiance with the colonies or with the British. Many tribes chose to side with the British because they believed that England would be more respectful of their property rights than the increasingly aggressive colonies. Yet the war went the other way, and most tribes were left standing on the wrong side of history. In the 1783 Treaty of Paris, Crown negotiators did nothing to protect the property rights of their Indian allies. The tribes were simply betrayed and abandoned.

In sum, the colonial approach to obtaining Indian land was opportunistic and contradictory. When Indians were willing to engage in land transfers, they were understood to have sufficient rights of ownership to sell, but they were not understood to have sufficient sovereignty to create any legal framework to regulate or interpret the terms of "sale." What was transferred in such sales was inventoried, defined, and incorporated within the property law principles of the colonial purchaser, which, not surprisingly, maximized the rights of the purchaser and ignored the rights (except the right of sale itself) of the "seller."[51]

If the Indians did not want to "sell," this was not necessarily a bar to obtaining Indian land. The doctrine of "discovery" was available to say that the Crown could claim such land because Indians did not "own" it, on account of the fact that they were non-Christians who lacked "civilization." In turn, the Crown could transfer the land to the colonies, and the colonies could transfer land to individual colonists. Sometimes colonies claimed an independent right of discovery to Indian land and the right to purchase or transfer it without Crown authorization. Mix this with the Indian concept of transferring nonexclusive use rights to more than one party, and there emerged a scheme of property law that was racist, contradictory, disordered, and confusing. This fractious taxonomy became the legacy that the newly formed republic of the United States would have to confront.

The haphazard colonial approach to land acquisition did not endure. After the formation of the republic in 1789, the primary vehicle for land acquisition became treaties. In *Johnson v. McIntosh*, the Supreme Court articulated the doctrine of discovery, which, among other things, foreclosed the ability of

Indian tribes and individual Indians to sell or transfer title to land to anyone *except* the federal government.[52]

Although the doctrine of discovery placed title to Indian land in the federal government, the remaining tribal property rights of use and occupancy could be obtained only through purchase or a just war. The primary legal vehicle for purchase was the act of entering into treaties. Treaties themselves varied significantly in their degree of mutuality and the relative power of the parties. The poles of this variance might be thought of as conquest and contract.[53] Treaties are thus about both law and power, and most land transactions with Indians took place in the middle ground where "Indians were not exactly conquered, but they did not exactly choose to sell their land title."[54] This often rough, sovereign-to-sovereign tumble was always mediated by law—a law that ultimately contained more and more power over Indians, but also established a framework to constrain the excesses of non-Indians.[55]

Governance

If the colonial goals were commerce and land acquisition and the Indian goals were commerce and the regulation of land usage, these goals were mediated through systems of governance. Systems of governance were often only dimly understood and were easily misunderstood on both sides. Such original misunderstanding and its contemporary legacy remain a significant cause of many ongoing issues within contemporary Indian law.

Colonial governance, not surprisingly, mirrored the rule of the home country in Europe. Colonial charters were essentially feudal in nature. They were issued directly from the king, and the chartered entity, whether personal or corporate, was directly responsible to the king rather than to Parliament. More practically, the local population was subject to rule of the "lord" or recipient of the charter, and as a necessary corollary, it was the local colonial officials who dealt directly with resident Indians. In fact, this feudal-like arrangement germinated the seeds of the American Revolution when Parliament sought to exercise internal control over the colonies in such matters as taxation, along with increasing royal encroachment on colonial self-government.[56]

The colonies generally lacked sufficient population or firepower to overwhelm local Indians and generally adopted two attendant strategies. The first attempt was to bring Indians within the feudal lord-vassal orbit.[57] Obviously, this was not attractive to native people and was largely unenforceable as well. The second way was to interact directly with tribal governing authorities. Yet this presented a twofold problem for the colonies: (1) squaring their rhetoric that tribes were insufficiently developed to have functioning governments and (2) when it was necessary to displace the rhetorical cant, the problem of discerning and identifying the structure and leadership of tribal government.[58]

This colonial confusion had several sources. One was the cultural inability to identify any kind of functioning tribal government that did not mirror the European model of monarchy and a developing, bureaucratic state. Another was the contradiction wrought by power and racism. As noted by the historian Francis Jennings, "The ideology of power produces many contradictions; Europeans' pronouncements that Indians had no government were contradicted by their practice of dealing with Indian chiefs through the protocol of diplomacy with sovereign states."[59]

Tribal governments in the New England region were largely decentralized and approximated a model known as a "kinship state," which functioned as "a community of families and clans in which some of the ordering functions of society are performed by the kin groups individually while others are assigned to officers and councilors chosen cooperatively."[60] In such contexts, tribal "kings" were not so easy to identify.

Despite such misperceptions, the key point of political interaction in these contexts was treaty making, where diplomatic necessity displaced (at least temporarily) cultural ignorance and racial animus. Yet this diplomatic necessity often did not assure colonial accuracy in identifying tribal leadership. As with the transfer of the land itself, the regulatory sovereign, whether colony or Crown, was little concerned with the legitimate *capacity* of the (apparent) tribal leadership from the tribal perspective, except in the context of military alliances. Colonial and Crown courts, including their successor state and federal courts, never invalidated a treaty based on the legal incapacity of the tribal leadership from the tribal perspective. For example, as Judge Boldt noted in the well-known case of *United States v. Washington*:

> No formal political structure had been created by the Indians living
> in the Puget Sound area at the time of initial contact with the United
> States Government. Governor Stevens, acting upon instructions from
> his superiors and recommendations of his subordinates, deliberately
> created political entities for purposes of delegating responsibilities
> and negotiating treaties. In creating these entities Governor Stevens
> named many Chiefs and sub-chiefs.[61]

Although colonial and tribal governmental interaction was often fraught with error and misconception, necessity left no other option except to stumble forward.

Culture

All of what has been described so far in matters of commerce, land transactions, and governance was substantially influenced by cultural attitudes. On the colonial side, these attitudes were seriously distorted by the pernicious mix of ignorance and racism. Primary ingredients in this mix were the debilitating notions of *civilization* and *Christianity*. The metaphor of Native "savagery" was central to this process. The term has at least two senses that both diverge from and ultimately converge with each other. The more obvious sense of the word was its use as a propaganda term employed by European nations, especially England, to justify aggressive and ruthless policies in the colonies.[62] The other sense is lexical. *Savage* derives from the Latin root "silva" (i.e., woods), which took two directions in English, the serenity of *sylvan* and the wilderness of *savage*.[63] At first, the notion of "savage" as wild did not even apply to persons but only to certain plants and animals.[64] Only later was it applied to people and twisted away from its ecological meaning into a racial configuration centering on "beastliness."[65]

The notion of savage as beastly and violent was easily expanded to encompass the characteristics of simple and heathen. *Simple* neatly fit the description of Indians as mere hunters and warriors. In part, this description was erroneous on its face, as many eastern tribes were engaged in much more sophisticated agriculture and ecological activities than the colonists were capable of practicing or understanding.[66] This description also denigrates "simple" and somehow posits "complexity" (i.e., "civilization") as superior. When recognition of people and societies departs from a horizontal description of difference and creates a vertical ranking of (real or imagined) differences, it often forms a pretext for exploitation. As to the warrior characterization, Europe was not notably pacific in its own history, and tribes were engaged in self-defense. They were being invaded.

The "heathen" idea also vigorously reinforced the notion of superiority and advantage. Christianity, more specifically Catholicism, was not only a theological force but also, perhaps more important, a political force. Christianity at its beginnings was no more than a small Jewish sect on the margins of both the Jewish and Roman worlds of the Middle East. Despite these humble beginnings, it grew rapidly and went from outsider to insider status with the conversion of the Roman Emperor Constantine in the fourth century.

Despite its own early history of persecution at the hands of the Roman Empire, Christianity developed its own prosecutorial mentality with its political ascendancy—an ascendancy marked by an increasing belief in its status as the one and only true religion. This was a belief that was particularly resonant with, and complementary to, European expansion. It provided a theological corollary to ideas of "savagery and backwardness." This is seen most forcefully in the actions of several popes who issued papal bulls granting authority to various European nations to claim territory and to convert the "heathens" they encountered in the process of "discovery."[67]

The pope's political authority was not readily acceded to in Protestant countries like England, the Netherlands, and most German states, but the theology of Native inferiority was readily endorsed. Christianity not only provided theological support for injustice but also was an on-the-ground force, with its missionary efforts to convert Indians to Christianity and in the process lessen their ability or willingness to resist or even question the political actions of colonial societies. No doubt many Christian missionaries thought that they were doing good, that they were doing God's work, and even that they were tempering the edges of colonial political aggression. Yet, Christian thought and practice became a primary, almost defining ingredient in eroding many tribal cultures and eviscerating tribal property rights.[68]

The power of language often directs and focuses cultural belief and action. Language not only describes but also creates "reality." The word *uncivilized* is a potent example. In the world of Enlightenment, the term possessed an inherently negative charge that placed Indian societies at an instant disadvantage as morally inferior and practically incompetent. Yet it can also be said that at earlier stages of colonial "contact," before raw power hardened such rhetoric into reality, Indians and non-Indians often inhabited parallel worlds of mutual need and accommodation. They had much in common that allowed their very real differences to be seen as a basis for living as rough equals in a multicultural world, rather than within a system of difference that posited colonial superiority and native inferiority.[69]

On the Indian side, cultural attitudes appear to have been remarkably different. To be sure, Europeans were seen as different. Yet they were understood by Indians to be viable trading partners, potential holders of reasonable property rights, and worthy of political alliance through the treaty-making process. They were not always to be trusted, of course, but they were not systematically rejected as being outside the human family.[70] In the end, these contending views produced some insightful commentary about the nature and source of both similarity and dissimilarity:

> What Locke failed to notice is that the Indians did not recognize
> themselves as poor. The endless accumulation of capital which he
> saw as a natural consequence of the human love for wealth made

little sense to them. Marshall Sahlins has pointed out that there are in fact two ways to be rich, one of which was rarely recognized by Europeans in the seventeenth century. "Wants," Sahlins says, "may be 'easily satisfied' either by producing much or desiring little." Thomas Morton was almost alone among his contemporaries in realizing that the New England Indians had chosen this second path. As he said, on their own understanding, they "lived richly," and had little in the way of either wants or complaints. Pierre Biard, who also noticed this fact about the Indians, extended it into a critique of *European* ways of life. Indians, he said, went about their daily tasks with great leisure,

for their days are all nothing but pastime. They are never in a hurry. Quite different from us, who can never do anything without hurry and worry; worry, I say, because our desire tyrannizes over us and banishes peace from our actions.

Historians often read statements like this as myths of the noble savage, and certainly they are attached to that complex of ideas in European thought. But that need not deny their accuracy as descriptions of Indian life. If the Indians considered themselves happy with the fruits of relatively little labor, they were like many peoples of the world as described by modern anthropologists.[71]

Perhaps the balance of power—if its trajectory had been more favorable to tribes—would have produced a different result. Perhaps, but that is not the history that occurred or the legacy that was bequeathed.

These initial colonial-Indian encounters in the matrix of commerce, land, governance, and culture had profound effects that changed each side. They constituted a course of dealings that over time tended to accrue more and more favorably to the colonial side but without the complete loss of significant Native authority.[72] This dynamic remained a powerful and unresolved force that had to be dealt with in the newly emerging context of the formation of the United States. This new nation-building phase brought forward the challenges of the colonial experience for review and potential adjustment, especially as to governmental and political legal interaction, as well as the issue of establishing a relationship between the states and the federal government in Indian affairs. These issues were initially confronted in the Articles of Confederation, the text of the Constitution, and then more fully in the Marshall trilogy of early Indian law cases,[73] which marked a significant turning point in creating the legal and constitutional baseline of Indian law.

Indians were neither savage nor noble, but rather distinct human communities who participated in history and acted with agency[74] with regard to both their environment and their encounter with other human communities, including newcomers from Europe. For many historians, this renewed understanding of Indian agency in early American history was deeply entwined with the formation of the republic. These historians "have increasingly sought to show, as James Axtell has put it, that the presence of the natives was 'essential...to the exploration, colonization, and national origins of America.'"[75] As the historian William Cronon has noted in the context of colonial New England:

> If Indians lived richly by wanting little, then might not it be possible
> that Europeans lived poorly by wanting much? The difference
> between Indians and Europeans was not that one had property and
> the other had none, it was that they loved property differently.[76]

This was the ground of the new nation as it turned to the postrevolution issue of national self-governance. Indians were not gone, and the challenge to include them or to exclude them was an important part of the process of nation building and the formation of a constitutional republic.

Articles of Confederation

The Revolutionary War was largely fought by the colonists to throw off the shackles of English oppression. There was no extensive thought about what would come next. After the Declaration of Independence and the Revolutionary War, a second primal, national undertaking—largely separate yet interrelated with the first—came to the fore. This second undertaking was the creation of a federal union that was ultimately to become the United States—a project not foreseen by Indians or the first explorers and settlers, and one not necessarily foreordained to succeed. In fact, the first attempt through the Articles of Confederation promptly and swiftly failed.

The establishment of an independent nation where there previously was none, especially when that nation was to be a union of recently liberated and independent colonies, presented a not inconsiderable task. The key political challenge was the willingness of the individual colonies, now sovereign states in their own right, to surrender some of their independent authority to a newly created national government, while retaining as much residual sovereignty as possible. In other words, the object was to unite the parts into a functioning whole that did not swallow the parts in the process, in essence to create a working nation that commanded allegiance and possessed legitimacy.

It was thus necessary to develop a political consensus and to translate it into an organic document and structure that reflected the political agreements of the participating parties. The resulting structure had to distribute power and responsibility in a coherent and effective way or risk dissolution and collapse.

The Articles of Confederation became the first post–Revolutionary War attempt to unite the former colonies based on both a political and a governmental consensus. The Articles of Confederation were developed in 1777 by the Continental Congress and took effect in 1781, when they were finally ratified by the state of Maryland, the last of the thirteen to do so. The Articles were *not* a true attempt to establish a new nation, but rather an effort among the thirteen states to affiliate without any significant surrender of power to the central government.

Despite the ardor of the revolutionaries and their celebration of values like liberty, freedom, and the sovereignty of the people, there was very little conception of, or agreement about, the best governmental structure to unify the states in a "more perfect union."[77] The initial attempt was the seriously flawed Articles of Confederation. The need for some kind of national plan of governance was recognized by the very Continental Congress that issued the Declaration of Independence on July 4, 1776. In early June of 1776, "the Congress voted to appoint a committee 'to prepare and digest the form of a confederation to be entered into between these colonies.' "[78]

The plan that emerged from the postindependence Congress became known as the Articles of Confederation. As their title indicates, they established a confederation, in essence an alliance, a multilateral treaty of sovereign nation states.[79] The Articles of Confederation did not really seek to create a union and did not formally go into effect until ratified by the vote of every state.[80]

The beginning passages of the Articles of Confederation variously describe the arrangement of the states as a "confederacy," a "confederation," and a "firm league of friendship with each other" in which "each state retains its sovereignty, freedom, and independence." All these terms suggest that this new "United States" would be a national entity in which the constituent states were already sovereign.[81]

The amendment process, which required unanimous approval by *all* the states, strongly confirmed its multilateral treaty–like structure based on the sovereignty of each state—as opposed to a national regime founded on ratification of a national people.[82] This basic multilateral treaty structure was further confirmed in the structure of the unicameral Congress. Each state would appoint a delegation of up to seven individuals, with each state casting a single vote regardless of its size. Delegates were paid by the states, often took their voting instructions directly from state government, and were subject to state recall.[83]

This union of "friendship" among the thirteen original states proved inherently flawed because the states were unwilling to transfer sufficient power to the central government. The states gave up little and retained much. Perhaps given their recent experience under British rule, the states were hesitant to cede any authority to a centralized power. Yet this reluctance created an unworkable system without unified governance, and it soon collapsed.

A view of these deficits is instructive. Congress was a unicameral body, with each state afforded one vote.[84] Congress possessed modest powers that were nevertheless significantly limited by the states. Any act of Congress could not become law until it was ratified by nine states.[85] In addition, the provision dealing with Indian tribes that the "legislative right of any state within its own limits be not infringed or violated" presaged serious conflict. Further confusion resulted from the authority of the Committee of States or any of the nine states to exercise the power of Congress when it was not in session.[86] The central government under this arrangement was clearly at the mercy of the states.

In addition, the Articles of Confederation did not establish any independent executive branch or any federal judiciary, with the exception of a complex scheme to resolve disputes between states. All of this was further complicated at the fiscal level because the central government possessed no direct power to tax and had to rely on the willingness and ability of each individual state to raise its share of the needed revenues. The central government was at the mercy of the states not only structurally but also fiscally.

In the structural mishmash of the articles, there was, however, express reference to congressional authority to deal with Indian tribes. Article IX provided that Congress should have "sole and exclusive right [of] ... regulating the trade and managing all affairs with the Indians not members of any of the States, provided that the legislative right of any State within its own limits be not infringed or violated."[87] What looks like an express "sole and exclusive" delegation to Congress was, of course, severely compromised by the dual proviso concerning "Indians not members of any state"[88] and the much more problematical notion that "the legislative right of any State within its own limits be not infringed or violated."[89] This severely compromised language was quite in line with the other structural deficits of the Articles of Confederation. What was apparently delegated to the federal government with one hand was reserved to the states by the other.

This very problem was expressly referred to in *Worcester v. Georgia*.[90] Chief Justice Marshall noted: "The ambiguous phrases which follow the grant of power to the United States, were so construed by the states of North Carolina and Georgia as to annul the power itself."[91] This impotency of the articles in Indian affairs was overcome, according to Chief Justice Marshall, by the Indian Commerce Clause and the treaty-making power in the Constitution such that

> These powers comprehend all that is required for the regulation of our intercourse with the Indians. They are not limited by any restrictions on their free actions. The shackles imposed on this power, in the confederation, are discarded.[92]

For our present purposes, it is enough to note that from the very beginning of the attempt to form something known as the "United States," the process required engagement with the question of how to deal with Indians and Indian tribes. Although the articles were short-lived and the provision dealing with Indians was hopelessly contradictory in apportioning authority between the federal and state governments, they do contain valuable lessons that form a baseline from which to examine the text of the Constitution as it addressed the same questions.

At the time of the adoption of the Articles of Confederation, it was absolutely clear that Indians and Indian tribes were not part of the "perpetual union."[93] Individual Indians were not citizens, and their tribes were not part of this "Confederation between States." The language of Article IX is quite precise on this issue. The authority described in Article IX is not authority "over" Indians or even "concerning" Indians but "with the Indians." This language—whatever its other shortcomings—locates Indians outside the Confederation and seeks to distribute authority (however unsuccessfully) between the sovereigns within (Congress and the states) the articles' structure. According to Robert Clinton, this reflected a nascent federal view of its relationship with Indian tribes as being one side of a "bilateral political, diplomatic, economic, and social relationship."[94] Yet as with many treaties—despite the *language* of bilateral respect—there was very little evidence of subsequent actions matching such commitments. In this instance, of course, time was short, and the Articles of Confederation proved almost totally ineffective. Their failure provided the backdrop for consideration and adoption of the U.S. Constitution. Yet Indians were clearly present as legally recognized sovereigns at the very beginning of the first attempt to establish a federal union.

There were two other documents in circulation at this time that reveal related thinking concerning the relationship of Indian tribes to the young post–Revolutionary War republic. In a 1775 speech to the Six Nations that was prepared by the Second Continental Congress, there was a pervasive call to the "brothers" in the Six Nations Iroquois Confederacy to provide support to the colonists in the Revolutionary War against Britain. This was a call that intimated the benefits of unification against the threat of Britain for *both* the colonies and the Indians: "For, if the King's troops take away our property, and destroy us who are of the same blood with themselves, what can you, who are Indians, expect from them afterwards?"[95] This was a fair enough question, to be sure, yet it was never to be answered because of the defeat of the British in the Revolutionary War. Of course, the unstated corollary question of what Indians might expect from the (victorious) colonists was subsequently answered. The answer was very little, and it was most often characterized by strife, exclusion, and deception. This problematic history is still working itself out today within and without a legitimate constitutional framework. When the weak become strong, do they remember their "promises" to the strong who have become weak?

Another revealing document containing some thoughts and early statements of the framers about Indians is Benjamin Franklin's draft of the Articles of Confederation. His Article X is exclusively devoted to the engagement of war with Indian nations.[96] No colony was allowed to engage in war with any Indian nation without the consent of Congress and the governing council of that specific Indian nation.[97] These councils were to meet and determine the "Justice and Necessity of such War."[98] This article expressed a great desire to keep peace with the Indian nations and to avoid the insurmountable costs of the inevitable large-scale war that would result from overtly hostile actions by the United States against Indians. Also, Franklin expressed sufficient respect for Indian nations to require them to consent to the necessity of war. War was not to be entered into unilaterally, and most certainly was not to be initiated by colonists. Each sovereign was to consult the other before engaging in such a drastic act.

Article XI stressed the need for peace by declaring that a "perpetual Alliance offensive and defensive, is to be enter'd into as soon as may be [sic] with the Six Nations."[99] Tribal territorial limits were to be established and not encroached upon, and no colony was to be able to purchase such lands.[100] This general rule was to be applied to all Indian nations. Further, Franklin placed in this article what appears to be the beginning of what later became known as the Bureau of Indian Affairs. A representative from the United States was to be appointed to live on each Indian Territory to "prevent Injustice in the Trade with them," and where necessary, the United States was to supply these Indian nations with necessities to "relieve their Personal Wants and Distresses."[101] The United States needed peaceful solutions to westward expansion because it could not afford a large-scale war, and the land cessions that Indian people would be likely to make would probably require aid in adjusting to the resulting new way of life.

All this swirled around in the context of uncertain nationhood, problematic western expansion, and the resulting tensions of the states with the national government and the tribes and of the national government with the states and the tribes. The nub of the western expansion issue was who would get to deal with the Indians concerning their land. Many states took the position that their Crown charters from England contained no fixed western borders and thus there was no such thing as national or Indian territory *outside* the boundaries of the original thirteen states. Only when the original states—as part of the ratification of the Articles of Confederation—agreed to fixed western borders was there some *partial* accommodation of federal and state interests.[102] Of course, as with so much of this early history, the interests and role of tribes in the emerging republic were definitely present and part of a new national agenda.

The Articles of Confederation failed because they were structurally ineffective, with too much power remaining with the states and too little going to the central government. In addition, they were often contradictory in that they seemed, in some cases, to transfer power to the federal government, only to have some proviso that appeared to retain it for the state. This latter was the situation in Indian affairs. Also, the articles failed to address such key issues as taxation or the meaningful establishment of an executive or judicial branch. In light of all that the articles failed to do, it remains all the more significant that they did address (albeit imperfectly) the issue of the governmental relationship with Indian tribes. The failure of the articles was soon apparent to all, and thus it was necessary to reassess their adequacy for the task of establishing a national governing structure sufficient to reliably guide the new and fragile republic of the "United States."

3

Second Opportunity

The Structure and Architecture of the Constitution

A T THE TIME LEADING UP TO THE ADOPTION OF THE CONSTITUTION, INDIANS and Indian tribes were often seen as the enemy, the "uncivilized," the "heathen," the other, but also the possessors of the land, desirable commercial partners, expert geographers, and people at home in their cultures. Diplomacy and war bracketed these perceptions. Indian tribes and Indians were outsiders, yet they were close at hand. This was the soil of constitutional encounter.

In the aftermath of the failure of the Articles of Confederation to effectuate a satisfactory union, the work of establishing the United States as a functioning republic continued. Initially, the goal was to amend the Articles of Confederation—particularly with reference to the economic problems created by their inability to put in place a means to pass uniform legislation to govern, even minimally, interstate, Indian, and international commerce. Conflict and trade barriers abounded. Regional conflicts were intense. Trade with Indians was unregulated.

The convention to amend the Articles of Confederation soon realized the necessity for something much broader. The necessity to draft and adopt an entirely new form of national governance became even more apparent. The convention to amend the Articles of Confederation is now known as the Constitutional Convention of 1787. Its work completely rethought the structure of the federal government in relation to the states (and, to a lesser extent, to Indian tribes), as well as the enumeration and distribution of powers within the federal government.

The constitution that emerged—while not without controversy and some ambiguity—did go a long way to identify a workable and enduring structural relationship between the federal government and the states, as well as the creation of the three branches of the federal government with an agreed-upon distribution of powers and appropriate checks and balances. As with the Articles of Confederation, there was concern, though admittedly subsidiary to the federal-state relationship, about the relationship of the federal government and the states to the tribes. These sovereign-to-sovereign concerns are most distinctly reflected in the federal-state and state-state context by the Interstate Commerce Clause, the Supremacy Clause, the Full Faith and Credit Clause, the Tenth Amendment, and Eleventh Amendment, and in the federal-tribal context by the Indian Commerce Clause and the treaty-making power.

This new and original architecture continues to cast lasting shadows over tribal sovereignty and contemporary Indian law. These shadows include the rich vitality of Interstate Commerce Clause jurisprudence and scholarship, which contrasts sharply with the largely inert body of Indian Commerce Clause jurisprudence and scholarship; the reach and effect of the Full Faith and Credit Clause, the Supremacy Clause, and the Eleventh Amendment on modern tribal sovereignty; and the exemplar of the Tenth Amendment's commitment to protect the state sovereign from an overreaching federal sovereign, suggesting the need for similar protection for the tribal sovereign.

Roots of the Constitution

The core of early colonial and revolutionary thought was largely dedicated to relocating the focus of governmental authority from the divine to the human, from far away to nearer at home. This transformation is most artfully described in Bernard Bailyn's *The Ideological Origins of the American Revolution*. In this seminal work, Bailyn locates the American transformation in the development of thought surrounding the issues of representation and consent, constitutional authority and individual rights, and sovereignty.[1] These questions were all part of Enlightenment discourse in England, as well as elsewhere, but they took on a particularized local coloring in the context of oppression in the colonies that was effectuated by the increased strictures on colonial self-rule emanating from England.

These changes in the colonies led many writers to stress that whatever the means for selecting representatives, the actual makeup of Parliament in England did not—indeed, could not—represent the interests of (disenfranchised) colonists. This thinking—however hesitant and uncertain—began a move to reconstitute law and governance away from a top-down model to an inside-out model premised on consent:

> The very nature and meaning of law was involved. The traditional sense, proclaimed by Blackstone no less than by Hobbes, that law was a command "prescribed by source superior and which the inferior is bound to obey"—such a sense of law as the declaration of a person or body existing independently above the subjects of law and imposing its will upon them, was brought into question by the developing notion of representation. Already in these years there were adumbrations of the sweeping repudiation James Wilson and others would make of Blackstone's definition of law, and of the view they would put in its place: the view that the binding power of law flowed from the continuous assent of the subjects of law; the view "that the only reason why a free and independent man was bound by human laws was this—that he bound himself."[2]

Such thinking was republicanism in the bud—a bud whose perfume would turn the English monarchy into something of a noxious weed, the smell of which had no place in the garden of liberty and self-rule.

This newly emerging discussion about representation and consent also gave rise to the issues of the source of governing authority and individual rights. Emerging—again tentative, confusing, fragmentary—thought began to identify the necessity of a document (England did *not* have one) to describe and distribute governmental powers that emanate from the *people* and were surrendered only with their consent:

> Thus created and thus secured, the constitution could effectively designate what "part of their liberty" the people are to sacrifice to the necessity of having government, by furnishing answers to "the two following questions: first, what shall the form of government be? And secondly, what shall be its power?" In addition, "it is the part of a constitution to fix the manner in which the officers of government shall be chosen, and determine the principal outlines of their power, their time of duration, manner of commissioning them, etc." Finally, "all the great rights which man never mean, nor ever ought, to lose should be *guaranteed*, not *granted*, by the constitution, for at the forming of a constitution, we ought to have in mind that whatever is left to be secured by law only may be altered by another law."[3]

A corollary to this nascent constitutional talk was a developing discussion that acknowledged that while individual rights were expressed in both positive and common law, their ultimate source was in the "abstract universals of natural rights."[4] There also appeared to be a developing consensus that the core of these individual rights involved "Life, Liberty, and Property."[5] The ensuing dialogue turned on the practical and pragmatic issue of whether such natural scripture could and should be reduced to written law. While not part of the Articles of Confederation or the original Constitution adopted in 1787, this platform became realized in the Bill of Rights, the first ten amendments to the U.S. Constitution, which was adopted in 1789.

Of particular relevance to the colonies was the emerging issue of defining state sovereignty beyond the notion of monarchical divine right. Hobbes and others had cut the divine cord and (re)conceptualized state sovereignty as characterized by two essential elements: a notion of some "unqualified, indivisible power" that had some identifiable "location."[6] And although this "location" shifted from the king to Parliament in England, this move highlighted its essential arbitrariness with respect to the colonies. Even though there was significant decentralized local control in many of the colonies, the taxing powers of Parliament highlighted in the infamous Stamp Act[7] essentially broke the back of England's colonial legitimacy. Such power was both absolute and arbitrary and was to be resisted and ultimately overthrown.

There was much discussion along the way about permissible "external" powers of Parliament vis-à-vis the colonies and impermissible "internal" powers interfering in the self-governance of the colonies. These distinctions ultimately did not hold for many colonists in the context of being the subjects of an empire. These variegated notions of sovereignty were nevertheless pivotal in the preparation of the U.S. Constitution, with its concerns for the dual sovereigns of the states and the (new) federal government and the shadow sovereign represented by Indian tribes. The identification and distribution of sovereignty among the state and federal sovereigns became the primary theme in the constitutional debates and in the constitution itself. This was especially true in the aftermath of the failure of the Articles of Confederation to deal adequately with federal, state, and tribal sovereignty.[8]

The Great Law of Peace

The conventional wisdom of the "democratic spirit" of the young republic of the United States is that it was the sole product of the thinking of the founding fathers enmeshed in the larger Enlightenment thinking of the era. No doubt there is much truth in this observation, but it may not be the whole truth, as it ignores the actual existence and potential influence of indigenous versions of constitutional governance and the democratic prospect. The most robust indigenous model in this area is that of the Iroquois Confederacy or Haudenosaunee, which was an alliance of the Seneca, Cayuga, Onondaga, Oneida, Mohawk, and Tuscarora located in northern New York, eastern Canada, and in and around the Great Lakes area.

Under the charismatic vision of the shaman and prophet Deganawidah, the confederacy ultimately adopted new rules of governance in what became known as the Haudenosaunee constitution, or the Great Law of Peace. The Great Law of Peace, which predates the U.S. Constitution by at least 400 years, bears the unmistakable stamp of both separation of powers and a "federalism" distribution of power between the confederacy and its constituent tribes:

> When issues came up before the alliance, the Tododaho [main
> speaker] would summon the fifty sachems who represented the clans
> of the Five Nations. Different nations had different numbers of
> sachems, but the inequality meant little because all decisions had to
> be unanimous; the Five Nations regarded consensus as the social
> ideal. As in all-consensus driven bodies, though, members felt
> intense pressure not to impede progress with frivolous objections.
> The heads of clans, who were all female, chose the sachems, all male.
> As a rule, sachems were succeeded by their nephews, but the system
> was not entirely hereditary—sachems could be impeached if they
> displeased their clan, and if their nephews were not deemed fit for
> office, someone outside the family could take over.[9]

Beyond this broad structural configuration, there were 117 codicils of the Great Law that not only granted much power to the great council but also limited it:

> Its jurisdiction was strictly limited to relations among the nations
> and outside groups; internal affairs were the province of the
> individual nations. Although the council negotiated peace treaties,
> it could not declare war—that was left to the initiative of the leaders
> of each of Haudenosaunee's constituent nations. According to the
> Great Law, when the council of sachems was deciding upon "an
> especially important matter or a great emergency," its members had
> to "submit the matter to the decision of their people" in a kind of
> referendum.[10]

Such native practices were regionwide and often caught the eyes of colonial leaders. Roger Williams, for example, commented that the sachems "will not conclude of ought...unto which the people are averse."[11] The consent of the governed was much more palpable in indigenous America than in the despotisms that governed in Europe.[12] The consent element also included a strong feminist component, where women had substantial, if not identical, power with men. Many feminists of the nineteenth century, such as Lucretia Mott, Elizabeth Cady Stanton, and Matilda Joslyn Gage, all of whom lived in the northeast region of the country, found inspiration in indigenous configurations involving the roles of women.[13]

Embedded in the structures of the Great Law and similar tribal confederations were a cluster of individual values that emphasized liberty, personal autonomy, and social equality. This, too, was not lost on some colonists. Benjamin Franklin, for one, was well aware of all this. In fact, a mainstay of his printing business was the publication of Indian documents and treaties as important public documents.[14] The sophistication and insight reflected in the Great Law of Peace was a powerful refutation to the stereotype of Indian "simplicity" and lack of agency in political affairs.[15]

This heady Indian liberty where "every man is free" was unknown in Europe and attractive to some but fearsome to others because "[t]he Savage does not know what it is to obey."[16] It also set up a kind of competition for colonists' allegiance and created an informal brake on excessive colonial oppression of its members because they might go over to the other side. Yet the attractiveness of these native values did little to temper colonial avarice for tribal resources, especially land.

To some, these encounters, especially with the Great Law of Peace, demonstrate direct native inspiration and influence on the U.S. Constitution. To others, not so.[17] Although the precise scholarly debate remains largely unresolved, "nobody disputes that the Haudenosaunee exemplified the formidable tradition of limited government and personal autonomy shared by many cultures north of the Rio Grande."[18] Regardless of where colonists and colonial thinkers actually looked, what they were seeking was close at hand.

The Constitution and Indian Tribes

The Constitution clearly recognized Indian tribes as sovereigns but *not* as sovereigns who participated in its creation, its ratification, or its compact for governance. Indian tribes were recognized sovereigns but largely as sovereigns *outside* and on the margins of the new republic and its Constitution. With this in mind, I examine each of the relevant constitutional provisions, with an eye to reviewing its analytical and doctrinal development, as well as assessing the

current parameters of each doctrine. My goal is to provide a review of the structure of the Constitution as it deals with the federal and state sovereigns, and to
demonstrate how this structure illuminates the constitutional status of the
tribal sovereign. The differences in constitutional text and resulting Supreme
Court jurisprudence are quite instructive.

These architectural joints in the Constitution are directed to describing a
blueprint for federalism—a federalism that allocates governmental authority
between the national and state sovereign. An extensive body of Supreme Court
jurisprudence concerned with the parameters and borders of these key federalism fittings has also developed. One of these core fittings is the Indian
Commerce Clause and the way in which the Court has parsed federal and state
authority in Indian country with regard to this constitutional provision. In addition, there is the fainter blueprint that deals with the nature of *tribal* sovereignty
itself, both within the Indian Commerce Clause and in treaty making. This is
something we might call Indian law federalism—an Indian law federalism that
constitutes a continuing shadow to mainline federalism.

Federal-State Relationship: Constitutional Federalism

Interstate Commerce Clause

The issue of national regulation of interstate commerce was not originally seen
as an issue of federalism or an area of potential conflict. During the colonial
period, trade among the thirteen original colonies was effectively regulated by
Britain itself. All colonial trade between the colonies and foreign nations was
regulated by the King's Privy Council and the British Board of Trade.[19] As a
result, there was very little economic conflict among the colonies at the time of
the Revolutionary War. In the aftermath of the Revolutionary War and during
the demise of British control of colonial trade, there was an unforeseen gap or
power vacuum. This potential problem went largely unnoticed in the Articles
of Confederation, which granted no interstate commerce regulatory authority
to Congress.

In the resulting gap, the newly formed states developed sharply different
economic interests, which were often advanced through programs of economic
protectionism and trade barriers. This was exacerbated by the loss of trade with
Britain and the resulting shortage of currency. "Economic chaos" was at hand.[20]
As a result, the regulation of commerce became a primary concern of the
Continental Congress—a concern that ultimately produced the Interstate
Commerce Clause. Despite some discussion in the Federalist Papers as to
the federal-state balance to be struck in this area, there was no extensive debate

over the issue at the Continental Congress that adopted the enumerated power set out in the Interstate Commerce Clause.[21]

The language of the Interstate Commerce Clause is plain enough. It grants Congress power to regulate commerce "among the several states."[22] Commerce Clause jurisprudence has long focused on two overriding themes: the meaning of the term *commerce* and whether federal control over interstate commerce is absolute or something less, with some authority potentially reserved to the states. The seminal case in the history of the meaning of the Commerce Clause is the 1824 decision of *Gibbons v. Ogden*.[23]

In *Gibbons*, the essential dispute was rather narrow in nature, but Chief Justice Marshall took the opportunity to establish some broad parameters for the congressional power that might properly be invoked by the Commerce Clause. The case involved the issue of whether a New York grant of an exclusive monopoly to engage in steamboat navigation in the waters of New York to a partnership (subsequently transferred to Ogden) could defeat the claim of a competitor (Gibbons), whose actions were authorized by a federal statute.[24] The Court answered in the negative, relying primarily on the force of the Supremacy Clause, which required the states to follow federal statutes as the supreme law of the land.[25]

Chief Justice Marshall went on to define the term *commerce* broadly as commensurate with any kind of "intercourse." Along with its attendant power to regulate "commerce which concerns more States than one,"[26] this understanding recognized that "the power of Congress may be exercised within a State."[27] With his characteristic craft, Marshall also conceded that states had (constitutionally) reserved authority over commercial activities "which are completely within a particular State, which do not affect other States, and with which it is not necessary to interfere for the purpose of executing some of the general powers of the government."[28] This standard was not defined and arguably set a rather high bar for states to overcome.

The Marshallian tact in *Gibbons* essentially followed the Madisonian lead that a strong federal hand in interstate commerce was necessary to avoid the dysfunction and chaos suggested by the failure of the Articles of Confederation.[29] Such a view was also quite compatible with the notion of a dormant (i.e., silent) Commerce Clause that acts as a barrier to state legislation that affects interstate commerce, even in the absence of express congressional legislation barring such state action.

The yang to this yin was the notion expounded by Marshall's successor, Chief Justice Taney, with his view that states could enact legislation that affected interstate commerce as long as that legislation did not conflict with express federal legislation. In this view, the negative implications of a dormant (i.e., silent) Commerce Clause were nonexistent.[30] This view has not prevailed, although there remains significant scholarly and jurisprudential concern about the bona fides of the dormant Commerce Clause doctrine.[31]

The other primary Interstate Commerce Clause issue was whether its grant of power to Congress was exclusive or concurrent. This is but another way of asking the doctrinal question about the existence of a "dormant" Commerce Clause and what, if any, its implications are. It goes without saying that federal legislation in interstate commerce is binding on the states under the Supremacy Clause. Yet, the text itself does not address the issue of exclusive or concurrent authority to regulate interstate commerce. As a result, the Court has had to face the issue of parsing the meaning of constitutional silence or dormancy. It has, for the most part, interpreted the silence as creating a negative implication against state forays into regulating interstate commerce, even when Congress has not acted.[32] Thus, the dormant Commerce Clause doctrine holds that the Interstate Commerce Clause bars any and all state legislation that affects interstate commerce, even if there is no federal legislation on the point.

The doctrine's current substance—though often criticized—is easy to summarize: "[w]hen a state statute clearly discriminates against interstate commerce, it will be struck down, unless the discrimination is demonstrably justified by a valid factor unrelated to economic protection. Indeed, when the state statute amounts to economic protection, a virtually *per se* rule of invalidity has applied."[33] Even when a state statute is facially neutral, it will be struck down if it imposes an undue burden on interstate commerce.[34] Yet the scholarly and jurisprudential debate continues as to exactly how "near" exclusive (yet not absolutely exclusive) the dormant Commerce Clause is.[35]

The final gradient to examine within the context of the Interstate Commerce Clause is whether there is any substantive limit to the plenary nature of Congress's authority to regulate such "commerce." The thrust of *Gibbons* in this regard was quite broad: "The wisdom and the discretion of Congress, their identity with the people, and the influence which their constituents possess at elections, are, in this, as in many other instances...the sole restraints...from its abuse."[36] This exceptional dictum regarded the interstate commerce power as absolute and "plenary,"[37] subject only to other *specific* restrictions in the Constitution, but not including the residual sovereignty reserved to the states in the Tenth Amendment.[38] In this view, the main restraint on the commerce power was the mechanism of electoral politics.

After almost 150 years, this absolutism has begun to buckle. In 1995, the Court in *United States v. Lopez*[39] struck down by a five-to-four vote the federal Gun-Free School Zones Act of 1990.[40] The Court held that the challenged statute was not within the parameters of the Interstate Commerce Clause because there was no demonstration that the regulated activity—*any* instance of the possession of a firearm near a school—"*substantially* affects," rather than merely affects, interstate commerce.[41]

In a complex, modern capitalist state, it is possible to argue that any and all activities affect—even "substantially" affect—interstate commerce. In fact, this was the position of the United States in *Lopez*. When queried at oral argument, counsel for the United States could not provide a single example of an action that would clearly be outside the purview of Congress's commerce power.[42] The resulting concern—ideology aside—is commonsensical. Without a recognizable border, an enumerated power can threaten to swallow the delegation that gave it birth in the first instance.[43] And because commerce is both practically and constitutionally an area of legitimate federal *and* state interest, it is an issue of federalism that requires the identification of constitutional borders between permissible federal and state activity. Congress's "plenary" power in interstate commerce, while extensive, is not infinite. *Lopez* reminds us that there is a minimal threshold relative to the subject matter (i.e., "interstate commerce") that must be satisfied before its plenary scope may be invoked.

The *Lopez* rationale was further advanced in *United States v. Morrison*,[44] when the Court struck down the remedial portion of the Violence Against Women Act because—despite contrary congressional findings—its focus on "[g]ender-motivated crimes" was not "economic activity."[45] As noted by Justice Souter in his dissent, the effect of *Lopez* and *Morrison* was to revive the competition of old rivals about whether the Interstate Commerce Clause power was plenary or categorically limited.[46] He did not think this new competition wise.

Despite this apparent jurisprudential shift in *Lopez* and *Morrison*, the Court appeared unwilling (or unable) to go further in the 2005 case of *Gonzales v. Raich*.[47] In that case, popularly known as the medical marijuana case, the Court upheld a federal criminal statute known as the Comprehensive Drug Abuse Prevention and Control Act of 1970,[48] which included marijuana as an illegal substance and recognized no exception for the "medical use" of marijuana. This ban conflicted with a California state statute known as the Compassionate Marijuana Use Act of 1990,[49] which under appropriate circumstances permitted the medical use of marijuana.

Despite the recognition that there was much evidence that marijuana does have "valid therapeutic purposes," the Court upheld the federal statute (and struck down the state statute) as a valid exercise of Congress's power to regulate interstate commerce.[50] The Court (surprisingly or not) found *Lopez* and *Morrison* inapposite because those cases did *not* involve commerce or any sort of economic enterprise, but rather the criminal possession of a firearm in a school zone in *Lopez* and gender-based assaults in *Morrison*.[51]

In sum, the jurisprudence and scholarship involving the Interstate Commerce Clause has been and continues to be varied, deep, and significant. Just a glance at the record demonstrates that since *Gibbons v. Ogden*, the Supreme Court has decided at least forty-two cases about its meaning. In addition, books and law review articles abound. The history of the Indian Commerce Clause, as we will see, is the exact opposite. There is not much jurisprudence and even less scholarship. As a result, the Indian Commerce Clause tends to be both ignored and little understood.[52]

Supremacy Clause

The Constitutional Convention readily decided—particularly in light of the shortcomings of the Articles of Confederation—on the necessity of establishing a federal judiciary. "William Randolph's resolution 'that a National Judiciary be established' was unanimously adopted early in the convention."[53] The ensuing discussion focused on whether the Constitution should specifically establish lower federal courts or merely authorize Congress to do so. A proposal to expressly establish lower federal courts in the Constitution was narrowly defeated. A compromise was then brokered by Wilson and Madison to have the Constitution expressly establish the Supreme Court with discretion reserved to Congress to establish lower federal courts. The proposed compromise was accepted by the convention delegates and became the basis for the text of Article III.[54] The first lower federal courts were established by the Judiciary Act of 1789.[55]

The text of the Supremacy Clause is direct and unambiguous:

> This Constitution, and the Laws of the United States which shall be
> made in Pursuance thereof; and all Treaties made, or which shall
> be made, under the Authority of the United States, shall be the
> supreme Law of the Land, and the Judges in every State shall be
> bound thereby, any Thing in the Constitution or Laws of any state to
> the Contrary notwithstanding.[56]

As noted earlier, there was no precursor version in the Articles of Confederation. This shortcoming was obviously problematic. It would be extremely difficult to maintain a union if state judges were free to disregard federal law. This point was particularly noteworthy at the time the Constitution was ratified because Article III of the Constitution did *not* establish lower federal courts. It was thus understood that state courts would be the primary vehicles for enforcing federal law and federal causes of action.

State courts have always been understood to have concurrent jurisdiction with federal courts over any federal claim unless a federal statute establishes exclusive federal jurisdiction. The more difficult issue is not whether state courts have concurrent jurisdiction, but whether they may decline to exercise it. The general answer is no.[57]

The Supremacy Clause also plays a significant role in the area of law known as federal preemption. Federal preemption describes the doctrine stipulating that as long as Congress acts within the parameters of one of its enumerated powers, its statutory enactments will displace any conflicting state legislation.[58] The Supremacy Clause, particularly its language "any thing in the Constitution or Laws of any state to the contrary notwithstanding," carries the day and resolves any conflict between federal and state law in favor of the federal legislation.

Litigation in this context has tended to focus on issues of statutory interpretation rather than any challenge to the constitutional roots of the doctrine. If there is a challenge to a federal statute as being outside the scope of Congress's authority, such a challenge does not involve Supremacy Clause preemption questions. Preemption questions only come to the fore after it is acknowledged that the federal statute is within the substantive ambit of proper congressional authority, with the sole remaining question being whether the statute—as properly interpreted—does or does not purport to "preempt" relevant state authority.

The most difficult cases in this area involve interpretations of the dormant (or negative) implications of congressional power such as those in the Commerce Clause.[59] In addition, there are related issues of interpretation in determining whether, despite state legislation that might well be consistent with federal legislation, the intent of Congress was to "occupy the field."[60] Where multiple federal regulations and statutes govern in a given field, it leads to the conclusion that Congress meant to exclusively control the field, and state regulation will be void.[61] Also, if the field is traditionally deemed "national," the Court is more likely to strike down state intrusions into areas that Congress has reserved to itself.[62] If Congress unambiguously declares that it constitutionally intends to occupy a field, then all state action in that area will be preempted.[63]

The constitutional glue of the Supremacy Clause is designed to bind the states to the observance of any federal law properly enacted and legitimately within the scope of Congress's constitutional authority.

THE SUPREMACY CLAUSE AND INDIAN TRIBES

Neither the text nor the history of the Supremacy Clause makes any express reference to Indian tribes. Yet there has been no significant litigation on this issue, and it has been routinely thought to apply to tribes. The key textual reference is to the "Judges in every State," which would not appear to include tribal judges on reservations and only state (or local) judges in "every State." However, it might also be argued textually that the Supremacy Clause language does not actually say state judges, but rather judges "in every State," which might be read to include tribal judges because they are geographically "in every State." This is admittedly a strained reading, especially in light of the Supremacy Clause's concluding language: "any Thing in the Constitution or Laws of any *State* to the Contrary notwithstanding."[64] Despite the absence of any textual or historical support, it seems unlikely at this juncture that any court would rule that the Supremacy Clause does not apply to Indian tribes.[65]

The anomalous issue of the Supremacy Clause and Indian tribes again harks back to the original position and status of tribes when the Constitution was adopted—that position being one as a recognized sovereign, but recognized as being *outside* (or on the margins), not part of the federal-state constitutional compact; instead, this sovereign was mainly dealt with through means of diplomacy, war, and treaties. In this regard, tribes were less like states that are bound by the Supremacy Clause and more like foreign nations that are not.

Although this description is undoubtedly true as an original matter, the Supreme Court has made it clear that it is essentially otherwise in the contemporary era. For example, in the case of *United States v. Wheeler*,[66] the Court noted that tribal "incorporation within the territory of the United States, and their acceptance of its protection, necessarily divested them of some aspects of the sovereignty which they had previously exercised."[67]

This "incorporation" was not the result of any constitutional adjustment or amendment. Nor was it the product of tribal consent. It was, rather, the result of national expansionary power exceeding the bounds of the Constitution:

> The sovereignty that the Indian tribes retain is of a unique and limited character. It exists only at the sufferance of Congress and is subject to complete defeasance. But until Congress acts, the tribes retain their existing sovereign powers. In sum, Indian tribes still possess those aspects of sovereignty not withdrawn by treaty or statute, or by implication as a necessary result of their dependent status.[68]

Robert Clinton is one of the few scholars who have examined the historical and constitutional relationship of Indian tribes to the Supremacy Clause. His in-depth analysis definitively demonstrates that neither the text of the Constitution (nor its predecessor Articles of Confederation) nor any surrounding writings such as the Federalist Papers reveal the slightest inkling that the Supremacy Clause was meant to include Indian tribal sovereignty within its purview.[69] And although this might strike many as unexpected, it is nevertheless of a piece with the broader understanding that tribes were not part of the constitutional compact between the federal government and the states and thus there was no (legitimate) authority *over* them, but only authority to deal *with* them through the Indian Commerce Clause and treaties. Of course, the operational reality (as opposed to constitutional legitimacy) from the very beginning has been that tribes are subject to expansive (perhaps even limitless) federal authority.

The basic function of the Supremacy Clause, as a key ingredient to foster a working relationship between the federal government and the states and as a means to resolve potential federal-state conflicts, is never even cited in Indian law jurisprudence. Federal "supremacy" is presumed as a necessary element of Congress's and the Supreme Court's "plenary" power in Indian affairs. The problem, of course, is that these conceptions of federal "plenary" authority in Indian affairs are not rooted in the Constitution and, in fact, exceed the relevant history and text of the Constitution in the Indian Commerce Clause and treaty-making power.[70] Plenary authority in Indian affairs is not rooted in the text or history of the Constitution but in the text and history of colonialism—a colonialism in which a "conquered people" only has authority at the "sufferance" of the "conqueror."[71]

Tenth Amendment

The text of the Tenth Amendment states: "The powers not delegated to the United States by the Constitution, nor prohibited by it to the States, are reserved to the States respectively, or to the people."[72] The amendment was ratified in 1791 and is the central constitutional embodiment of the basic understanding that the powers of the federal government are limited to its enumerated powers granted to it by the states (and the people), with all that remains reserved to the states (and the people). That is the essential compact of the states and "founding fathers," a compact grounded in skepticism and concern for the potential overreaching of a too powerful central government.

The jurisprudence involving the Tenth Amendment tends to reflect one of two approaches. One approach tends to view the Tenth Amendment as simply expressing the constitutional postulate that the federal government is indeed a government of limited and enumerated powers, and if the federal government exceeds its limited and enumerated authority, such action should be (judicially) found unconstitutional. The second approach understands the Tenth Amendment as an independent textual limit that "preserves a field of autonomy"[73] for states, even when there is a potential conflict with an enumerated power.

Laurence Tribe has described these approaches as choosing between two sides of the same coin. If Congress exceeds its authority, the Court may strike it down as either exceeding its enumerated powers or as violating the Tenth Amendment. For example, in *Bailey v. Drexel Furniture Co.*,[74] the Court held that the Child Labor Tax violated the Tenth Amendment because it exceeded Congress's taxing power.[75]

The Court itself has used the analogy of the half-empty or half-full cup to describe this approach:

> In the end, just as a cup may be half empty or half full, it makes no difference whether one views the question at issue in these cases as one of ascertaining the limits of the power delegated to the Federal Government under the affirmative provisions of the Constitution or one of discerning the core of sovereignty retained by the States under the Tenth Amendment.[76]

In other circumstances, the Court has pushed beyond this approach to locating some independent doctrinal force in the Tenth Amendment. This was particularly true in an early line of cases running from the 1870s to the 1930s. For example, in *Collector v. Day*,[77] the Court held that Congress could not tax the salary of a state judge. The theory was that despite Congress's enumerated power to tax, the exercise of the power in this instance would be inconsistent with principles of state sovereignty because "any government...if subject to the control of another and distinct government, can exist only at the mercy of that government."[78]

This jurisprudential approach is generally referred to as "dual federalism" and defined under the rubric that "the powers of the General Government, and of the State, although both exist and are exercised within the same territorial limits, are yet separate and distinct sovereignties, acting separately and independently of each other, within their respective spheres."[79] The essential operative principle is that there exists a kind of interdependent reciprocity where the federal government "in its appropriate sphere is supreme; but the States within the limits of their powers not granted, or, in the language of the [T]enth [A]mendment, 'reserved,' are as independent of the general government as that government within its sphere is independent of the States."[80]

This early waxing of a vital Tenth Amendment jurisprudence ultimately waned. The Tenth Amendment was scaled back to limit its reach to nonenumerated powers, while enumerated powers—especially the Commerce Clause—were greatly expanded and effectively reduced the Tenth Amendment to a constitutional shadow. The *Collector* case was overruled in *Graves v. New York*,[81] and the Tenth Amendment was further limited with the Court's pronouncement in *United States v. Darby*[82] that it merely "states but a truism that all is retained which has not been surrendered."[83]

This waning of the Tenth Amendment has begun, in recent times, to mildly shift. The Court has decided cases that move back toward an operational Tenth Amendment. In cases such as *New York v. United States*[84] and *Printz v. United States*,[85] the Court held that federal legislation, admittedly within the scope of Congress's enumerated powers, could nevertheless not "commandeer" state legislatures or state executive officials to carry out federal functions. As the Court stated in the *New York* case, "[s]tates are not mere political subdivisions of the United States,"[86] and the challenged legislation improperly invaded state sovereignty and violated the Tenth Amendment.

The Tenth Amendment is also the repository for a key philosophical and political ingredient in the Constitution, namely, that national sovereignty derives not just from the constitutional compact of the states, but directly from the people themselves. This idea reflects the concern of many participants in the early revolutionary and constitutional dialogue that a national sovereignty grounded solely in the consent of the state sovereigns could hold the people and their liberty hostage to some governmental authority independent of their will. In other words, without governmental authority firmly rooted in the people, tyranny was always close at hand. This philosophical underpinning has had little direct impact on constitutional jurisprudence. Yet, it is the essential core that provides political and legal legitimacy to the constitutional enterprise as a whole. Without it, the federal government would lack the dignity and respect necessary to advance, and even expand, the democratic prospect.[87]

Eleventh Amendment

There is no greater fervor in contemporary federalism discussions than that surrounding recent Supreme Court jurisprudence and the contours of the Eleventh Amendment.[88] The text of the Eleventh Amendment states: "The Judicial power of the United States shall not be construed to extend to any suit in law or equity, commenced or prosecuted against one of the United States by Citizens of another State, or by Citizens or Subjects of any Foreign State."

The Eleventh Amendment was not part of the original Constitution or the Bill of Rights. It was adopted and ratified in 1798 in direct response to the Supreme Court's decision in *Chisholm v. Georgia*.[89] In *Chisholm*, the Court decided that it had original jurisdiction pursuant to Article III of the Constitution to entertain a lawsuit brought by two South Carolina citizens against the state of Georgia for a debt owed on an estate.[90] The general reaction to the decision was "swift and hostile," and the proposed (Eleventh) amendment found its final form (after six drafts) within a year. The negative reaction to *Chisholm* came from a widespread state fear of potential state liability in a federal forum for Revolutionary War debts.[91]

The plain text of the Eleventh Amendment, according to most scholars, is subject to either of two plain meaning interpretations: namely, that either it repealed the Citizen-State Diversity Clauses of Article III for all cases in which a state appears as a defendant (while retaining potential federal question jurisdiction in lawsuits brought by out-of-state or foreign citizens) *or* it repealed both diversity and federal question jurisdiction when out-of-state or foreign citizens were plaintiffs.[92]

The current Court, however, does not accept this either-or textual formulation; rather, it has proceeded in the direction that the key to the Eleventh Amendment is found not in what it says but rather in the "presupposition...which it confirms"[93]—a presupposition that focuses on discerning the Constitution's understanding of state sovereign immunity, which is *not* expressly identified anywhere within the text of the Constitution. This "presupposition," as it is currently understood by the Court, is that when the states formed the union and joined its constitutional compact, their (common law) sovereign immunity remained completely intact.

Despite the fact that there is little direct historical evidence for such a wide-sweeping presupposition, this possibility has always lurked in the tantalizing penumbra surrounding the enigmatic case of *Hans v. Louisiana*.[94] In *Hans*, the Court held that Eleventh Amendment sovereign immunity protected a state from a federal lawsuit by one of its own citizens on a land obligation. Since such a lawsuit (citizen against his own state) does *not* implicate diversity jurisdiction, *Hans* was generally understood to (improperly) *extend* state sovereign immunity to federal question lawsuits brought by a state's own citizens. Although the Court often appeared ready to overrule *Hans*[95] as (constitutionally) misdirected, it never has, and *Hans* now appears even more firmly ingrained in the center of current Eleventh Amendment jurisprudence.

With *Hans* no longer subject to jurisprudential doubt, the Supreme Court has decided a group of cases in which it has reinvigorated and extended Eleventh Amendment sovereign immunity protection for states. These cases include

Blatchford v. Native Village of Noatak and Circle Village,[96] *Seminole Tribe of Florida v. Florida*,[97] *Idaho v. Coeur d'Alene Tribe of Idaho*,[98] *Florida Prepaid Postsecondary Education Expense Board v. College Savings Bank*,[99] and *Alden v. Maine*.[100] It is worth noting in this context that the first three cases in this series, *Blatchford*, *Seminole Tribe of Florida*, and *Coeur d'Alene Tribe of Idaho*, are all Indian law cases in which the advance of Eleventh Amendment protection of states worked directly against tribal sovereignty.

In *Blatchford*, the Court held that the Eleventh Amendment barred direct suit by Indian tribes against states in federal court without state consent. In fact, *Blatchford* enthusiastically resuscitated *Hans* with the observation that "[d]espite the narrowness of its terms, since *Hans v. Louisiana*, we have understood the Eleventh Amendment" as confirming "the presupposition of our constitutional structure...that the States entered the federal system with their sovereignty intact" and "that the federal authority in Article III is limited by this sovereignty."[101]

In *Seminole Tribe of Florida*, the Court overruled its decision in *Pennsylvania v. Union Gas Company*[102] that the Congress could waive a state's sovereign immunity through legislation enacted pursuant to the Interstate Commerce Clause. It also struck down that part of the Indian Gaming Regulatory Act that authorized tribes to sue states that failed to negotiate a tribe-state gaming compact in good faith.[103] This decision significantly limited the ability of tribes to deal adequately with recalcitrant states in the gaming context.[104]

In the *Coeur d'Alene* case, the Court held that a state's Eleventh Amendment protection barred a tribe from suing a state to resolve title to a disputed piece of land (e.g., ownership of a lake bed) within the reservation. The Court observed that such an action, despite its equitable nature seeking injunctive relief, was the functional equivalent of a quiet title action that had substantial implications for state sovereign interests.[105]

In these cases, there is little to no discussion of their implications for tribal sovereignty, a sovereignty that apparently is without constitutional resonance, much less any constitutional solidity. The denial of a federal forum in which tribes might sue states severely limits the ability of tribes to hold states federally accountable for the violation of tribal or individual Indian federal rights. The sole alternative is for the United States to sue the state in its capacity as trustee for the beneficiary tribe.[106] The Eleventh Amendment does not protect states from lawsuits brought by the federal government in federal court. Conversely, tribes, like states, possess (common law) sovereign immunity, but they, unlike states, do not possess any *constitutional* protection of their sovereign immunity. The point to note is that some of the most significant cases in contemporary Eleventh Amendment jurisprudence inflict extensive damage on the tribal sovereign. This collateral damage has been little noticed outside the field of Indian law.[107]

State-State Sovereignty

Full Faith and Credit Clause

While the other provisions under discussion in this book are directed to issues of federalism, concerning the relationship of the federal government to the states and the federal government to the tribes, the Full Faith and Credit Clause focuses primarily on the relationship of the states to each other. If there was to be an effective union, not only would there have to be a workable relationship between the federal government and the states but also there would have to be an effective and respectful interaction among the states themselves and their citizens.

This element of state-to-state comity was recognized in the Articles of Confederation in Article IV, which provided for "full faith and credit" in each state of the "acts, records, and judicial proceedings" of every other state.[108] This language was directly incorporated in Article IV of the Constitution and, along with the "privileges and immunities" and "fugitive from justice" clauses,[109] forms the core of Article IV's primary purpose, "to help fuse into one Nation a collection of independent, sovereign States"[110] by guaranteeing the basic rights of individuals as they move from state to state.

These clauses, taken in full, deal not only with the relationship of the states to one another (the Full Faith and Credit Clause) but also with the relationship of the states to citizens of another state (Privileges and Immunities Clause and Fugitive from Justice Clause). The concern here—given the focus on the (constitutional) relationship of tribes to the federal and state governments—will be with the Full Faith and Credit Clause. The text of the Full Faith and Credit Clause is clear and direct: "Full Faith and Credit shall be given in each state to the public acts, records, and judicial proceedings of every other State. And the Congress may by general Laws prescribe the Manner in which such Acts, Records, and Proceedings shall be proved, and the Effect thereof."[111] This constitutional provision by its terms is not self-executing. The implementing statute was passed in 1790 and its text reads:

> The Acts of the legislature of any State, Territory, or Possession of
> the United States, or copies thereof, shall be authenticated by affixing
> the seal of such State, Territory or Possession thereto.

The records and judicial proceedings of any court of any such
State, Territory or Possession, or copies thereof, shall be proved or
admitted in other courts within the United States and its Territories
and Possessions by the attestation of the clerk and seal of the court
annexed, if a seal exists, together with a certificate of a judge of the
court that the said attestation is in proper form.

Such Acts, records and judicial proceedings or copies thereof, so
authenticated, shall have the same full faith and credit in every court
within the United States and its Territories and Possessions as they
have by law or usage in the courts of such State, Territory or
Possession from which they are taken.[112]

The implementing statute expands the constitutional text from "each state"
to include "Territory or Possession," thus requiring, for example, the state of
New Jersey to give full faith and credit to a Puerto Rican judgment.[113] The full
faith and credit guarantee also applies to federal judgments[114] and federal court
enforcement of state judgments.[115]

The provisions of the full faith and credit guarantee are essentially twofold
in nature: Each state and federal court must give the judgments of other states
(including federal judgments) the same conclusive effect between the parties
and their privies as is given such judgments in the state (or federal district)
where they were rendered, and they must allow the bringing and maintenance
of actions based on out-of-state judgments to the extent it has judicial machin-
ery for that purpose.[116]

Foreign Judgments

Judgments rendered by foreign courts are outside the textual reach of the Full
Faith and Credit Clause and the implementing statute at 28 United States Code
(hereinafter U.S.C.) § 1738. The result has been generally to provide such foreign judgments comity rather than full faith and credit. The leading case in this
area is *Hilton v. Guyot*.[117] The *Hilton* Court identified the elements of comity for
foreign judgments to include four general conditions, namely, that (1) the foreign court possessed personal and subject matter jurisdiction; (2) the judgment
was not procured by fraud; (3) the court provided essential due process, that is,
notice and opportunity to be heard; and (4) the judgment did not offend or
conflict with the public policy of the enforcing state. The general respect
accorded to foreign judgments as reflected by the doctrine of comity still leaves
the individual states with flexibility in deciding particulars in the enforcement
of foreign judgments. However, in the growing interdependence of a global

economy, there is a move toward more reliability and uniformity through several model federal statutes, such as the Uniform Foreign Country Money Judgments Recognition Act.[118]

Tribal Court Judgments

As with foreign judgments, the text of the Full Faith and Credit Clause makes no reference to Indian tribes. The implementing statue, 28 U.S.C. § 1738, also makes no express reference to tribes, but its language relative to "territory" is sufficiently ambiguous to suggest the potential for including tribal court judgments within its scope. The Supreme Court has not directly ruled on this issue.

There is little doubt that the basic text of the Full Faith and Credit Clause guarantee in the Constitution is limited to states. The language is plain and unambiguous and certainly reflects the fact that tribes were *not* part of the original union. In addition, it was certainly inconceivable to the founding fathers that tribes had courts capable of issuing judgments that could or should be enforced in state courts.

The principal means of dealing with such issues were through *treaty* provisions that often identified the specifics of federal-tribal cooperation in matters involving the conduct and actions of Indians and non-Indians in Indian country. For example, the Fort Laramie Treaty of 1868 provided that:

> If bad men among the whites, or among other people subject to the authority of the United States, shall commit any wrong upon the person or property of the Indians, the United States will, upon proof made to the agent and forwarded to the Commissioner of Indian Affairs at Washington city, proceed at once to cause the offender to be arrested and punished according to the laws of the United States, and also reimburse the injured person for the loss sustained.

> If bad men among the Indians shall commit a wrong or depredation upon the person or property of any one, white, black, or Indian, subject to the authority of the United States, and at peace therewith, the Indians herein named solemnly agree that they will, upon proof made to their agent, and notice by him, deliver up the wrongdoer to the United States, to be tried and punished according to its laws; and in case they willfully refuse so to do, the person injured shall be reimbursed for his loss from the annuities or other moneys due or to become due to them under this or other treaties made with the United States.[119]

Such agreements with states were largely unnecessary because states were not recognized as having any legitimate interest or concern in what was happening in Indian country. It was an exclusive federal-tribal matter.[120]

The implementing statute first passed in 1790 clearly expanded the constitutional language of full faith and credit to include territories and possessions. Given the fact that even at this early period, Congress often passed statutes that dealt directly with tribes, it seems unlikely that Congress intended to include tribes within the statute without making any express reference to them. The statute was most likely directed to the reality of existing territory east of the Mississippi River but outside any state, and of acquiring territory—such as the Louisiana Purchase in 1803—that would add land to the United States that was outside the boundaries of any state.

Despite this likelihood, there is sufficient textual ambiguity in the implementing statute that some courts have found it sufficient to support full faith and credit for tribal court judgments. The leading case from this perspective is *United States ex rel Mackey v. Coxe*.[121] In *Mackey*, the Supreme Court construed an 1812 federal statute with a provision to recognize the grant of letters of administration by the proper authority in any of the "United States or the *territories* thereof" to include letters of administration granted by Cherokee Nation law: "The Cherokee country, we think, may be considered a territory of the United States, within the act of 1812. In no respect can it be considered a foreign State or a territory, as it is within our jurisdiction and subject to our laws."[122]

This case standing alone—which does not even directly involve the full faith and credit statute—seems a rather thin reed on which to rest the argument that the full faith and credit statute encompasses tribes. This reed is sometimes then tethered to the text of 28 U.S.C. § 1738 by noting that the language relevant to the *rendering* court—"The records and judicial proceedings of *any* court of *any* such State, Territory, or Possession" is similar but not identical to the language pertinent to the *enforcing* court—"shall have the same full faith and credit in every court within the United States and its Territories and Possessions."[123] In this interpretation, it is argued that a tribal court is geographically located within the terms identified in the statute and hence legally "*any* court of *any* state, territory or possession." This linguistic fact appears to be less than compelling. Such a convoluted reading has not had much support.

The more accepted understanding is that neither the Full Faith and Credit Clause nor its implementing statute pertains to tribal court judgments. In this view, it is up to each state (and the federal government) to formulate its own rules with respect to enforcing tribal court judgments. The converse is also true with regard to the enforcement of state court judgments by tribal courts. In a few instances, there are *specific* federal statutes that require states to give full faith and credit to tribal court judgments. Such statutes include the Indian Child Welfare Act,[124] the Violence Against Women Act,[125] the Full Faith and Credit Act for Child Support,[126] the Indian Land Consolidation Act,[127] the National Indian Forest Resources Management Act,[128] the American Indian Agricultural Resource Management Act,[129] and the Maine Indian Claims Settlement Act.[130] The very existence of these specific federal statutory provisions would seem to indicate a congressional understanding that full faith and credit does not exist generally for tribal court judgments. In addition, these statutes also contain express reference to territories and possessions, which would seem to undermine the claim that the territory and possession language of 28 U.S.C. § 1738 includes tribes.

States have taken various approaches to this issue. These approaches include a *state* guarantee of full faith and credit, comity, or decisions on a case-by-case basis. The specific legal mechanisms include state statutes, state supreme court decisions, and state supreme court rule-making authority.[131] There is no clear general rule for federal courts to follow, and at least one circuit court has adopted the comity model.[132] Several states, such as Alaska[133] and South Dakota,[134] have adopted a judicially created comity approach; New Mexico[135] and Washington[136] have adopted a full faith and credit approach. State statutory enactments include full faith and credit in states such as Wyoming[137] and Arizona[138]; state supreme court rules requiring full faith and credit include Alaska[139] and North Dakota.[140]

There is also the converse issue of whether tribal courts must provide full faith and credit, comity, or only a case-by-case determination in the enforcement of state court judgments in tribal courts. Obviously, tribal courts (as the states) are bound by any specific federal statutes that require tribal courts to give full faith and credit to state court judgments, but there is no general federal rule on the issue. Most tribes have taken no definitive action in the area. The few that have taken action have adopted the comity model. Tribes must also deal with judgments from other tribal courts and generally treat them similarly to state court judgments. For example, see *In re Marriage of Red Fox*,[141] where the Court of Appeals for the Crow Tribe of Montana recognized that it had to respect a judgment of a Northern Cheyenne Tribal Court unless that judgment had been obtained by fraud, the judgment conflicted with another final judgment entitled to recognition, or recognition of the judgment was contrary to tribal public policy.

A few states and tribes condition their provision of full faith and credit or comity on reciprocity.[142] In such an instance, a state or tribe will provide full faith and credit or comity only if that particular state or tribe provides full faith and credit or comity to its judgments. A good example in this regard is South Dakota. In *Mexican v. Circle Bear*,[143] the South Dakota Supreme Court adopted the comity model as identified in the seminal international comity case of *Hilton v. Guyot*.[144] Nevertheless, the South Dakota legislature promptly adopted a statutory modification of *Mexican v. Circle Bear*, which made comity discretionary rather than mandatory, and outside of domestic relations, the statute was limited to "exceptional circumstances" and conditioned on "reciprocity" from the issuing tribal court.[145] South Dakota provides the classic form of comity to foreign nation judgments but is more circumspect and cautious concerning tribal court judgments rendered within its own borders. Legal respect, it seems, emerges piece by piece from the exigencies of the past.

The full faith and credit or comity issue also presents important policy concerns for all involved, particularly tribes. Full faith and credit and comity are hinges of respect and parity. If the federal government or state provides full faith and credit to tribal court judgments, the tribes are receiving the highest form of legal respect in this area of the law. If tribal court judgments are receiving comity, they are receiving a substantial amount of respect. If neither, they are receiving little or no respect. This issue of respect and governmental parity harks back to one of our initial themes concerning the ability of the dominant society to accurately perceive and honor tribal governance and performance.

The full faith and credit or comity issue also challenges tribes to decide difficult issues of reciprocity, particularly in a context that for many tribes involves a long legacy of legal and racial animosity with states. There is also the more indirect and nuanced issue of assimilation and autonomy. Do tribes have to play too much by someone else's rules to obtain full faith and credit or comity? Do they need to be given enduring respect before they can be expected to return it? This debate has sometimes been cast in the scholarly literature as whether a strict (reciprocal) full faith and credit or symmetrical approach for all is (or is not) preferable to an asymmetrical comity approach that would mandate comity on the state or federal side but make it only discretionary on the tribal side.[146] In the end, the respect embedded in full faith and credit and comity is surely essential for tribal court development and enhanced sovereignty, but it must also preserve a certain flexibility with room to evolve in order to achieve a mutually satisfactory result to both tribes and states.

The full faith and credit or comity quandary in Indian law further illustrates a central paradox of contemporary Indian law. Although it is clear that the Full Faith and Credit Clause was never intended as originally written to apply to tribes, Congress nevertheless may use its plenary power to enforce such a regime in whole or in part. As noted before, Congress has done this on a number of occasions at least to require full faith and credit be accorded *to* tribal court judgments, and presumably it could extend such legislation across the board to all situations involving tribes and states, requiring full faith and credit *from* tribes as well.

Yet this still leaves two important questions relative to policy and constitutional doctrine. First, one might think such a move to be good policy but nevertheless constitutionally flawed because such plenary power is not constitutionally justified. It thus presents a theoretical and practical conundrum whether plenary power can even be used to achieve "good" policy objectives that advance respect for tribal sovereignty. It seems that real-world considerations involving the precarious nature of contemporary tribal sovereignty counsel an affirmative response. Yet such a response—at least at the scholarly level—needs to indicate the essential conceptual contradiction and the continuing risk of such extensive power.

Second, and oddly enough, there indeed might be a fully constitutional approach in this area that would authorize Congress under the Indian Commerce Clause to enact legislation that would bind the federal government and the states but not the tribes. Yet one doubts whether such a one-sided approach would be politically possible, given the likely strong opposition by the states. Practical advance will eventually need constitutional reform.

Federal-Tribal Relationship: Indian Law Federalism

Although it is routine to speak of federalism in the context of the Constitution's division of authority between the federal government and the states, such an observation is almost never made with respect to the federal government and tribes. This is unfortunate in that it avoids a valuable opportunity to identify such contours, however faint they may seem, about the federal-tribal relationship as it is outlined in the Constitution. The development of constitutionally based Indian law federalism would be a significant step forward in securing a reliable foundation for the potential and reality of tribal sovereignty.

The Indian Commerce Clause

The text of the Indian Commerce Clause—like the Interstate Commerce Clause—is direct and succinct. Congress shall have the power to regulate commerce "with the Indian tribes."[147] However, unlike the Interstate Commerce Clause, it does have a predecessor version in the Articles of Confederation. As noted in chapter 2, that version was hopelessly contradictory: "Congress assembled shall also have the sole and exclusive right and power of...regulating the trade and managing all affairs with the Indians, not members of any of the states, provided that the legislative right of any State within its own limits be not infringed or violated...."[148]

The "exclusive" right granted to Congress nevertheless cannot "infringe" on the legislative right of the states. This obvious contradiction was noted by Madison in The Federalist No. 42:

> The regulation of commerce with the Indian tribes is very properly unfettered from two limitations in the articles of Confederation, which render the provision obscure and contradictory. The power is there restrained to Indians, not members of any of the States, and is not to violate or infringe the legislative right of any State within its own limits. What descriptions of Indians are to be deemed members of a State, is not yet settled, and has been a question of frequent perplexity and contention in the federal councils. And how the trade with Indians, though not members of a State, yet residing within its legislative jurisdiction, can be regulated by an external authority, without so far intruding on the internal rights of legislation, is absolutely incomprehensible. This is not the only case in which the articles of Confederation have inconsiderately endeavored to accomplish impossibilities; to reconcile a partial sovereignty in the Union, with complete sovereignty in the States; to subvert a mathematical axiom, by taking away a part, and letting the whole remain.[149]

Madison clearly wanted to resolve the ambiguity and confusion in Article IX of the Articles of Confederation, and he wanted to resolve the problems in favor of the national government. Madison's views—as with the Interstate Commerce Clause—prevailed without much debate at the Constitutional Convention, and the Indian Commerce Clause was redrafted to excise any reference to state authority in Indian commerce or Indian affairs generally.

It is also worth noting that the text of Article IX of the Articles of Confederation conferring authority on Congress was not limited to commerce per se but also to "managing all affairs with the Indians." Although there is no indication what this phrase in the Articles of Confederation meant or what its redaction in the Constitution means, it was probably related to the other primary colonial activities with Indians, namely, war, diplomacy, and treaty making. These activities are all forbidden to the states in other parts of the Constitution. States are expressly prohibited from entering into treaties and expressly prohibited from declaring war.[150]

The Indian Commerce Clause poses two distinct conceptual issues. The first is whether it provides any effective limit on federal authority in Indian affairs. Despite its clear text and surrounding history, the answer, at least since the 1903 decision in *Lone Wolf v. Hitchcock*,[151] has been no. Congress's plenary power has transformed a limited power to regulate *trade with* Indian tribes to complete authority *over* Indian tribes.

The second issue is whether it provides any effective bar to state authority in Indian country. The answer is yes when Congress expressly enacts legislation to curb such authority. For example, the Non-Intercourse Act expressly forbids private or state land transactions with tribes that are not approved by the federal government.[152] In addition, the Court has sometimes viewed other less express federal legislation as preempting any state authority in that general subject matter area. For example, in *McClanahan v. Arizona State Tax Commission*,[153] the Court struck down the applicability of state income tax to income earned by a tribal member who lived and worked on the reservation. The Court found federal preemption emanating from the interplay of the 1868 Navajo Treaty and the Buck Act.[154]

The more challenging variant of this question is whether the Court has ever used the concept of a dormant Indian Commerce Clause to strike down state authority in Indian country. This line of analysis takes its lead from dormant Interstate Commerce Clause jurisprudence that holds that even when Congress does *not* act, the dormant or silent element of constitutional provision forecloses state authority in areas textually assigned to Congress. In this view, Congress must expressly authorize state authority in the areas related to interstate commerce before the state can act. For example, in the case of *Kassel v. Consolidated Freightways Corp.*,[155] the Court struck down the attempt of the State of Iowa to regulate the use of double-length tractor-trailers, despite the fact that Congress had enacted no legislation on the matter.[156]

In the context of the Indian Commerce Clause, Clinton valiantly makes the case for a dormant Indian Commerce Clause jurisprudence. The core of his argument centers on a rather broad interpretation of cases that turn aside state authority over Indians and Indian tribes in Indian country. The cases relied on—by Clinton's own admission—do not even cite the Indian Commerce Clause, much less discuss its "dormant" component. Such a view strains credulity. For example, in the seminal case of *Williams v. Lee*,[157] the Court held that the states, including state courts, had no authority over a commercial transaction involving an Indian and a non-Indian in Indian country because such "state action infringed on the right of reservation Indians to make their own laws and be ruled by them."[158] There is no citation to, or discussion of, the Indian Commerce Clause, yet Clinton finds that "the *Williams* infringement test, while not clearly announced and labeled as a dormant Indian Commerce Clause test, is best understood in this light."[159]

The Indian Commerce Clause was formulated to resolve an issue of federalism between the federal government and the states. It was *not* designed to invade the province of tribal sovereignty. The issue of trade and commercial intercourse with Indian tribes was important both as an element of economic development and as a risk to political stability. Trade and land transactions were of immense economic interest in the early republic, and at some level these activities were to be encouraged. Yet American citizens, corporate interests, and the states themselves could not be trusted to carry out their endeavors without firm federal regulation. Greed, cultural insensitivity, and racism constantly threatened to push commerce and land transactions with Indians into political instability and war.

The core of the Indian Commerce Clause reflects a recognition of federal authority to regulate its side of commercial interaction with Indians and Indian tribes. This authority also included the ability to regulate states and private interests and further foreclosed any independent state authority in Indian country. It was up to tribes as functioning sovereigns to regulate their side of commercial interaction with non-Indian citizens and their governments.

Congressional authority deriving from the Indian Commerce Clause was pivotal in the early days of the republic. Trade was the preeminent activity involving Indians and non-Indians (and the states) during these early times. Yet as a result of greed, racial antipathy, and cultural misunderstanding, violence and conflict were often close at hand. Despite treaties, strict regulation at the individual level was necessary to ensure a modicum of stability and regularity.

The first of these federal laws, known as the Non-Intercourse Act, was passed in 1790 and was directed against "obstreperous whites." Regardless of the government-to-government nature of the treaties, "white settlers and speculators ignored the treaties and guarantees. Plainly, something more was needed than the treaties, which had been so largely disregarded."[160] Initially, the trade and intercourse law's primary thrust was to regulate trade by providing federal licensing of traders and establishing penalties for trading without a license. In addition, to discourage private (and state) land speculators (including states) from dealing directly with the Indians and Indian tribes, the statute prohibited such private land transactions unless expressly approved by some public act of federal recognition or federal treaty.[161] Subsequently, as alcohol became an increasing problem in Indian country, the Trade and Intercourse Acts were amended to make it a federal offense to bring liquor into Indian country.[162]

The purpose of these statutes was not to regulate Indian conduct (which, of course, would have raised its own constitutional problems) but rather to regulate individual non-Indian (and state) conduct in dealing with Indians and tribes.

During this era, even when there was federal government intent to abide by its legal commitments and responsibilities to Indian people and tribes, such intent was often undermined by the unscrupulous (and illegal) behavior of many white traders, speculators, and settlers. In many instances, the federal government was in conflict with its own citizens about how to deal with Indians.[163]

As these statutes plainly indicate, the power conferred on Congress by the Indian Commerce Clause was limited to the federal and state side of the equation. The Indian Commerce Clause did not (and could not) confer authority to regulate the trade *of* Indians, but only *with* Indians. There is, of course, the identical language in the Foreign Nation Commerce Clause, to regulate trade "*with* foreign Nations." Certainly a sovereign may regulate its own conduct and that of *its* citizens when interacting with sovereigns who are not part of the nation-state. When the Constitution was adopted in 1789, both Indian tribes and foreign nations were recognized as sovereigns, but not as sovereigns who were part of the constitutional process or compact. Individual Indians, like "foreigners," were neither federal nor state citizens.

The Constitution did not *include* Indians or Indian tribes but *excluded* them, hence the necessity of the Indian Commerce Clause as a means of dealing with them as *outsiders* to the Constitution and the constitutional process. The Indian Commerce Clause recognized tribal sovereignty as a reality that existed *outside*, not *inside*, the Constitution. This constitutional reality was complemented by the treaty-making provision of the Constitution and the ensuing 350 plus treaties entered into by the federal government with Indian tribes.

As a result of this array of factors, the history and text of the Indian Commerce Clause are much different from the Interstate Commerce Clause. And yet jurisprudentially, the history and text of the Indian Commerce Clause have been both ignored and turned inside out when necessary to serve federal interests. Despite the early seminal cases of *Cherokee Nation v. Georgia*[164] and *Worcester v. Georgia*,[165] in which tribes were recognized as "domestic dependent nations" and states were deemed without authority in Indian country as a result of treaties and the strictures of the Indian Commerce Clause, there was no concomitant recognition of any limit on federal authority.

In *Kagama v. United States*,[166] the Court was faced with a constitutional challenge to the then recently passed (1885) Major Crimes Act, which made it a federal offense for an Indian to commit one of the enumerated major crimes against another person in Indian country. The constitutional challenge was that the statute was beyond what was permitted to Congress under the Indian Commerce Clause. The Court readily agreed with this claim, noting commonsensically that the regulation of criminal conduct did not amount to the regulation of commerce.[167]

Yet instead of simply declaring the statute unconstitutional, the Court upheld it on nonconstitutional or perhaps more accurately extraconstitutional grounds. The Court noted in a rather truncated fashion that the statute was needed to protect Indians from the states as their "deadliest enemy" and therefore justifiable on the amorphous—but clearly nonconstitutional—grounds of a trust duty owed to Indians by the U.S. government.[168] The *Kagama* case is mentioned here simply to locate the first and last time that the Indian Commerce Clause appeared to have (but then really did not have) constitutional limits. The *Kagama* case remains good law to this day.

Kagama is also important because it established the precedential ground-work for the plenary power doctrine that was established in *Lone Wolf v. Hitchcock*.[169] The plenary power doctrine is the fulcrum of the extraconstitutional regime in Indian law today and is discussed in detail in chapter 5. The *Kagama* Court was not insensitive to its own doctrinal strain when it noted: "The relation of the Indian tribes living within the borders of the United States, both before and since the Revolution, to the people of the United States has always been an anomalous one and of a complex character."[170] It was only a matter of time before this "anomalous" relationship completely departed from the text and history of the Constitution in the 1903 decision of *Lone Wolf v. Hitchcock*.

In the modern era, the Indian Commerce Clause morphed from a textual constraint on federal power in Indian affairs to a textual accelerant of federal authority. For example, in 1973, in the case of *McClanahan v. Arizona State Tax Commission*,[171] the Court held that a state may not assert its income tax against a tribal member living and working on the reservation. The Court forthrightly admitted some doctrinal inconsistencies of the past, which it attempted to correct with the observation "[t]he source of federal authority *over* Indian matters has been the subject of some confusion, but it is now generally recognized that the power derives from federal responsibility for regulating commerce with Indian tribes and for treaty making."[172] The Court made no effort in *McClanahan* to demonstrate how the Indian Commerce Clause provided Congress with authority *over* Indians and Indian tribes. As set out in ensuing chapters, it will be demonstrated that congressional and Supreme Court authority in Indian affairs remains unchecked and without limit, constitutional or otherwise.

In distinction to the jurisprudence of the Interstate Commerce Clause, the jurisprudence of the Indian Commerce Clause is remarkably sparse and doctrinally thin. It has occasionally, as in *McClanahan* itself, been indirectly used to limit state authority in Indian country, but it has never limited federal authority over Indians and Indian tribes in Indian country. The word *indirectly* is particularly important in that the Court in *McClanahan* made no reference to matters of commerce but rather to broad notions of federal preemption in Indian affairs. In fact, there is not a single case after *Kagama* that even discusses how the Indian Commerce Clause came to regulate not only trade *with* Indians but *all* activities *of* Indians.

However, recently, in *United States v. Lara*,[173] while the majority ratified Congress's plenary power to expand (or contract) "inherent" tribal sovereignty, Justice Thomas punctured the unanalyzed assumption concerning the reach of the Indian Commerce Clause:

> The Court utterly fails to find any provision of the Constitution that gives Congress enumerated power to alter tribal sovereignty. The Court cites the Indian Commerce Clause and the treaty power. I cannot agree that the Indian Commerce Clause "provide(s) Congress with plenary power to legislate in the field of Indian affairs." At one time, the implausibility of this assertion at least troubled the Court, *see, e.g. United States v. Kagama*, 118 U.S. 375, 378–379 (1886) (considering such a construction of the Indian Commerce Clause to be "very strained"), and I would be willing to revisit the question. Cf., *e.g., United States v. Morrison*, 529 U.S. 598 (2000); *United States v. Lopez*, 514 U.S. 549 (1995).[174]

No member of the Court joined Justice Thomas's opinion concurring in the judgment, and it thus appears unlikely that the questionable jurisprudence involving the Indian Commerce Clause will be judicially reexamined in the near future.

Treaties

The authority to make treaties is found in Article II of the Constitution: "He [the President] shall have the Power, by and with the Advice and Consent of the Senate, to make Treaties, provided two thirds of the Senators present concur...."[175] Treaties were the primary form of legal interaction between the federal government and tribes from the founding of the republic to 1871. Treaties were the primary legal mechanism used to reflect and to record the results of Native-white diplomacy. During that time, the United States entered into more than 350 treaties with Indian tribes. Many of these treaties were promptly broken, but tribes were left without legal recourse because of the sovereign immunity of the United States. This history may be summarized:

Before 1946, Indian claims against the United States could be litigated only if Congress had passed special legislation authorizing suit to be brought by a particular tribe. The Court of Claims had been established in 1855 to permit many types of claims against the United States, thus affording a partial waiver of sovereign immunity. 10 Stat. 612. In 1863, however, all claims based on treaty violations were excluded from the jurisdiction of the Court of Claims. 12 Stat. 765, 767. Statutes of limitations also were impediments to most non-treaty Indian claims.

By the 1940s, a consensus had been reached that a better mechanism was needed to resolve Indian claims. The process of enacting special legislation for each Indian claim had proved cumbersome—a total of 142 such acts had been passed. There was also widespread sentiment among Indians and in Congress that past moral wrongs should be legally redressed. Further, the idea of a "final settling" of obligations to Indians complemented the mounting pressure for termination.

The Indian Claims Commission Act of 1946, 25 U.S.C.A. §§ 70–70v, established a three-(later five-) member commission to adjudicate Indian claims. Tribes were allowed to prosecute specified claims arising before the passage of the Act. All claims were required to be filed with the Commission by August 13, 1951, but old claims would not be subject to any other statute of limitations or to the defense of laches. Review of Commission decisions was to be by the Court of Claims and then by the Supreme Court. Claims arising after the passage of the Act were to be filed in the Court of Claims. Initially, the Commission was to complete its work within five years. But the complex cases moved slowly and Congress continually extended the life of the Commission. Finally, Congress dissolved the Commission and transferred all pending cases to the Court of Claims as of September, 1978. Several cases arising under the 1946 Act remain on the docket of the reconstituted Court of Claims.[176]

In 1871, Congress enacted a statute ending the treaty-making process with Indian tribes. The statute did not represent any major policy shift in Indian affairs by the federal government, but rather it reflected a squabble between the Senate and House of Representatives. The dispute focused on the ability of the Senate alone to ratify treaties and thereby obligating the House of Representatives to authorize legislation to appropriate the necessary funds to meet any federal financial commitment incurred in a treaty. The House of Representatives became increasingly antipathetic to the process of being obligated to authorize expenditures for political and fiscal commitments it had no say in. The 1871 statute was attached as a rider to an appropriations bill. The statute reads in its entirety:

> No Indian nation or tribe within the territory of the United States shall be acknowledged or recognized as an independent nation, tribe, or power with whom the United States may contract by treaty; but no obligation of any treaty lawfully made and ratified with any such Indian nation or tribe prior to March 3, 1871 shall be invalidated or impaired.[177]

Two important points—one express, one implied—result from the statute. The statute expressly recognized the validity of existing treaties; it did *not* terminate or abrogate any treaty. The statute further implicitly recognized the continuing ability of the federal government to execute bilateral agreements with tribes. These bilateral agreements would differ from treaties only in the ratification process of requiring the approval of both houses of Congress.[178] The federal government has entered into numerous agreements with tribes since 1871.[179]

Little remarked anywhere[180] is the fact that the statute is probably unconstitutional. This is so because the primary effect of the statute is to strip the president of his Art. II, § 2 power to enter into treaties with Indian tribes. Under the Constitution, treaty making is an executive power, not a congressional power. Congress has no authority to limit the constitutional authority of any coordinate branch of the federal government, including that of the chief executive.[181] This is the quintessence of checks and balances and the separation of powers doctrine. Yet perhaps, as elsewhere, basic constitutional principles do not appear to have much traction in Indian law.

This issue has never reached the Supreme Court or even any federal courts of appeal. President Grant, who signed the legislation in 1871, was apparently willing or sufficiently ignorant to surrender executive constitutional authority without a qualm. Obviously a president's acquiescence or even his endorsement cannot make constitutional what is unconstitutional. Such is the core of constitutional integrity. It is to retain the structural unity of the original compact, regardless of moves to the contrary.

The two most significant legal issues with treaties generally involve the status of treaties in the federal hierarchy of law and the appropriate standard for treaty interpretation, including treaty abrogation. These are particularly central matters within Indian law because of unique historical and cultural concerns and their contemporary reverberations. Treaties are expressly mentioned in the Supremacy Clause and are therefore directly binding on the states. The Supremacy Clause language is sometimes misunderstood as placing treaties *above* other federal law, including congressional legislation. The constitutional "supremacy" of treaties is only true vis-à-vis state law. The Supremacy

Clause itself does not address the question of any hierarchy of federal law.[182] Within the hierarchy of federal law, treaties are generally regarded as the equivalent of federal statutes enacted by Congress. As Chief Justice Marshall noted, a duly enacted treaty must "be regarded in courts of justice as equivalent to an act of the legislature."[183] This not surprising result flows directly from the text of the Supremacy Clause, which states, "This Constitution, and the laws of the United States which shall be made in pursuance thereof; and all Treaties made, or which shall be made, under the Authority of the United States, shall be the supreme Law of the land...."[184]

A treaty, despite its bilateral nature, may be unilaterally abrogated by Congress, as long as the statute is enacted after the treaty and represents "the last expression of the sovereign."[185] The converse is true as well. A duly enacted treaty supersedes any contrary prior statute, whether federal or state. However, a treaty that is not self-executing becomes effective only when authorizing legislation is passed, and then it is the statute rather than the treaty itself that supersedes the prior statute.[186]

The ability to make treaties with Indian tribes is coextensive with treaty making with foreign nations.[187] Treaties with Indian tribes also have the same binding effect on states as treaties with foreign nations.[188] The treaty-making power can be regarded as wide but not limitless. In addition to the procedural requirements of Article II, § 2, which require that "two-thirds of all senators present concur," there are both structural and substantive limitations. The structural limitation is embedded in the notion that the treaty-making power must concern itself with questions "properly the subject of negotiation with a foreign country."[189] This includes Indian tribes but would not include states or municipalities.

The substantive cap reflects the understanding that while a treaty may expand federal power beyond any enumerated power, it cannot circumvent any express (constitutional) limitation on federal authority. As the Court noted in *De Geofroy v. Riggs*, a leading case on treaty interpretation:

> The treaty power...is in terms unlimited, except by those restraints
> which are found in that instrument against the action of the government,
> or its departments, and those arising from the nature of the government
> itself and of that of the states. It would not be contended that it extends
> so far as to authorize what the constitution forbids, or a change in the
> character of the government, or in that of one of the states, or a cession
> of any portion of the territory of the latter, without its consent.[190]

The Court in *Reid v. Covert* expressly held that a treaty cannot "confer power on the Congress, or any other branch of Government, which is free from the restraints of the Constitution."[191]

Models of Treaty Interpretation

Although the Supreme Court itself has not made such a distinction, there have been two primary models of treaty interpretation employed by the Court in Indian law. These models are best denominated as the reserved rights approach and the enumerated rights approach. In the reserved rights approach, the tribe is truly regarded as a complete sovereign with the full power of any national sovereign. In this view, the treaty reflects what a tribe has given up, with everything else not so surrendered as reserved.

The classic case for this model of treaty interpretation is *United States v. Winans*,[192] which involved the meaning of an 1859 treaty between the Yakima Nation and the United States. Although the treaty expressly recognized an off-reservation right to fish in the tribe and its members, it said nothing about access to these "usual and accustomed" places that were often owned and controlled by non-Indians. The lower court had held that the non-Indians had acquired "perfect, absolute title" to the lands in question and therefore had the right to exclude Yakima tribal members from the land.[193]

The Supreme Court reversed, noting that to hold otherwise would be an "impotent outcome," which "seemed to promise more, and give the word of the nation for more."[194] The treaty was not "a grant of rights to the Indians, but a grant of rights from them, a reservation of those not granted."[195] Not having ceded their treaty right to fish off reservation, the Indians had also not ceded their right to access their usual fishing places, even though the treaty made no express reference to the right of access.[196]

This mode of treaty interpretation reflects a true sovereign-to-sovereign approach, wherein the distinctive markers are what each side cedes to the other and what, if anything, they jointly undertake. What remains is what is reserved; that which is not expressly ceded is reserved to the tribe. Another example of reserved rights interpretation is the case of *United States v. Winters*,[197] in which the Court held that an 1888 agreement establishing the Fort Belknap Reservation in Montana reserved water rights to the tribe, despite the fact that the agreement made no express reference to water rights.[198] Note, however, that the Court in both *Winans* and *Winters* created a limitation on the rights of private non-Indians under state law, but it might well have been reluctant to enforce such reserved rights against a state, much less against the federal government itself.

The enumerated rights approach in treaty interpretation proceeds in the opposite manner. The only treaty rights that exist in the tribe are those that are expressly enumerated in the treaty. This approach is especially prevalent in the modern era, when tribes seek to assert treaty rights as the basis of tribal authority over non-Indians. A classic case in this regard is *Montana v. United*

States.[199] In *Montana*, despite language in the 1868 Fort Laramie Treaty with the Crow Tribe describing the reservation in Article II as "set apart for the absolute and undisturbed use and occupation of the Indians herein named,"[200] the Court found that the tribe had lost its ability to regulate the hunting activities of non-Indians on fee land within the reservation.[201] This was so despite the fact that there was no cession by the Crow Tribe in the treaty of its (inherent) authority over non-Indians within the Crow Reservation.

Instead of the reserved rights approach, the Court opted for an enumerated rights approach when it stated that the

> exercise of tribal power beyond what is necessary to protect tribal self-government or to control internal relations is inconsistent with the dependent status of the tribes, and so cannot survive without express congressional delegation. Since regulation of hunting and fishing by nonmembers of a tribe on lands no longer owned by the tribe bears no clear relationship to tribal self-government or internal relations, the general principles of retained sovereignty did not authorize the Crow Tribe to adopt Resolution 74–05.[202]

The *Montana* approach has subsequently been elevated by the Court to "pathmarking" status regarding tribal civil jurisdiction over nonmembers.[203] This enumerated powers approach has thus been exceptionally effective in limiting treaty-based claims of retained or reserved tribal authority over non-Indian activities on nontrust land within the reservation.

The Court has never articulated a consistent way to interpret treaties. It has oscillated between the reserved rights and enumerated rights approaches without even noticing the oscillation. In the modern era—especially when dealing with non-Indians—treaties provide no convincing rationale to the Court for jurisdictional authority over non-Indians. Despite this slight, treaties remain central to most Indian tribes as a cornerstone of their legal identity and the basis of the government-to-government relationship with the United States. For the United States, treaties are certainly not a cornerstone, but rather something more like an inconvenience—an inconvenience that sometimes pricks its conscience, but often does not.

Treaties in Indian Law Jurisprudence

The fate of treaties in Indian law, while subject to the models of interpretation described previously, was often tragic not only legally but also socially and culturally. At times, the trail of broken treaties has threatened to upset any claim for federal legitimacy within Indian law. This is so as a matter of doctrine, policy, and culture.

DOCTRINE

Treaty law doctrine in the context of Indian law is extremely pliable—at times, so pliable that it is better described not as doctrine, but as a chimera totally at the service of national objectives. Treaty interpretation in Indian law is bracketed by two major cases: *Lone Wolf v. Hitchcock*[204] and *United States v. Dion*.[205] *Lone Wolf* authorized unilateral congressional abrogation of Indian treaties, and *Dion* set the contemporary standard for treaty abrogation.

The *Lone Wolf* decision in 1903 held that Congress could unilaterally abrogate treaties with Indian nations. Without much discussion, the Court simply cited the Chinese exclusion case of *Chae Chan Ping v. United States*[206] for the necessary principle. The Court made no real effort to discern whether the relevant statute, the General Allotment Act,[207] even authorized treaty abrogation. Nor did it touch on the issue of how the statute, rather than abrogating a specific treaty, abrogated *all* treaties with Indian tribes. In *Chae Chan Ping*, the specific question was whether the relevant statute abrogated a particular treaty:

> Here the objection made is that the act of 1888 impairs a right vested under the treaty of 1880, as a law of the United States, and the statutes of 1882 and of 1884 passed in execution of it. It must be conceded that the act of 1888 is in contravention of express stipulations of the treaty of 1868 and of the supplemental treaty of 1880, but it is not on that account invalid or to be restricted in its enforcement. The treaties were of no greater legal obligation than the act of congress. By the constitution, laws made in pursuant thereof, and treaties made under the authority of the United States, are both declared to be the supreme law of the land, and no paramount authority is given to one over the other. A treaty, it is true, is in its nature a contract between nations, and is often merely promissory in its character, requiring legislation to carry its stipulations into effect. Such legislation will be open to future repeal or amendment. If the treaty operates by its own force, and relates to a subject within the power of congress, it can be deemed in that particular only the equivalent of a legislative act, to be repealed or modified at the pleasure of congress. In either case the last expression of the sovereign will must control.
>
> The effect of legislation upon conflicting treaty stipulations was elaborately considered in *The Head-Money Cases*, and it was there

adjudged "that so far as a treaty made by the United States with any foreign nation can become the subject of judicial cognizance in the courts of this country, it is subject to such acts as congress may pass for its enforcement, modification, or repeal." 112 U.S. 580, 599.[208]

Treaty abrogation in the Indian context is different than most treaty abrogation with foreign nations. In the former, the United States *extends* its authority over the *people* and *land* of the tribe and even takes tribal land without consent; in the latter there is no *extension* of U.S. authority over foreign nation lands and citizens. There is simply, in most cases, a breach of a promise to perform some duty outside the borders of the foreign country such as, for example, in the *Chae Chan Ping* case, permitting a certain number of Chinese citizens to immigrate to the United States. Thus, treaty abrogation in Indian affairs often is more like an act of war than a simple breach of legal obligation.

The *Lone Wolf* case was not only jurisprudentially wanting but also brazen in its announcement that the decision was in the best interest of the Indians despite their opposition to it. The fact that Indian lands could be unilaterally "purchased" by the United States at whatever price offered occasioned nothing more than the observation that it was "a mere change in the form of investment of Indian tribal property."[209] Indians could not know what was best for themselves, because they "were in substantial effect the wards of the government."[210] All of this came with an irrefutable presumption of good faith that foreclosed judicial review:

> We must presume that Congress acted in perfect good faith in the dealings with the Indians of which complaint is made, and that the legislative branch of the government exercised its best judgment in the premises. In any event, as Congress possessed full power in the matter, the judiciary cannot question or inquire into the motives which prompted the enactment of this legislation.[211]

The issue of treaty abrogation was essentially a "political question," and relief, if any, was available only by appeal to Congress and "not to the courts."[212]

Over time, the sharpest edges of *Lone Wolf*'s doctrine of treaty abrogation have been modified but not abolished. The modifications include the judicial rollback of the political question doctrine and irrefutable presumption of congressional good faith in treaty abrogation, as well as the judicial development of canons of construction to modify the often disadvantageous negotiating position of tribes in the treaty-making process.[213] Yet the threat of treaty abrogation remains a lethal jurisprudential weapon.

In subsequent cases, particularly *Delaware Tribal Business Committee v. Weeks*[214] and *United States v. Sioux Nation of Indians*,[215] the Court essentially did away with the political question doctrine in Indian law and replaced it with the rational basis test for evaluating the constitutionality of legislation, including treaty abrogation. As the court noted in *Weeks*:

> The standard of review most recently expressed is that the legislative judgment should not be disturbed "[a]s long as the special treatment can be tied rationally to the fulfillment of Congress' unique obligation toward the Indians...."[216]

This change, however, is more illusory than real. The rational basis test sets an exceptionally low threshold for the constitutionality of federal statutes. No congressional enactment in Indian affairs has ever been set aside or declared unconstitutional for failure to satisfy the rational basis test.

While the substantive threshold for treaty abrogation remains de minimis, the procedural barriers to permitting challenge in the first instance have been ameliorated to a considerable degree. As noted earlier, the problem of the federal government's sovereign immunity has been quite problematic in Indian law matters. Today, the ability of Indian tribes to sue the United States is expressly recognized in both the federal question and civil rights statutes set out at 28 U.S.C. § 1331[217] and 28 U.S.C. § 1345.[218]

This earlier jurisdictional bar was devastating. It permitted de facto treaty abrogation and the confiscation of tribal land without judicial remedy, indeed without even the hallowed right to have one's day in court. Obviously, the mere lifting of a jurisdictional bar does not itself create a substantive right of recovery, including that of money damages. What is needed is both a waiver of federal sovereign immunity and the existence of a statutory (or common law) basis for recovery. The Tucker Act[219] creates the necessary waiver of federal sovereign immunity for jurisdictional purposes. Many individual federal statutes grant the required substantive basis for potential recovery. Examples of such statutes include the Indian Claims Commission Act[220] and the Non-Intercourse Act.[221] In other situations such as quiet title actions[222] and breach of trust responsibility,[223] recovery is often limited to declaratory and injunctive relief. The right to sue for breach of the trust responsibility or treaty abrogation is, where authorized, often limited to money damages without the possibility of more appropriate remedies, such as land return.

The Court has not always been insensitive to these problems.[224] As a counterweight, the Court created a set of canons of construction to guide treaty interpretation. These canons of treaty interpretation are threefold in nature: ambiguous expressions must be resolved in favor of the Indian parties concerned,[225] Indian treaties must be liberally construed in favor of the Indians,[226] and Indian treaties must be interpreted as the Indians themselves would have understood them.[227]

These canons derive from the unequal bargaining position of the tribes in many treaty-making situations and from the recognition of the unique trust relationship that exists between the federal government and tribes.[228]

The ability of tribes to negotiate on equal terms with the federal government changed significantly over time. In the earliest days of the republic (and before), Indian tribes often had the upper hand in terms of resources and military might, including the advantages of coalitions with the British (and the French) to advance favorable leverage in the treaty-making process. This leverage waned over time, and many (but not all) tribes found themselves with less and less bargaining power and more and more subject to treaties that were imposed on the most unfavorable terms without meaningful negotiations. Tribes could not easily resist or opt out of treaty making when it was most disadvantageous to them.

Many scholars have noted that such negotiations were almost always unsatisfactory to the Indians. Friendly Indians were commonly selected as chiefs by federal officials and given power and prestige over tribes that had their own methods of selecting leaders. Some treaties purported to bind Indian tribes not present at negotiations by the signatures of unauthorized headmen who were unaware that their signatures would bind those tribes. There are numerous accounts of threats, coercion, bribery, and outright fraud by the negotiators for the United States.[229] Given these factors, it is natural that the Indians often felt abused and angry at the close of negotiations. Indian tribes at treaty negotiations also faced a language barrier. The treaties were written only in English, making it a certainty that semantic and interpretational problems would arise. When several Indian tribes were involved, the government negotiators would sometimes use a language they believed to be common to all tribes but in fact carried different meanings to each. The very serious language problems have been emphasized by the Supreme Court:

> [T]he negotiations for the treaty are conducted, on the part of the
> United States, an enlightened and powerful nation, by
> representatives skilled in diplomacy, masters of a written language,
> understanding the modes and forms of creating the various technical
> estates known to their law, and assisted by an interpreter employed
> by themselves; ... the treaty is drawn up by them and in their own
> language; ... the Indians, on the other hand, are a weak and
> dependent people, who have no written language and are wholly
> unfamiliar with all the forms of legal expression, and whose only
> knowledge of the terms in which the treaty is framed is that imparted
> to them by the interpreter employed by the United States. ...[230]

It is impossible to avoid the conclusion, therefore, that the young nation's ideals were often subservient to its ambitions when it came to honoring the solemn promises contained in the treaties. Breach by the United States was common; in one case, a treaty was respected for only twelve days before it was violated by the government negotiator.[231]

Such treaties became analogous to contracts of adhesion that merited close judicial scrutiny to ensure a minimum standard of reasonableness, if not fairness, in their interpretation. Of course, there were always exceptions, such as the Fort Laramie Treaty of 1868, which was negotiated between the federal government and the Great Sioux Nation after their military standoff resulting from Red Cloud's War.[232] This treaty has been the centerpiece and hallmark of the Sioux Nation's legal existence and interaction with the federal government ever since.

The Court's use of the canons of construction has been checkered at best. On the positive side, there is the view that the Court has put teeth into these rules of construction:

> For example, the Supreme Court concluded that the treaty phrase "to be held as Indian lands are held" also reserved hunting and fishing rights to the Indians. In construing treaty language reserving to the Indians the right to fish at "usual and accustomed places" on lands relinquished to the United States, it held that the language included an easement to cross over these lands to reach traditional fishing grounds, even after they had become privately settled by whites. Recently, the Court found that general provisions in the Navajo Treaty of 1868, which set aside the reservation "for the use and occupation of the Navajo tribe of Indians" and provided for the exclusion of non-Navajos from the reservation, must be construed as excluding the operation of state laws, including state tax laws, upon Indians living on the reservation.[233]

A competing view suggests that the canons are more variable in the vigor with which they are applied. In some cases, for example, they are simply ignored; in others, they are deemed inapplicable because they do not satisfy certain threshold requirements such as the "ambiguity" necessary for their invocation and applicability. For example, Chief Justice Rehnquist observed in *DeCoteau v. District County Court*[234] that the canon according to which ambiguities are resolved to the benefit of Indian tribes is not "a license to disregard clear expressions of tribal and congressional intent."[235] In the end, the applicability of the canons often turns on what is in the eye of the beholder.

It is also important to note that the Court's strongest pronouncements in favor of upholding treaties have tended to be in the context of tribal claims against private individuals and the states, rather than against the federal government itself. For example, in the classic 1905 case of *United States v. Winans*,[236] the Court upheld an 1859 treaty with the Yakima Nation that guaranteed tribal members access to "traditional and customary" fishing spots off the reservation, even when that involved recognizing an equitable servitude on non-Indian fee land in order to guarantee access to these spots.

In other cases, where actions involving treaty abrogation are brought against the United States, the Court has been much more parsimonious in determining whether the United States breached the treaty. This is especially true in cases like *Lone Wolf v. United States* and the Sioux Nation case involving the taking of the Black Hills. The Court has occasionally used the canons of construction against the United States, but only in cases seeking money damages rather than land return or injunctive relief.[237]

The most recent case of treaty interpretation was resolved in favor of the tribe against the state. In *Minnesota v. Mille Lacs Band of Chippewa Indians*,[238] the Court held in a five-to-four vote that an 1837 treaty with several bands of Chippewa Indians that guaranteed to the Indians certain off-reservation hunting, fishing, and gathering rights on land ceded by the treaty was not abrogated by an executive order in 1850, an 1855 treaty, or the admission of Minnesota into the union in 1858.[239] The Court did employ the canons of construction to aid in its interpretation. The Court said:

> In this case, an examination of the historical record provides insight
> into how the parties to the Treaty understood the terms of the
> agreement. This insight is especially helpful to the extent it sheds
> light on how the Chippewa signatories to the Treaty understood the
> agreement because we interpret Indian treaties to give effect to the
> terms as the Indians themselves would have understood them.[240]

Treaty interpretation involves two additional problems—one practical and one doctrinal. The practical concerns (or maybe they are really political in nature) center on the role of the passage of time. Most often, treaty cases require a determination about what the treaty means as to land cession, reservation borders, jurisdiction, or hunting and fishing rights anywhere from 50 to 150 years *after* the signing and ratification of the treaty. This often takes the Court into the realm of vast demographic changes and accommodation (or deference) to state authority in contested areas. The Court is often powerfully affected by such facts. For example, in a series of contemporary cases involving acts of Congress that permitted non-Indians to homestead on portions of the reservation in the last decade of the nineteenth century through the first decade of the twentieth century, the Court has uniformly found that where the *current* demographics favored non-Indians, it was the intent of Congress to abrogate the relevant treaty and diminish the reservation. Conversely, if *current* demographics still favored the tribe, treaty abrogation was not found, and there was no "diminishment" of the affected reservation.[241] This may sound exaggerated, but it is not. In fact, the Court itself admits that the use of current demographic data to discern legislative intent more than a century ago is "an unorthodox and potentially unreliable method of statutory interpretation."[242] The Court, of course, does not admit that demographics are *dispositive*, but that is the empirical reality.[243]

The Court has also used brazen fictions to justify treaty abrogation long after the fact. For example, in the well-known Black Hills case,[244] after treaty negotiations with the Sioux Nation failed to yield a treaty for cession of the Black Hills, Congress simply passed a statute in 1877 annexing 7.7 million acres that were part of the Great Sioux Nation Reservation, established as part of the Fort Laramie Treaty of 1868. This confiscation of Sioux Nation lands was without compensation. It was also not subject to litigation because of U.S. sovereign immunity, which was not waived until 1920, when a special jurisdictional statute was passed by Congress. Litigation began in 1923 and culminated in a 1980 Supreme Court decision that held that when the United States "took" the Black Hills in 1877 it was exercising its power of eminent domain under the Fifth Amendment, and the federal government's only error was its failure to provide "just compensation."[245] The treaty abrogation issue was dismissed in a footnote.[246]

There was no discussion—much less any evidence—that Congress ever considered its actions based on its power of eminent domain. The problem here, of course, is that when the federal government confiscates Indian land, no court is going to order its return, especially if it was expropriated more than a hundred years ago. The best a court can do is to bemoan the inimical history of an earlier era, order compensation, and direct the tribe to Congress for potential land return.[247]

The other issue—more doctrinal in nature—is what legal standard controls determination of whether Congress intended to abrogate a treaty. This standard has varied significantly, while consistently remaining fuzzy and abstract. Such phrases as "clear expression to the contrary,"[248] "sufficiently clear and specific,"[249] and "explicit statement"[250] have all had their moments.

In the 1986 case of *United States v. Dion*,[251] the Court acknowledged this inconsistency and its determination to ameliorate it:

We have enunciated, however, different standards over the years for determining how such a clear and plain intent must be demonstrated. In some cases, we have required that Congress make "express declaration" of its intent to abrogate treaty rights. In other cases, we have looked to the statute's "legislative history" and "surrounding circumstances" as well as to "the face of the Act." Explicit statement by Congress is preferable for the purpose of ensuring legislative accountability for the abrogation of treaty rights. We have not rigidly interpreted that preference, however, as a *per se* rule; where the evidence of congressional intent to abrogate is sufficiently compelling, "the weight of authority indicates that such an intent can also be found by a reviewing court from clear and reliable evidence in the legislative history of a statute."[252]

The Court then stated: "What is essential is clear evidence that Congress actually considered the conflict between its intended action on the one hand and treaty rights on the other, and chose to resolve that conflict by abrogating the treaty."[253]

In *Dion*, the Court went on to hold that the 1940 Eagle Protection Act, which made no reference to Indians or treaties, as amended in 1962, in part, to permit the Secretary of the Interior to exempt the taking of bald or golden eagles for Indian religious purposes, abrogated the 1858 treaty (and by extension all Indian treaties) with the Yankton Sioux tribe in regard to the hunting of bald and golden eagles by tribal members on the reservation. Whatever one might think of the result as a practical or policy matter, the Court's analysis appeared deeply flawed in light of its own newly minted standard of treaty abrogation. The Court found treaty abrogation when neither the text of the amended statute nor any legislative history even mentions treaties, much less treaty abrogation.[254] It is hard to fathom the effort to fashion an explicit rule for treaty abrogation and then to apply it so dismally in the very case that created the rule.

POLICY AND CULTURE

Great nations, like great men, should keep their word.
—*Justice Hugo Black*[255]

If the federal side of treaty making is characterized by an admixture of meretriciousness, weak promises, and periodic attempts to hew to the letter of its commitment, how does it look from the tribal side? What were tribal goals and objectives (whether the product of choice or necessity) in the treaty making process? The differences turn out to be vast and hark back to one of our original themes of cultural contact and difference.

The federal view from the beginning was almost wholly political and instrumental in nature. The federal side was mostly committed to ending hostilities, getting as much land as possible, and giving up as little possible in return. The tribal side also sought to end hostilities, as well as retain as much land as possible and obtain adequate consideration for the land surrendered in terms of compensation and the provision of services.[256]

As noted, the results of particular treaty negotiations were often determined by the relative power of the two sides at that particular historical moment. Yet, the tribal side often had a broader, more cultural conception of what treaties involved. This is perhaps best understood by the term *covenant*. The federal view was often reductionist in nature. Treaties were no more than contracts and could be breached at will with the sole remedy (once there was a waiver of sovereign immunity), if any, being money damages. The tribal view was often expansive in nature, understanding treaties as binding two cultures and peoples in a set of interdependent promises.

This more expansive view often characterized the period from 1600 to 1800. According to Robert Williams, treaties may be viewed—from the tribal perspective—as sacred texts, as stories, and as constitution.[257] More precisely, they may be seen as the cutting edge of diplomacy on a multicultural frontier. In this context, the essential constitutive elements of treaties were obligations of hospitality and mutual aid in times of war and difficulty. Treaties provided the basis for connection, continuance, renewal, and even forgiveness.[258] Changing circumstances or loss of strength in bargaining power was irrelevant to the binding obligations. The two sides, from this perspective, are better understood as relatives, rather than (competing) nation-states.[259]

If constitutions are understood as establishing overarching structural relationships between sovereigns occupying the same territory, treaties with Indian tribes certainly have the potential to meet this definition. This did not happen to any noticeable extent with regard to early federal-tribal relations but, as this book hopes to demonstrate, treaties may yet provide the groundwork for forging a legitimate and enduring constitutional relationship between the federal government (including the states) and the tribes.

At the time of treaty making, there was not only the obvious political encounter but also the subtler notion of societies engaged in various kinds of contact and evolving along quite different governmental lines. Most tribal societies were essentially kinship states in which the key relationships were personal, familial, and decentralized in nature; colonial societies (including the United States) were beginning to diverge from this model toward one that was increasingly impersonal, bureaucratized, and centralized.[260] These changes, which were to become increasingly significant differences, were often unrecognized by both sides and fueled the misunderstanding already developing in the commercial and diplomatic context.[261]

For example, the Lakota (Sioux) people did not see the treaty as mere expedience and the power politics of the day, subject to future accommodation to other emerging national interests. Every treaty was settled with the smoking of the pipe. As insightfully noted by Father Peter John Powell, the well-known historian and anthropologist:

> [W]hites rarely, if ever, have understood the sacredness of the context in which treaties were concluded by the Lakota people.... "The pipe never fails," my people the Cheyenne say. For the pipe is the great sacramental, the great sacred means that provides unity between the Creator and the people. Any treaty that was signed was a sacred agreement because it was sealed by the smoking of the pipe. It was not signed by the Chief and headman before the pipe had been passed. Then the smoking of the pipe sealed the treaty, making the agreement holy and binding.
>
> Thus, for the Lakota, the obligations sealed with the smoking of the pipe were sacred obligations.[262]

From the tribal perspective, such views are not mere romantic artifacts of the past but rather present realities that might become the cornerstone of the future. For many tribes, there continues to be a strong legal and cultural commitment to the importance of treaties. In this view, treaties form the constitutional horizon that most approximates the true "government to government" relationship at the root of authentic constitutional governance and cultural respect.[263]

Although the federal perspective on treaties was and is exceptionally narrow and formalistic, the tribal perspective has been exceptionally wide and richly particularistic, reflecting not mere legal agreement but rather the binding together of two distinct communities. In this view, treaties are seen more like sacred texts than like mere political agreements between sovereigns. In many treaty contexts, the signing of the treaties was solemnized by the smoking of the sacred pipe. To restate for the sake of emphasis, for the plains Lakota (Sioux), the smoking of the sacred pipe—a divine gift from the White Buffalo Calf Woman—was designed to commemorate the significance of the mutual commitment of two peoples and to invoke the assistance of Wakan Tanka or the Great Spirit in their joint undertakings.[264]

For many Indian tribes, particularly in the northeast in the late eighteenth and early nineteenth century, treaty making in the narrow sense of signed agreements was enveloped in an extensive "treaty protocol" that was designed to satisfy the necessary conditions precedent and to create the necessary degree of relationship required before a treaty could be signed. Such a process often took several days and involved as many as nine stages. Quoting such a protocol in detail is necessary to provide an adequate sense of its detail and breadth of concern:

> At the height of its development, the treaty protocol ideally consisted of nine stages. First came a formal invitation to attend a meeting at a recognized or "prefixed" place or "council fire." This invitation, accompanied by strings or belts of wampum (Dutch colonists called the beads *zewant*), established a right for the hosts to set the agenda and speak first; it also obliged them to provide ritual and material hospitality for the visitors. Second was a ceremonial procession, by foot or canoe, by which the visitors arrived at the site of the council. Third was the "at the Wood's Edge" rite, in which the hosts offered rest and comfort to visitors presumed to be tired from a long journey. Each side offered the other the "Three Bare Words" of condolence, to clear their eyes, ears, and throats of the grief-inspired rage that prevented clear communication—the rage that, if unchecked, provoked mourning wars and spiraled into endless retaliatory feuds. After at least one night's rest, the council itself began with, fourth, the seating of the delegations and, fifth, an extensive Condolence ceremony, in which tearful eyes were again ritually dried, minds and hearts cleansed of the "bile of revenge," blood wiped "from the defiled house," graves of the dead "covered" to keep grief and revenge out of sight, clouds dispelled to allow the sun to shine, and fire kindled to further illuminate the proceedings. Sixth came a "recitation of the law ways," a rehearsal of the history of two peoples' relationships with each other, the basis of their peaceful interactions, and the way in which their forebears had taught them to behave. Almost universally, the connection was described in terms of fictive kinship; two peoples were "Uncle" and "Nephew," or "Father" and "Child," or "Brother" and "Brother," and addressed each other with the authority or deference appropriate to the power relationship inherent in such terms. The recitation of the law ways articulated ideals rather than grubby realities. Kinship terms and other names by which relationships were described served an educative function to

remind participants of what their attitudes toward each other *ought* to be.

Only in the seventh stage, after the ritual requirements for establishing a peaceful environment had been fulfilled, could what Europeans considered the business of a treaty council—the offering of specific "propositions"—take place. To be considered valid, each "word" had to be accompanied by an appropriate gift, usually of wampum strings ("fathoms") or belts prepared specially for the occasion. "Presents among these peoples dispatch all the affairs of the country," explained a French missionary who understood the process much better than Livingston. "They dry up tears; they appease anger; they open the doors of foreign countries; they deliver prisoners; they bring the dead back to life; one hardly ever speaks or answers, except by presents." Wampum gifts in particular confirmed the validity of a speaker's words in several interrelated ways. As a sacred substance, wampum underscored the importance of what was being said. As a valuable commodity, it demonstrated that the speaker was not talking only for himself or on the spur of the moment, but that he had the considered support of the kin and followers who had banded together to collect the treasured shells and have them strung. And, as carefully woven patterns of white and black beads, wampum also became a mnemonic device, allowing belts or strings to be "read" accurately both by a speaker delivering a message as instructed and by a recipient recalling promises made years before.

While propositions and wampum were offered by the hosts, visitors were to listen politely but not respond substantively until at least the next day. Hasty replies were not only disrespectful but indicated that the negotiator had not conferred with his colleagues and therefore could not be speaking with their approbation or with properly prepared wampum. Only when each of the hosts' propositions had been answered could the visitors introduce new points. The same expectations of polite listening and postponed responses applied throughout a treaty conference. Thus, as at Albany in 1679, the whole affair could last for weeks. Once the substantive dialogue finally ended, the eighth step was the affixing of marks to any documents Europeans might insist upon. The ninth step consisted of a feast and the presentation of final gifts from the hosts. Unlike symbolic wampum, these tended to be of more material value: food, cloth, tools, weapons, and, too often, liquor—all of which leaders would redistribute to their followers.[265]

Such things as drying tears, setting minds straight, establishing reliable channels of communication, and exchanging gifts were not mere window dressing but rather the cultural core of tradition: a tradition that binds tribal people who, because of their sense of individual liberty and decentralized political structure, were not under the thumb of any political or military hierarchy.[266] The extensive treaty protocol sought to invoke the sacred cultural bonds of connection rather than the secular bonds of hierarchy and control.

Treaty making—especially during the period of 1600 to 1800—was a necessary ingredient in achieving survival on a multicultural frontier made up of the English, French, and a wide configuration of tribes. In this context, the essence of treaties—at least from the tribal side—was to establish bonds of connection, continuance, renewal, and forgiveness.[267] These bonds were often mediated by the practices of hospitality and mutual aid. As the Miami Chief Le Gris explained to General Authority at the Treaty of Grasonville:

> When brothers meet, they always experience pleasure. As it is a
> cool day, we would hope you would give us a little drink; you
> promised to treat us well, and we expect to be treated as warriors,
> we wish you to give your brother a glass of wine. I hope you are
> pleased with this visit of your brothers. You have some things
> which we have not yet had any; we would like some mutton and
> pork occasionally.[268]

A Choctaw leader visiting Savannah, Georgia, in 1734 to request assistance stated, "We are surrounded with white people and the French are building forts which we do not like. We have come to see who are our friends and whose protection we may rely on."[269]

A group of Canastoga chiefs described their treaty relationship to William Penn and the colony of Pennsylvania in 1712 with the observation that they should "Live as friends and Brothers, and be as one Body, one heart, one mind, and as one Eye and Ear." According to Williams, such a view rises to the level of constitutional principle and obligation. This was the heart of Indian diplomacy:

> [C]ustomary bonds created by a treaty relationship were relied on, as
> a matter of constitutional practice, in times of need or crisis. This
> principle meant that the relationship of multicultural unity created
> between treaty partners should be continually reaffirmed and
> strengthened. The customary terms used to describe the

connections maintained by a treaty, the frequent conferences, the binding of future generations, and the forgiveness of past transgressions were seen as acts of renewal between treaty partners. They sustained the sacred bonds that, as a matter of constitutional principle, could be relied on for survival in a hostile and chaos-filled world.[270]

Treaties, in this broader context, have also been described as compacts that transcend their narrow particulars to create a relationship that reworks the contours of sovereignty itself:

> Compacts differ in origin, nature and effect. Their object is to restructure the parties and create or enlarge some common, national sovereignty. Treaties are agreements between existing sovereigns; compacts create new sovereigns. Since compacts alter the fabric of government, they require the consent of the people themselves, the same as an internal amendment of either party's constitution. Once ratified by the people, a compact cannot be modified, dissolved or superseded except by the same process. It is not alliance, but the constitution of an amalgamated body politic.[271]

In this view, such treaty federalism provides the basis for new and enduring relationships of (almost) coequals within a common system, rather than the current system where tribes are often seen as no more than "dependent" entities subject to national whims.[272]

Treaties and Political Arrangements between Tribes and the United States

Although much of the preceding might seem unlikely to move the rather narrow current views to some broader view, it is worth recalling that some early Indian treaties did contain imaginative political suggestions and arrangements. These political arrangements included the possibility of statehood and representation in Congress. For example, the 1778 Fort Pitt Treaty with the Delaware Nation, the very first treaty negotiated by the United States with an Indian tribe, not only contained a clause authorizing General Washington's troops to pass through its territory to reach British outposts[273] but also held out the promise of statehood:

> [S]hould it for the future be found conducive to the mutual interest of both parties to invite any other tribes who have been friends to the interest of the United States, to join the present Confederation, and

to form a *state* whereby the Delaware nation shall be head, and to have representation in Congress.[274]

Thus, at the very beginning of this nation's history, it was well understood that Indian tribes were outside the national polity and its constitutional structure but might yet enter into it on mutually agreeable grounds. Yet, there has never been any constitutional adjustment or amendment to accomplish such inclusion, except the dubious notions of dependency and plenary power.[275]

The Cherokee Nation's right to a delegate in the U.S. House of Representatives, which is part of the 1835 Treaty of New Echota, is another example of unique political configurations contemplated by treaties. The Cherokee Right to a congressional delegate is provided for in Article 7 of that treaty:

> The Cherokee nation having already made great progress in
> civilization and deeming it important that every proper and laudable
> inducement should be offered to their people to improve their
> condition as well as to guard and secure in the most effectual manner
> the rights guarantied to them in this treaty, and with a view to
> illustrate the liberal and enlarged policy of the Government of the
> United States towards the Indians in their removal beyond the
> territorial limits of the States, it is stipulated that *they shall be entitled*
> *to a delegate in the House of Representatives of the United States whenever*
> *Congress shall make provision for the same.*[276]

This delegate right was included in the treaty as part of the federal government's commitment to the Cherokee Nation for its "agreement" in the treaty to surrender its land and be subject to removal—the infamous Trail of Tears—to the Indian Territory west of the Mississippi River.[277] The key point is not, of course, to justify removal but to demonstrate the range of political configurations envisioned in treaties to deal with Native nations, who were not within the bounds of the original constitutional compact. As with so much within treaties and Indian law generally, the Cherokee right to a congressional delegate has never been realized.[278]

There was also a flurry of proposals for Indian statehood during the latter part of the nineteenth century, before the Oklahoma Indian Territory became its own multiracial state. As stated by Clinton, such various proposals contemplated:

> (1) the consent of the tribes through treaty and (2) representation in
> Congress as *separate* constituent Indian states within the union. It
> did not assume the exercise of direct federal power over Indian
> nations without their consent or representation. Such proposals,

therefore, were advanced in a manner consistent with the basic
Lockean social compact notions of popular delegation that animated
early American constitutional theory.[279]

Such diverse treaty-based and other political arrangements between tribes and
the United States not only are a source of historical interest but also serve as a
potential basis from which to reconsider the fractured political and constitutional relationship that continues to exist today between Indian tribes and the
federal government.

Summary

The original structure of the Constitution created a number of structural relationships between the federal government and the states. These provisions—
the Interstate Commerce Clause, the Full Faith and Credit Clause, the
Supremacy Clause, the Tenth Amendment, and the Eleventh Amendment—
whatever their doctrinal warp or woof, have resulted in a sizable body of constitutional jurisprudence and scholarship explicating the dynamic nature of
the federal-state (and state-state) relationship. The constitutional fate of the
two primary provisions—the Indian Commerce Clause and treaties—dealing
with the federal-tribal relationship has been otherwise. The resulting jurisprudence has little or no *constitutional* vigor because neither section has created any boundary to limit the federal authority in Indian affairs. There is no
dialogue, only ratification of federal objectives.[280] Very little scholarship—
especially from constitutional law scholars—has focused on this important
terrain.

The architecture and structure of the (original) Constitution have proven
inadequate to support the edifice of tribal sovereignty in the modern era. The
original architecture has largely been set aside by extraconstitutional moves
primarily designed to ensure national objectives and to erode tribal sovereignty, notwithstanding constitutional recognition and treaty commitments
to the contrary. This architecture is in serious need of reworking to (re)estab-
lish a viable structure to validate and support contemporary exercise of tribal
sovereignty and self-governance.

Despite the Constitution's recognition of *three* sovereigns, its architecture reveals essentially a *two*-sovereign model that focuses primarily on the
relationship between the federal and state sovereigns. When the Constitution
was adopted, this two-sovereign model was appropriate because the tribal
sovereign was really not part of, or included in, the republic. It largely func-

tioned outside and independent of the Constitution. This is no longer true. Tribes (without their consent) have been absorbed and incorporated into the republic but without the necessary constitutional adjustment and recognition. This has resulted in a perverse legacy of exclusion and constitutional injustice, which needs increased jurisprudence and scholarly concern in an attempt to identify new pathways to constitutional balance and respect.

4

The Marshall Trilogy

Foundational but Not Fully Constitutional?

THE NATIVE AND EARLY AMERICAN ENCOUNTER ORIGINATED IN NAVIGATIONAL error and took root in the activities of trade and land acquisition that were transacted primarily through acts of war and diplomacy. All of this was, in turn, refracted through the lens of culture and mediated by the institution of law. Many of these recurring themes are manifested in three early U.S. Supreme Court cases that established the foundational principles of Indian law: *Johnson v. McIntosh*,[1] *Cherokee Nation v. Georgia*,[2] and *Worcester v. Georgia*,[3] collectively known as the Marshall trilogy because Chief Justice John Marshall wrote the majority opinion in each case. These cases not only established some of the basic principles of Indian law but also provide an enduring legacy and challenge in the modern era of Indian law. Therefore, consideration and engagement with them will not only illuminate the roots of Indian law but also shed light on some of their tangled contemporary branches.

Land acquisition, as previously discussed, was a pervasive activity in colonial and early America. From the non-Indian side, everyone was more or less engaged in acquiring land, not just the federal government (and before the federal government, the Crown) in its activities of war, diplomacy, and treaty making. Many states (and before the states, the colonies) were also engaged in land acquisition from Indians, despite the strictures of the Constitution and the Non-Intercourse Act.[4] There were also many private land speculators and syndicates—including some of the founding fathers—who acquired land directly from Indians and Indian tribes both before and after the Revolutionary War.

This kind of land speculation by private individuals and corporate entities, at least prior to the Non-Intercourse Act of 1790, was not illegal under U.S. law. However, private purchases west of the Appalachian Mountains did violate the Proclamation of 1763 issued by King George III of England. Thus it was only a matter of time before there would be a conflict between a private speculator's claim and the federal government's claim to Indian land. This was the case of *Johnson v. McIntosh*. In fact, many people thought that *Johnson v. McIntosh* was, indeed, manipulated to get this very issue before the Court in an attempt to vindicate the speculators' pre-Revolutionary War purchases.[5] The fact that it became the seminal case defining Indian property rights surprised many. No doubt Indians themselves were flabbergasted to learn that *their* property rights were at the heart of a lawsuit in which they were not a named party and did not participate.

Johnson v. McIntosh

Johnson v. McIntosh was, in part, a case that stemmed from the resolution of the claims of many of the original thirteen states that their western borders extended infinitely westward to the Pacific Ocean in accordance with the boundaries described in their original colonial charters.[6] This issue of where state borders ended and federal "Indian territory" began was of considerable significance to all concerned. The Articles of Confederation compromise, with its ambiguous "legislative right" provision in Article IX, failed to provide any resolution.[7]

This absence of any national power to regulate the state purchase of Indian lands threatened the very notion of a workable union and balanced federalism. For example, the State of Virginia initially refused to give up its western lands, its far western boundary, and the concomitant authority to regulate Indian land transfers within its far-reaching borders. As a result, the Continental Congress was poised to declare null and void all pre–Revolutionary War purchases of Indian lands by frontier speculating companies and other private individuals, as well as clamp down on state authority to ratify or participate in Indian land transfers.

These actions were staunchly opposed by the powerful land speculators and syndicates who had purchased lands in these areas and counted well-known individuals such as George Washington, Thomas Paine, and Benjamin Franklin among their shareholders. Finally, a binding compromise was struck. Virginia (and other states) agreed to recognize narrow western borders in exchange for the federal government's agreement to forgive state Revolutionary War debt and not to investigate conflicting claims in the region, as well as a promise by Congress that the ceded lands would be used for the common good, thus obviating any necessity to specifically invalidate anyone's prior title.[8]

The territory ceded by Virginia in 1784 became known as the Old Northwest and included land purchased from Indians by land speculators prior to the Revolution. This process culminated in the Northwest Ordinance of 1787, which provided that western Indian lands were no longer subject to direct conquest or private purchase but rather negotiation and federal purchase: "The utmost good faith shall always be observed toward the Indians; their lands and property shall never be taken from them without their consent...."[9] *Johnson v. McIntosh* thus represented a case of first impression about the nature of federal claims to Indian lands not located within the borders of any state.

Johnson v. McIntosh was brought in the form of an ejection action involving lands located in the district of Illinois territory. The plaintiffs, Joshua Johnson and Thomas Grahame, were descendants of an original grantee who claimed title under a direct purchase and conveyance from the Illinois and Piankeshaw Indians. The defendant, William McIntosh, claimed title under a grant from the United States. Judgment was granted in favor of the defendant at the trial level.

Since the case was heard on stipulated facts, there was no dispute as to whether the plaintiffs had received conveyance from the Illinois and Piankeshaw Indians. Recognized chiefs had the capacity to convey tribal land and apparently did so on two different occasions, as evidenced by appropriately recorded deeds in 1773 and 1775. These deeds reflected consideration in the amount of $24,000 and $31,000, respectively. The deeds conveyed title to W. Murray (1773) and Louis Viviat (1775), acting for themselves and others. All of these individuals were citizens of England. None of these individuals took actual possession of this land because of the commencement of the Revolutionary War. From 1781 until 1816, the original grantees petitioned Congress to confirm their titles to these lands under the deeds in question, but without success.[10]

The United States subsequently received title to the same lands pursuant to the Treaty of Greenville after defeating the Illinois and Piankeshaw tribes in the Battle of Fallen Timbers in 1794. In 1818, the federal government conveyed approximately 11,560 acres of this land to one William McIntosh. McIntosh took actual possession of these lands before the institution of the lawsuit by several heirs of William Johnson, one of the original grantees. Because no facts were in dispute, the Court framed the dispositive issue clearly: What is "the power of Indians to give, and private individuals to receive, a title which can be sustained in the Courts of this country"?[11] The Court's answer was blunt. No such power existed.[12]

The legal rationale employed by the Court to support this result was the doctrine of "discovery." The doctrine of discovery had two components: one external or international and one internal or domestic. The external element was the basic international law convention within the European family of nations that whichever European nation got to a portion of the New World first had prior claim:

> But, as they were all in pursuit of nearly the same object, it was
> necessary, in order to avoid conflicting settlements, and consequent
> war with each other, to establish a principle, which all should
> acknowledge as the law by which the right of acquisition, which they
> all asserted, should be regulated as between themselves. This
> principle was, that discovery gave title to the government by whose
> subjects, or by whose authority, it was made, against all other
> European governments, which title might be consummated by
> possession.[13]

This approach proceeded from the understanding that "discovery of this immense continent" offered "an ample field to the ambition and enterprise of all" and was justified because the "character and religion of its inhabitants afforded an apology for considering them as a people over whom the superior genius of Europe might claim an ascendancy."[14] The European convention of thought was that there was plenty of land for the "discoverers" to divide among themselves and that those who were already on the land were inferior to the discoverers. The young republic of the United States, despite its own recent revolution, decided to accept this questionable doctrine.[15] This element of the discovery doctrine was an essential customary norm of early international law.[16] Its blatant self-interest is readily apparent. It was not part of the Constitution or any federal statute.

The interior or domestic aspect of the doctrine of discovery focused on the relationship of the "discoverer" to the "natives," not to other "discoverers." In this realm, the "discoverer's" rights were "exclusive, no other power could interpose between them."[17] The potential choices were relatively straightforward: Native people and nations could be seen as having identical property rights to those of "discoverers," having no property rights at all, or something in between.

Chief Justice Marshall attempted to strike a middle course but ultimately succumbed to an undertow of racism, false anthropology, and questionable history. The racism component was standard for the times: Native people lacked both civilization and Christianity, and the European willingness to bestow, and not to withhold, these "gifts" was "ample compensation" for any resulting loss of land. The false anthropology centered on the notion that Indians were "fierce savages, whose occupation was war, and whose subsistence was drawn chiefly from the forest. To leave them in possession of their country, was to leave the country a wilderness...."[18] This characterization appeared without citation to any authority and was quite false. It is difficult not to see this as a transparent manipulation and misunderstanding of basic reality. The invaders justified themselves by the "warlike" nature of those that were being dispossessed, without even the slightest recognition of the possibility of self-defense. Yet Chief Justice Marshall almost did so with his terse acknowledgment that Indians were brave and "were ready to repel by arms every attempt on their independence."[19]

As to "subsistence" in the "wilderness," such an observation also appeared far from the mark, at least by today's understanding that Indian tribal life in the early Americas was exceptionally rich and diverse. In fact, some Indian societies were as, if not more, agriculturally sophisticated and "urbanized" as any European society at that time,[20] but such was the process of expansion. No serious qualms or impediments were permitted. "Conquest," according to Chief Justice Marshall, brooked no challenge to its legality or rightness:

> Conquest gives a title which the Courts of the conquerer cannot
> deny, whatever the private and speculative opinions of individuals
> may be, respecting the original justice of the claim which has been
> successfully asserted.[21]

Indeed, the Court expressed the view that what was done was done. "Although we do not mean to engage in the defense of those principles which Europeans have applied to Indian title, they may, we think, find some excuse, if not justification, in the character and habits of the people whose rights have been wrested from them."[22] In the end, as to the internal or domestic aspects of "discovery," the Court decided that tribes had lost title to the land (and thus could not alienate or sell it) but retained the rights of use and occupancy, which could only be extinguished by "purchase or conquest."[23] This view created the right of "preemption" in the discoverer against all others to potentially obtain and extinguish the tribal rights of use and occupation.

As part of this exegesis on the doctrine of discovery, the Court also struck down the right of non-Indians to purchase land directly from Indians. This was seen as a necessary corollary to their loss of title.[24]

In the final analysis, the opinion had a sense of inevitability about it:

> However extravagant the pretension of converting the discovery of an
> inhabited country into conquest may appear; if the principle has been
> asserted in the first instance, and afterwards sustained; if a country
> has been acquired and held under it; if the property of the great mass

of the community originates in it, it becomes the law of the land, and cannot be questioned. So, too, with respect to the concomitant principle, that the Indian inhabitants are to be considered merely as occupants, to be protected, indeed, while in peace, in the possession of their lands, but to be deemed incapable of transferring the absolute title to others. However this restriction may be opposed to natural right, and to the usages of civilized nations, yet, if it be indispensable to that system under which the country has been settled, and be adapted to the actual condition of the two people, it may, perhaps, be supported by reason, and certainly cannot be rejected by Courts of justice.[25]

As noted by many scholars, this case is remarkable from several perspectives. It carried forward a medievally inspired view of property rights that endorsed the extinguishment of indigenous title (as nonexistent) without moral qualm.[26] This appears especially hypocritical from the perspective of a new (revolutionary) nation steeped in the ideals of freedom, liberty, and fair play. At the same time, the case dealt a severe blow to the investment-backed expectations of land speculators, including such well-known political figures as George Washington, Benjamin Franklin, and Thomas Paine.

The opinion, whether consciously or not, studiously avoided going too far by either declaring that Indians had no property rights at all or were possessed of the full complement of rights recognized in non-Indians. The ground established in the opinion was pragmatic but without a horizon of legitimate moral merit. In the words of the seminal Indian law scholar, Felix Cohen, these divergent positions "produced a cruel dilemma: either Indians had no title and no rights or the Federal land grants on which much of our economy rested were void."[27] Chief Justice Marshall struck an uneasy middle ground that Indians did not have title but did have the rights of use and occupancy. Indians retained some sticks in their bundle of property rights but had lost the quintessential stick of title.

The opinion reflected a blend (or concoction?) of ascendant federalism concerns to ensure national (over state and private) hegemony in Indian affairs, to establish a practical, coherent system of land tenure, and to recognize a residual moral concern with the status of Indians and their property rights.[28] Yet Chief Justice Marshall's opinion does *not* read like something that was brimming with great legal confidence and political brio; rather, it contains an undertone of misgiving that could not transcend its historical circumstances.[29] A fledgling Court in a fledgling nation did not dare go too far in taking on the powers that be.

The Roots of the Doctrine of Discovery

Chief Justice Marshall's opinion, standing alone, does not reveal the depth and insistent presence of the doctrine of discovery in early colonial and American history. The doctrine of discovery was deeply rooted not only within the European family of nations that included England, France, Spain, Portugal, Holland, and Sweden but also within early colonial and state law within America. Although there were variations and occasional dissent, the ubiquity of western commitment to the doctrine of discovery made it one of the first principles of international law.

The foundation of the doctrine of discovery as a primary international law principle was first established by Spain, Portugal, England, and the Roman Catholic Church in the fifteenth and early sixteenth centuries.[30] It was also firmly embedded in early colonial and American law—even before *Johnson v. McIntosh*—as a crucial rationale to support early "land acquisitions" by the original thirteen colonies and the Crown and the individual states and the United States itself in such areas as the lands of the Louisiana Purchase in 1803 and the Pacific Northwest Territories. In fact, President Jefferson used and invoked the Lewis and Clark Expedition of 1803–1805 as the basis for the U.S. discovery claim to the Pacific Northwest.[31]

The international principle of discovery rested, of course, on the remarkable convergence of self-interest of Western nations (including the United States) to justify their exploitation—particularly in the area of land acquisition—of indigenous societies around the globe. One of the myths of law is that it is neutral and detached from the baser human attributes such as greed, racism, and the will to power. The doctrine of discovery is a brutal rejoinder to that myth.

The doctrine of discovery was first elaborated by the papacy to justify the Crusaders' invasion of "infidel" lands held by Muslims in the Middle East. According to Pope Innocent's commentary in 1240, the rationale of discovery was justified to "dispossess pagans." The papacy's "divine mandate" concerning the spiritual well-being of *all* humankind automatically displaced any competing secular or non-Christian religious claims.[32]

The Church continued to refine this doctrine. One of its major developments was to focus more directly on the question of what rights in the land, if any, were held by non-Christians. The answer was that non-Christians did possess natural law rights, similar to those of Christians, to "lordship and property," with the significant proviso that the pope could invade foreign lands to punish violations of the natural law or to spread the gospel.[33] The self-serving rationale was that any deviance from the papal script was grounds for invasion or dispossession.

Despite this generally accepted rubric, there was conflict about its particulars among Catholic countries such as Spain, Portugal, England, and France. As to conflict between Spain and Portugal, a 1493 papal bull of Pope Alexander VI divided the world in half, granting Spain the right of discovery to all lands west of the Canary Islands and granting Portugal all lands east of the Azore Islands.[34]

There was also a seeming moment of dissent in 1532 when the king of Spain's chief legal advisor and a leading theologian and Dominican priest, Francisco de Vitoria, gave a series of lectures entitled "On the Indians Lately Discovered," which addressed the natural rights of indigenous people in the Americas. The core of Vitoria's discourse centered on three conclusions, namely, that indigenous people of the west "possessed natural legal rights as free and rational people," that the pope's grant of title to lands in America to Spain was invalid and could not affect the inherent rights of Indians, and that violations by Indians of the natural law principles of the law of nations might justify a Christian nation's conquest and colonial empire in America.[35]

Although this formulation looked—at first blush—like it might undermine the views of the papacy, the king of Spain's careful, if not esoteric, interpretation avoided any real conflict. The potential loophole, of course, was the definition of natural law principles. In accordance with European views (no indigenous views were solicited or considered), natural law precepts included the right to travel in indigenous lands, mandatory trade with indigenous peoples, and acceptance of the gospel by indigenous peoples. Violation of any of these principles by indigenous peoples as determined by European nations justified conquest and empire.[36]

England and France were both Catholic countries at this time, but neither had a papal bull from the pope to justify their colonizing activities in the New World. Therefore, reconsideration of the doctrine of discovery was in order, but war came first. The French and English conflict over discovery claims in North America was resolved by the French and Indian War. In the Treaty of Paris that concluded the Seven Years War in 1763, France ceded its discovery claim to Canada and east of the Mississippi to England, and its claims southwest of the Mississippi to Spain.[37]

A lingering question—left to the legal theorists—was how the claim of discovery was to be perfected. Did it require mere assertion, a wave of a papal bull from a ship docked in the bay, physical occupancy, or actual rape and plunder? The answer that was forged by legal scholars, especially in England and France, was the requirement of current occupancy and actual possession. This view was complemented by the development of the doctrine of *terra nullius* that held that lands not put to the highest agricultural use (again, as defined by

Europeans) were essentially "vacant" or in a state of "waste," subject to European discovery and occupation. In essence, no European country disputed the applicability of the doctrine of discovery in the New World. Of course, there were disagreements about its application in particular instances, and its fine doctrinal points. Yet, its core was never in doubt. The property rights of indigenous people were minimal to nonexistent.

The doctrine of discovery was also actively embraced by the original thirteen colonies, as well as the early post-Revolutionary individual states and the United States itself, well in advance of *Johnson v. McIntosh*. The English colonies pursuant to their royal charters granted by the king routinely invoked the doctrine of discovery to justify the acquisition of Indian lands. For example, the colony of Maryland enacted a law in 1638 to control land acquisition and trade with Indians, which was based on the Crown's "right of first discovery," by which the king had become "lord and possessor" of Maryland and had gained outright ownership of the real property in Maryland.[38]

The colonies were also concerned with preemption and regulation of the purchase of Indian lands by individuals. Many colonies enacted legislation requiring non-Indian purchasers of Indian land to obtain licenses or the permission of the governor or colonial legislature before buying, leasing, or occupying Indian land. Sanctions included forfeiture, fines, and even imprisonment.[39] Such regulatory schemes were deemed essential to establish order in the context of booming "land fever" in the colonies. There was also growing tension between the colonies and the Crown itself about the right of preemption. Was it the colonies or the Crown who ultimately regulated the purchase of Indian land? The friction around this issue was a contributing factor to the Revolutionary War.

These issues of trade and land acquisition were so prevalent in colonial America that every one of the thirteen original colonies had multiple laws dealing with these problems.[40] These issues that so bedeviled the colonies and the Crown constituted a veritable template of colonial settlement and expansion that was directly replicated with the post-Revolution creation of the United States and its individual states. This template involved a set of contentious problems that centered on questions of land ownership, the nature of Indian property rights, federal or state preemption, the regulation of land acquisition and transfer, and the governance of commerce. These issues were often prefigured in much colonial litigation.[41] Indeed, this template was a significant matter of concern within the Articles of Confederation, the Constitution, and the Marshall trilogy itself. Neither the Articles of Confederation nor the Constitution was adequate to the task, and it took the Marshall trilogy, for better or worse, to resolve most of what was at issue.

The doctrine of discovery also played a significant role in the western expansion of the young United States. This was especially true during the presidency of Thomas Jefferson. President Jefferson was adept and prescient in his use of the discovery doctrine. Both as a practicing attorney and as governor of the State of Virginia, he was quite cognizant of the role the doctrine of discovery played in land conveyances that involved the extinguishment of Indian title.[42]

President Jefferson's understanding and use of the doctrine of discovery are best illustrated by examining details of the Louisiana Purchase from France. President Jefferson was well aware that this 1803 transaction with France did not convey true fee simple title of the subject lands from France to the United States. The doctrine of discovery did not really give France meaningful fee simple title to this land, but only the preemptive right to secure potential sale of the use and occupancy rights of the various tribes. Jefferson's understanding of this legal reality was demonstrated by his writing to the Senate in 1808 that it was now incumbent upon the United States to purchase these lands west of the Mississippi from their "native proprietors."[43]

This necessity was a significant though often underplayed element of the rationale for the Lewis and Clark Expedition. Although the Lewis and Clark venture certainly had an exploratory and scientific element, it was also essentially designed to establish contact with the various tribes for commercial purposes and eventual land transfer and to perfect claims under the discovery doctrine. Jefferson also intended to use the travels of Lewis and Clark to establish discovery claims to the Pacific Northwest territory that was not part of the Louisiana Purchase.[44]

The national objectives to expand, to consolidate land acquisitions, and to advance legal stability were all deeply embedded in the doctrine of discovery. Without it, legal uncertainty and moral debate threatened the essential bedrock of a developing nation. The contours of the doctrine of discovery itself were unclear. Did it extinguish Native title and recognize the right of the discoverer to transfer Native lands without Native consent, or did it merely create the right of preemption in the "discoverer" to purchase Indian land? Prior to *Johnson v. McIntosh*, both understandings were at work at different times and places.

This story was also fraught with a certain chaos and silence. There is little doubt that the acquisition of Indian land was chaotic with private acquisition by non-Indians, acquisition by colonies and states, and acquisitions by the Crown and the federal government, often competing with each other. Many such acquisitions were often contradictory and overlapping, as in *Johnson v. McIntosh* itself. There was also uncertainty as to which sovereign, if any, could regulate Indian land transactions—was there no regulation except pure market forces, or was there regulation by the colonies and individual states or by the Crown and the federal government? Did such regulation limit the ability of non-Indians to purchase Indian land? Did such regulation limit the abilities of Indians to sell land to non-Indians? All sides claimed the right to purchase, and all governments the right to regulate. These were the clamoring voices of the buyers and regulators. Without predictable order of some kind in land tenure—particularly in a capitalist society where land is a premier commodity—these nascent colonial and independent societies could not long function.

The silence amid this chaos was the voice of the Indian sellers. What did they think they were "selling"? Regulating? Did they think they were "selling" at all? Were these transactions, voluntary or involuntary, the product of consent or force? This mixture of many contending voices on one side and the absence of voice on the other side was the essential backstory of *Johnson v. McIntosh.*

Johnson v. McIntosh brought order by recognizing the sole authority of the federal government to regulate and control the transfer of Indian land. Private purchases and the states as buyers and Indians themselves as sellers[45] were all subject to paramount federal authority. This was the essential result of *Johnson v. McIntosh.* This is a legal story that reverberates and haunts to this day, not only because of its essential drama and inhumanity but also because title to Indian lands continues to be held by the United States. As a result, tribes continue to have no authority to sell, lease, or otherwise develop their land and resources without express federal government approval.[46]

Johnson v. McIntosh: An Alternative View

It has also been suggested by some scholars that *Johnson v. McIntosh* was never intended to be the leading case about Indian property rights; rather, it was directed, even manipulated, toward a narrow pre–Revolutionary War issue involving the validity of the Proclamation of 1763, which forbade the private purchase of property directly from Indians in Indian territory, that is, land west of any of the original thirteen colonies. In this view, the case was not directed toward any broad issue of Indian property rights to sell in the early post-Revolutionary era[47] but rather toward the authority of non-Indians to purchase, particularly in the pre-Revolutionary era.

This view of *Johnson v. McIntosh* highlights the tension between different non-Indian purchasers of Indian land, as opposed to the tension between non-Indian buyers and the Indian sellers. In other words, it revealed the tension between individual non-Indian (or syndicate) purchasers and their rights, if any, vis-à-vis their local and/or national sovereigns, and not the tension between non-Indian purchasers (including non-Indian sovereigns) and Indian sellers. The issue in this view focuses on which sovereign (colony or crown, state or federal government) had the authority to regulate land purchases by non-Indians from Indians, rather than on the issue of the rights and capacity of Indians to sell or transfer their land in the first instance.

This new perspective on *Johnson v. McIntosh* draws widely on information not contained in the stated facts of the case. According to the extensive research of Lindsay Robertson and a fortuitous windfall of heretofore unknown documents, the case may be seen as a collusive attempt by the named parties to seek vindication of an Illinois and Wabash Land Companies (a well-known land syndicate) pre-Revolutionary purchase of two extensive parcels of land from the Illinois and Piankeshaw Indians. These were purchases that violated the terms of the Proclamation of 1763.[48]

The legal barrier to these purchases was King George III's Proclamation of 1763, which expressly prohibited private land purchases from Indians in the trans-Appalachian west:

> The Proclamation of 1763 declared the lands west of the Allegheny Mountains to be reserved for the use of the Indians; barred colonial governors from authorizing surveys or issuing patents establishing title to these lands; forbade individual colonists to purchase, settle, or take possession of any of them without a license from the Crown; and ordered squatters to leave immediately. The Crown claimed a "preemption" or "preemptive" right to those lands (i.e., an exclusive right to purchase, whenever the Indian owners should be willing to sell). East of the mountains, the Crown's governors and commanders in chief were authorized to exercise the preemption right to purchase Indian lands on the Crown's behalf, but west of the mountains, the right belonged to the Crown alone. Neither colonial governors nor individual colonists had any right to claim title to Indian lands west of the mountains. The Proclamation of 1763 was the first of many British moves that would lead to the American Revolution.[49]

Despite this bar, some land speculators were willing to take their chances that the Proclamation of 1763 would be withdrawn or otherwise declared illegal as beyond the Crown's legislative authority, and they began purchasing land directly from Indians in the western territory. This was the attitude of the Illinois and Wabash Land Companies, in which Thomas Johnson was a shareholder. As the pool of potential purchasers was exceedingly narrow, potential profits for speculators were exceptionally high.

The speculators' gamble that the Proclamation of 1763 would fail as a matter of law never materialized. Therefore, their strategy became to seek confirmation of their title from an appropriate sovereign. Numerous attempts from 1775 to 1816 all failed. The speculators' petitions for confirmation of their title were rejected by the Crown, the Continental Congress, the State of Virginia, and the U.S. Congress.[50] All these sovereigns rejected the legitimacy of these private purchases because they were illegal under the Proclamation of 1763 when they were made and were also contrary to the law and public policy of the State of Virginia and the United States.[51]

Litigation was a last grasp to secure recognized title, and little was left to chance. The architect of this approach was Robert Goodloe Harper, and his strategy—admittedly a long shot—was to recruit a compliant defendant, proceed on a stipulated (and collusive) set of facts, and find a favorable judge in a federal district court. Surprisingly, this strategy initially worked. Pursuant to design, the (recruited) defendant prevailed at the trial level, the judge entered a judgment but wrote no opinion, *and* the lone issue involving the validity of the Proclamation of 1763 was preserved on appeal. Harper, the key actor behind the scenes, also hired and paid for McIntosh's counsel before the Supreme Court.[52]

Despite this convergence of collusion and deception, the Court—especially Chief Justice Marshall—though probably unaware of the cross manipulation of the judicial process, proceeded with dispatch. According to a number of court observers, several members of Court, as well as McIntosh's esteemed counsel, raised unexpected questions about the Indian capacity to sell land, in addition to the basic issue of the validity of the Proclamation of 1763. As to this basic issue, the Court held that the Proclamation of 1763 was valid as to all western, pre-Revolutionary land transfers. Johnson and his syndicate lost in a case of minor importance, but the Court went needlessly, even dangerously, further into the realm of post-Revolutionary land transfers involving Indians. Here, the Court, in Robertson's view, went astray with its bold declaration about the doctrine of discovery, with its eye on the quandary of the land warrants made by the State of Virginia to members of its Revolutionary War militia on Chickasaw lands that were now part of the State of Kentucky.[53]

In the end, Chief Justice Marshall wrote the unanimous opinion of the Court in eight days. Much of the questionable authority cited by the Chief Justice came from his own biography of George Washington.[54] According to Robertson, the Chief Justice seized on *Johnson v. McIntosh* as a vehicle to establish a narrow precedent to validate the claims of Virginia militia veterans in his home state. These veterans were given land grants by the State of Virginia on Chickasaw lands now located in, and contested by, the new State of Kentucky.[55] In this view, Chief Justice Marshall seized the opportunity—in dicta—to announce that the doctrine of discovery put title to Indian lands in the original states as well as the federal government.[56] This rationale would confirm the authority of the State of Virginia to transfer Chickasaw land, without purchase or conquest, to its Revolutionary War veterans, and these transfers would be binding on the new State of Kentucky.[57]

Robertson notes that Chief Justice Marshall probably did not foresee the immense implications of *Johnson v. McIntosh*. In fact, he tried to retract much of its extensive rhetoric in the Cherokee Nation cases, especially *Worcester v. Georgia*,[58] but it was too late. Chief Justice Marshall died in 1835, and the new Court fully embraced the Marshallian version of the doctrine of discovery that put *title* to Indian land in the federal government or even the states.[59] It provided a devastating and self-deluding rationale for removal and much of the tragedy that followed. History is inevitably about forks in the road and the attendant *choices* that are made, and it needs to emphasize the choices, not any alleged inevitable destiny. *Johnson v. McIntosh* was (and is) a case about choices and their fateful aftermath.[60]

The Doctrine of Discovery: A Postscript

The active use of the doctrine of discovery is by no means dead or relegated to the past as a cruel artifact. It was, for example, resurrected by Canada when the high Arctic areas of the most northern territory in Canada were drawn into the Cold War.[61] Canada feared the increasing U.S. presence, namely, its plan "to build airstrips capable of landing heavy jets and cargo planes at the remote northern Ellesmere Island weather stations of Alert and Eureka, points on the North American continent only 1200 miles across the Arctic Ocean from the plains of Siberia."[62]

Because Ellesmere Island was largely uninhabited, Canada felt its "sovereignty" potentially threatened by U.S. encroachment. As a way of dealing with this predicament, Canada "recruited" a small number of Inuit to relocate to Ellesmere Island in 1953. They were promised much, but given little. Despite their Arctic residency, almost 700 miles to the south, the new environment was qualitatively different, hellish in the extreme, with six months of darkness, brutal cold and wind, and very little fish or game. Suffering was extreme.[63]

The doctrine of discovery was reborn anew with its macabre commitment to use Native people, where no non-Native would go, to reestablish the sovereignty of one Western country against another. This bizarre cruelty did not go unnoticed by the Inuit, and with incessant persistence from some of the descendants of the original Inuit, Canada slowly came to realize the mistake and the arrogance of its overreaching. By the mid-1970s, it was clear that those Inuit "families had planted the flag for Canada and Canada had the duty to return the favour."[64]

Initially, little of immediate substance occurred. Progress was glacial. Yet by the early 1990s, as a result of substantial investigation and publicity, Canadian public opinion rapidly changed and culminated in the Nunavut Land Claims Agreement of 1993, which

> gave the Inuit title to 137,355 square miles of territory, an area nearly as large as the state of California, along with a share of federal government royalties from oil and mineral development on federal lands and the right to harvest and manage wildlife. This Agreement put the future of the Inuit people in their own hands for the first time since the Vikings had arrived in the Arctic a thousand years ago. It also made Inuit the largest private landowners in North America.[65]

The burdens and obfuscations of history do occasionally change for the better. "The history of the Arctic had been given back to the people it belonged to. In the most profound sense, the people of the Arctic had, finally, come home."[66]

Cherokee Nation Cases

The Cherokee Nation cases consist of *Cherokee Nation v. Georgia*[67] and *Worcester v. Georgia*.[68] These cases, which were decided in 1831 and 1832, respectively, dealt with matters of jurisdiction and authority in Indian affairs but nevertheless were deeply colored by the continuing pressure, this time from the state of Georgia, to limit tribal territory and to reduce tribal and federal zones of authority within Indian country.

The background to the *Cherokee* cases involved the efforts of eastern (especially in the South) states, epitomized by Georgia, to obtain more and more Indian land for themselves and their citizens. In this regard, such activity was a kind of corollary to the private land speculation pressure at the heart of *Johnson v. McIntosh*. Despite the federal attempts to keep the states at bay, including, for example, a resolution by the Continental Congress in 1788 directing Secretary of War Henry Knox to prepare to remove non-Indian intruders in Indian country, as well as President Washington's appearance before the Senate in 1789 decrying the fact that "the treaty with the Cherokees has been entirely violated by the disorderly white people on the frontiers,"[69] states such as Georgia ignored these warnings.

Despite these pleas, the federal government did *not* secure any voluntary compliance by, or assistance from, the states. In fact, the federal government often buckled under state pressure. For example, the United States entered into a compact with the State of Georgia in 1802 that obligated the federal government to extinguish Indian title to lands within Georgia in exchange for Georgia ceding its western land claims.[70]

The federal government was nevertheless hemmed in by its own treaty commitments to protect and respect tribes, including the Cherokee Nation,[71] but it soon became amenable to a removal policy, which would relocate the Five Civilized Tribes west to Indian territory, *outside* the borders of any state. The justification for removal was found in familiar stereotypes, as these excerpts suggest, bracketing the harsh as against the "tender." In 1830, Georgia Governor George Gilmen stated:

> [T]reaties were expedients by which ignorant, intractable, and savage people were induced without bloodshed to yield up what civilized peoples had a right to possess by virtue of that comment of the Creator delivered to man upon his formation—be fruitful, multiply, and replenish the earth and subdue it.[72]

Georgia Congressman (later governor) Wilson Lumpkin put it more tenderly:

> The practice of buying Indian lands is nothing more than the substitute of humanity and benevolence, and has been resorted to in preference to the sword, as the best means for agricultural and civilized communities entering into the enjoyment of their natural and just right to the benefits of the earth, evidently designed by *Him* who formed it for purposes more useful than Indian hunting grounds.[73]

Georgia itself also enacted a number of laws to dismantle the Cherokee Nation. These statutes sought to abolish Cherokee government, annul its laws, and forbid its legislature and courts from meeting, while also purporting to distribute Cherokee lands over five Georgia counties and to extend Georgia land onto Cherokee territory.

Congress ultimately capitulated to these pressures and narrowly passed the Removal Act, which was signed by President Jackson in 1830. It stated:

> That it shall and may be lawful for the President of the United States to cause so much of any territory belonging to the United States, west of the river Mississippi, not included in any state or organized territory, and to which the Indian title has been extinguished, as he may judge necessary, to be divided into a suitable number of districts, for the reception of such tribes or nations of Indians as may choose to exchange the lands where they now reside, and remove there....[74]

The Cherokee Nation reacted as best it could. It carried on with dignity and resolve, relying on its own written constitution and treaties with the United States government. It sent a memorial to Congress that stated:

> We wish to remain on the lands of our fathers. We have a perfect and original right to remain without interruption or molestation. The treaties with us and the laws of the United States made in pursuance of treaties guarantees our residence and privileges, and secures us against intruders. Our only request is, that these treaties may be fulfilled, and these laws executed.[75]

Congress was not moved. President Jackson also refused a direct appeal by the Cherokee Nation to uphold its treaty rights against the State of Georgia.[76] The Cherokee Nation, having exhausted its appeals to Congress and the president, turned to the Court. The Cherokee Nation, represented by William Wirt and John Sargeant, filed an original action against the State of Georgia in the U.S. Supreme Court to seek injunctive relief to prevent Georgia from executing or enforcing any of its laws within the Cherokee territory, as recognized by treaty between the United States and the Cherokee Nation.

All federal courts, including the Supreme Court, are courts of limited jurisdiction, and the burden of establishing jurisdiction is on the plaintiff. Article III of the Constitution defines the original jurisdiction of the U.S. Supreme Court. It provides:

> In all Cases affecting Ambassadors, other public Ministers and Consuls, and those in which a State shall be Party, the supreme Court shall have original Jurisdiction. In all the other Cases before mentioned, the supreme Court shall have appellate Jurisdiction, both as to Law and Fact, with such Exceptions, and under such Regulations as the Congress shall make.[77]

The Cherokees complained before the Supreme Court that they

> [e]xpected protection from these unconstitutional acts of Georgia, by the troops of the United States; but notice has been given by the commanding officer of these troops to John Ross, the principal chief of the Cherokee Nation, that "these troops, so far from protecting the Cherokees, would co-operate with the civil officers of Georgia, in enforcing their laws upon them." Under these circumstances it is said that it cannot but be seen that unless this court shall interfere, the complainants have but these alternatives: either to surrender their lands in exchange for others in the western wilds of the

continent, which would be to seal, at once, the doom of their civilization, Christianity, and national existence; or to surrender their national sovereignty, their property, rights and liberties, guaranteed as these now are by so many treaties, to the rapacity and injustice of the state of Georgia; or to arm themselves in defence of these sacred rights, and fall sword in hand, on the graves of their fathers.[78]

The Cherokee Nation invoked the Supreme Court's original jurisdiction based on the claim that its lawsuit was one involving an action brought by a foreign nation against a state. Thus the case turned on a jurisdictional question.

The jurisdictional analysis—and hence constitutional analysis in this instance—was remarkably straightforward. The Cherokee Nation argument was lean, direct, and to the point. It was a "foreign state" in Article III terms because its treaty history with the United States, as reflected in such treaties as the 1785 Treaty of Hopewell and the 1791 Treaty of Holston, recognized the Cherokee Nation as "sovereign and independent; with the right of self govern-ment, without any right of interference with the same on the part of any state of the United States."[79] Because this condition of independence rested, in part, on the fact the Cherokee people were noncitizens or "aliens," the Cherokee Nation must certainly be, not a state of the union, but a foreign state in Article III terms.

Chief Justice Marshall found this argument "imposing" but noted that "we must examine it more closely before we yield to it."[80] This examination began with the telling observation that "[t]he condition of the Indians in relation to the United States is perhaps unlike that of any other two people in existence...the relation of the Indians to the United States is marked by peculiar and cardinal distinctions that exist nowhere else."[81] Having noted the relational quandary, the Court proceeded to find that the Cherokee Nation was not a "foreign state" in Article III terms.

The core analysis relied on the language found in an examination of the text of the Commerce Clause.[82] The Court noted that the text of Article I, sec-tion 8, treats Indian tribes and foreign nations as discrete, not identical, entities:

Had the Indian tribes been foreign nations, in view of the convention [i.e., the commerce clause]; this exclusive power of regulating intercourse with them might have been, and most probably would have been, specifically given, in language indicating that idea, not in language contradistinguishing them from foreign nations. Congress might have been empowered "to regulate commerce with foreign nations, including the Indian tribes, and among the several states."

This language would have suggested itself to statesmen who considered the Indian tribes as foreign nations, and were yet desirous of mentioning them particularly.[83]

The motion for the injunction was denied with the observation:

If it be true that wrongs have been inflicted, and that still greater are to be apprehended, this is not the tribunal which can redress the past or prevent the future.[84]

If this was all there was to *Cherokee Nation*, the decision would be wholly unremarkable. What gives the case its enduring significance is a series of observations and pronouncements about the nature of tribes, their relationship to the federal government, and the relationship of the federal government to the states in Indian affairs. These statements of Chief Justice Marshall—while merely dicta in a case that issued no affirmative order—have become foundational principles in Indian law.

At the outset, Chief Justice Marshall noted that the facts in the case elicit much sympathy for the plight of the Cherokee Nation, but that sympathy could not be "indulged" until the jurisdiction issue was resolved.[85] Despite resolving the jurisdictional issue against the Cherokee Nation, the Court described tribes as "domestic dependent nations" with territorial integrity and powers of self-government, who nevertheless had a unique relationship with the federal government described as one of "pupilage. Their relation to the United States resembled that of a ward to its guardian."[86]

Despite the lack of elucidation, these phrases and analogies entered directly into the stream of Indian law as core precepts that tribes possess sovereignty yet are reliant on the national government's "kindness and its power."[87] The nature of a tribe's sovereignty or its domestic dependent nationhood status remains as unclear in the year 2009 as it was in 1831. It continues to exist, but its particulars, its contours, and its borders remain elusive.

The guardian-ward analogy eventually became doctrine in the development of the trust relationship, in which the United States acts as the trustee for the beneficiary tribe (and individual Indians) in regard to matters of (trust) land and natural resources, as well as "protecting" tribes from their "deadliest enemies," the states. Yet, the precise standard of care for the trustee was, and is, by no means clear. And although the trust relationship might be best understood as a "shield" to protect tribal resources from jurisdictional encroachments by the states, it has often been used as a "sword" by the federal government against the tribes to advance its own agenda, which has often been adverse to tribal resources and tribal authority.[88]

As a shield to protect tribal resources and authority from outside forces, the trust relationship is arguably rooted in both treaty guarantees and the Indian Commerce Clause. Yet it remains to be determined how *constitutionally* rooted this doctrine is, when it is distorted into a doctrinal platform for expansive federal authority in Indian affairs to deal adversely with tribal land and natural resources and to limit tribal sovereignty within Indian country.[89] This "sword" has no constitutional roots, except extraconstitutional self-dealing and violation of tribal sovereignty.

The majority opinion in *Cherokee Nation* also recognized the unusual fact that the Cherokee Nation was in court at all because

> at the time the constitution was framed, the idea of appealing to an American court of justice for an assertion of right or a redress of wrong, had perhaps never entered the mind of an Indian or of his tribe. Their appeal was to the tomahawk, or to the government. This was well understood by the statesmen who framed the Constitution of the United States, and might furnish some reason for omitting to enumerate them among the parties who might sue in the courts of the union.[90]

This observation reflects one of the principal themes of encounter identified earlier as that of diplomacy and war.[91] Tribes were sovereigns outside, not inside, the Constitution. By 1831, some of these elements were already under stress. Congress and the president refused the invitation of diplomacy, including treaty enforcement, and the Cherokee Nation was incapable of waging war, hence its turn to the Court. This turn to the Court became an increasingly predominant theme of Indian law in the modern era.

Cherokee Nation did not result in a unanimous opinion. Justice Johnson concurred but wrote a separate opinion. It emphasized that the Treaty of Hopewell, rather than reflecting tribal sovereignty, reflected an inordinate dependence of the tribe on the federal government—dependence wholly inconsistent with nationhood, and a nationhood that, if recognized, threatened the integrity of the family of nations:

> Where is the rule to stop? Must every petty kraal of Indians, designating themselves a tribe or nation, and having a few hundred acres of land to hunt on exclusively, be recognized as a state? We should indeed force into the family of nations, a very numerous and heterogeneous progeny.[92]

Justice Johnson also would have rejected the case on the grounds that it raised a political question in that it sought an order commanding the executive branch to take action, including the possible use of force, against a state—a course of action already rejected by the president as fraught with incalculable evils that threatened the delicate federal-state balance of the early republic.[93]

Justice Baldwin also concurred in the judgment but wrote separately to emphasize the critical importance of the case:

> As the reasons for the judgment of the court seem to me more important than the judgment itself, in its effects on the peace of the country and the conditions of the complainants, and as I stand alone on one question of vital concern to both; I must give my reason in full. The opinion of the court is of high authority in itself; and the judge who delivers it has a support as strong in moral influence over public opinion, as any human tribunal can impart. The judge, who stands alone in decided dissent on matters of the infinite magnitude which this case presents, must sink under the continued and unequal struggle; unless he can fix himself by a firm hold on the constitution and laws of the country. He must be presumed to be in the wrong, until he proves himself to be in the right.[94]

The core of Justice Baldwin's concern was that to recognize Indian tribes as "foreign nations" would imperil all previous actions by the colonies, states, and the federal government itself in dealing with tribes, wherein ascendant (federal) sovereign authority was always asserted over Indian tribes and their territory.[95]

According to Justice Baldwin, the Court's

> judicial power cannot divest the states of rights of sovereignty, and transfer them to the Indians, by decreeing them to be a nation or foreign state, pre-existing and with rightful jurisdiction and sovereignty over the territory they occupy. This would reverse every principle on which our government have [sic] acted for fifty-five years; and force, by more judicial power, upon the other departments of this government and the state of this union, the recognition of the existence of nations and states within the limits of both, possessing dominion and jurisdiction paramount to the federal and state constitutions.[96]

Justice Thompson dissented. He found that the Cherokee Nation was a "foreign state" for Article III purposes, the key determinant being that "[i]t is sufficient if it be really sovereign and independent: that is, it must govern itself by its own authority and laws."[97] Such was the Cherokee Nation. Whatever its governmental weakness, or "dependence" on the federal government—as evidenced by certain language in the Treaties of Hopewell and Holston—its self-governance and independence remained.[98] These were essential international law maxims described and catalogued by the eminent international law scholar Vattel.[99]

While acknowledging the doctrine of discovery, Justice Thompson rejected the claim that conquest had in fact occurred, and the continued negotiation and application of treaties were proof to the contrary.[100] The essence of Georgia statehood, Thompson opined, is its "political character," not its boundaries. The Cherokee Nation likewise retained its essential right of self-governance through the treaties, and the federal government had a corollary duty within the treaties to assist in protecting this right. Therefore, it was proper to issue an injunction against the state of Georgia.[101]

The Court thus split into three pairs, with Justices Marshall and McLean viewing the tribes as "domestic dependent nations" (without detail or any operational definition), Justices Johnson and Baldwin viewing them without any sovereignty, and Justices Thompson and Story viewing them as foreign nations in the context of early international law principles.

There are several noteworthy elements in this opinion that bear the characteristic stamp of Chief Justice Marshall, including the establishment of core substantive principles without the necessity of issuing any affirmative order that had to be enforced and deciding a case in which the dicta is more important than the holding. In this regard, it is much like the seminal case of *Marbury v. Madison*,[102] which established the foundational concept of judicial review to determine the constitutionality of any federal or state legislation but, as in *Cherokee Nation*, without issuing any affirmative order. Such jurisprudential moves were particularly adroit in the early days of the republic, when the Supreme Court lacked the institutional resources and established power of Congress and the president. The opinion in *Cherokee Nation* recognized an essential tribal sovereignty, created a unique tribal-federal relationship, and established a basic federalism in Indian law that the federal government, not the states, had exclusive authority in Indian affairs. These principles were further recognized and extended in *Worcester v. Georgia*.[103]

Worcester v. Georgia

Not surprisingly, the decision in *Cherokee Nation* did little to quell the vigor of Georgia's animus toward the resistance of the Cherokee Nation to its expansionary agenda. *Worcester v. Georgia* came to the Court a year later with essentially the same issue as *Cherokee Nation*, but this time in the context of an appeal of a criminal case in which the Supreme Court's (appellate) jurisdiction was clear and unequivocal. The sole *substantive* issue was whether the State of

Georgia had legitimate (criminal) jurisdiction to prosecute a non-Indian for preaching within the Cherokee Nation reservation without a state license to do so.[104] The Court answered in the negative. The State of Georgia did not have criminal jurisdiction to prosecute such a state offense that occurred in Indian country. Chief Justice Marshall wrote the majority opinion, but this time jurisprudential finesse would not suffice; an affirmative order would have to be issued.

The defendants, Samuel Worcester and Elizur Butler, worked and preached on the Cherokee lands with the permission of the Cherokee Nation. They lacked any state license and were convicted in a jury trial and sentenced to four years of hard labor in the state penitentiary. The defendants appealed, and a writ of error was issued by the U.S. Supreme Court. The appellate jurisdiction of the Supreme Court was properly invoked to challenge the state statute as "repugnant to the constitution, laws and treaties of the United States."[105]

In the early part of the opinion, Chief Justice Marshall reprised the doctrine of discovery, but with a decidedly lighter, almost revisionary, touch:

> It is difficult to comprehend the proposition, that inhabitants of either quarter of the globe could have rightful original claims of dominion over the inhabitants of the other, or over the lands they occupied; or that the discovery of either by the other should give the discoverer rights in the country discovered, which annulled the pre-existing rights of its ancient possessors.[106]

Yet, of course, there was "reality" as well: "But power, war, conquest, give rights, which, after possession, are conceded by the world; and which can never be controverted by those on whom they descend."[107] The doctrine of discovery's theoretical and practical vacuity (which did *not* undermine its "reality") was nevertheless abundantly clear to the Court:

> The extravagant and absurd idea, that the feeble settlements made on the sea coast, or the companies under whom they were made, acquired legitimate power by them [i.e., royal charters] to govern the people, or occupy lands from sea to sea, did not enter the mind of any man.[108]

The Court then proceeded to its treaty analysis. Chief Justice Marshall discerned in both the Treaty of Hopewell and the Treaty of Holston a recognition of tribal sovereignty and federal protection of that sovereignty. The Treaty of Hopewell in "its essential articles treat the Cherokees as a nation capable of maintaining the relations of peace and war, and ascertain the boundaries between them and the United States."[109]

The Court's language is even stronger in characterizing the Treaty of Holston:

> This treaty, thus explicitly recognizing the national character of the Cherokees, and their right of self government; thus guaranteeing their lands; assuming the duty of protection, and of course pledging the faith of the United States for that protection; has been frequently renewed, and is now in full force.[110]

The treaty analysis was complemented with a discussion of the federal Trade and Intercourse Acts, which

> treat them as nations, respect their rights, and manifest a firm purpose to afford that protection which treaties stipulate. All these Acts, and especially that of 1802, which is still in force, manifestly consider the several Indian nations as distinct political communities, having territorial boundaries, within which their authority is exclusive, and having a right to all the lands within those boundaries, which is not only acknowledged, but *guarantied* by the United States.[111]

The cumulative effect of treaties and the trade and intercourse acts recognized Indian nations as "distinct, independent political communities, retaining their original natural rights"[112] in which "the laws of Georgia can have no force."[113] The authority to deal with tribes, indeed, the "whole intercourse between the United States and this [Indian] nation, is, by our constitution and laws, vested in the government of the United States."[114] The state criminal convictions of Worcester and Butler were therefore reversed.

Justice McLean concurred. Much of his opinion is taken up with the appropriateness of federal review of state criminal convictions. Although in most circumstances federal review is not permitted, it is most certainly available when a state's penal laws "infringe upon the [C]onstitution of the United States, or some treaty or law of the union."[115] Conditions change, but the "principles of justice are the same. They rest upon a base which will remain beyond the endurance of time."[116]

The Cherokee Nation Cases and Constitutional Crisis

At the time of their decision, the *Cherokee Nation* and *Worcester* cases threatened a constitutional crisis—a crisis that involved the federal government and the State of Georgia and a crosscutting crisis between the Supreme

Court and the president. The State of Georgia refused to submit briefs and did not appear at oral argument in either of these cases.[117] In addition, prior to the *Cherokee Nation* case, Chief Justice Marshall issued a writ of habeas corpus in the case of George Corn Tassel, a Cherokee, who was convicted in Georgia state court of killing another Cherokee on Cherokee land. The Georgia state legislature was not impressed. It condemned the chief justice's "interference," and Corn Tassel was hanged five days later.[118] Georgia's bold refusal to appear before the Supreme Court in both *Cherokee Nation* and *Worcester* and its violation of the Supreme Court's order in the Corn Tassel case threatened the very existence of the early republic. No republic can hold if its constituent entities owe no deference or allegiance to the central government.[119] The tender fabric of early constitutional federalism was at risk of being ripped apart.

In addition to the constitutional tension between the Supreme Court and the State of Georgia, there was a constitutional clash involving the separation of powers between the Supreme Court and the president. Unlike *Cherokee Nation*, the *Worcester* decision resulted in an affirmative order mandating the release of Worcester and Butler. The Court's mandate was not self-executing, and due to an apparent gap in the Judiciary Act of 1789, there was apparently no procedural mechanism to obtain the necessary order to direct the federal marshals. Meanwhile, the Court had adjourned until the next regularly scheduled session in 1833.[120]

At this time, President Jackson purportedly said, "John Marshall has made his decision; now let him enforce it."[121] Although others consider the statement apocryphal, there is no doubt that President Jackson supported Georgia's claimed sovereignty over Cherokee land.[122] A constitutional imbroglio was averted only when the impending nullification crisis triggered by the threat of several southern states to withdraw from the union convinced President Jackson that such a constitutional crisis was not in the national interest. As a result of this turn of events, President Jackson personally urged the governor of Georgia to pardon Worcester and Butler. The missionaries had initially resisted the offer of pardons, but they subsequently changed their minds and were pardoned by Governor Lumpkin in 1833.[123]

This original constitutional crisis at the very beginning of Indian law has transmogrified in a quite different, but just as potent, way to the constitutional crisis of contemporary Indian law, in which the Constitution as currently interpreted by the Supreme Court provides no effective limits to *federal* power in Indian law. As a result, there is growing constitutional tension between the federal government and the tribes.[124]

The Foundation and Legacy of the Marshall Trilogy

The early constitutional crisis abated. Foundational principles of Indian law emerged. These principles are generally understood to include the recognition of tribal sovereignty and self-government, the existence of a unique federal-tribal relationship often identified as the trust relationship, federal exclusivity in dealing with Indian tribes as a basic tenet of a developing federalism, and as a necessary corollary, the absence of any inherent state authority in Indian affairs.[125] To these should be added *Johnson v. McIntosh*'s denigration of tribal property rights, which rested on a mélange of colonialism, racism, and cultural misunderstanding.

Although the opinions in the Marshall trilogy were often somewhat sketchy and thin in their citation to precedent and other authority (not surprising for early cases of first impression), certain constitutional roots are apparent. This was particularly true in *Worcester*, where the Court was adamant in recognizing that tribal sovereignty and tribal self-government inhere in the constitutionally authorized treaties the Cherokees made with the federal government. Mere dependence or reliance on the federal government for assistance does not impair tribal authority.[126]

Federal authority in Indian affairs derives from treaty making and the Indian Commerce Clause. Yet it is important to remember that this federal authority was understood as *limited* to regulate interaction *with* tribes through treaties and commerce but not to regulate the trade and self-governance *of* tribes. These sources, particularly the Indian Commerce Clause, also serve to divest the states from any claim of authority in Indian country. This is apparent from both history and the constitutional text, especially in light of the more ambiguous predecessor version that appeared in the Articles of Confederation.[127] States cannot point to any constitutional recognition supporting their legal and political forays into Indian country. The *structure* of the Constitution confirms this basic element of federalism.

The unique federal-tribal *trust* relationship is more problematic. Although such a relationship often inheres in the *text* of treaties, it is obviously neither required nor prohibited by the Constitution, and it is rooted in its commitment to serve a protective function, safeguarding tribal land and resources from non-Indian and state predation. Yet this limited view of the trust relationship ultimately was transmogrified into a *generalized* (indeed, limitless) federal power, uncoupled from treaties and the Constitution, that justified wide-ranging congressional (and judicial) initiatives that clearly were *not* beneficial to tribes. This most unfortunate legal development crystallized into Indian law doctrine with the announcement of the plenary power doctrine in the 1903 decision of *Lone Wolf v. Hitchcock*.[128] The shield of the trust relationship became the sword of plenary power. Its protective focus, which was rooted in treaties and the Indian Commerce Clause, was transformed into a vehicle of excessive federal power to limit tribal sovereignty and to further erode the tribal land and natural resource base of Indian tribes.[129]

Johnson v. McIntosh, of course, has no express constitutional roots. It is rooted in the bitter soil of colonialism and the ragweed of "discovery." Yet it was *not* a rogue doctrine, but rather one of the first principles of international law, an international convention within the European family of nations—a "family" that a young United States readily joined, despite just having thrown off the shackles imposed by British tyranny. The United States occasionally had its qualms about "discovery," but it did not let them interfere with its expansionary agenda.

Although *Johnson v. McIntosh* defies contemporary justification, even in its original form it was not elevated to become constitutional principle. In this regard, it is a dark parallel to slavery. While there was no affirmative discussion or per se endorsement of slavery in the Constitution as originally adopted, there was enough constitutional silence to tolerate and even to condone it. So, too, with the evisceration of tribal property rights. Nothing in the Constitution expressly required or prohibited the result in *Johnson v. McIntosh*. The closest thing—and it is only tangential—is treaty making, which, of course, provided the *only constitutionally* recognized vehicle for the potential sale or transfer of Indian land, to the federal government.

Certain elements of *Johnson v. McIntosh*, notably the tribal land rights of use and occupancy, were also mixed with the fledging identification of the trust relationship that emanated from the *Cherokee Nation* cases. This mix yielded the not unreasonable notion that the federal government had affirmative duties to safeguard tribal land and natural resource interests from unwarranted encroachment by state and private interests. Although this responsibility was (and is) discharged with varying degrees of (legal) zeal, little was done to protect the beneficiary tribes (and individual Indians) from the self-dealing of the federal government trustee with respect to tribal land and resources.[130] And with ultimate title to Indian lands still held by the United States, effective tribal sovereignty remains substantially compromised.

The trust relationship, especially in its most hierarchical and vertical form, also serves to undercut tribal sovereignty by effectively foreclosing the ability of tribes to use, improve, lease, and even sell their land and resources without federal government approval. Yet this problem is not insurmountable, and there have been a number of reforms—especially within the practices of the Bureau of Indian Affairs—to restructure the trust relationship into a more cooperative, horizontal relationship[131] that is less like the relationship of a "ward to its guardian" and more like the relationship of junior and senior partners. This trajectory of change is far from complete, but it is heading in the right direction, and with a continued commitment to a meaningful self-determination, along with increasing infusion of federal services and financial resolve, positive change is likely to continue. Yet there is no guarantee in the shifting world of federal Indian law policy that such will be the case, especially when there are no adequate constitutional limits on federal power. In addition, there is a need to examine the difficult question of when the trust responsibility—at least in its management[132] capacity—might well come to an end, not in abandonment to likely failure and renewed land loss, but in the realization of effective tribal autonomy.

The Marshall trilogy also established some overarching practices, if not actual principles, in Indian law. These practices include identifying the role of Congress and the Supreme Court as the prime, if not sole, arbiters of what the state and tribal sovereign may do in Indian country. As a necessary corollary, it is the federal government that serves as the final umpire on the field of Indian law dreams and reality—an umpire that both makes the rules (i.e., Congress) and interprets them (i.e., Supreme Court), but without any authorizing rulebook (i.e., Constitution). In the trilogy, the Constitution appears to constrain the states, but there is no express discussion about whether it constrains the federal government to any significant degree. This is the principal doctrinal weakness of the Marshall trilogy. Thus it remains unclear how much of the Marshall trilogy is truly constitutional in nature and how much of it is essentially a mélange of statutory and common law doctrine.

Modern Supreme Court jurisprudence clearly regards the Marshall trilogy as subject to change and lacking "Platonic" status:

> This is not to say that the Indian sovereignty doctrine, with its concomitant jurisdictional limit on the reach of state law has remained static during the 141 years since *Worcester* was decided. Not surprisingly, the doctrine has undergone *considerable evolution in response to changed circumstances.*[133]

The foundational core of the Marshall trilogy rests on generalizations, both constitutional and otherwise, and not on detailed jurisprudence; therefore, it can lead to different (operational) interpretations. In addition, the trilogy is grounded in a view of Indian tribes as not fully integrated into the new republic but rather on its margins with their own land, their own government, their own culture, and their own constituents. This static landscape did not long remain but underwent rapid legal, political, social, and economic change, evolving as it went into a process that absorbed tribes more and more into the republic. This was the "new" landscape that ultimately confronted the Supreme Court in the seminal case of

Lone Wolf v. Hitchcock in 1903. At that crossroads, the Court bid a firm farewell to the Constitution as the necessary marker of metes and bounds in Indian law.

History and Indian Law

History is the propaganda of the victors.
—Simone Weil

Many Indian law scholars and much Indian law jurisprudence note that history is a central component of Indian law.[134] The history (and anthropology) of who Indians were and the present understanding of past events and incidents are often pivotal in much modern Indian law decisionmaking. Yet, there is seldom any discussion of the nature of the historical enterprise itself in the cases or scholarly literature. What exactly history is, what its methods are, and what it tells us are therefore key aspects of Indian law that are worthy of closer attention.

Given the significance of land in Indian law, it is particularly useful and resonant to analogize the work of the historian to that of a mapmaker. The essence of making maps is like writing history: it is to represent, not to replicate. It is a distillation of the past. Historians "distill the experiences of others for the purpose of helping you get from where you are to where you want to go."[135] In this sense, "the past is a landscape and history is the way we represent it."[136] The way we represent it is through "pattern recognition as the primary form of human perception and the fact that all history—even the most simple narrative—draws upon the representation of such patterns."[137] For history or maps to work, their representations must "fit" reality, and the maps may thus vary with the particular reality they seek to represent. For example, maps for highway travel, maps for air travel, maps for hiking, and maps for drilling oil describe the same landscape differently:

> Cartographic verification is, therefore, entirely relative: it depends upon how well the mapmakers achieve a fit between the landscape being mapped and the requirements of those for whom the map is being made.[138]

Such narratives or maps of *human* history that concern the interaction of human groups presumably are equally concerned with matters of "fit," "requirements," and "verification."

This process of "verification" often falls to the courts in Indian law. For example, when the federal government took possession of the Sioux Nation's Black Hills in 1877 in violation of the Fort Laramie Treaty of 1868, was it simply working out the particulars of manifest destiny or engaging in manifest injustice?[139] As noted by the historian E. H. Carr, "Every great period of history has its casualties as well as its victories."[140]

Thus one of the key questions becomes what are the "requirements of those for whom the map is being made"? For example, there is little doubt that one of the "requirements" of the (dominant) national society at the time of the federal taking of the Black Hills in 1877 was unimpeded western expansion. And thus the "fit" provided by the explanation of manifest destiny was sufficiently adequate. Yet were these the same "requirements" of the (multicultural) national society in 1980, when the Supreme Court considered the events of 1877? Presumably, the answer was no, and indeed, that was one of the issues the Court had to confront.

The Black Hills case is quite instructive in this regard. In fact, it is one of the few cases in Indian law that actually engages the quandary of the nature of the historical enterprise. This is particularly true in Justice Rehnquist's dissent. In the majority opinion written by Justice Blackmun, the Court found that the United States had legitimately used its power of eminent domain to take 7.7 million acres of the Black Hills in violation of the Fort Laramie Treaty of 1868.[141] The federal government's sole legal shortcoming was the failure to pay just compensation, but its moral shortcomings were extensive.[142] Justice Blackmun quoted approvingly the conclusion of Judge Nichols of the Court of Claims that "a more ripe and rank case of dishonorable dealings will never, in all probability, be found in our history."[143]

Justice Rehnquist strenuously opposed this characterization. His opposition was essentially twofold. The first was his disdain for revisiting history, and the second was the attendant uncertainty it created that he regarded as fixed in place and not in need of "revision":

> There were undoubtedly greed, cupidity, and other less-than-
> admirable tactics employed by the government during the Black Hills
> episode in the settlement of the West, but the Indians did not lack
> their share of villainy either. It seems to me quite unfair to judge by
> the light of "revisionist" historians or the mores of another era actions
> that were taken under pressure of time more than a century ago.[144]

Apparently, when there is "cupidity" on both sides, the old status quo ought to prevail. Justice Rehnquist felt no need, for example, to distinguish between invasion and self-defense, gain and loss, or a (treaty) promise and its breach. The "pressure of time" (i.e., manifest destiny?) excuses then and *now*. But why?

An essential aspect of law is its deference to the past, but an unbending rigidity toward, and rejection of, evolving notions of what is just in a particular set of circumstances merely capitulates to continuing injustice. Think of *Brown v. Board of Education*,[145] for example. Without the Court's willingness to confront the past, the blatant injustice of "separate but equal" would have remained the norm.

Justice Rehnquist did *not* argue that there was a unitary view of history. Different views inhere "since history, no more than law, is not an exact (or for that matter an inexact) science."[146] History perforce is inexact, and therefore we should tread lightly in its presence. This does not seem an unreasonable dictum. Yet there needs to be some accountability and review of cited sources. Justice Rehnquist's own citations to historical sources are quite problematic in this regard.[147]

Rehnquist faulted the majority for apparently relying on historians "writing for the purpose of having their conclusions or observations inserted in the reports of congressional committees."[148] The reliability of such historians, if they existed, would be a legitimate concern. However, as the majority points out, this allegation is "puzzling because, with respect to this case, we are unaware that any such historian exists."[149] The majority, in contrast, actually cited numerous primary sources contemporaneous with the events of the 1870s. The alleged revisionism appears chimerical.[150]

Rehnquist then offered the proposition that "the confrontations in the West were the product of a long history, not a conniving Presidential administration," citing historian Ray Billington as his authority.[151] The Billington language is from an *introduction* to the first edition of *Soldier and Brave*.[152] Even if introductions were prized for their scholarly value, it is important to note that this particular introduction was *entirely* omitted from subsequent editions of the book.[153]

More important, the proposition Rehnquist attempts to advance is simply *inconsistent* with the remainder of Billington's book. Even though "confrontations in the West" were the product of a "long history," Billington actually *acknowledges* the "conniving" nature of the Grant administration in its attempts to acquire the Black Hills.[154] He writes: "In 1874 discovery of gold in the Black Hills, a part of the Great Sioux Reservation, set off an invasion of miners and a Government effort to buy the hills from the Sioux. These events led to the Sioux War of 1876–77, a *scarcely disguised attempt to clear the unceded territory and to frighten them into ceding the Black Hills*."[155]

Furthermore, this scholar, whom Rehnquist calls a "respected student of the settlement of the American West," provides ample ammunition to refute other elements of his dissent. For example, Rehnquist uses the well-known historian Samuel Eliot Morison to argue that the Plains Indians were bloodthirsty and violent.[156] Billington, in contrast, noted that the Sioux Indians "regarded their guns as cherished possessions and means of livelihood."[157]

Other historians and writers, writing forty and fifty years prior to the Rehnquist dissent, also refute those and the other claims of Morison.[158]

Justice Rehnquist also quotes Samuel Eliot Morison for evidence of the "cultural differences which made conflict and brutal warfare inevitable" on the Great Plains:[159] "They lived only for the day, recognized no rights of property, robbed or killed anyone if they thought they could get away with it, inflicted cruelty without a qualm, and endured torture without flinching."[160] This work was published in 1965 (not 1865!), and it appears racist, as well as anthropologically unsound, and it harks all the way back to eighteenth- and early-nineteenth-century views of savagery and the absence of civilization.[161] Morison's claims are patently in error. All societies have concepts of property and self-defense. This basic proposition appears to have eluded both Morison and Justice Rehnquist. In the end, Justice Rehnquist, apparently despairing over the historical enterprise, abjures it completely:

> That there was tragedy, deception, barbarity, and virtually every other vice known to man in the 300-year history of the expansion of the original 13 Colonies into a Nation which now embraces more than three million square miles and 50 States cannot be denied. But in a court opinion, as a historical and not a legal matter, both settler and Indian are entitled to the benefit of the Biblical adjuration: "Judge not, that ye be not judged."[162]

Certainly, the view that legal judgments about history, both then and now, are somehow beyond the pale flies in the face of a core ingredient of modern Indian law, which is the very meaning of time and history in the context of changing circumstances. Many Indian law cases, such as the *Sioux Nation Black Hills* case itself, require the Court to revisit events and encounters that took place more than a hundred years ago. Although this is a daunting prospect, it is inevitable and bears some reflection. Some of the potential ingredients to aid in the difficult process of historical interpretation include empathy, moral sensitivity, and alertness to the tyrannies of the past. No doubt there are complicated issues as to remediation and the role of the judiciary,[163] but it seems normatively problematic in the extreme to stubbornly cling to the inequities of the past. To do so allows the oppression of past history to continue to oppress, rather than be transformed in the present.

History is not a catalogue of facts but a selection of facts that forms a pattern that is tied together in a narrative to identify and "explain" the past. The quality of empathy (not sympathy or sentimentalism) directs writers (or readers) of history to open their minds to the *other* side, to "their hopes and fears, their beliefs and dreams, their sense of right and wrong, their perception of the world and where they fit within it."[164] In neither the Marshall trilogy nor Justice Rehnquist's dissent in the Sioux Nation case is there any empathy as to how this "history" looked to Indians from *their* viewpoint. The value of empathy is that it adds balance to much of the historical inquiry. It might, of course, make the task of achieving historical assessments more complex, but in the context of legal adjudications, presumably concerned with justice, this does not seem an unreasonable requirement.

Although the majority opinion in the *Sioux Nation Black Hills* case may be regarded as an example of seeking to balance the scales of history, it is necessary to remember that the question in the case was not whether the United States could take the Black Hills without tribal consent; rather, the question was only whether the United States had paid for it.[165] Given that the Court awarded only money damages and no land return, Justice Rehnquist's dissent is all the more troublesome, even virulent.

In other cases, it is routine for the Court to state that it cannot remake history, particularly when it would disturb the expectations of the non-Indian majority. For example, in a 2005 case involving the Oneida Indian Nation of New York, the Court opined that the tribe could not "rekindle the embers of a tribal sovereignty long grown cold" because of its likely adverse effect on the settled expectations of the dominant community. In such a jurisprudence, history often conspires with law to perpetuate, rather than reconsider, the inequities of the past.[166] In this view, the "old" maps of colonialism and dominion continue to be legible and adequately verified for present purposes.

Yet, there are other ways to approach the history of past events when dealing with Native people. The case of *Mabo v. Queensland* from Australia is instructive in this regard.[167] In this case, which involved the nature of land title, if any, of the Meriam people to the Murray Islands, the Australian High Court observed:

> The peace and order of Australian society is built on the legal system. It can be modified to bring it into conformity with contemporary notions of justice and human rights, but it cannot be destroyed. It is not possible, a priori, to distinguish between cases that express a skeletal principle and those that do not, but no case can command unquestioning adherence if the rule it expresses seriously offends the values of justice and human rights (especially equality before the law) which are aspirations of the contemporary Australian legal system. If a postulated rule of the common law expressed in earlier cases seriously offends those contemporary values, the question arises whether the rule should be maintained and applied. Whenever such

a question arises, it is necessary to assess whether the particular rule is an essential doctrine of our legal system and whether, if the rule were to be overturned, the disturbance to be apprehended would be disproportionate to the benefit flowing from the overturning.[168]

In this framework, there is a frank acknowledgment of the possibility of jurisprudential change in order to achieve "conformity with contemporary notions of justice and human rights." To be sure, it is a possibility to be carefully weighed against potential harm resulting *from* such a change, but it is a possibility nevertheless. Such a possibility is not even on the horizon of American Indian law jurisprudence.

An ethos of moral sensitivity probably strikes many as inappropriate to history's domain of factual inquiry. Yet this is really not so. Most history—including most Indian law history—is primarily about how groups of people treat each other. Thus it is necessary and inevitable to confront the moral context of these encounters. In this view, the historian's job would appear to be twofold: to describe the moral climate at the time of the historical events in question and to view the historical events in light of contemporary moral standards.[169] These two strands of moral and factual inquiry, while necessary, are discrete and not to be confused or run together,[170] for to do so distorts and unsettles the location of the present and the past. Such a historical inquiry may, when properly carried out, help to illuminate possibilities within the law for balm and amelioration. If historical choices made in the past no longer retain moral vigor and persuasion in the present, how are better legal or political choices to be made in the present? Such is the challenge of history, with its ongoing commitment to learn from the "representations" and "fit" of the past in order to make better maps with which to forge a more meaningful future. Such actions are not about assessing social guilt but about fashioning law to meet the new "requirements" of a society committed to respect and fairness to all.

History rescues events from oblivion but not necessarily from tyranny. Oppression in the past can remain in the present—despite its disavowal—if the terms of contemporary judgment continue to be "imported from other times and places."[171] In this context, history and law need a vocabulary and grammar to set individuals and groups next to each other in a (new) horizontal relationship of respect and equality rather than (even inadvertently) replicating the (old) vertical relationship of dominance and inequality.

This is indeed a tall order. Perhaps it is largely unachievable in Indian law, especially in light of law's unflinching commitment to the past. Yet the law is also forward-looking; therefore, yoked to our respect for the past must be a commitment to hold it accountable in the present.[172] History cannot be coerced, but it can be moved forward with respect and hard work if we keep to the goal of a collective well-being of all.

Cartography and Translation: A Note on Ireland and the Middle East

The analogy of the historian's task in writing history to the craft of the cartographer in making maps finds specific examples in the histories of both Ireland and the Holy Land, with their own quite powerful attachment of indigenous peoples to the local landscape. With the centrality of landscape in the Indian experience squarely in mind, an examination of the mapping of these places is uniquely instructive in the sense that cartographers' mapping of an actual landscape can be used to harm and dispossess indigenous people.

In Ireland, in the early nineteenth century, British soldiers of the Royal Engineers and their Irish assistants set out "to transliterate the local Gaelic placenames and Anglicize them, in the process of mapping for the Ordinance Survey."[173] This mapping was complemented with the establishment of national schools run by the British, where instruction would take place only in English and the system would replace any local schools where the language of instruction was Gaelic.[174]

The dynamics and challenges of this process are dramatically evoked in Brian Friel's play *Translations*.[175] In this play, the Irish characters enact and debate the pros and cons of this transforming process in the context of their nineteenth-century rural circumstances. Are the name changes and new schools a way to move forward from a limiting past or, rather, just additional ways to undermine traditional language and cultural lifeways? The play doesn't provide any easy answers, but the playwright has indicated elsewhere that looking back is not a simple either-or proposition but rather a complex undertaking to better understand the present: "the only merit in looking back is to understand who you are and where you are at this moment."[176] Friel has written that he

> believes that culture can be causative, can have political
> consequences: so, when he discusses language, he sees it as a
> specific basis for all the politics which may ensue...because they
> grew up in a state where the speaking of Irish was a political act, and
> where a person who gave a Gaelic version of a name to a policeman
> might expect a cuff on the ear or worse.[177]

To preserve the best of tradition, there must also be an understanding of the best (and worst) of modernity and the most fruitful way to translate the best of both into a creative synthesis. The ever-present danger is simply to impose a dominant grid over indigenous complexities or indigenous nostalgia over modern complexities.[178]

In the context of such colonial contact between societies, mapping and education are inevitable but fraught with risk to advance an insidious imperialism—a stultifying British imperialism characterized by "its desire not so much to translate Irish values into English words as to translate English values into Irish terms" and thus failing to preserve Irish values and linguistic content within English.[179]

This is the treacherous process of translation:

And the attempt to write all the new names into a book represents the colonizer's benign assumption that to name a thing is to assert one's power over it and the written tradition of the occupier will henceforth enjoy primacy over the oral memory of the natives.
A map, in short, will have much the same relation to a landscape as the written word has to speech. Each is a form of translation.
    Such translation has always been an act of imperialism, for as Edward Said has written: "…cultures have always been inclined to impose concrete transformation on other cultures, receiving those other cultures not as they are but as, for the benefit of the receiver, they ought to be."[180]

The key, therefore, is to find balance with its commitment to grow and to adapt but also to avoid both "regressive nostalgia" and "assimilative suffocation."[181]

This same process has also been identified in the Holy Land of the Middle East. Changes in place-name identification from Arabic to Hebrew began to eviscerate the Arabic past: "Local names are the essence of the cultural heritage of a place; they commemorate *historical* events and open the way to an understanding of the local population's worldview."[182] The Israeli maps of name changes were met with Palestinian mapmaking:

On the Palestinian maps, reality is frozen in 1946. Hundreds of villages and towns, ruins, and hollowed graves that no longer exist fill the map of Palestine, whereas the Jewish settlements appear under the classification of "Jewish colonies, divided according to the stages of the Zionist conquest, from 1882 to the present." Everything created in Palestine by the Jews was considered an aberration. The Palestinians created their own "sacred geography." They had no interest in the "current map," only in the "historical map" that, in their opinion, proved "the flawless Hebrew map" to be a fabrication and evidence of the plundering of their land, its history, and its civilization. The symbolic act of taking possession, expressed through the assignment of names, was answered by the converse symbolic act, whose purpose was to deny the right to take possession. And the maps became a battleground: I'll destroy your map just as you destroyed mine.[183]

This process of renaming is a cornerstone of colonial displacement and empire that reaches far back:

> As is well known, the British had made mapping the cornerstone of their dominion throughout the Empire. The first official maps they prepared were of Ireland, in 1653, when they wished to confiscate the landholdings of the rebellious Irish and to bestow them on English soldiers and settlers. Ever since then, the surveyor has walked beside the British officer, and sometimes has gone before him.[184]

Mapmaking and the assignment of place-names are acts of proprietorship, acts of transfer, symbolic deeds. "Mapmaking...was one of the specialized intellectual weapons by which power could be gained, administered, given legitimacy and codified."[185] The entire western movement in the United States was accompanied by such acts of mapmaking and translation. Just look at any map of the times, and it is apparent that Indian lands and names are almost never identified or represented.[186]

An essential point about maps and history, however, is that they need not be permanent. They are subject to translation and revision, and it is possible to reverse the negative processes to achieve a new balance. Renaissance and reform may be realized through acts of translation and retranslation:

> by writing their own history and then rewriting it. This would be a literal re-membering—not a making whole of what was never whole to begin with, but a gluing together of fragments in a dynamic recasting....
>
> Since absolute forgetting is as impossible as total recall, the need is to bring elements of the past into contact with the present in a dynamic constellation.[187]

Although such work appears to point to a multiplicity of histories that create more divergence, if not divisiveness, that need not be so. What is necessary is the commitment to dialogue:

> But today he is prepared to share the love of the landscape, on condition that a dialogue take place between the two interpretations:

"You claim that this land has been yours always and forever, as if history did not continue [to unfold] when you were not there, as if nobody was there, and the land had but one role—to wait for you. Don't impose your version on me and I won't impose mine on you...and history will laugh at us both. It has no time for Jews and Arabs." Speaking as a person who does not thrust his identity on the landscape, but draws his from it, he put words in the mouth of "the place." "The geography within history is stronger than the history within geography...because the place itself is neutral. Despite the wind and rain of thousands of years, it receives all comers. It is cynical. I am referring to a place that is stronger than what has gone on in it throughout the course of history."[188]

Much of the work of Indian law is to resolve such contending views over the meaning and interpretation of the maps of history, and the likely key is a commitment grounded in rigor and belief that there is "enough space, physical and historical,"[189] with which to construct a mutual and just future.[190] Without such (re)translation and dialogue, the tyranny and injustice of the (dominant) past will continue.

5

Lone Wolf v. Hitchcock

The Birth of Plenary Power, Incorporation, and an Extraconstitutional Regime

THE HINGE OF MODERN INDIAN LAW IS THE CASE OF LONE WOLF V. HITCHCOCK.[1] *Lone Wolf* has aptly been referred to as Indian law's *Dred Scott*[2] decision, yet it remains little known outside the field of Indian law. The decision upheld the authority of Congress to allot reservations without tribal consent, confirmed the power of Congress to unilaterally abrogate treaties, and inaugurated an extraconstitutional regime within the field of Indian law through the doctrine of plenary power.

A proper understanding of *Lone Wolf* begins with a discussion of the case's historical context in the rapidly expansive moves of the federal government to obtain Indian land *within* the borders of Indian reservations for non-Indian settlement. Prior to the allotment era of 1887–1934, all lands within Indian country were Indian lands. Non-Indians were not permanent residents or land-holders in Indian country. The rough borders of Indian country consisted of an informal line running north and south through the republic, separating states and tribes, and non-Indians and Indians from each other.

Expansion abounded and redoubled national and local pressure in Indian country. The United States acquired the Pacific Northwest through the Treaty with Great Britain of 1846. As a result of the Treaty of Guadalupe Hidalgo with Mexico in 1848, the United States annexed California, Nevada, Utah, most of Arizona, and large areas of New Mexico and Colorado. Gold was discovered at Sutter's Mill in California in 1848, spurring one of the largest human migrations in American history. California (1852), Oregon (1859), and Nevada (1864) achieved early statehood. The General Homestead Act of 1862, the Desert Land Act of 1877, and other federal land disposition programs lured settlers west.[3]

The Background of the Allotment Process

As western expansion continued in the latter part of the nineteenth century, two things became apparent to the federal government, namely, the need for additional land for non-Indians (potentially including land *within* Indian reservations) and the increasing tension with Indians over communal ownership of land. The federal government sought to resolve these problems with the enactment of the Dawes Severalty Act, popularly known as the General Allotment Act, in 1887.

Supporters of the legislation were an odd coalition of Indian rights groups (which were largely non-Indian Christian-based organizations working to "help" Indians) and (non-Indian) land speculators. How could this be? The largely non-Indian Indian rights groups saw Indians sinking rapidly under the continued onslaught of non-Indian settlement, exacerbated by Indian stubbornness in clinging to their communal ways, especially in matters of (collective) land tenure. From this perspective, hope, if there was to be hope, would require Indians to change their ways, especially in regard to landholding patterns. Assimilation in land tenure patterns was the necessary survival accommodation to Manifest Destiny.

The motives of these proponents of allotment, according to most scholars, were unassailable. A member of Congress, speaking on the Dawes bill in 1886, said, "It has...the endorsement of the Indian rights associations throughout the country, and of the best sentiment in the land."[4] The aim of these "friends" to the Indians was to change the Indians by substituting white "civilization" for tribal culture. There was no question as to the unalloyed blessing of this policy. It was self-evident, and allotment was to be the primary tool to break up tribal life. As the agent for the Yankton Sioux wrote in 1877:

> As long as Indians live in villages they will retain many of their old
> and injurious habits. Frequent feasts, community in food, heathen
> ceremonies, and dances, constant visiting—these will continue as
> long as the people live together in close neighborhoods and
> villages.... I trust that before another year is ended they will generally
> be located upon individual land [or] farms. From that date will begin
> their real and permanent progress.[5]

This policy was rife with both racial condescension and naivety. It harked back to the tainted ethnocentric view that Indians were inferior and engaged in backward economic pursuits. This view predominated, despite the reality that much of Indian agriculture and hunting and gathering was as productive and efficient as anything in the non-Indian community. The pressure on, and faltering of, much tribal economic activity was not due to intrinsic tribal shortcomings but rather extrinsic in the form of increased encroachment by outside forces.

The naivety flowed from the almost total lack of discussion and understanding of how to implement such a policy. There was little understanding of Indian culture and almost no communication with Indian people about what they wanted. There was also little or no understanding of the semiarid landscape of much of the West, where the average rainfall was less than ten inches per year and where 160-acre farms were not going to survive. In addition, the appropriations to facilitate such a large undertaking were grossly inadequate.

The Bureau of Indian Affairs (BIA), the agency to be charged with carrying out this responsibility, would have unfettered discretion in implementing this policy, but it had no administrative competence or legislative oversight in carrying out this massive undertaking. As a result, the allotment policy was ultimately implemented rather haphazardly and without much planning. Some reservations were completely allotted, some partially, and some almost not at all. For example, the Navajo and Hopi Reservations were only slightly allotted, the Blackfeet and Fort Peck Reservations in Montana were substantially allotted, and the Sisseton-Wahpeton Reservation in South Dakota was completely allotted, while the Jicarilla, Mescalero, and White Mountain Apache Reservations in New Mexico were *not* allotted at all.[6]

The supporters of allotment included not only misguided "friends" of the Indians but also their "enemies." These enemies were the land speculators who were clearly interested in obtaining Indian lands for sale to non-Indian homesteaders. This did not go unnoticed, but such concern did little to slow passage of the Allotment Act. Senator Teller from Colorado referred to an 1881 precursor of the General Allotment Act as "a bill to despoil the Indians of their lands and to make them vagabonds on the face of the earth."[7] Senator Teller also said:

> If I stand alone in the Senate, I want to put upon the record my
> prophecy in this matter, that when 30 or 40 years have passed and
> these Indians shall have parted with their title, they will curse the
> hand that was raised professedly in their defence to secure this kind
> of legislation and if the people who are clamoring for it understood
> Indian character, and Indian laws, and Indian morals, and Indian
> religion, they would not be clamoring for this at all.[8]

Senator Teller strongly believed that allotment was mostly in the interest of land-grabbing speculators, but the minority House Report in 1880 had even gone further:

The real aim of this bill is to get at the Indian lands and open them
up to settlement. The provisions for the apparent benefit of the
Indian are but the pretext to get at his lands and occupy them. . . . If
this were done in the name of greed, it would be bad enough; but to
do it in the name of humanity, and under the cloak of an ardent
desire to promote the Indian's welfare by making him like ourselves
whether he will or not, is infinitely worse.[9]

The Indians were clearly opposed to allotment. The Senecas and Creeks sent
memorials to Congress disapproving of allotment as contrary to their traditions
of common landholding. The Creek, Choctaw, and Cherokee Memorial of 1881
warned: "The change to an individual title would throw the whole of our domain
in a few years into the hands of a few persons."[10]

There were also Indian voices set against allotment that never made it to
Congress. For example, from the Rosebud Sioux Reservation, Chief Hollow
Horn Bear said:

My friends, you have all heard what my father-in-law says, but I do
not think he is right. He believes what the white people tell him; but
this is only another trick of the whites to take our land away from us,
and they have played these tricks before. We do not want to trust the
white people. They come to us with sweet talk, but they do not mean
it. We will not sign any more papers for these white men.[11]

His audience reacted:

All the Indians grunted "Hau!" ("How!"), which meant that they agreed
with what Hollow Horn Bear said. The other chiefs arose and spoke. So
many of them were against the allotment that it seemed we were not to
get it. But these councils which the Indians held among themselves
were not recorded, as there were no white persons present.[12]

A Hopi by the name of Albert Yava stated:

I don't know where [Senator] Dawes [the bill's sponsor] got his
knowledge of Indian ways, but he was dead set against a tribe or clan
owning communal lands. . . . [T]he Government began to survey the
Hopi lands to divide them up, and they did all this without any
consultations with responsible Hopi leaders. . . . They only stirred up
confusion and resentment by what they were doing.[13]

The implementation of allotment was characterized by haste and a lack of pre-
paredness. This was not surprising, given the ardent support of both its friends
and enemies. Allotment had become an article of faith with reformers and

rested on the belief that Indian progress was inexorably linked to an ethic that derived solely from individual ownership of property:

> The upsurge of humanitarian concern for Indian reform in the post–Civil War era gave new impetus to the severalty principle, which was almost universally accepted and aggressively promoted, until Congress finally passed a general allotment law. Allotment of land in severalty, however, was part of the drive to individualize the Indians that became the obsession of the late-nineteenth century Christian reformers and did not stand by itself. The breakup of tribalism, a major goal of this Indian policy, had been moved forward by the abolition of the treaty system and would be carried on by a government educational system and by the extension of American law over the Indian communities. Yet for many years the dissolution of communal lands by allotment, together with the citizenship attached to provide landowning, was the central issue.[14]

General Allotment Act (Dawes Severalty Act)

President Cleveland signed the Dawes Act on February 8, 1887.[15] The statutory specifics were quite straightforward:

1. A grant of 160 acres to each family head, of 80 acres to other single persons over 18 years of age and to each orphan under 18, and of 40 acres to other single persons under 18 when the allotment was ordered.
2. A patent in fee to be issued to every allottee, but to be held in trust by the Government for 25 years, during which time the land could not be alienated or encumbered.
3. At the expiration of the trust period, the Indian would get the land in fee simple.
4. Indians who received their allotments became U.S. citizens. This provision was changed by a 1906 amendment to the Allotment Act, which required the issuance of a patent in fee before eligibility for citizenship.
5. The process of allotment was not mandatory, but was left to the discretion of the President acting through the Secretary of Interior.
6. Neither tribes nor individual Indians were required to consent to allotment. It was a unilateral process.
7. After a reservation was allotted, the Secretary of Interior could negotiate with the tribe for the purchase of the remaining "surplus"

land. Such transactions required the consent of the tribe and ratification by Congress.[16]

The promise of federal assistance to assist individual Indians in the allotment process in order to advance agricultural self-sufficiency was severely undercapitalized. For example, in 1888 the total congressional appropriation was $30,000. Given the fact that that in 1888 alone 3,568 allotments were created, the per capita federal expenditure was less than $10 per allotment. It subsequently dipped to $15,000 per year in the period 1891–1893. There was no funding at all during the next seven years from 1893 to 1900.[17]

The results of the allotment process were truly devastating. The national Indian land estate diminished from 138 million acres in 1887 to 48 million acres in 1934, a staggering loss of 90 million acres. Of the 90 million acres, approximately 26 million acres were transferred from the tribes to individual Indian allottees and then passed to individual non-Indians through sale, fraud, mortgage foreclosure, or tax sales.[18] The remaining 64 million acres were obtained through federal purchase of tribal "surplus" lands. Despite the statutory requirement of tribal consent, this requirement was effectively set aside in the *Lone Wolf* decision.

This grim policy was expressly halted as part of the Indian Reorganization Act of 1934 (IRA). The statute ended the process of granting allotments and further mandated that any allotment still in trust at the time of the passage of the IRA would remain in trust indefinitely. Those lands that remained in trust were, however, further undermined by the process of fractionalism, in which growing numbers of heirs inherited a smaller and smaller amount of undivided land interests in the original allotment. For example, a father's five children each would inherit a one fifth individual interest in their father's allotment. In time, if each of these five children had five heirs, twenty-five grandchildren would inherit a land interest of 4 percent of 160 acres or a little more than 6 acres. If each grandchild had five children, there would be 125 heirs, whose individual interest would be less than 1.3 acres. The problem of fractionalism remains unresolved to this day.[19]

The legacy of allotment is thus not only the severe loss of land *within* Indian reservations but also the crushing legal burden on most individual Indian allotments that remain in trust. The fractionalism issue has rendered most individual Indian allotments unavailable for any actual use by the heirs of the original allottee, except through leasing the (individual) allotments and parsing out the limited lease income among all the heirs. The vision of the Indian reformers of developing "yeoman" Indian farmers as friends and competitors of their non-Indian neighbors never materialized in the real world outside the imagination of the reformers. The reformers were brokers of loss and despair, not gain and prosperity. The loss of land, political autonomy, and self-governance are the true legacy of allotment.

The policy of allotment evoked strong characterization. President Theodore Roosevelt called allotment "a mighty pulverizing engine to break up the tribal mass. It acts directly upon the family and the individual."[20] More recently, an Indian law scholar put it in more blunt contemporary terms: "allotment was ethnic cleansing by eminent domain."[21]

The Lone Wolf Decision

The Lone Wolf case was the pivotal decision to ratify and to aid and abet the allotment process. Lone Wolf did not directly involve allotment under the General Allotment Act, but rather whether Congress could unilaterally abrogate the 1867 Treaty of Medicine Lodge without tribal consent,[22] acquire tribal land within the Kiowa-Comanche Reservation for non-Indian settlement without tribal consent, and make allotments to tribal members against their will in accordance with the Act of June 6, 1900. The decision clearly answered yes and established a federal regime of law that disposed of any tribal consent provision for land cession or the imposition of allotment. Treaty and statutory provisions to the contrary were swept aside by the Court without qualm.

Tribal members led by Lone Wolf and others did not readily accept this assault and attempted to resist by standing on the two guarantees contained in the Treaty, namely, the Article II guarantee that promised the Indians "absolute and undisturbed use and occupation of the reservation" and the Article XII requirement of the "approval of three-fourths of the adult male population to approve any land cessions."

The engine used by the federal government to obtain this land was the Jerome Commission, which came to the reservation in 1892. The mission of the commission was straightforward: "to gain Indian consent to change Medicine Lodge Treaty guarantees and Indian acquiescence to the opening of the reserves to whites."[23] At the public meetings held on the reservation on September 26–27, Judge Sayre, one of the commissioners, sternly noted that the president in the past had forced allotments on reluctant Indians and could do so again if the gathered Indians were not cooperative.[24]

Various tribal leaders, including Lone Wolf, spoke against the proposed allotment scheme. Lone Wolf addressed the commissioners on September 28. He represented those individuals in strong opposition to allotment. He noted that tribes were striving to change their old way of life and were making "rapid progress."[25] He requested that the commission not "push" the Indians and noted that enforced allotment would mean sudden downfall for the three tribes (Kiowa, Comanche, and Apaches). Because of this, he said, all three tribes had decided "not to sell the country."[26]

Land prices and payment formulas dominated the proceedings. The federal negotiators were evasive, going no further than an offer of a $2 million lump sum for the approximately 1.75 million acres and using the extravagant illustration that such a generous figure would fill 2,000 money boxes with silver dollars and require twenty-six six-mule-team wagons to haul all that sudden wealth.[27] When pressed, however, the commissioners admitted that the per-acre amount was between $1.00 and $1.10 (or about $665 per capita).[28]

The commissioners' goal was to obtain approval of the three fourths of the adult male population in accordance with Article XII of the Medicine Lodge Treaty. The commissioners had only two carrots to dangle: the amount of the total payment for the "surplus" land and the size (and number) of allotments to be provided to tribal members.

The commissioners did not have authority to offer more than $2 million and thus craftily urged approval of the $2 million figure, with the right to seek more from Congress. The commissioners also stated incorrectly that the proposed allotments were larger than those available under the Dawes Act. The commissioners did allow the Indians to include an additional number of white people (approximately twenty-five) who would be eligible for allotments should the proposed agreement be approved by the Article XII figure of three fourths of the adult male population. The commissioners also added some names on their own motion.[29]

Behind the scenes, it was all about getting the necessary number of signatures. Obviously the numbers, especially the total number of the adult male population, were rather imprecise. The working figure for required signatures was 450.[30] The meetings in early October grew more heated and frenzied. There were accusations of fraud and chicanery all around.[31] Much of it was directed against Joshua Givens, one of the Indian interpreters, who blatantly obtained signatures under false pretenses and also forged the signatures of others. As a result of the uproar, a guard had to be posted to protect him.[32]

The commissioners themselves apparently grew more frustrated. After a sharp verbal exchange about the quality of Joshua Givens's translating skills, a vexed Chairman Jerome announced at one open meeting, "Congress has full control of you, it can do as it is of a mind to with you."[33] He dropped the pretense of negotiations when he decreed, "Congress has determined to open this country."[34]

Accusations by Lone Wolf and others continued. When the commissioners returned to Washington, they switched versions of the agreement, cut and pasted various signatures and marks, and developed a composite document containing mostly counterfeit signatures.[35] The commissioners were confident they had the requisite number of signatures, and Agent George Day falsely certified that the 1892 Agreement had the required number of signatures. An official copy of the agreement was supposed to have been left by the commissioners with the agent for the Indians or their attorneys to examine. When controversy ensued, the agent "lost" the original for eight years.[36] Despite the rampant deceit and manipulation, "the Jerome Agreement was between 21 and 91 signatures short of the needed three-fourths depending on whether age 18 or 21 was the cutoff for adult status."[37]

Lone Wolf himself was one of the casualties of this process. At a meeting of about 400 Kiowa at Fort Sill after the departure of the commission, Lone Wolf was ousted as chief because he had agreed to a more expansive proposal developed by the Comanche leader, Quannah Parker. This proposal for increased compensation and delayed implementation was never really considered by the commissioners, and Lone Wolf (and others) demanded that their names be stricken.[38]

All the wrangling, chaos, and deceit involving the Jerome Commission was only the beginning. Bills were introduced in both the House and Senate to "ratify" the Jerome Agreement. One of the sponsors on the Senate side was Senator Henry Dawes of Massachusetts, whose name gave the General Allotment Act its more common title, the Dawes Act.[39]

Although a bill to enact the Jerome Agreement passed the House, it was stalled and delayed in the Senate. A Kiowa and Comanche delegation traveled to Washington to protest. At the heart of the congressional dispute was not whether to pass legislation, but what its terms would be. The core of the disagreement was between those groups such as the Indian Rights Association (mostly non-Indian missionary people) that wanted to expand the size of the proposed individual allotments and others such as the Rock Island Railroad that wanted to contract the size of the proposed allotments in order to expand opportunities for non-Indians as potential customers and homesteaders.[40]

Changes were made. The size of the individual allotments was expanded from 160 to 320 acres. Of the approximately 2.9 million acres on the reservation, 480,000 acres were retained as common (tribal) grazing lands, and 445,000 acres were allotted to individual tribal members. That left approximately 2 million acres that were transferred from the tribes to the federal government as "surplus" land for non-Indian settlement under public land homesteading laws. The total price was $2 million (for per capita distribution) or about $1 per acre paid in two installments more than ten years apart. These terms were enacted into law as part of the Act of June 6, 1900.[41] Almost 3,000 Indian allotments were made in less than a year.[42]

These changes were never presented to the tribes for their approval under Article XII of the Medicine Lodge Treaty of 1867 and the Springer Amendment of 1889. Perhaps federal officials knew that tribal consent was highly unlikely, or maybe they simply decided not to bother with such a "formality" anymore. This shift in policy did not go unnoticed. In a letter printed in the *Washington Post*, Samuel Brosius, chief lobbyist for the Indian Rights Association, noted that the June 6 Act was "the first instance in which Congress has amended an Indian agreement without the changes being submitted for agreement by the tribe interested."[43] The Indian Rights Association feared that this apparent shift to no longer seeking tribal consent presaged potential unilateral confiscation of Indian lands and the wholesale violation of Indian rights.[44] This fear was confirmed and given the judicial imprimatur of the Supreme Court in the *Lone Wolf* case itself.

Lone Wolf and his followers did not accept the new regime of deceit, manipulation, and unilateral treaty abrogation. Lone Wolf became resurgent as a tribal leader seeking to halt implementation of the 1900 Act. In the always curious world of coalitions and supporters of Indian causes, Lone Wolf found (financial) support for his resistance within the cattle industry, which opposed land opening because it would threaten its ability to graze cattle and lease substantial amounts of Indian land.[45]

Lone Wolf eventually retained the well-known Washington lawyer William Springer, a colorful character in his own right. The legal strategy that emerged was to seek a temporary restraining order and a permanent injunction halting the cession and the opening of the "surplus" lands for non-Indian settlement. Springer filed the *Lone Wolf* action in the equity division of the Supreme Court in the District of Columbia on June 6, 1902, naming Secretary of the Interior Ethan Hitchcock, a new appointee, as the primary defendant.

Relief was promptly denied by Justice A. C. Bradley, who rejected the claim that the 1900 Act deprived the tribes of their property without due process of law in violation of the Fifth Amendment. Justice Bradley described the allotment procedure in this instance as "the usual process" in which misunderstanding, deception, and lack of consent were not relevant, as the matter was within the exclusive purview of Congress. Justice Bradley opined that "it is to be assumed" that Congress made its decision "with due regard to the public interests of and the rights of the Indian."[46]

The Court of Appeals affirmed, with Justice Alvey writing for the Court:

[R]eservations are held by the Indians subject to the control and dominion of the United States, and such Indian tribes are subject to be changed from one locality or reservation to another, as may best serve the purpose and policy of the government.... They have no title in the lands which they occupy.[47]

While the appeal was pending before the Supreme Court, President McKinley issued the proclamation opening the ceded and surplus lands on August 6, 1901. In contrast to past methods of settlement involving the chaos and confusion of a "land run," where settlers were simply let loose to stake their claims, officials decided to hold a preliminary registration and then a lottery. Federal officials moved swiftly to survey, prepare, and clear the way for non-Indians to enter claims for homesteads on the "surplus" lands. Thirty-three land clerks from the Department of Interior were detailed from Washington, D.C.[48]

Once allotments to Indians were completed as described in the Jerome Agreement, 2 million acres of surplus remained. This was expected to yield from 12,500 to 13,000 homesteads. Excitement mounted as the registration process loomed. The railroad took in $2 million in ticket sales in transporting people to the reservation sites. From July 10–26, 1902, more than 165,000 registrants filed for the 12,500 parcels, a ratio of about thirteen registrants for each available parcel.[49] Non-Indians now engulfed the Kiowa, Comanche, and Apache tribes and breached the wall that heretofore had separated them. Indian country would never be the same.[50]

Later in the year, the case reached the Supreme Court. The core of Lone Wolf's argument remained as it was in the beginning, namely, that the allotment of Indian land and the opening of the remainder for non-Indian homesteading was a denial of due process and an express violation of the tribal consent requirement that was set out in Article XII of the Medicine Lodge Treaty of 1867. Lone Wolf and his attorneys were relatively confident that the Supreme Court would not endorse such an unprecedented move by the federal government. The federal government had often acted in a peremptory fashion in regard to Indian land, but never so blatantly when a treaty was involved.[51] Beyond this broad treaty-based assertion was the claim that the federal government had paid inadequate compensation and hence had "taken" Indian land in violation of the Fifth Amendment's guarantee of due process and "just compensation."

The federal government's argument relied heavily on the lower courts' decisions, with their focus on the paramount authority of Congress in Indian affairs. The government also presented the factual claim of tribal consent as demonstrated by the local BIA agent's "certification" of the necessary number of signatures and the subsequent tribal input concerning the changes made in the penultimate 1900 Act.[52]

The Court handed down its opinion in *Lone Wolf* on January 5, 1903, a unanimous opinion authored by Justice Edward Douglas White. The opinion was only fourteen pages long. Justice White acknowledged, but promptly rejected, Lone Wolf's core argument that the unconsented provision of allotments to individual tribal members and the unconsented sale of "surplus" tribal land to the federal government for non-Indian settlement were violations of Article XII of the Medicine Lodge Treaty of 1867 and by extension constituted a "taking" of tribal land without "just compensation" in violation of the Fifth Amendment. The Court turned aside this view because it "ignored" the status of the contracting Indians and the relation of dependency they have and continue to bear toward the government of the United States.[53] Avoiding the issue of consent was necessary in order not to "materially limit and qualify the controlling authority of Congress in respect to the care and protection of the Indians."[54]

Well? True or false? Principle or sophistry? At best, perhaps it was some of both, though certainly not in equal proportions. The principal rationale of the Court is embedded in the trust relationship, as seen in the context of the allotment period. In this view, it might be argued that the trustee federal government decided what was best for the beneficiary Indians, and if it thought that a better future for Indians involved individual ownership of property, so be it. What sufficed for non-Indian homesteading constituents of the federal government ought to suffice for constituents of an allotted tribe. Allotment, in this view, is seen as a gateway to individual landholding and the laudable goal of assimilation, a step of inclusion and incorporation. For diverse reasons, allotment failed to achieve its noble goal,[55] but standing alone, it probably was not a breach of trust at that time. Despite its condescension, perhaps it was not a strict violation of trust.

Yet, it is considerably more difficult, if not impossible, to see the unconsented cession of the "surplus" land as being in the beneficiary's best interest, especially when the trustee had a blatant conflict of interest in wanting to secure tribal land for its own expansionary agenda to aid its own non-Indian citizens at the direct expense of the tribes and their members. That the Court does not even identify, much less address, the issue of conflict of interest blinks reality. Perhaps more likely, the opinion studiously ignores this reality, because it could not handle or justify it. In addition, of course, there is no constitutional provision that grants Congress plenary power in Indian affairs but rather only the ability to regulate "trade with Indians" and make treaties with Indians.

The Court did not stop here but went even further. It insulated Congress's actions with regard to treaties and Indians from *any* judicial review:

Plenary authority over the tribal relations of the Indians has been exercised by Congress from the beginning, and the power has always been deemed a political one, not subject to be controlled by the judicial department of the government.[56]

Such extravagant power was now denominated as "plenary" and placed beyond judicial review. This jurisprudential dagger was not seen as lethal but as merely "administrative," constituting "a mere change in the form of investment of Indian tribal property" and thereby creating an irrebuttable presumption that "Congress acted in perfect good faith."[57] When read as a whole, there is a breathtaking formalism in Lone Wolf that keeps reality completely out of sight. But how could it be otherwise? The violation of treaty guarantees, taking another's property without consent, and blatant self-dealing constituted the reality to be avoided, not confronted. This is the jurisprudence of Lone Wolf.

Treaty Abrogation

The treaty abrogation aspect of Lone Wolf, however, requires further analysis. The opinion cited a single case, the Chinese Exclusion Case,[58] for the authority of Congress to unilaterally abrogate treaties. Although the case does stand for the broad proposition cited, it does not so easily cover the Lone Wolf situation. The Chinese Exclusion Case involved an 1868 treaty with China that dealt in part with the free flow of Chinese immigrants into the United States,[59] and subsequently, there was much objection in California and other parts of the northwest about the adverse effect of this immigration.[60] This concern resulted in renewed discussion with China in an attempt to modify the treaty to permit the United States to enact legislation to "regulate, limit, or suspend, the coming of Chinese laborers, or their residence therein."[61] No such agreement was forthcoming, but nevertheless, several such statutes were enacted, at least one of which, passed in 1888, specifically offended guarantees under the treaty.[62]

The Court agreed that this was so, yet held that it was not legally impermissible to do so, reasoning that the United States does its best to honor its treaty obligations, but Congress may enact statutes that contravene treaty obligations if it is in the national interest to do so. The Court noted that this was especially true in this instance because Congress's authority in the regulation of immigration and deportation of aliens was a quintessential congressional prerogative.[63] The application of this principle in the Lone Wolf case was arguably quite different and problematic. The Medicine Lodge Treaty of 1867 had an express requirement of tribal consent for future land cessions, which Congress either ignored or acquiesced in the executive branch manipulation of the Jerome Commission. In addition, the treaty abrogation was in part in direct conflict with the federal government's own affirmative trust responsibility to the tribes to protect their land base.

Treaty abrogation in the Indian law context is generally different from treaty abrogation in the foreign nation context. Treaty abrogation in the Indian law context *extends* U.S. authority over the people and land of the tribe. Conversely, in the foreign nation context, there is usually no extension of U.S. authority over a foreign land and its citizens within their homeland. The sole case cited for the proposition in *Lone Wolf* proves this point. The "abrogated" treaty was between the United States and China and focused on conditions of immigration. The U.S. abrogation did not (could not) extend U.S. authority over the territory of China and its citizens there. Nor could such abrogation result in the U.S. annexation of part of the land base of China. But this is exactly what happened in *Lone Wolf*. The United States annexed Indian land and extended its authority over Indian lands and Indian individuals. This is more analogous to an act of war than to an act of law.

This was particularly ironic in the context of the overall allotment policy, which had as one of its central elements the conferral of U.S. citizenship on Indian allottees. The privilege of citizenship was thus often predicated on the unconsented taking of the collective land interests of those soon-to-be citizens. The "privilege" of citizenship thus had an unexpected and very high hidden cost.

In addition, *Lone Wolf* did not purport to be limited to the unique facts of that case, but rather it created a *universal* rule of abrogation of Indian treaties. This rule did not even require express congressional intent to abrogate. *Lone Wolf* thus effectively struck down *all* (350 plus) Indian treaties in regard to the potential unconsented taking of tribal land. After the decision in 1903, there was never any judicial inquiry, concerning the taking of "surplus" land, as to whether Congress even intended to abrogate any specific treaty in the context of allotment. It was merely assumed, and it was beyond judicial review anyway.[64] This extraordinarily expansive view of *Lone Wolf* does not appear to be justified by its facts, Congress's intent, or the relevant precedent. Yet because of the application of the political question doctrine, *Lone Wolf*–style treaty abrogation remained hermetically sealed from judicial inquiry for more than seventy years.[65]

Lone Wolf also needs to be examined as to whether it was an unwarranted extension of the rationale that was articulated in *United States v. Kagama*.[66] Recall that in *Kagama*, the Supreme Court found the Indian Commerce Clause to be an insufficient constitutional basis for the enactment of the Major Crimes Act[67] but nevertheless upheld the legislation as a legitimate exercise of the federal government's trust responsibility to protect Indians from outside forces, namely, the states. In *Kagama*, the trust responsibility was used as a shield to protect Indians:

> It seems to us that this is within the competency of Congress. These Indian tribes *are* the wards of the nation. They are communities *dependent* on the United States, dependent largely for their daily food; dependent for their political rights. They owe no allegiance to the states, and receive from them no protection. Because of the local ill feeling, the people of the states where they are found are often their deadliest enemies. From their very weakness and helplessness, so largely due to the course of dealing of the federal government with them, and the treaties in which it has been promised, there arises the duty of protection and with it the power. This has always been recognized by the executive, and by Congress, and by this court, whenever the question has arisen.[68]

This portion of *Kagama* is quoted approvingly in *Lone Wolf,*[69] but it is then used without qualm or analysis to permit the transformation of the trust responsibility from a protective shield to a destructive sword with which to carve up and dispose of the tribal land estate. All of this is cloaked in arid formalism that is a toxic mix of deceit and evasion. In *Kagama*, treaties and the trust responsibility are a source of duty for the protection of tribes by the United States. In *Lone Wolf*, treaties and the trust responsibility are merely disposable impediments that may be ignored in the invasion of tribal land interests by the federal government.

In *Kagama*, the Court acknowledged: "The relation of the Indian tribes living within the borders of the United States, both before and since the Revolution, to the people of the United States, has always been an anomalous one, and of a complex character."[70] By the time of *Lone Wolf*, what was "anomalous" and "complex" had became lethal and ruthless, a deadly sword of exploitation.

Constitutional Crossroads

Lone Wolf is perhaps best thought of as the case that placed the field of Indian law at a constitutional crossroads: the crossroads at which, in one direction, lay adherence to the limits of the Constitution imposed by the Indian Commerce Clause and treaties, and in the other direction lay the road of extraconstitutional governance and plenary power. The Court never even acknowledged the crossroads but rather considered it a clear highway, whose sole purpose was to facilitate the unilateral expansion of federal land acquisition and power in Indian affairs.

In addition to the boldly imperial elements embedded in *Lone Wolf*, there is another complementary and perhaps more salient, but seldom observed, aspect of a missed constitutional moment. Indeed, it is the legacy of that missed constitutional moment that is most revealing about the current flux of much recent Indian law jurisprudence.[71] A rethinking of *Lone Wolf* further suggests that the primary hinge of Indian law is often found in Supreme Court decisions rather than in the more common scholarly notion of congressional policy.[72] Most distressing, of course, is that current Supreme Court jurisprudence is neither anchored in, nor constrained by, any constitutional norms or limits, and therein lies its ongoing perniciousness.

The critical problem posed by the *Lone Wolf* case was not really the issue identified by the Court of whether Congress could unilaterally abrogate a treaty between the federal government and an Indian tribe[73] but rather the much broader question of the nature of the *changing* legal relationship of the federal government to Indian tribes. In this pivotal moment in Indian law, the Supreme Court chose to focus on a symptom, not the underlying cause. The press in the late nineteenth and early twentieth centuries of American history placed Indian tribes, particularly in the West, in a much different geographical, social, and political relationship to the federal government than at the time of the seminal Marshall trilogy[74] of the early nineteenth century. At that time, Indian tribes were largely located physically, culturally, and politically outside the orbit of, and insulated from, undue encroachment by both the federal and state governments. These sovereigns were, for all practical purposes, separated by a vertical line that ran from north to south, dividing Indian country and Indian territory from the rest of the country.[75] Tribal self-government and autonomy remained extensive.

Yet this basic pattern soon began to change. The design and reality of significant separation gave way more and more to a pattern of expansion and encirclement; non-Indian country began to surround Indian reservations with greater frequency. Much of this territory soon became the new states of the West.[76] The reservation itself was undergoing a fundamental change from a homeland held in common with few, if any, non-Indian residents to a place (in many situations) with a growing land tenure class of individual Indian allottees, who might sell or otherwise lose their allotments to non-Indians.[77] Added to this was the presence of a significant number of non-Indians who purchased federal homestead allotments on the reservation from the federal government, which acquired this "surplus land" directly from the tribe. This latter situation describes, of course, the *Lone Wolf* case, in which the Supreme Court approved federal acquisition of surplus land from the tribe through a process of treaty abrogation and unilateral congressional action.

One way of thinking about this process—call it manifest infamy, if you will—is to view it as creating a new setting in which the legal regime of old was, at least from the federal perspective, insufficient to meet the new demands of the day. Tribes—geographically, politically, and socially—were less and less outside or on the margins of the republic and increasingly inside the republic. They were, apparently with little notice or fanfare, increasingly being *absorbed* into the dominant society, and as a result, both sides were drawn into an uncharted legal realm.[78] It is this uncharted legal realm that confronted the Supreme Court in *Lone Wolf*, but which the Supreme Court (and the country as a whole) conveniently ignored.

As the federal government began to act more and more directly to establish a legal regime *within* Indian country, as opposed to at the interface[79] between itself and tribes, the existing foundational rules established in the Marshall trilogy began to buckle. The beginning of this shift is readily discernible in the case of *United States v. Kagama*.[80] In *Kagama*, the Supreme Court confronted the issue of whether Congress could pass legislation that created federal criminal jurisdiction over acts committed by one Indian person against another Indian person *within the reservation*.[81] The Court could find no authorization for such legislation within the Constitution itself and had to settle on some vague notion of dependence and necessity.[82] As the Court itself (unconvincingly) noted:

> The power of the general government over these remnants of a race once powerful, now weak and diminished in numbers, is necessary to their protection, as well as to the safety of those among whom they dwell. It must exist in that government, because it never has existed anywhere else; because the theatre of its exercise is within the geographical limits of the United States; because it has never been denied; and because it alone can enforce its laws on all the tribes.[83]

It was apparent in *Kagama* that a new doctrinal footing would be necessary to justify the likely continuance and growth of federal legislation to be deployed on the reservation. *Kagama* made it clear that no adequate conceptual mooring could be located in the Constitution. *Lone Wolf* answered *Kagama*'s source-of-authority dilemma with its identification of plenary power, which is clearly an extraconstitutional notion.

The point is not to rehash the extensive critique[84] of *Lone Wolf*'s plenary power doctrine, but to note that this formulation also included a subtext that signaled the need for a constitutional reassessment of the status of Indian tribes and tribal individuals within the republic. Presumably, such reassessment would have led to the conclusion that the process of absorption, for better or worse, required some equivalent constitutional incorporation.[85] However, this subtext went unrecognized and unacknowledged.

The General Allotment Act[86] and the 1900 statute at issue in *Lone Wolf* were also creating momentum in the direction of (federal) citizenship for all Native people.[87] So as tribes and tribal people were coming more and more into the federal system, instead of calling attention to the necessity of the appropriate constitutional adjustments and amendments to vouchsafe tribal sovereignty and individual integrity in order to demonstrate the true grandeur of this republic's core organic document, the Court reached into the ether of fable and unconstrained power.

The danger of such fable and unconstrained power has erupted yet again in Indian law, this time in a particularly virulent form. In a series of cases, beginning with *Oliphant v. Suquamish Indian Tribe*[88] in 1978, then *Montana v. United States*[89] in 1981, and culminating with *Plains Commerce Bank v. Long Family Land and Cattle Co.*[90] in 2008, the Supreme Court has again taken it upon itself to unilaterally abrogate tribal authority, especially in regard to non-Indians. It has done so without reference to any constitutional justification—indeed, without reference to any apposite congressional enactments, and ultimately without reference to any coherent doctrinal underpinning. The Court accomplished this through a quite brazen manipulation of precedent and an incessant repetition of the mantra that it has always been thus.[91] The distinction between *Lone Wolf* and these recent cases is that the Court in its current jurisprudence has arrogated the power to itself rather than deferring to Congress.

All of this has been thoroughly noted in recent Indian law scholarship with such phrases as the "new subjectivism,"[92] "a common law for our age of colonialism,"[93] and "judicial plenary power."[94] This scholarship, for the most part, does not call attention to the constitutional moment at hand. If *Lone Wolf* was "necessary" to devise some (extraconstitutional) rationale to justify *unbounded* congressional authority in Indian affairs in order to reconfigure the federal-tribal relationship for "new" times, are we not witnessing a similar process now to again reconfigure the federal-tribal relationship to extirpate tribal authority over non-Indians through a jurisprudential sleight of hand? This is apparently the "new necessity" of the times, at least as seen from the rather insular, if not colonialist, vantage point of the Supreme Court.

The present predation of Indian law jurisprudence is *Lone Wolf* dressed up in a new and false pedigree that attempts to hide the constitutional vacuity at its core. The attempt to update the *Lone Wolf* style of constitutional avoidance does not work in the present day because the counterfeit thinking is so transparent. In this light, it is difficult to see how essential tribal sovereignty can be vouchsafed in any enduring way, without a recognition of the "necessity" of constitutionalizing it in a mutually acceptable way.[95]

Is not the way forward likely to be both surer and more honorable if it is grounded in the aspirations and potential of a *living* Constitution rather than in the amnesia or historical exigencies of the various branches of the federal government? The lessons of *Lone Wolf* and its current avatars seemingly leave no doubt in their wake. The way forward is a journey back to the Constitution, lest another constitutional moment be lost in some plenary haze of common law obfuscation.

Lone Wolf, "Foreigners," and Foreign Affairs

The decision in *Lone Wolf* also closely parallels several other expansive—essentially imperial—jurisprudential moves of the era to facilitate the advance of empire abroad and to stem the flow of "undesirable" immigration at home. These expansive powers were not readily discernible from the text or history of the Constitution, but where there is a political will, as in *Lone Wolf*, there is often a jurisprudential way.

Immigration

In regard to federal authority to regulate immigration, the Alien Act of 1798 was the first statute that joined the question of whether the power to regulate immigration was an enumerated federal power.[96] Congressional discussion was wide-ranging over whether such federal power could be located in any grant of express (or implied) authority or whether the power was impliedly reserved to the states. Although international law appeared to recognize the regulation of immigration as an essential attribute of national sovereignty, it was difficult to pinpoint any such express federal authority within the Constitution.[97] There was also rousing discussion as to whether the Constitution protected only citizens and not persons generally (including aliens).[98] The Act was enacted into law, but expired by its own terms in 1800 without any Supreme Court resolution of these issues.

Subsequent Supreme Court jurisprudence wobbled on this issue, before appearing to settle on the Foreign Commerce Clause as the constitutional source for exclusive federal authority over immigration. The premier case in this regard is the 1875 case of *Henderson v. New York*.[99] In this case, Justice Miller, writing for a unanimous Court, struck down New York and Louisiana statutes that required shipmasters to post a bond or pay a specified sum per passenger to alleviate the state's burden in caring for immigrants. The Court concluded that these state statutes impermissibly burdened the exclusive regulation of foreign commerce by Congress:

> [T]he transportation of passengers from European ports to those of the United States has attained a magnitude and importance far beyond its proportion at that time to other branches of commerce. It has become a part of our commerce with foreign nations, of vast interest to this country, as well as to the immigrants who come among us to find a welcome and a home within our borders.[100]

Despite the apparent safe haven of the Foreign Commerce Clause, the federal government did not seek shelter there nine years later in its first appearance in an immigration case.[101] Instead, in a four-page brief in the *Head Money Cases*,[102] it relied on a theory of inherent sovereign powers.[103] Despite the government's claim, the Court hewed to its Foreign Commerce Clause analysis.[104]

The Court turned away from this enumerated powers approach in the original Chinese Exclusion Case, *Chae Chan Ping v. United States*.[105] In this case, the Court upheld in sweeping terms the power of Congress to retroactively terminate the right of an alien resident to reenter the United States.[106] The Court, without any *constitutional* analysis, merely adopted the international law principle that a necessary incident of national sovereignty is the ability to regulate immigration.

It is the notion of *necessity*, not constitutional analysis, that is paramount:

> [T]he United States, in their relation to foreign countries and their subjects or citizens are one nation, invested with powers which belong to independent nations, the exercise of which can be invoked for the maintenance of its absolute independence and security throughout its entire territory. The powers to declare war, make treaties, suppress insurrections, repel invasion, [and] regulate foreign commerce...are all sovereign powers, restricted in their exercise only by the constitution itself and considerations of public policy and justice which control, more or less, the conduct of all civilized nations.[107]

The parallel to Indian law jurisprudence of the time is eerily resonant. Recall, for example, the concluding tautology concerning necessity in *United States v. Kagama*, the influential case that preceded *Lone Wolf v. Hitchcock* and upheld the constitutionality of the Major Crimes Act:

The power of the General Government over these remnants of a race once powerful, now weak and diminished in numbers, is necessary to their protection, as well as to the safety of those among whom they dwell. It must exist in that government, because it has never existed anywhere else, because the theatre of its exercise is within the geographical limits of the United States, because it has never been denied, and because it alone can enforce its laws on all the tribes.[108]

The *Chae Chan Ping* case is also a leading precedent for the right of Congress to unilaterally abrogate treaties, and it was the sole precedent cited in *Lone Wolf v. Hitchcock*[109] for this very proposition.

In the end, plenary power can seldom be truly absolute for long because it then appears more despotic than democratic. Yet the arc toward despotism extends further when noncitizens (including Indians during this era) are involved, especially in territory outside the continental United States (but including Indian country during this same period in the late nineteenth and early twentieth centuries). The Court found plenary power in immigration to be most absolute in the context of issues of entry to and expulsion from the United States and less so as to some constitutional protection to immigrants—especially Chinese—who were legally present in the country.[110] As noted by Sarah Cleveland, these cases created a rough compromise between an extreme Federalist social contract theory that would deny (noncitizen) immigrants basic constitutional protections because they were outside the social contract embodied in the Constitution, and the Jeffersonian vision of limited government, which closely circumscribed the enumerated powers of the federal government and did not include an express right to federal control over immigration.[111] This was a compromise that was practical, perhaps, but not constitutionally coherent.

Governance and the Territories

As with Indian tribes, the Articles of Confederation failed to provide an adequate answer to the means and authority for the governance of territories. In fact, the Articles were completely silent as to the governance of territories and admission of new states.[112] The response to this gap was the inclusion of the Territory Clause of Article IV in the Constitution, which provides that "Congress shall have power to dispose of and make all needful rules and regulations respecting the Territory or other property belonging to the United States."[113]

As with questions of Indian law and immigration, there were serious constitutional questions about both the acquisition of new territory and its governance. In fact, President Jefferson himself had serious qualms about the constitutional basis for such actions, so much so that he believed that a constitutional amendment was necessary to authorize the Louisiana Purchase from France.[114]

In this regard, it is worthwhile to note the rapid increase of territorial acquisition immediately after the adoption of the Constitution:

> Among the criticisms directed at the proposed Constitution in 1787 was the alleged ungovernability of "the great extent of country which the Union embrace[d]." Nevertheless, the United States grew rapidly over the course of the 1800s as a result of western and colonial expansion. In the fifty years between 1803 and 1853, the land area of the United States increased by over three hundred percent. In 1803, the United States acquired the Louisiana Territory, which added 822,000 square acres to the new nation, nearly doubling its size. The Red River Basin was acquired in 1818, and in 1819 Florida was purchased from Spain. Texas was annexed by joint resolution in 1845, and the Oregon Territory was acquired in an 1846 settlement with Britain. The Mexican Cession of 1848 (following the Mexican-American War) and the 1853 Gadsden Purchase from Mexico largely completed the acquisition of the forty-eight contiguous states.[115]

President Jefferson, under pressure from both Congress and his own cabinet, soon abandoned his call for a constitutional amendment and gave way to expedience rather than constitutional principle.[116] Jefferson himself put it well: "The Executive, [i]n seizing the fugitive occurrence which so much advances the good of their country, have done an act beyond the Constitution."[117]

Although the acquisition question—at least for territories contiguous with the original thirteen states—was no longer considered to be encumbered by constitutional impediment, there remained the separate questions of governance and citizenship. Most participants in the governance debate conceded that Article IV, section 2 of the Constitution indeed authorized some kind of governance over the Louisiana Territory, but there was sharp disagreement as to the legal, even constitutional, ingredients of this governance.

The initial congressional compromise established a nonrepresentative form of government for the territory, which allowed the president to appoint the governor for the territory with only minimal constitutional protections for the (non-Indian) residents of the territory, who were not considered citizens of the United States. Some thought this was probably unconstitutional; others regarded it as a *temporary* expedient justified by the general incapability of the largely French and Spanish non-Indian residents to engage in self-governance. President Jefferson regarded this populace as being as "incapable of self-government as children."[118] This temporary government approach provoked much opposition from the press and from residents within the territory. Congress quickly modified its approach by extending the principles of the 1787 Northwest Ordinance to the Louisiana Territory, including the privileges and immunities of citizenship and a bill of rights. This also included provisions for a general assembly of twenty-five elected members and, upon achievement of a certain population, a probable chance at statehood.[119] As Cleveland noted, "The imperial colonial model had been rejected, at least momentarily. The question of the constitutionality of statehood for Louisiana, which was so hotly contested when the treaty was first considered, was never expressly revisited, and Congress admitted Louisiana as a state in 1812."[120]

The trajectory of western expansion did not, of course, end with the Louisiana Purchase, and therefore the unresolved questions about governance in the western territories continued to reappear. The original tension was still manifest regarding whether the Constitution applied in full to the western territories in accordance with a strict view of enumerated powers or whether the Constitution's applicability was rather minimal and Congress's authority relatively unchecked.[121]

The key pre–Civil War decision in this regard was the *Dred Scott* case.[122] Although it is better known for its infamous holding that Scott, a "free black," was not a citizen and hence not a "person" capable of suing in U.S. courts, it also created an important precedent about the applicability of the Constitution in the territories. Chief Justice Taney took the strict view that the Constitution did apply in full to the territories and, indeed, that the federal government was a government of "enumerated" powers not subject to enlargement by any reference to the international law of national sovereignty:

> [I]t is sovereign and supreme in its appropriate sphere of action, yet it does not possess all the powers which usually belong to the sovereignty of a nation. Certain specified powers, enumerated in the Constitution, have been conferred upon it; and neither the legislative, executive, nor judicial departments of the government can lawfully exercise any authority beyond the limits marked out by the Constitution.[123]

This view was not, however, as straightforward as it seemed. Given its focus on race, slavery, and the constitutionality of the Missouri Compromise, which had outlawed slavery in the northern Louisiana Territory, the case did not proceed in a strictly constitutional manner.

The fact that the Constitution did apply in full in the territories preserved the property rights of John F. A. Sanford as a citizen and slaveholder of Scott under the Due Process Clause. As a result of this line of thinking, the case effectively struck down the Missouri Compromise banning slavery in part of the Louisiana Territory. It was only upon statehood that any part of a territory could exercise independent judgment about the propriety or legality of slavery. These troubling issues—at least as manifest in the western territory—did not persist for long, as all of these territories became states (and their residents citizens) by the end of the nineteenth century.

This tangle of issues, however, did not completely disappear. The post–Civil War amendments[124]—especially the Fourteenth Amendment—were necessary to set aside the holding of the *Dred Scott* case that freed slaves could *not* be citizens. The key language of the Fourteenth Amendment in this regard was the extension of citizenship to all persons "subject to the jurisdiction" of the United States.[125] This included former slaves, as well as all residents of the territories, but not Indians.[126]

This general consensus about the full applicability of the Constitution to the territories also began to give way. The paradigm began to shift from the narrow text of the Constitution to the wide-open spaces of inherent powers. The 1879 case of *National Bank v. County of Yankton*[127] is indicative of the developing trend. The Court upheld in no uncertain terms the power of Congress to set aside an act of the Dakota Territorial Legislature:

> Such a power is an incident of sovereignty, and continues until
> granted away. Congress may not only abrogate laws of the territorial
> legislatures, but it may itself legislate directly for the local
> government. It may make a void act of the territorial legislature valid,
> and a valid act void. In other words, it has full and complete
> legislative authority over the people of the Territories and all the
> departments of the territorial governments.[128]

This expanded language was still tethered to some constitutional restraint: "Congress is supreme [over the territories] and...has all the powers of the people of the United States, *except such as have been expressly or by implication* reserved in the *prohibitions* of the Constitution."[129]

This developing jurisprudential ambiguity continued in several cases involving the Mormon Church in the Utah Territory. In both *Murphy v. Ramsey*[130] and the *Church of Jesus Christ of Latter Day Saints v. United States*,[131] the Court upheld the right of Congress to prohibit bigamists and polygamists from voting, to rescind the charter of the Mormon Church, and to take church property in enforcing antipolygamy statutes.

The federal government invoked "plenary" power in its widest form as necessary in the absence of any state power in the territories:

The United States, in turn, asserted a modest sovereign authority over the territories that was both derived from and constrained by the Constitution. The government contended that the power to legislate arose from the Territory Clause and the power to acquire, that Congress had reserved the power to nullify territorial legislation in Utah's organic act, that the Mormon Charter violated the Establishment Clause, and that the promotion of polygamy constituted abuse of corporate powers warranting dissolution under Congress's police powers.[132]

This view forms an interesting corollary to the view of the Court in *Kagama*. In the *Mormon* cases, extensive inherent federal power is necessary in the *absence* of any state power; in *Kagama*, extensive inherent federal power is necessary to protect (Indians) against deadly state power.[133]

With the closing of the western frontier toward the end of the nineteenth century, U.S. territorial expansion was no longer limited to areas contiguous with the original thirteen states. The search for raw materials and markets brought the United States into conflict with Hawaii and Colombia and into war with Spain. As a result of these encounters, the United States annexed and/or acquired Hawaii, Puerto Rico, Guam, the Philippines, Panama, and the eastern Samoan Islands.[134]

Not surprisingly, all this new imperial effort raised again the not so uncommon question about the extent of congressional authority and constitutional limitations (if any) in the context of the governance of these new territories. As usual, there was a contending mix of nativism, racism, capitalism, and empire and its relationship to the social contract and limited federal powers described in the Constitution. These questions were largely played out in the *Insular* cases, a series of Supreme Court decisions between 1901 and 1905 regarding the application of federal tariff law and constitutional criminal procedure practices to the new territories.[135]

In these cases, the Court continued its expansive view of inherent powers moving along a general arc that (select) U.S. law applied automatically to these territories upon cession to the United States, that constitutional limitations on this authority were vague and sporadic at best, and that the inhabitants of the possessions were not citizens and had no guarantee of ever becoming citizens.[136]

These cases echoed—even cited—seminal Indian law cases such as *Johnson v. McIntosh* for the proposition that "the government of the United States, in virtue of its sovereignty...has the full right to acquire territory enjoyed by every other sovereign nation"[137] and *Kagama v. United States* for the holding that the federal government had complete authority over territorial inhabitants.[138]

As Cleveland noted:

> In the course of resolving national authority over the new territories, the court revisited U.S. territorial doctrine from the Louisiana Purchase forward, drawing repeatedly from Chief Justice Marshall's opinion in *Johnson v. McIntosh* that sovereign states could govern conquered territories as they saw fit. The decisions that resulted were largely motivated by the expansionist desire to acquire territory in the far reaches of the earth, with all the benefits of commerce and international status that this entailed, and a xenophobic desire not to allow the inhabitants of such regions to partake of the American birthright.[139]

The *Insular* cases found extensive (negative) common ground with Indian law cases of the era, namely, *United States v. Kagama* and *Lone Wolf v. Hitchcock*. The individuals involved were *not* citizens, their territory was not theirs, and they were subject to the unconstrained "plenary" power of Congress. There was, however, an important conceptual, if not operational, distinction. Acquired territories had no sovereignty except as granted by Congress, whereas Indian tribes possessed a preexisting, preconstitutional form of sovereignty that nevertheless existed "only at the sufferance of Congress and... subject to complete defeasance."[140]

Very little, if any, of this was actually tethered to the text of the Constitution. Where necessary, the demands of empire and expansion converted the *limited* constitutional powers of the federal government into a vessel for *all* the sovereignty *international* law afforded. The basic precepts of federalism that recognized some identifiable constitutional division of authority between the federal government and the states and hence created a two-sovereign checks-and-balances model were not present in Indian country and the acquired territories. As a result, more often than not, an unconstrained unitary (federal) sovereign model resulted. This was all the more unfortunate when the motive to expand was conjoined with nativism and a convenient racial animus to abet the exploitation.

Indian law jurisprudence in the modern era does not invoke this unsavory past, except for one glaring exception. In the 2004 case of *United States v. Lara*,[141] the majority opinion of Justice Breyer upheld Congress's plenary authority to "relax" federal constraints on tribal sovereignty. Yet Justice Breyer went on to state not only that Congress possessed such plenary power but also that the federal government possessed a *preconstitutional* authority over Indian tribes that was an inherent component of nationality. The authority for this startling proposition derived in part from the *Insular* cases.[142] The Court seems poised, if necessary, to conjoin the extraconstitutional regime of *Lone Wolf* with a new preconstitutional source. In this new movement, federal authority in Indian law is to be found above and below, outside and under, but *not in* the Constitution.

PART II

Individual Indians and the Constitution

6

Elk v. Wilkins

Exclusion, Inclusion, and the Ambiguities of Citizenship

L IKE MUCH OF THE REST OF INDIAN LAW, THE STORY OF INDIANS AND
citizenship is a mixture of exclusion and inclusion, separation and
assimilation, racism and respect, and abandonment and belonging. All of this
admixture was reflected in the shifting policy and conceptual inconsistency
taken in the various federal approaches to citizenship. Many of these patterns
were repeated and exacerbated in the context of Indians and state citizenship.
In addition, the entire process of conferring citizenship was thoroughly
insensitive to issues of tribal belonging and membership.

The Constitution, as adopted in 1789, makes no textual reference to Indians
and citizenship but does include much more ambiguous language in Article
I, Section 2 in the context of apportioning representatives among the states:

> Representatives and direct Taxes shall be apportioned among the
> several States which may be included within this Union, according to
> their respective Numbers, which shall be determined by adding to
> the whole number of free Persons, including those bound to service
> for a Term of years, *and excluding Indians not taxed*, three fifths of all
> other Persons.[1]

This language is the only textual reference to individual Indians in the Constitution
and sets the basic constitutional marker for considering issues of Indian citizenship. Though inexact, this language was generally understood to mean that individual Indians who had left the reservation permanently (and presumably severed
their bonds with the tribe) and were subject to state taxes, would be counted for
purposes of establishing a state-by-state census figure for ascertaining the number

of representatives each state was entitled to in the House of Representatives.[2] Indians who remained with their tribes would not be counted.

At the time, this constitutional language was understood neither to expressly confer U.S. citizenship on Indians nor to expressly prohibit extending citizenship to Indians. This power to confer citizenship was understood to reside with Congress's lawmaking authority[3] and the president's authority to enter into treaties with Indian tribes.[4] Both approaches were used in dealing with various segments of the Indian population. It was not until 1924 that a federal statute conferring U.S. citizenship on *all* Native Americans was enacted.[5] Issues of state citizenship for Indians took even longer. The early statutes and treaties took a wide array of approaches—but all of them required fulfillment of some condition precedent by the individual Indian before citizenship was conferred. Examples of such conditions included renouncing tribal membership, accepting an allotment, marrying a non-Indian male, and serving in the U.S. military.[6]

Treaties

Not all treaties between the federal government and Indian tribes provided an option for citizenship, but those that did were remarkably similar. They always involved accepting an individual land allotment and often, but not always, required the individual to sever his or her connection to the tribe. Such provisions in the earliest treaties were in the context of particular federal policies, such as removal, termination, and assimilation.

During the removal process in the early nineteenth century, for example, when the federal government was forcibly relocating a number of the southeastern tribes west of the Mississippi River, a number of treaties provided for the possibility of citizenship. The 1817 treaty with the Cherokees is illustrative:

> And to each and every head of any Indian family residing on the east side of the Mississippi river, on the lands that are now, or may hereafter be, surrendered to the United States, *who may need to become citizens of the United States*, the United States do agree to give a reservation of six hundred and forty acres of land, in a square, to include their improvements, which are to be as near the centre thereof as practicable, in which they will have a life estate, with a reversion in fee simple to their children, reserving to the widow her dower, the register of whose names is to be filed in the office of the Cherokee agent, which shall be kept open until the census is taken as stipulated in the third article of this treaty. Provided, That if any of the heads of families, for whom reservations may be made, should

remove therefrom, then, in that case, the right to revert to the United States.[7]

The 1830 Treaty of Dancing Rabbit Creek with the Choctaws is unique in that it is one of the few treaties that offered the possibility of federal (and state) citizenship but expressly reserved tribal affiliation:

> Whereas the General Assembly of the State of Mississippi has extended the laws of said State to persons and property within the chartered limits of the same, and the President of the United States has said that he cannot protect the Choctaw people from the operation of those laws; Now therefore that the Choctaw may live under their own laws in peace with the United States and the State of Mississippi they have determined to sell their lands east of the Mississippi and have accordingly agreed to the following article of treaty.
>
> ....
>
> Article XIV. Each Choctaw head of a family being desirous to remain and *become a citizen of the States*, shall be permitted to do so, by signifying his intention to the Agent within six months from the ratification of the Treaty, and he or she shall thereupon be entitled to a reservation of one section of six hundred and forty acres of land, to be bordered by sectional lines of survey.... If they reside upon said lands intending to become citizens of the States for five years after the ratification of this Treaty, in the case a grant in fee simple shall issue; said reservation shall include the present improvement of the head of the family, or a portion of it. Persons, who claim under this article *shall not lose the privilege of a Choctaw citizen*, but if they ever remove are not to be entitled to any portion of the Choctaw annuity.[8]

Sometimes a removal treaty contained an express provision whereby certain Indians could become citizens if they did not remove with their tribe and also dissolved their tribal relationship. For example, an 1867 treaty with numerous tribes residing in Kansas provided "which portions of certain tribes, parties hereto, now residing in Kansas, should be enabled to remove to other lands in the Indian country south of that State, while other portions of said tribes desire to dissolve their tribal relations and *become citizens*...."[9] The treaty went on to expressly describe the relevant procedure in Article XVII:

> [B]ut any time previous to that date any member of the tribe may appear before the United States district court for Kansas, and declare

his intention to *become a citizen, when he shall receive a certificate of citizenship*, which shall include his family, and thereafter be disconnected with the tribe....[10]

Other treaties that involved the termination and end of the tribe's legal existence often provided for citizenship. For example, the 1855 Treaty with the Wyandotts provided:

> The Wyandott Indians having become *sufficiently advanced in civilization, and being desirous of becoming citizens*, it is hereby agreed and stipulated, that their organization, and their relations with the United States, as an Indian tribe, shall be dissolved and terminated on the ratification of this agreement...the said Wyandott Indians, and each and every of them, except as hereinafter provided, shall be deemed, and are hereby declared, to be *citizens of the United States*, to all intents and purposes; and shall be entitled to all the rights, and privileges, and immunities of such *citizens*; and shall in all respects be subject to the laws of the United States and of the Territory of Kansas, in the same manner as other citizens of said Territory; and the jurisdiction of the United States and of said Territory, shall be extended over the Wyandott country in the same manner as over other parts of said Territory.[11]

Yet other treaties expressly identified certain elements of character as necessary for citizenship:

> [A]fter which any of said Delawares, being adults, may appear before the said judge in open court, and make the same proof and take the same oath of allegiance as is provided by law for the naturalization of aliens, and also make proof, to the satisfaction of said court, *that he is sufficiently intelligent and prudent to control his own affairs* and interests, that he has adopted the habits of civilized life, *and has been able to support, for at least five years, himself and family....*[12]

Notice here that there is a direct comparison to the naturalization of aliens and the further condition of the acceptance of an allotment with fee patent status, along with termination of tribal membership. This treaty was enacted in the context of removal.

Treaties providing for allotment and citizenship did not involve removal and did not require any particular character traits or the severing of tribal bonds, but they did require the acceptance of an allotment and its subsequent fee patent.[13] Such an example is the Fort Laramie Treaty of 1868:

And any Indian or Indians receiving a patent for land under the foregoing provisions, shall thereby and from thenceforth become and be a *citizen of the United States*, and be entitled to all the privileges and immunities of such citizens, and shall, at the same time, retain all his rights to benefits accruing to Indians under this treaty.[14]

It has also been held that a treaty with a foreign nation can confer U.S. citizenship on the foreign nation's indigenous people if they were recognized as citizens by the foreign country before the land transfer to the United States. Such was the interpretation of the Treaty of Guadalupe Hidalgo between the United States and Mexico involving Pueblo Indians in a case decided by the Supreme Court of New Mexico Territory.[15]

In sum, treaties with Indian tribes conferred citizenship in a variety of ways in a variety of contexts. The key triggering event that invokes the potential of citizenship is whether the treaty deals in part with the status of individual Indians in addition to the status or situation involving the tribes as a whole. Examples, as the previous treaties indicate, include the status of individual Indians who do not remove with their tribe, such as the Choctaw in the Treaty of Dancing Rabbit Creek; individuals whose tribe is otherwise terminated, such as the Wyandott in the 1855 treaty; and individuals who accept an allotment, such as Sioux in the Fort Laramie Treaty of 1868. Once the triggering event occurs, there also may be *additional* requirements, such as the renunciation of tribal membership typified in the 1867 treaty with numerous tribes in Kansas and/or the demonstration of competency to confirm that the individual Indian was "sufficiently intelligent and prudent to control his own affairs."[16] These latter requirements appeared rooted in a naturalization model of citizenship that requires a "naturalized" citizen to renounce "foreign" (i.e., tribal) citizenship and demonstrate basic literacy or competence. There was also out-and-out racism that viewed Indians as largely inferior to non-Indians and thus could obtain citizenship only by coming up to the standards of competence and civilization.

Statutes

Federal statutes, prior to the Citizenship Act of 1924, provided a slightly overlapping but significantly different approach to citizenship for Indians than treaties did. The bridge statute that continued part of the treaty approach, but also marked the end of it, was the Dawes Severalty Act (or General Allotment Act) of 1887.[17] The specifics of allotment in the context of citizenship are contained at Section 6, which states:

And every Indian born within the territorial limits of the United
States to whom allotments shall have been made under the
provisions of this act, or under any law or treaty, and every Indian
born within the territorial limits of the United States who has
voluntarily taken up, within said limits, his residence separate and
apart from any tribe of Indians therein, and has adopted the habits of
civilized life, is hereby declared to be a citizen of the United States,
and is entitled to all the rights, privileges, and immunities of such
citizens, whether said Indian has been or not, by birth or otherwise, a
member of any tribe of Indians within the territorial limits of the
United States without in any manner impairing or otherwise
affecting the right of any such Indian to tribal or other property.[18]

Many in Congress came to feel that granting citizenship as soon as the allotment
was issued, but before expiration of the twenty-five-year trust period and its attendant limitations on alienability and taxation,[19] was precipitous and unwarranted.[20]
The 1906 Burke Act amended the Dawes Severalty Act to withhold citizenship
until a fee (as opposed to a trust) patent was issued.[21] The Allotment Act did not
require renunciation of tribal membership as a condition of citizenship. Nor did
it require any knowledge about the U.S. government or its Constitution.

Citizenship that was conferred as a result of allotment was often accompanied by elaborate and revealing ritual that not only celebrated citizenship and
patriotism but also joined it to the virtues of work, saving, and "whiteness." The
shooting of a final arrow and placing a hand on the plow by Indian men and the
taking of "this work bag and purse" by Indian women were the symbolic acts.
The "Citizenship Ritual" oath was a pageant of transformation:

Citizenship Ritual

For men: (Read name.) _____ (white name). What was your Indian
name? (Gives name.) _____ (Indian name). I hand you a bow and an
arrow. Take this bow and shoot the arrow. (He shoots.)

_____ (Indian name). You have shot your last arrow. That means that
you are no longer to live the life of an Indian. You are from this day forward to live the life of the white man. But you may keep that arrow, it will
be to you a symbol of your noble race and of the pride you feel that you
come from the first of all Americans.

_____ (White name). Take in your hand this plow. (He takes the han-
dles of the plow.)

This act means that you have chosen to live the life of the white man—
and the white man lives by work. From the earth we all must get our living,

and the earth will not yield unless man pours upon it the sweat of his brow. Only by work do we gain a right to the land or to the enjoyment of life.

_____ (White name). I give you a purse. This purse will always say to you that the money you gain from your labor must be wisely kept. The wise man saves his money so that when the sun does not smile and the grass does not grow, he will not starve.

I give into your hands the flag of your country. This is the only flag you have ever had or ever will have. It is the flag of freedom, the flag of free men, the flag of a hundred million free men and women of whom you are now one. That flag has a request to make of you, _____ (white name); that you take it into your hands and repeat these words:

"For as much as the President has said that I am worthy to be a citizen of the United States, I now promise to this flag that I will give my hands, my head, and my heart to the doing of all that will make me a true American citizen."

And now beneath this flag I place upon your breast the emblem of your citizenship. Wear this badge of honor always; and may the eagle that is on it never see you do aught of which the flag will not be proud.

(The audience rises and shouts: "_____ (white name) is an American citizen.")

For women: (white name). Take in your hand this work bag and purse. (She takes the work bag and purse.)

This means that you have chosen the life of the white woman—and the white woman loves her home. The family and the home are the foundation of our civilization. Upon the character and industry of the mother and the home maker largely depends the future of our Nation. The purse will always say to you that the money you gain from your labor must be wisely kept. The wise woman saves her money, so that when the sun does not smile and the grass does not grow, she and her children will not starve.

I give into your hands the flag of your country. This is the only flag you have ever had or ever will have. It is the flag of freedom, the flag of free men, the flag of a hundred million free men and women of whom you are now one. That flag has a request to make of you, _____ (white name); that you take it into your hands and repeat these words:

"For as much as the President has said that I am worthy to be a citizen of the United States, I now promise to this flag that I will give my hands, my head, and my heart to the doing of all that will make me a true American citizen."

And now beneath this flag I place upon your breast the emblem of your citizenship. Wear this badge of honor always; and may the eagle that is on it never see you do aught of which the flag will not be proud.

(The audience rises and shouts: "_____(white name) is an American citizen.")

Of Utmost Good Faith, 93–94 (Vine Deloria Jr.,
ed., Straight Arrow Books, 1971).

In contrast, a naturalization oath from the same era was decidedly less ritu-
alistic. It was about giving up citizenship from elsewhere and embracing a new
citizenship and patriotism. It was not about adopting a "virtuous" new life that
involved work, saving, and character:

Naturalization Oath

Be it remembered, That on this _____ day of the Month of _____ in the year
of our Lord _____ and of the Independence of the United States
the _____, an alien, being a free white person, appeared before the
Circuit Court of the State of Wisconsin, for Chippewa County, and applied
to the Court to be admitted to become a citizen of the United States, and the
said _____ having, more than two years ago, made a declaration of
his intended application as aforesaid, in the manner and form proscribed in
an Act of Congress entitled "An Act to establish an uniform rule of
Naturalization, and to repeal the Acts heretofore passed on the subject;" and
the Court being satisfied by the testimony of _____ and
_____, citizens of the United States, that the said _____
has resided within the United States for the continued term of five years last
past, and within the State of Wisconsin one year at least; and that during that
time he has behaved as a man of good moral character, attached to the principles of the Constitution of the United States, and well disposed to the good
order and happiness of the same; and the said applicant declaring on oath
before the Court that he will support the Constitution of the United States,
and that he doth absolutely and entirely renounce and abjure all allegiances
and fidelity to every foreign Prince, Potentate, States, or Sovereignty whatever, and particularly Victoria whereof he was before a subject.
   Thereupon the Court admitted the said _____ to become a
citizen of the United States of America.
   _____, Clerk

> http://www.wisconsinhistory.org/genealogy/natlzn/
> images/pre1906cert.jpg

The core view of (non-Indian) citizenship then (and now) may be
summarized:

> In 1795, Congress extended the residency requirement to five years
> and clarified and underscored the requirements of character and
> allegiance. In the law, particular emphasis was placed repeatedly on an
> oath of citizenship. The applicant must declare an oath not only "that
> he will support the Constitution of the United States," but also "that he
> doth absolutely and entirely recuse and abjure all allegiance and fidelity

to every foreign prince, potentate, State or sovereignty whatsoever." This language is the core of the Oath of Renunciation and Allegiance still taken by all new citizens. The 1795 law also required that, during the time of residency (or "probation," as some called it), the applicant must have "behaved as a man of good character, attached to the principles of the Constitution of the United States, and well disposed to the good order and happiness of the same." These remain requirements for citizenship in the United States.[22]

There is also the critical distinction to note that the statutory process of granting citizenship to Indians was largely "involuntary," not requiring consent, whereas the naturalization process of all other individuals was largely based on individual voluntary consent.

Soon after the allotment era, Congress began to pass statutes with the sole purpose of conferring citizenship on certain segments of the Indian population. None of these statutes required the surrender of tribal membership. Taken as a whole, they reflect movement away from the naturalization model and the attendant elements of racial animus. Examples of such legislation include the statute that conferred citizenship on all Indian women who married non-Indian male citizens[23] and the statute that conferred citizenship on all Indians who enlisted and fought in World War I.[24]

It soon became apparent that there was no longer (if there ever was) any legitimate reason to withhold federal citizenship from *any* Native Americans. As a result, and with little fanfare, Congress passed the Indian Citizenship Act of 1924. It provides:

The following shall be nationals and citizens of the United States at birth:...

A person born in the United States to a member of an Indian, Eskimo, Aleutian, or other aboriginal tribe: *Provided*, That the granting of citizenship when this subsection shall not in any manner impair or otherwise affect the right of such person to tribal or other property.[25]

This legislation clearly reflects an assimilative and inclusive view of Native Americans within the national polity. This inclusiveness did not require any forfeiture of tribal membership, yet it nevertheless raised or reraised questions relative to the constitutional status of Native American citizenship and the status of Native Americans as state citizens. As to the former, the 1924 statute was clearly necessary because the Supreme Court had rejected the argument that the Fourteenth Amendment conferred U.S. citizenship on Native Americans in the case of *Elk v. Wilkins*.[26] Many states also rejected the notion that the

Fourteenth Amendment conferred *state* citizenship on Native Americans. The text of the 1924 Act itself makes no reference to states or state citizenship.

Elk v. Wilkins

Because the Fourteenth Amendment is generally understood as a proscription against limiting citizenship based on race, it might be assumed that the Fourteenth Amendment removed any such bar to the citizenship of native people. *Elk v. Wilkins* expressly held to the contrary.

In this case, the plaintiff John Elk brought his action in the Circuit Court of the United States for the District of Nebraska against the registrar of one of the wards of the City of Omaha for refusing to register him as a qualified voter in a city election. Elk averred that the sole reason for not accepting his registration was that he was an Indian and therefore was not a citizen of the United States and not entitled to vote. He claimed that the action taken was in direct violation of the Fourteenth and Fifteenth Amendments. Specifically, he alleged that such action contravened the first section of the Fourteenth Amendment, which provides: "All persons born or naturalized in the United States and subject to the jurisdiction thereof, are citizens of the United States and of the State wherein they reside,"[27] and that part of the Fifteenth Amendment that provides "the right of citizens of the United States to vote shall not be denied or abridged by the United States or by any state on account of race, color or previous condition of servitude."[28] The Circuit Court dismissed Elk's complaint without an opinion.

The essential facts were not disputed. Elk was an Indian born in the United States who had fully severed his relationship to his tribe. In addition, he had "completely surrendered himself to the jurisdiction of the United States" and was a bona fide resident of the city of Omaha and the state of Nebraska.[29] With these facts uncontested, the Supreme Court characterized the dispositive issue as

> whether an Indian, born a member of one of the Indian tribes within the United States, is, merely by reason of his birth within the United States, and of his afterwards voluntarily separating himself from his tribe and taking up his residence among white citizens, a citizen of the United States, within the meaning of the first section of the Fourteenth Amendment of the Constitution.[30]

The core of the Court's analysis centered on the retention in the Fourteenth Amendment of the "Indians not taxed" language found in the unamended Constitution[31] and the meaning of the Fourteenth Amendment text that states "born or naturalized in the United States and *subject to the jurisdiction thereof*."[32] The original text of the Constitution in the apportionment clause dealt with slavery in the context of the "three-fifths rule" and Indians in the context of the "Indian not taxed" clause. Such phrases were clear limitations on the potential for citizenship. The Fourteenth Amendment eliminated the "three-fifths rule" language completely but retained the "Indians not taxed" language verbatim. The controlling question then became what the import was of change in text for one group (i.e., slaves) and retention of text for another group (i.e., Indians).

According to the Court, the retention of the "Indians not taxed" language in the Fourteenth Amendment was strongly indicative of intent not to confer citizenship. Slavery having been abolished by the Thirteenth Amendment and the persons formerly held as slaves made citizens by the Fourteenth Amendment, the original clause fixing the apportionment of representatives was necessarily abrogated, as it counted only three-fifths of such persons. Indians were a different matter:

> But Indians not taxed are still excluded from the count, for the reason that they are not citizens. Their absolute exclusion from the basis of representation, in which all other persons are not included, is wholly inconsistent with their being considered citizens.[33]

In addition, the Court decided that Indians were not "born in the United States and subject to the jurisdiction thereof" within the meaning of the first section of the Fourteenth Amendment. Persons not subject to the jurisdiction of the United States at the time of birth cannot become so afterward, except by being naturalized individually or collectively through the force of treaty.[34] The Court reasoned that Indians born within the territorial boundaries of the United States nevertheless owed immediate allegiance to their tribe and not the United States and were thus properly analogized to such noncitizens as children of foreign ambassadors born within the United States. They were thus not subject to the jurisdiction of the United States.[35]

The Court found such a construction supported by other contemporary actions of Congress taken at that time. For example, the very Congress that drafted the Fourteenth Amendment also passed the 1866 Civil Rights Act, which declared that "all persons born in the United States, and not subject to any foreign power, excluding Indians not taxed,"[36] shall be citizens of the United States. In addition, the Court referred to treaties entered into with tribes while the amendment was pending that continued to hew to a naturalization model. Such an example was the treaty with the Kansas Indians, which permitted individual Kansas Indians to apply for citizenship.

The Court also pointed out that even after ratification of the Fourteenth Amendment, Congress enacted several statutes that conferred citizenship on certain Indians in accordance with the naturalization model. Such legislation included an 1870 statute dealing with the Winnebago Indians in Minnesota[37] and an 1873 statute dealing with the Miami Tribe in Kansas.[38] These statutes required any tribal member of these tribes desiring U.S. citizenship to make application in open court at the local federal district court in such manner that:

> [M]ake[s] the same proof, and take[s] the same oath of allegiance as is provided by law for the naturalization of aliens, and should also make proof to the satisfaction of the court, that they were sufficiently intelligent and prudent to control their affairs and interests, that they had adopted the habits of civilized life, and had for at least five years before been able to support themselves and their families; and thereupon they should be declared by the court to be citizens of the United States, the declaration entered of record, and a certificate thereof given to the applicant; and the Secretary of the Interior, upon presentation of the certificate, might issue to them patents in fee simple, with power of alienation, of the lands already held by them in severalty...and thereupon such persons should cease to be members of the tribe, and the lands so patented should be subject to levy, taxation, and sale, in like manner with the property of other citizens.[39]

The majority's reading of the text of the Fourteenth Amendment, and subsequent statutes and treaties, was augmented by considerations of dependence and "pupilage"; such conditions could be adjusted only by "the nation whose wards they are and whose citizens they seek to become, and not by each Indian for himself."[40] Wardship was an impediment to citizenship and could be changed only by the guardian federal government and not by the individual Indian ward himself.

Justice Harlan (along with Justice Woods) dissented. The dissent did not contend that the Fourteenth Amendment standing alone conferred U.S. citizenship on Indians but rather that it lifted any bar against citizenship and positioned each individual Indian to *choose* citizenship without any further action required by the United States. This interpretation of the Fourteenth Amendment was largely undergirded by Justice Harlan's close analysis of the Civil Rights Act of 1866 and its legislative history.

Although this statute employed the "Indians not taxed" language of the Fourteenth Amendment, the legislative history strongly demonstrated Congress's intent to change the rules governing citizenship for Indians. The statute provided that "all persons born in the United States and not subject to any foreign power, excluding Indians not taxed, are hereby declared to be citizens of the United States."[41] According to the dissent:

This, so far as we are aware, is the first general enactment making persons of the Indian race citizens of the United States. Numerous statutes and treaties previously provided for all the individual members of particular Indian tribes becoming, in certain contingencies, citizens of the United States. But the act of 1866, reached Indians not in tribal relations. Beyond question by that act, national citizenship was conferred upon all persons in this country, of whatever race (excluding only "Indians not taxed"), who were born within the territorial limits of the United States, and were not subject to any foreign power. Surely every one must admit that an Indian, residing in one of the States, and subject to taxation there, became, by force alone of the act of 1866, a citizen of the United States, although he may have been, when born, a member of a tribe.[42]

According to Justice Harlan, it is this understanding that permeated the very same Congress when it drafted and adopted the text of the Fourteenth Amendment. "Those who sustained the former [Act of 1866] urged the adoption of the latter [the Fourteenth Amendment]."[43] Hence, the effect of the Fourteenth Amendment was to confer citizenship on all Indians except those "Indians not taxed."

Finally, the dissent noted that the interpretation of the majority led to the unseemly result that Indians such as John Elk, who had given up tribal affiliation and become state residents and taxpayers, became "stateless" persons in the constitutional sense. Under this most odd of constructions, according to the dissent, the effect of the Fourteenth Amendment was to maintain

a despised and rejected class of persons, with no nationality whatsoever; who, born in our territory, owing no allegiance to any foreign power, and subject, as residents of the States, to all the burdens of government, are yet not members of any political community nor entitled to any of the rights, privileges, or immunities of citizens of the United States.[44]

The travail of John Elk was perhaps foretold in the infamous case involving Standing Bear, a Ponca tribal leader. Standing Bear led a small group of tribal members from the Oklahoma Indian Territory back to the tribe's traditional homestead in Nebraska. He and his band were detained and incarcerated by the U.S. Army, but he attempted to challenge his incarceration through a habeas corpus action filed in federal court. The key issue in the case was whether Standing Bear was entitled to file his habeas petition, inasmuch as the relevant statute permitted such actions to be brought only by "persons." In other words, the question was whether the Indians were "persons" under U.S. law. The Court did not find the answer obvious and had to turn to Webster's dictionary for crucial assistance. Webster's dictionary described a person as a "living soul; a self-conscious being; a moral agent; especially a living human being; a man, woman, or child; an individual of the human race." This is comprehensive enough that it would seem to include even an Indian.[45] A person, but not yet a citizen.

Cases after Elk v. Wilkins

Between *Elk v. Wilkins* and the Citizenship Act of 1924, the federal courts focused largely on the effects of citizenship (via treaty or allotment) on jurisdiction. The principal issue in these cases was often reconciling the "emancipation" of citizenship with the dependency of "wardship."[46]

The best examples in this context are the cases that considered whether the federal criminal statute banning the sale of liquor to Indians in Indian country applied to Indians who had received allotments and citizenship under the Dawes Severalty Act of 1887. The 1905 case of *In re Heff*[47] held that Indian citizenship was incompatible with wardship, and hence the federal Indian liquor laws did not apply to citizen Indians:

> Of late years a new policy has found expression in the legislation of Congress—a policy which looks to the breaking up of tribal relations, the establishing of the separate Indians in individual homes, free from national guardianship and charged with all the rights and obligations of citizens of the United States. Of the power of the government to carry out this policy there can be no doubt. It is under no constitutional obligation to perpetually continue the relationship of guardian and ward. It may at any time abandon its guardianship and lead the ward to assume and be subject to all the privileges and burdens of one *sui juris*. And it is for Congress to determine when and how that relationship of guardianship shall be abandoned.[48]

Section 6 of the Dawes Act expressly conferred federal citizenship on allottees, and this citizenship became operational at the time of allotment, not twenty-five years later when the fee patent was awarded.[49] With federal citizenship in hand, the Fourteenth Amendment necessarily provided state citizenship.[50] State citizenship—at least in the context of the general state police power to regulate the sale of intoxicating liquor—must be duly respected, and hence federal jurisdiction could not reach the Indian (state) citizens.[51] Principles of federalism and the potential contradiction between federal and state law on the matter supported the finding of state rather than federal authority in this area of jurisdiction.[52]

Eleven years later in *United States v. Nice*,[53] the Supreme Court overruled *In re Heff* and found *no* incompatibility between citizenship for Indians and continued federal jurisdiction based on their wardship status. In this case, the defendant challenged his federal prosecution under the 1897 Act for the sale of liquor to a Rosebud Sioux allottee who was also a federal citizen. This time the Court agreed and reversed the dismissal of the defendant's conviction.[54] The Court reiterated the essential power of Congress to regulate the sale of intoxicants involving Indians "under national guardianship" and noted that such power "is not debatable."[55]

As to whether such federal authority was still incompatible with citizenship, the Court reversed the view it espoused in *In re Heff*. Citizenship was not incompatible with tribal membership or continued guardianship, and so citizenship might be conferred without completely emancipating the Indians or placing them beyond the reach of congressional regulations adopted for their protection.[56]

In the eight years leading up to the comprehensive Citizenship Act of 1924, the Court never wavered again. Citizenship was not inconsistent with dependency, and extensive (and potentially unlimited) federal authority in Indian affairs went unchecked. This, of course, was the era of plenary power that was established by the Supreme Court's 1903 decision in *Lone Wolf v. Hitchcock*.[57] Congress was the sole arbiter of its authority over Indians and Indian tribes. It and it alone ruled in Indian affairs. Citizenship, like everything else in Indian affairs, was to be regulated by Congress and, when necessary, endorsed by the courts. The Constitution, particularly the Fourteenth Amendment, according to the Court, had nothing to say in this area of law.

By the time of the 1924 Citizenship Act, assimilation through citizenship appeared to be inevitable. Neither the alleged "wildness" nor the "tribal loyalty" of Indians any longer stood in the way of a swift and universal conferral of U.S. citizenship on *all* Indians. Yet the historical residue was less than flattering to all concerned. The United States—particularly Congress—maintained its exorbitant power over Indians and Indian tribes, and Indian tribes and Indians were still subject to the full brunt of its power. Citizenship did not ameliorate the grand imbalance of power.

Citizenship is generally understood as a society's hallmark of respect for its members. It is the ultimate marker of inclusion. Yet in the Native American context, it was (and is) not without its ambiguities. For most of the time prior to the Citizenship Act of 1924, citizenship for Indians required a quid pro quo, usually the surrender of tribal membership and affiliation. A tribal membership and affiliation that were generally demeaned as primitive, wild, and uncivilized. It was *not* a citizenship negotiated between two sovereigns increasingly occupying the same landscape, but a status conferred by one at the expense of the other. It was plenary rather than consensual.

There have been a few legal challenges to the constitutionality of the Citizenship Act of 1924, but they all have failed. Indeed, no such challenge has ever reached the U.S. Supreme Court. Those few challenges—often brought by members of the Iroquois Confederacy—focused on the absence of tribal consent and the existence of treaty-based relations.[58] Such challenges have been found insufficient in light of Congress's plenary power in Indian affairs.

In addition to the absence of tribal consent, there is the problem of *individual* Indian consent, as is usually required under the naturalization model. The Supreme Court has nevertheless recognized Congress's authority to confer collective citizenship without direct individual consent. In *Boyd v. Nebraska*,[59] the Court held that in the context of newly admitted states, the individuals comprising the political community seeking statehood would be deemed to have effectively consented to U.S. citizenship.[60]

The Court noted that in the treaty context, whether with tribes or foreign nations, the sovereign to whom the naturalized individual had formerly owed allegiance either disclaimed continuing "foreign" dominion by treaty or was incorporated as a state of the union.[61] Despite the absence of either of these in the Citizenship Act of 1924, there is little doubt that plenary power suffices to insulate it from constitutional infirmity. In fact, it would probably be unconstitutional to deny Indian people citizenship.

The most prevalent nagging undercurrent involving Indians and citizenship was not so much the *fact* of citizenship itself, which standing alone represents respect and incorporation into the (national) body politic, but rather the price it exacted. Until the Citizenship Act itself, citizenship was largely extended to Indians on the condition that they surrender tribal membership as either incompatible with U.S. citizenship as a matter of divided loyalty or as a badge of inferiority or both. For many Indians, if not most, the price was too high and lacked fundamental respect and understanding of who Indian people were.

By way of comparison, in the context of slavery, for example, there was no divided loyalty or badge of inferiority except slave status itself. With the passage of the Thirteenth and Fourteenth Amendments to the Constitution, slavery was eliminated and citizenship for African Americans was at hand. The end of slavery quickly materialized into citizenship for former slaves, yet the process was neither as swift nor as unitary for Indians. The infamous *Dred Scott* case itself made this dichotomy painfully clear. Chief Justice Taney determined that the original Constitution (unless amended) permanently withheld citizenship from freed slaves, but it did not foreclose potential citizenship to Native Americans:

> The situation of this population was altogether unlike that of the Indian race. The latter, it is true, formed no part of the colonial communities, and never amalgamated with them in social connections or in government. But although they were uncivilized, they were yet a free and independent people, associated together in nations or tribes, and governed by their own laws....
>
> But they [i.e., Indians] may, without doubt, like the subjects of any other foreign government, be naturalized by the authority of Congress, and become citizens of a State, and of the United States; and if an individual should leave his nation or tribe, and take up his abode among the white population, he would be entitled to all the rights and privileges which would belong to an emigrant from any other foreign people.[62]

The ultimate conferral of federal citizenship on all Native people was a first step of national inclusion, yet the surrounding historical process was tarnished by racism and a derogatory attitude toward tribal membership and affiliation. On one hand, citizenship may be seen as a badge of inclusion and respect; on the other hand, it may be seen as advancing undue assimilation and even colonialism. This is especially true in the Native American context, where very often inclusion demanded the surrender of tribal membership, that citizenship of the heart.

Although citizenship is generally understood as empowering in its recognition of formal equality, it can also be seen as creating a potential bar to legislative or judicial action designed to redress *continuing* inequities concerning treatment of individual Indians and their tribes. For Native Americans, citizenship is perhaps best understood as a necessary yet insufficient step in the process of creating an equality and respect that is neither static nor self-satisfied, but rather dynamic in providing the vantage from which to confront the residue of the past that occludes and impedes the future of meaningful inclusion, an inclusion that does not demean the individual right of tribal membership and the collective right of tribal self-determination.

State Citizenship

The issue of state citizenship for Indian people raised similar as well as *additional* issues not addressed in the context of U.S citizenship. State citizenship issues reflected, in part, their own localized versions of alleged incompatibility

with tribal membership and the "down home" version of racism. State jurisprudence on this issue often involved interpretation of state constitutional provisions and state statutes, along with exigencies relative to the applicability of
federal cases and statutes.

Several states such as Minnesota, New Mexico, Idaho, Washington, and
North Dakota had express constitutional provisions dealing with the right of
Indians to vote, which, in turn, served as the dispositive marker in regard to
state citizenship. The issue for states was not so much whether Indians were
citizens per se, but what disabilities and limitations potentially attached to the
citizenship of certain subgroups of Indians who, for example, did not pay taxes
or had not given up tribal membership.

The 1890 Idaho Constitution in its section on suffrage and election provided:

> No person is permitted to vote, serve as a juror or hold any civil office
> who is under guardianship, idiotic or insane, or who has, at any
> place, been convicted of treason, felony, embezzlement of the public
> funds, bartering or selling, or offering to barter or sell his vote, or
> purchasing or offering to purchase the vote of another, or other
> infamous crime, and who has not been restored to the rights of
> citizenship, or who, at the time of such election, is confined in prison
> on conviction of a criminal offense, or who is a bigamist or
> polygamist, or is living in what is known as patriarchal, plural or
> celestial marriage, or in violation of any law of this state, or of the
> United States, forbidding any such crime; or who, in any manner,
> teaches, advises, counsels, aids, or encourages any person to enter
> into bigamy, polygamy, or such patriarchal, plural, or celestial
> marriage, or to live in violation of any such law, or to commit any
> such crime; or who is a member of, or contributes to the support, aid
> or encouragement of, any order, organization, association,
> corporation, or society which teaches or advises that the laws of this
> state prescribing rules of civil conduct, are not the supreme law of
> the state; nor shall Chinese, or persons of Mongolian descent, not
> born in the United States, *nor Indians not taxed, who have not severed
> their tribal relations, and adopted the habits of civilization*, either vote,
> serve as jurors, or hold any civil office.[63]

This section was amended in a state constitutional referendum in 1950 to elim-
inate the italicized language.[64]

The 1857 Minnesota Constitution contained this provision on Indian citizenship and voting:

[E]very male person of the age of twenty-one years or upwards belonging to either of the following classes who shall have resided in the United States one year, and in this state for four months next preceding and election, shall be entitled to vote at such election in the election district of which he shall at the time have been for ten days a resident, for all officers that now are, or hereafter may be, elective by the people. *1. White citizens of the United States. 2. White persons of foreign birth, who shall have declared their intentions to become citizens, conformably to the laws of the United States upon the subject of naturalization. 3. Persons of mixed white and Indian blood, who have adopted the customs and habits of civilization. 4. Persons of Indian blood residing in this state who have adopted the language, customs and habits of civilization, after an examination before any District Court of the State, in such manner as may be provided by law, and shall have been pronounced by said court capable of enjoying the rights of citizenship within the State.*[65]

This provision has since been amended to remove the italicized language.[66]

The New Mexico Constitution originally contained a provision which stated:

Every male citizen of the United States, who is over the age of twenty-one years, and has resided in New Mexico twelve months, in the county ninety days, and in the precinct in which he offers to vote thirty days, next preceding the election, except idiots, insane persons and persons convicted of a felonious or infamous crime unless restored to political rights, *and Indians not taxed* shall be qualified to vote at all elections for public officers.[67]

This provision was amended in 1967 to remove the italicized language.[68]

The 1889 North Dakota Constitution provided as follows:

Every male person of the age of twenty-one years or upwards belonging to either of the following classes, who shall have resided in the State one year, in the county six months and in the precinct ninety days next preceding any election, shall be a qualified elector at such election:

First. Citizens of the United States.

Second. Persons of foreign birth who shall have declared their intention to become citizens, one year and not more than six years prior to such election, conformably to the naturalization laws of the United States.

Third. *Civilized persons of Indian descent who shall have severed their tribal relations two years next preceding such election.*[69]

The North Dakota Constitution was amended in 1922 to remove the italicized language.[70]

The 1889 State of Washington Constitution contained the imperative declaration: "Provided, That Indians not taxed shall never be allowed the elective franchise."[71] The Washington Constitution was amended in 1974 to remove this disability on the Indian franchise.[72]

The constitutional provision for such states as Idaho, New Mexico, and Washington used verbatim the "Indian not taxed" language that appears in the original text and Fourteenth Amendment to the U.S. Constitution. These states generally followed the arc of federal court interpretation until such language was essentially rendered inoperative by the Citizenship Act of 1924. Yet as late as 1948, New Mexico often denied the right to vote to Indians based on this state constitutional provision. This practice was ultimately challenged and set aside by a federal court in the case of *Trujillo v. Garley.*[73] The three-judge panel registered its dismay at such an incongruous practice:

> Any other citizen, regardless of race, in the State of New Mexico who has not paid one cent of tax of any kind or character, if he possesses the other qualifications, may vote. An Indian, and only an Indian, in order to meet the qualifications to vote, must have paid a tax. How you can escape the conclusion that makes a requirement with respect to an Indian as a qualification to exercise the elective franchise and does not make that requirement with respect to the member of any [other] race is beyond me.[74]

The District Court struck down this portion of the New Mexico State Constitution as violative of the Fourteenth and Fifteenth Amendments.[75]

The state of Arizona embarrassed itself in the case of *Porter v. Hall*,[76] which was decided in 1928. The Arizona Supreme Court held that Native Americans could *not* vote because they were similar to minors and the mentally incompetent and fell under the state constitutional proscription denying the franchise to "person[s] under guardianship."[77] The Court explained:

> The person falling within any of the classes is to some extent and for some reason considered by the law as incapable of managing his own affairs as a normal person, and needing some special care from the state. . . . The man who for any reason is exempt from responsibility of the law for his acts, who cannot be trusted to manage his own person or property, certainly as a matter of common sense cannot be trusted to make laws for the government of others. . . .[78]

Despite the perverse interpretation, this case remained good law in Arizona until 1948, when it was overturned by the case of *Harrison v. Laveen*,[79] in which the Supreme Court of Arizona observed:

> We have made an extensive search of the proceedings of the Arizona Constitutional Convention and are unable to find the slightest evidence to indicate that the framers of our constitution in specifying that "persons under guardianship" (Sec. 2, Article 7) should be denied the right of franchise, thereby intended that this phrase be applied to Indians as such.[80]

The Court went on to hold "that the term 'persons under guardianship' has no application to the plaintiffs or to the Federal status of Indians in Arizona as a class."[81]

Minnesota's Constitution contained an express citizenship provision that stated:

> Persons of mixed White and Indian blood who have adopted the habits and customs of civilization.... Persons of Indian blood...who have adopted the language, customs and habits of civilization, after an examination before any district court of the state, in such manner as may be provided by law, and shall have been pronounced by said court capable of enjoying the rights of citizenship within the state.[82]

In 1917, the Supreme Court of Minnesota interpreted this provision in a case-specific way. In *Osphal v. Johnson*, the Court found that many Indians at issue did not meet the constitutional requirements of citizenship and hence the right to vote. The Court noted:

> It cannot for a moment be considered that the framers of the Constitution intended to grant the right of suffrage to persons who were under no obligation to obey the laws enacted as a result of such a grant.... The idea is repugnant to our form of government. No one should participate in the making of laws which he need not obey. As truly said by contestant: "The tribal Indian contributes nothing to the state. His property is not subject to taxation, or to the process of its courts. He bears none of the burdens of civilization, and performs none of the duties of citizens."[83]

The Court found that six Indians who had completed the allotment process under the Dawes Act satisfied the state constitutional requirement for citizenship and the franchise, but fifty-two Indians who had not completed the allotment process did not.[84] In the context of the fifty-two Indians denied citizenship, the Court noted that they still clung to some of the customs and habits of their race and were governed in their relation with each other by their peculiar tribal rules and practices, subject in a certain sense, to the advice and supervision of the federal authorities.[85]

The Court also observed that many of the fifty-two Indians denied citizenship and the franchise had nevertheless *"reached a degree of civilization superior to that manifested by many white men,* yet the facts warrant no other conclusion except that they are tribal Indians and subject to the disabilities incident to their status as such."[86] The Court further opined that the state franchise was in the nature of an "inducement" to Indians to sever their tribal ways and adopt the habits of "civilization."[87]

In these statements, we can see the divided and even contradictory impulses involved in state citizenship and the franchise for Indians. The "incentive" approach focuses not so much on forward-looking inclusion per se but rather on the backward-looking jettison of tribal relations. This is state citizenship with a steep cultural price tag. Yet the Court also perceived the essential perversity of such individual case-by-case determinations involving the adoption of the "customs and habits of civilization," when many white men manifestly lacked these qualities.

The knot of state citizenship and the right to vote persisted into the 1950s and 1960s and even the 1970s. For example, a Utah state statute provided: "Any person living upon any Indian or military reservation shall not be deemed a resident of Utah within the meaning of this Chapter, unless such person had acquired a residence in some county in Utah prior to taking up his residence upon such Indian or military reservation."[88] This statute was upheld by the Utah Supreme Court in the 1956 case of *Allen v. Merrell.*[89] The Court did not question the fact that Indians were state citizens, but that was not enough to guarantee the right to vote:

> That Indians are entitled to the rights and privileges bestowed upon
> citizens by the Federal and State constitutions, we do not question.
> But the right to vote is not vested absolutely in any citizen.... It is
> well settled that the right thus granted is subject to reasonable
> qualifications imposed by the state.[90]

The Court rejected challenges under both the Fourteenth and Fifteenth Amendments and found justification in the following:

> (1) That most persons residing on reservations are members of Indian
> tribes which have a considerable degree of sovereignty independent of
> state government; (2) That the Federal Government maintains a high
> degree of interest in and responsibility for their welfare and thus has
> potentially a substantial amount of influence and control over them,

and (3) That they are much less concerned with paying taxes and otherwise being involved with state government and its local units, and are much less interested in it than are citizens generally.[91]

The Court seemed to think that, on one hand, Indians had too little interest in state and local government (but why, then, did they want to vote?), while on the other hand they might have too much interest that resulted in "substantial control of the county government and the expenditures of its funds in a group of citizens who, as a class, had an extremely limited interest in its functions and very little responsibility in providing the financial support thereof."[92] In the end, it seemed a paradox of wanting too little or too much—either of which, apparently, sufficed as grounds for exclusion. No other group of citizens was subject to such inconsistent grounds for disenfranchisement. The U.S. Supreme Court granted review, but while the appeal was pending, the Utah legislature repealed the statute.

In New Mexico, there were several attempts to deny Indian citizens the right to vote based on residency and tax immunity issues. In Montoya v. Bolack,[93] the right of reservation Indian citizens to vote was challenged on residency grounds. The New Mexico Supreme Court easily decided that reservation residents were also state residents for the purpose of exercising the franchise. Yet the Court also noted with some asperity that Navajos who resided on the reservation had secured an asymmetrical advantage with respect to off-reservation residents: "[T]he anomalous situation [in which Indians can vote but are not subject to control by elected officials] places the Navajo in a more favored position than other legal residents of the state."[94]

Thirteen years later in 1975, the state sought to deny Navajo people the right to vote in a local school board election and attendant bond issue based on the tax immunization of trust land. The New Mexico Supreme Court again struck down the state's claim on equal protection grounds. The Court went on to observe that the "taxation without representation" canard, while superficially attractive, was empirically not well established in the case at bar, insomuch as the bulk of the repayment of the bond indebtedness was to be derived from corporations that leased Navajo lands.[95]

As these cases indicate, despite state citizenship and the grudging recognition of a general right to vote, there was continued (though generally unsuccessful) resistance to the Indian right to vote on more limited grounds such as residency and (property) tax-paying status. Yet even as that era came to a close, a new area of concern has come more and more to the fore. The new area does not involve the right to vote per se, but rather the myriad issues related to fair representation and the establishment of voting districts at the school board, municipal, county, and state levels.

South Dakota is a textbook example of this new zone of encounter involving the status of Indians as full-fledged state citizens. The primary federal statute designed to protect the voting franchise under the Fifteenth Amendment is the Voting Rights Act of 1965.[96] The statute was amended in 1975 to expressly include Indians and to expand the preclearance provisions of Section 5 to include Shannon County and Todd County, located on the Pine Ridge and Rosebud Sioux Reservations in South Dakota.[97]

This was not well received in South Dakota. Attorney General William Janklow referred to these changes in a formal letter to the (South Dakota) Secretary of State as a "facial absurdity." And in language eerily resonant of anti–civil rights sentiment in the South, he condemned the Voting Rights Act as an unconstitutional federal encroachment that rendered state power "almost meaningless."[98] Janklow approvingly quoted Justice Black's dissent in *South Carolina v. Katzenbach*,[99] which contended that Section 5 treated covered jurisdictions as "little more than conquered provinces."[100] This was not mere rhetoric, as Janklow advised the secretary of state not to comply with the procedural requirement. "I see no need," he wrote, "to proceed with undue speed to subject our State's laws to a 'one-man veto' by the United States Attorney General."[101] From 1976 to 2002, South Dakota enacted more than six hundred statutes and regulations having an effect on elections on voting in Shannon and Todd Counties but submitted fewer than ten for preclearance by the Attorney General of the United States.[102]

Despite the 1960s vintage of the Voting Rights Act statute, there was little litigation in Indian country generally and South Dakota particularly until the 1980s. Since then, a number of lawsuits have been brought by Indian plaintiffs, challenging various voting and districting practices in Indian country in South Dakota. They include successfully challenging (public) school board representation and voting in Roberts and Marshall Counties on the Sisseton-Wahpeton Indian Reservation, successfully challenging (public) school board voting practices in Ziebach County on the Cheyenne River Sioux Reservation, successfully challenging voter registration practices in Dewey County on the Cheyenne River Sioux Reservation, and successfully asserting the right to vote in elections for a sanitation district in the area of the Enemy Swim Lake and Campbell Slough on the Sisseton-Wahpeton Indian Reservation.[103]

Successful lawsuits were also brought by Indian plaintiffs against the districting of the Wagner School Board on the Yankton Sioux Reservation and the districting scheme in Buffalo County on the Crow Creek Reservation, in which the county divided itself into three districts for electing county commissioners, with the 83 percent Indian population packed in one district and the 17 percent non-Indian population controlling the other two districts.[104] Most recently, there has been a successful challenge to the state legislative redistricting plans on both the Cheyenne River Sioux Reservation and the Rosebud/Pine Ridge Sioux Reservations.[105] This is the new landscape of state citizenship and political participation for Indians.

Yet this is not the worst of it. As the number of Indian citizens registering and seeking to vote has increased in South Dakota, there has been a considerable increase in the claims of Indian voter fraud. In the 2002 reelection bid of Senator Tim Johnson, it was generally conceded that his narrow margin of victory by 524 votes was provided by voters in Indian country. Instead of applauding this increased participation by Indian citizens in the electoral process, there were widespread allegations of fraud by Indians.[106] The claims of fraud were even picked up by national commentators such as Robert Novak and Pat Robertson.[107]

The allegations of fraud were ultimately shown to be untrue, and State Attorney General Mark Barnett and Secretary of State Chris Nelson admitted as much. In fact, the sole criminal case brought by the state against an Indian person for the improper registration of Indian voters was dismissed on the state's *own* motion, when its *own* expert witness divulged he could not detect any fraud in the contested registration forms.[108]

The state legislative response to all this was not to call for an examination of the remaining state and local election laws or to call for a study of the related problems, but rather to pass a law requiring, for the *first* time in the state's history, the possession of photo identification in order to vote.[109] This was not a welcome of Indian citizens to a community of fellow citizens, but rather an insult to the integrity of Indian voters, many of whom lack photo identification.[110]

The state of South Dakota persists in its unfriendly ways. For example, there was additional federal litigation in which Charles Mix County, also the location of the Yankton Sioux Reservation, was found to have failed to redistrict after the 2000 Census in violation of both state and federal law. Its initial redistricting plan also failed to provide Native Americans (28 percent of the county population) with an opportunity to elect a candidate of their choice. A subsequent court-approved redistricting plan in *Blackmoon v. Charles Mix County* (with three county commissioner districts) led to the election of the first ever Native American county commissioner.

Arguably, this would have been seen as a meaningful step forward and a source of local pride. Apparently, it was not. There was an immediate move to expand the three districts to five, thereby diluting the Native American vote. The signatures for this referendum petition were allegedly solicited by the sheriff and his deputies while in uniform. The referendum passed in November 2006.

Because South Dakota is subject to the authority of § 5 of the Voting Rights Act,[111] certain local redistricting plans must be precleared by the U.S. Attorney General. In early 2008, the new redistricting plan was *rejected* because the county did not meet "its burden of showing that the proposed change does not have a discriminatory purpose." The letter from the Attorney General's office also noted that

> Charles Mix County and the State of South Dakota have a history of
> voting discrimination against Native Americans. Native Americans
> could not vote in the County until 1951. Even when Native Americans
> received the right to vote, they were discriminated against in
> registration and other parts of the voting process.[112]

At the edge of the prairie, a regrettable denial of full political rights and progressive history continues.

State and tribal citizenship also reflect an element of asymmetry and misunderstanding because the state and the tribe are separate sovereigns who nevertheless occupy common territory. For example, a tribal member who lives on a reservation is both a reservation and state *resident* and is both a tribal and state *citizen*. A non-Indian who resides on the reservation is also both a reservation and state resident but is only a state citizen and *not* a tribal citizen. This asymmetry often causes jurisdictional confusion as well.

This, too, lest we forget, is the legacy of allotment. Although the Allotment Act[113] was a significant vehicle bringing federal citizenship to Indians, it was also a mighty engine bringing significant numbers of non-Indians as permanent residents to the reservation. Yet the Allotment Act addressed neither the issue of state citizenship for Indians nor tribal jurisdiction over non-Indians. As a result, this tangle of Indians and non-Indians as permanent residents of both Indian country and their respective states has yet to be fully parsed and understood as it pertains to matters of citizenship, voting, and representation. Perhaps this is part of an unfortunate but all too predictable trajectory. The barbs of race and ignorance created resistance, in many instances, to the movement of Indian people to become (state) citizens with the right to vote, along with the right to fair and adequate representation on state (and local) elected bodies. Much of this resistance has slowly been cauterized and largely overcome, but not completely, as the situation in South Dakota amply demonstrates.

In sum, the road to state citizenship and the attendant franchise was not unlike the road to federal citizenship, except that it took longer and was often subject to local qualms over whether Indians satisfied residency requirements and were sufficiently engaged with state and local government issues. These concerns became manifest only upon the exhaustion and final rejection of the more traditional claims relative to the alleged incompatibility of tribal membership with state citizenship and the alleged shortfall on the scale of "civilized" status. Yet the journey to *full* state citizenship is by no means over, as the recent growth of litigation for full and fair representation indicates.

Even in this complex, contemporary milieu, there is still opportunity to pursue the path of education and cooperation rather than the ignorance and antagonisms of the past. In the end, it is necessary to fully understand and comprehend the *tripartite* nature of citizenship for Indian people as federal, state, *and* tribal citizens. Mutual respect, dialogue, and a commitment to problem solving are the necessary guideposts for a meaningful future for all.[114]

7

Indians and the First Amendment

The Illusion of Religious Freedom?

ALTHOUGH THE LANGUAGE OF THE FIRST AMENDMENT[1] IS DESIGNED TO BE universal and to protect *all*, it has often proved problematical in protecting the free exercise religious rights of Native Americans. This has been true from the earliest days of the republic to the contemporary era. Although the rationales have varied, courts (and Congress) have struggled to locate Indian religious practices within (or without) the protection of the Free Exercise Clause. These legislative and judicial struggles have grappled—knowingly and unknowingly—with a theme embedded in the initial "contact" encounter, and that is the theme of "difference." Are Indians and their religious practices so different from the Judeo-Christian mainstream that the First Amendment does not reach them or reaches them only sporadically and inconsistently?

This theme manifests itself within the interrelated questions of whether individual Indians are generally protected by the First Amendment and, if so, whether they are protected in a specific instance involving a specific practice. Although the answer to the first question would seem to obviously be yes, it has not always been so, particularly in the eighteenth and nineteenth centuries. And while no court would deny the applicability of the Free Exercise Clause to Indians, the right often fails to protect Indians in particular circumstances. These varied circumstances include Native American free exercise claims in the context of religious practices on public lands owned by the United States or individual states, the use of peyote, the use of eagle feathers, and incarceration. The results to date have been quite mixed and certainly lack any kind of coherent Indian First Amendment jurisprudence.

There is also the related conceptual issue of whether there are any notable free exercise issues involving Indians (or non-Indians) in the context of potential infringement by *tribal* government restrictions. While the answer to this question might also appear to be found within the same First Amendment jurisprudence mentioned before, the answer is *not* found there. The First Amendment strictures do not apply against the tribes. Tribes predate the Constitution and are not subject to its limitations, although they are subject to the paramount legislative authority of Congress. This is the holding of the classic case of *Talton v. Mayes*.[2]

Given the rationale of *Talton v. Mayes*, tribes are nevertheless subject to the federal *statutory* constraints of the Indian Civil Rights Act of 1968.[3] These statutory protections contain a free exercise guarantee but do *not* contain any establishment prohibition.[4] Tribes may also have their own tribal constitutional guarantees relative to freedom of religion.[5] To date, there is no significant body of *tribal* court jurisprudence on free exercise issues within Indian country.[6]

Early Free Exercise and Establishment Law and Jurisprudence in the Eighteenth and Nineteenth Centuries

If the "promise" of *Johnson v. McIntosh*[7] was to "Christianize" Indians as partial compensation for the loss of fee title to their lands, how was that to take place? Allison Dussias describes this process thusly:

> The federal government provided funding for Christian missionaries' activities and, from 1869 to 1882, used members of Protestant religious groups as government agents on many reservations. With the help of Christian churches, the government also endeavored to suppress Native American religious beliefs and practices: the goal of both church and state was to assimilate the Indians by destroying Indian religion and culture and replacing them with Christianity and "American" culture. From a twentieth-century perspective, these joint efforts to destroy Native American beliefs and practices and replace them with Christianity raise serious constitutional concerns. Yet this entanglement of church and state went largely unquestioned for most of the nineteenth century. For nineteenth-century Native Americans, the free exercise of religion meant freedom to practice the Christian religion. The government was deemed to have the authority to suppress traditional religious practices and establish Christianity among the Indians, the Constitution notwithstanding.[8]

From today's perspective, direct government funding of religious instruction and missionary activities would clearly appear to violate the Constitution's prohibition against the establishment of religion. Yet in the context of Indian affairs, no such objection was made in the eighteenth and nineteenth centuries. In fact, as early as 1776, Congress passed resolutions directing the establishment of missions among certain tribes and funding missionaries.[9]

The federal government's policy in this area became particularly active after the Civil War. Having ended slavery, there was renewed governmental attention to the plight of Indians, particularly in the West. Several government studies revealed extensive poverty and federal government incompetence and corruption in Indian country.[10] In 1869, President Grant inaugurated what became known as the Peace Policy, which was generally committed to a policy of "civilization and ultimate citizenship" for Indians. One key approach to remedy the federal government's incompetence and corrupt administration in Indian country was to turn this function over to religious groups and individuals.[11]

Congressional legislation authorized the president to establish a ten-member Board of Indian Commissioners. A chief responsibility of the board was to reform local Indian agencies by replacing local administrative leadership with individuals from Christian religious groups. Initially, there was a mix of Army officers and Quakers. In 1870, Congress prohibited military appointments, and President Grant reached out to other Christian groups. The job of these individuals was to "convert and educate the Indians at the agencies."[12] The Peace Policy never truly caught hold and faded by 1881.

The Peace Policy was replaced by a federal policy that focused intently on schools; federal schools for Indians were characterized by a distinct and pervasive Christian influence. In 1886, for example, almost a third of the federal schools in Indian country were operated by religious groups funded by Congress.[13] None of this caused a constitutional stir until there was inter-Christian rivalry and hostility. This hostility was largely Protestant hostility directed toward Catholic groups, who by the end of the 1880s were receiving almost two thirds of the federal contract funds.[14]

This conflict was epitomized by Commissioner of Indian Affairs Thomas Morgan's virulent anti-Catholicism in a speech in which he described the Catholic Church "as an alien transplant from the Tiber ... recruiting her ranks by myriads from the slums of Europe."[15] By 1890, this clash led to the end of direct funding of religious schools in Indian country by Congress. Yet the issue of government funding of religious schools for Indians sprang up in another context. Catholics cut out from direct federal funding began to seek funding from tribal trust and treaty funds that were held by the federal government for the benefit of Indian tribes. In 1904, President Theodore Roosevelt approved granting such contracts as long as the affected Indians consented.[16]

The Protestants, especially those in the influential Indian Rights Association, were outraged and eventually provided legal counsel to several members of the Rosebud Sioux Tribe to challenge this practice. The resulting case reached the Supreme Court in 1908. The essential claim of the plaintiffs in *Quick Bear v. Leupp*[17] was that government funding of sectarian religious schools violated the Establishment Clause of the First Amendment, as well as several federal statutes that expressly forbade that practice.[18] The Court turned aside those claims by converting the case from an Establishment Clause case against the federal government into a free exercise case protecting the free exercise rights of Indians:

> [I]t seems inconceivable that Congress should have intended to prohibit them from receiving religious education at their own cost if they so desired it; such an intent would be one "to prohibit the free exercise of religion" amongst the Indians, and such would be the effect of the construction for which the complainants contend.[19]

As late as 1909, Congress granted (tribal) land on the Rosebud Sioux Reservation to the Bureau of Catholic Missions for the provision of religious and educational activities to members of the Rosebud Sioux Tribe.[20] All of this took place in the context of the "right" to government-funded *Christian* education. All this federal government activity occurred outside the pale of traditional Indian education and religious practices, but that was soon to change.

Government Discrimination against Traditional Indian Religious Practices

If the thrust of federally funded education for Native Americans was to *advance Christian*-based education and conversion, there soon developed a complementary federal move to *suppress traditional* Native American religious expression, especially in the context of tribal dances and ceremonies. This was *Johnson v. McIntosh*'s commitment to "civilize" Indians in recompense for the "uncompensated" taking of title to their land. Such sentiments were expressed at the highest levels of the federal government. For example, Secretary of the Interior Henry Teller stated in 1883: "If it is the purpose of the Government to civilize the Indians, they must be compelled to desist from the savage and barbarous practices that are calculated to continue them in savagery, no matter what exterior influences are brought to bear on them."[21]

These perverse sentiments were converted into practice, if not law, in Indian country without the benefit of congressional legislation. In 1883, the secretary of the interior established courts on most reservations with express authority to prosecute Indians for engaging in tribal dances and other traditional religious activities. The "rules" for these courts, known as Courts of Indian Offenses, defined participation in the Sun Dance, Scalp Dance, and War Dance as criminal offenses. Other offenses prohibited the practices of medicine men and the distribution of property that accompanied ceremonial dances.[22] Responsibility for establishing such courts and appointing Indian judges to staff them was delegated by the secretary of the interior to the local BIA agent in charge of the reservation. These courts were not authorized by any congressional enactment.

Although this policy caused considerable harm to many Native American individuals, it was not particularly successful because of substantial Indian resistance on many reservations and the unwillingness of many Indian judges to interfere with the religious practices of friends and neighbors. Yet as late as 1921, the commissioner of Indian affairs remained adamant in his commitment to the suppression of Native American religious rights:

> The sun-dance, and all other similar dances and so-called religious
> ceremonies are considered "Indian Offences" [sic] under existing
> regulations, and corrective penalties are provided. I regard such
> restrictions as applicable to any [religious] dance which
> involves...the reckless giving away of property...frequent or
> prolonged periods of celebration...in fact any disorderly or plainly
> excessive performance that promotes superstitious cruelty,
> licentiousness, idleness, danger to health, and shiftless indifference
> to family welfare.[23]

The concerns of the commissioner ran wide and deep and reflected a significant "civilizing" program that contained substantial components of fear, misunderstanding, and ignorance. Government officials, odd as it may seem from a contemporary perspective, seldom saw the religious or sacred components of the dances but rather only the "secularized" components relevant to the "reckless" giving away of personal property and the militant celebration of tradition. They also saw such practices as a means of avoiding work and as a rebuff to conversion efforts. There was little success in such government efforts, but even where there was, it tended to create Indians who were dispirited and without energy for the assimilative program of self-empowerment.[24] Government officials, for the most part, saw no free exercise issue. Free exercise meant free exercise of *Christian* religion. The First Amendment stopped at the Cross.

Two examples are illustrative. In the late 1880s, many Lakota people in South Dakota took up the Ghost Dance religion, which held that an Indian messiah was soon to appear who would deliver Indian people from their dire straits. Core teachings of the Ghost Dance religion were: "You must not hurt anybody or do harm to anyone. You must not fight. Do right always."[25] An essential element of the Ghost Dance religion was a dance in which participants wore white garments known as "ghost shirts," painted with stars, the moon, and the sun, which were believed to make them immune to bullets.[26]

As the Ghost Dance spread throughout the Dakotas, it was largely perceived as militant and troublesome rather than religious (with strong Christian overtones).[27] The U.S. Army was called out. Sitting Bull, a leading Lakota chief and adherent of the Ghost Dance religion, was killed in the course of an attempt to arrest him on the Standing Rock Reservation. His followers fled and joined Big Foot and his band of Sioux, fleeing to the Pine Ridge Reservation.

At Wounded Knee, a massacre ensued when the Army used two Hotchkiss artillery guns to open fire on the Sioux after an insufficient surrender of weapons by the encamped Sioux families. Three hundred unarmed individuals, including many women and children, were slain.[28] The free exercise of religion did not include the right to Ghost Dance, much less protection against federal government violence.

Although the Ghost Dance soon disappeared from the scene in a thicket of violence and failed messianic hopes, religious persecution of the Sioux and other Plains Indians did not. "The 1904 regulations of the Court of Indian Offenses provided that the sun dance 'and all other similar dances and so-called religious ceremonies' were 'Indian offenses,' participation in which was punishable by the withholding of rations or incarceration."[29]

If the Ghost Dance was met with inexcusable and deadly violence, the Pueblo dances of the southwest Pueblo Indians were met with the most blatant forms of cultural racism. The moving force in this crusade came from the Indian Rights Association, a "pro-Indian" Christian missionary group, who "knew" what was best for Indians—and that did not include ceremonial dancing. The pressure exerted by the Indian Rights Association resulted in 1921 in the issuance of Circular No. 1665 on Indian dancing by Commissioner of Indian Affairs Charles Burke.[30] The circular rested in part on a collection of statements and descriptions concerning the alleged lurid aspects of many of those dances. This collection was known as the "Secret Dance Files."[31] None of these reports was independently corroborated or submitted to experts or impartial observers for confirmation of their accuracy.[32]

The object of Circular No. 1665 was not to engage in religious discrimination per se but rather to halt or severely limit practices that interfered with the Christianizing and assimilative missions of the federal government and Christian missionaries. The concerns included that such dancing ceremonies took valuable time away from work in the fields, often resulted in the reckless giving away of property, were generally immoral because they involved excess, and were not Christian.[33]

The single word that most permeates these various government and field reports is *superstition*. But that, too, carries its own irony, when at least from today's vantage, the real superstition was *not* the Indians in their dances, but the non-Indians' own "superstition" about the religious practices of others. Non-Indians could not see any practice as religious unless it was Christian. Christianity and religion were synonymous and identical. There was no religious expression outside Christianity. This view was at once impoverished, self-laudatory, and extremely parochial. Government practices that enforced these views were presumably unconstitutional as well, but no court ever pronounced them as such.

Yet these extreme views and practices also finally began to give way. By the time of the 1934 Indian Reorganization Act, Commissioner of Indian Affairs John Collier, a progressive, issued orders that supported Indian religious liberty and curtailed missionary activities in Indian schools.[34] Although such actions were an important (and long overdue) step forward, they did not by any means usher in an era of newfound respect and vindication of Native American free exercise claims. The struggle continued, but the new landscapes of encounter were different. These landscapes include sacred sites in the public domain, the use of peyote, the possession of eagle feathers, and the religious rights of Native Americans in prison.

Sacred Sites

Many Native Americans do not consider themselves as people of the book (i.e., Bible) but rather as people of the land, whose central religious rituals and practices take place at particular sacred places. Oftentimes, these sacred places are located in the public domain and are owned by the federal (or state) government. This has given rise to significant First Amendment concerns and litigation by Native Americans in light of the government's oft-made claim that it has the right to use public land for legitimate government purposes, even if this infringes on the right of Native Americans to freely practice and exercise their religious rights.

In the context of government regulation and ownership of public lands, these Native American First Amendment claims have been almost uniformly unsuccessful. Several circuit court decisions in the 1980s set a rather high bar for Native American plaintiffs to satisfy. In *Sequoyah v. Tennessee Valley Authority*,[35] the Sixth Circuit decided against the attempt by Cherokee Indians to block the flooding by the Tellico Dam because the flooding of their "sacred homeland" would violate their free exercise rights. In accordance with the recognized First Amendment jurisprudence of the time, the circuit court decided that the Cherokee plaintiffs did not adequately demonstrate that the land in question was of religious "centrality or indispensability" to the "religious ceremonies and practices" of the plaintiffs.[36] The plaintiffs did not meet their burden in demonstrating that the "particular geographic location in question is inseparable from the way of life, the cornerstone of their religious observance, or plays the central role in their religious ceremonies and practices."[37]

In *Badoni v. Higginson*,[38] the Tenth Circuit ruled against the Navajo attempt to limit the federal government's authority to regulate the water level of the Lake Powell Reservoir because it encroached on free exercise rights at the Rainbow Bridge National Monument, a sandstone arch 309 feet high with a span of 278 feet. The Navajos also claimed that by encouraging tourism, federal officials had "permitted desecration" and denied Navajos the right to conduct ceremonies there.[39]

In this case, the Tenth Circuit acknowledged that the particular Navajo beliefs and practices at issue were central and indispensable religious beliefs and practices and that the government's activities at Lake Powell did create a burden on their beliefs and practices. Nevertheless, the court ruled against the Navajo claimants by finding in the context of the applicable standard of strict scrutiny that the federal government had a "compelling state interest" in maintaining the water levels of Lake Powell to provide water for Western states.[40]

The court also rejected the claim that government-facilitated increased access by tourists would infringe on the free exercise rights of the plaintiffs. The court noted that any government regulation of tourist access to the Rainbow Bridge National Monument would raise serious Establishment Clause issues relative to the government's "favoring" one religion at the expense of others.[41]

Although these lower court cases all found against the Native American plaintiffs, the judicial test that was applied appeared remarkably straightforward and identical to the First Amendment free exercise test used in other free exercise claims cases involving other religions, such as the Amish and Seventh-Day Adventists.[42] In these cases, the Court required the plaintiffs to show that the religious practices at issue were central to the plaintiff's religious beliefs and practices and that the government's actions significantly impaired that practice. If this was satisfied, the burden of proof would shift to the government—in accordance with strict scrutiny analysis applicable to constitutional claims involving fundamental rights—to show that there was a compelling state interest that superseded the limitation on free exercise rights. Although such a test—like any judicial test—left much room for interpretation, the basic analytical framework for the application of the test was clear.

In the *Sequoyah, Bandoni,* and *Block* cases, there was also a major practical problem. In all these cases, the plaintiffs were seeking to halt or slow down massive federal projects that involved expenditures of tens of millions of dollars, and the various circuit courts showed little interest in halting such long-standing projects and improvements involving substantial federal expenditures. This political reality complicated, perhaps doomed, the purely legal analysis.

When the first (and only) sacred site case reached the Supreme Court in 1988, the Court substantially revised (even overturned) previous First Amendment jurisprudence in this area and delivered a near-fatal blow to *any* Native American free exercise claim involving lands in the public domain. In *Lyng v. Northwest Indian Cemetery Protective Association,*[43] a number of Native Americans and several environmental groups sought to stop the building of a road running through the Six Rivers National Forest, which adjoins the Hoopa Valley Indian Reservation in California. Of particular concern to the Native American plaintiffs was that the proposed road would go through the Chimney Rock area, which was used for religious purposes by Yurok, Karok, and Tolowa Indians.[44]

This was part of a project to create a paved seventy-five-mile road linking two California towns, Gasquet and Orleans. In total, the U.S. Forest Service upgraded forty-nine miles of previously unpaved roads on federal land. To complete this project (the G-O road), the Forest Service planned on building a six-mile paved segment through the Chimney Rock section of the Six Rivers National Forest.[45]

As part of its draft environmental impact statement, the Forest Service commissioned a study of American Indian cultural and religious sites in the area. The study, which was completed in 1979, found the area to be an "integral and indispensable" part of Indian religious conceptualization and practice. In addition, it found that the construction of the road "would cause serious and irreparable harm to the sacred areas which are an integral and necessary part of the belief systems and lifeway of Northwest California Indian Peoples."[46] The report ultimately recommended that the G-O road not be completed.

Three years later, the Forest Service rejected this conclusion and decided to complete the G-O road. It did make minor changes in its original plan in order to avoid some archaeological sites, and it slightly increased the distance of the proposed road from portions of the Chimney Rock area, but it also adopted a management plan to allow harvesting significant amounts of timber in this area of the forest.[47]

Both the district court and the Ninth Circuit Court of Appeals granted permanent injunctive relief that prohibited completion of the G-O road or putting the timber-harvest management plan into effect. Both courts applied what they believed to be the applicable free exercise analysis involving the centrality of the plaintiffs' practice to their religious beliefs, the significant adverse effects on such practices by the government's plan, and the absence of a compelling state interest to overcome the adverse impact on plaintiffs' free exercise rights.[48]

In a six-to-three vote, the Supreme Court reversed the lower courts' decisions and found no violation of the plaintiffs' free exercise rights under the First Amendment.[49] The most startling element in the Court's opinion, authored by Justice O'Connor, was its analytical framework, which significantly departed from the approach of the lower courts and even its own previous jurisprudence. The Court announced that what was key in its (new) analysis was not related in any manner to the degree of governmental interference with plaintiffs' free exercise but only whether the government's action was coercive or imposed a penalty on the plaintiffs. Justice O'Connor wrote:

> [T]he challenged government action would interfere significantly
> with private persons' ability to pursue spiritual fulfillment
> according to their own religious beliefs. In neither case, however,
> would the affected individual be *coerced* by the Government's action
> into violating their religious beliefs; nor would either governmental
> action *penalize* religious activity by denying any person an equal
> share of the rights, benefits, and privileges enjoyed by other
> citizens.[50]

The Court nevertheless admitted that government projects "could have devastating effects on traditional Indian religious practices"[51] in the Chimney Rock area. Yet somewhat incongruously, the Court noted that such results constituted mere "incidental effects"[52] of legitimate government programs and hence were not prohibited under the First Amendment. Justice O'Connor's opinion appeared to want to hold its ground on the slippery slope to save the government from being rendered inoperable "if it were required to satisfy every citizen's religious needs and desires."[53] This was, apparently, especially grating to Justice O'Connor in this instance: "Whatever rights the Indians may have to the use of the area, however, those rights do not divest the Government of its right to use what is, after all, *its* land."[54]

Justice O'Connor did not believe that the government should be grossly insensitive to such Native American concerns and should be reasonably accommodating whenever possible. In this case, the limited Forest Service accommodation was adequate, especially because doing more would result in "leaving the two existing segments of road to dead-end in the middle of a National Forest."[55] In the end, the majority's opinion drove Native American religion even further to the margins of American society, even beyond the First Amendment itself, reducing it to a minor irritant that had to give way before all governmental "progress" that transpired in the public domain.

Justice Brennan wrote a blistering dissent, not so much in the form of a jeremiad, but more in the form of a lament. He began with a discussion of the differences between Native American religion and "traditional western religions." Native American religion is pervasive and does *not* easily recognize the sacred-secular distinction. It is "inextricably" bound to the use of the land, where rituals must be performed in prescribed locations to protect humankind from discord and other catastrophes. Failure to conduct these ceremonies in the manner and place specified, adherents believe, will result in great harm to the earth and to the people whose welfare depends on it.[56]

Western religions are different. They do not center on the land, but rather focus on sacred texts such as the Bible, which are the source of governing dogma and creed. They also tend to be hierarchical, with a clear distinction between the sacred and secular. In essence, their adherents are people of the book rather than people of the land.[57] Justice Brennan contended that the majority does not really grasp these distinctions, and as a result, they are insensitive to what is at stake for the plaintiffs. The majority lacks any sense of empathy with the plight of these Native Americans and therefore is indifferent to the resulting harm.[58]

Justice Brennan's dissent then proceeded to link this insensitivity to the majority opinion's avoidance of the essential constitutional issue:

> [T]he Court argues that the First Amendment bars only outright prohibitions, indirect coercion, and penalties on the free exercise of religion. All other "incidental effects of government programs," it concludes, even those "which may make it more difficult to practice certain religions but which have no tendency to coerce individuals into acting contrary to their religious beliefs," simply do not give rise to constitutional concerns.[59]

This was inconsistent, according to the dissent, with:

> our recognition nearly half a century ago that *restraints* on religious
> conduct implicate the concerns of the Free Exercise Clause, see
> *Prince v. Massachusetts*, 321 U.S. 158 (1944), we have never suggested
> that the protections of the guarantee are limited to so narrow a range
> of governmental burdens. The land-use decision challenged here will
> restrain respondents from practicing their religion as surely and as
> completely as any of the governmental actions we have struck down
> in the past, and the Court's efforts simply to define away
> respondents' injury as nonconstitutional are both unjustified and
> ultimately unpersuasive.[60]

The majority's opinion exalted form over substance. It constricted free exercise protection with its coercion-penalty formulation, even while acknowledging that its effect would be devastating to the Native Americans' ability to practice their religion in the "high country" area within the Blue Creek Unit of the Six Rivers National Forest. Justice Brennan found such a result "cruelly surreal" with its bizarre logic that "governmental action that will virtually destroy a religion is nevertheless deemed not to 'burden' that religion."[61]

Justice Brennan's dissent located the refusal of the majority to even recognize the constitutional dimension of the Native Americans' claim because of its concern for government property rights. The core of this exclusionary analysis "stems from its concern that acceptance of respondents' claim could potentially strip the government of its ability to manage and use vast tracts of federal property."[62] Native American free exercise rights were uncoupled from the Constitution because they (potentially) intrude on nonconstitutional property rights of the government.

There is also the attendant slippery slope concern that the nature of such site-specific religious practices "raises the specter of future suits in which Native Americans seek to exclude all human activity from such areas."[63] Justice Brennan did not dismiss these concerns as illegitimate but rather argued that this "stress point"[64] must be resolved within, rather than blindly dismissed as outside, the constitutional balancing involved in free exercise jurisprudence.

To be sure, such cases may be far from easy to resolve, but to place them *outside* the Constitution is institutionally indefensible and an abdication of constitutional responsibility.[65] Justice Brennan concluded his dissent with the painful observation that the majority's ruling that the constitutional right of the free exercise of religion for Native Americans in this case "amounts to nothing more than the right to believe that their religion will be destroyed."[66]

The dissent reiterated what Justice Brennan regarded as the appropriate strict scrutiny constitutional analysis involving a fundamental right:

> [A]dherents challenging a proposed use of federal land should be required to show that the decision poses a substantial and realistic threat of frustrating their religious practices. Once such a showing is made, the burden should shift to the Government to come forward with a compelling state interest sufficient to justify the infringement of those practices.[67]

The "sensitivity" to Native American free exercise claims called for by the majority and reflected in federal statutes such as the American Indian Religious Freedom Act[68] are not to be negated. Yet they must not be confused with, or substituted for, appropriate *constitutional* analysis, which the *Lyng* majority jettisoned as no longer required. The bald holding of *Lyng* should give pause both constitutionally and ethically. What is most sacred to these Native Americans—a sacred site located on federal land—does *not* rise to a level sufficient to even *invoke* the First Amendment. For these First Americans, the First Amendment must seem hollow indeed.

Although direct attempts by Native Americans and their supporters, in such groups as the American Indian Religious Freedom Coalition, failed in their attempts to have Congress overturn the result in *Lyng*, there was some limited and progressive reform. This included, for example, obtaining a designation of the high country area in *Lyng* for permanent wilderness protection under the Smith River National Recreation Area Act,[69] which effectively closed future development in the area. In addition, Congress amended the National Historic Preservation Act of 1966[70] to include "properties of traditional religious and cultural importance to an Indian tribe" for protection. President Clinton also issued Executive Order 13,007,[71] titled "Indian Sacred Sites," which requires federal agencies to "accommodate access to and ceremonial use of Indian sacred sites by Indian religious practitioners" on federal land.

If such sacred site Native American free exercise claims ever reconnect with the First Amendment, there are likely to be additional conceptual challenges, the principal one being how far federal "sensitivity" and accommodation may go before it trenches the other religious clause in the First Amendment, namely, the Establishment Clause. A good example of navigating these pitfalls may be found in the Devils Tower climbing controversy in Wyoming.

Devils Tower[72] is a national monument established in 1906. It is a sacred site to a number of tribes, including the Lakota and Northern Cheyenne, and it is located within the aboriginal homelands of these tribes—but it is *not* within the borders of any current Indian reservation. It is also a premier rock-climbing destination for many non-Indians and a site for related commercial activities.

In 1995, the National Park Service—in accord with the recent policy directives for consultations with Indian groups—adopted a policy that banned rock climbing during the month of June, the time of greatest Native American ceremonial use. This action was challenged by a group of rock climbers as contrary to the Establishment Clause. The National Park Service's policy was struck down as violating the Establishment Clause because it "favored" one (Indian) religion over all other religions.[73]

The National Park Service revised its policy and announced a request that climbers "voluntarily" choose not to engage in rock climbing during the month of June. This policy was also challenged by the climbers on Establishment Clause grounds, but this time the challenge was struck down and the policy upheld as permissible accommodation in accord with federal congressional and executive policy.[74] Many have praised this result stemming from the cooperation of various federal agencies and Native American groups and tribes for its pragmatic effectiveness:

> The courts and Congress have left sacred sites protection in the
> hands of land management agencies, and although many feared this
> decision would be disastrous, land agencies have actually embraced
> their role and sought to accommodate Indian religions and protect
> their sacred sites. Furthermore, agency accommodation is actually
> better for society as a whole than the broader judicial and legislative
> protections typically advocated by sacred sites supporters. Agency
> accommodation avoids the disadvantages of broad categorical
> protection while still serving as a strong method for preserving
> sacred sites. Although land agencies have had the role of sacred sites
> protectors thrust upon them, they seem to have turned out to be
> ideally suited for the job.[75]

Such praise is no doubt justified, yet it begs an essential question. Why does such religious protection not emanate from the Constitution itself, but rather only from executive branch discretion and agency good will? Such executive branch discretion and good will that are not constitutionally required are, of course, not a guarantee or right. Discretion and good will are subject to revocation or change at any time. Such a secondhand protection for those who were here first hardly accords the constitutional dignity and respect normally associated with the First Amendment.

The Use of Peyote

If the *Lyng* case placed Native American free exercise claims on federal land *outside* the purview of the Constitution, the *Smith*[76] case eschewed the conventional compelling state interest analysis altogether and, with a constitutional sleight of hand, fashioned a new "test." This new test erected a standard that did *not* protect the use of peyote by members of the Native American Church. The purported universality of the First Amendment to protect the free expression rights of *all* Americans failed again to vindicate a Native American claim.

Although the *Smith* case was the first case involving Native American use of peyote to reach the Supreme Court, earlier cases, both state and federal, applied the strict scrutiny and compelling state interest test, with results generally favorable to Native Americans. The premier case in this regard is *People v. Woody*.[77] In this case, the California Supreme Court reversed the conviction of a Native American member of the Native American Church for possession of peyote, a controlled substance under California state law. The court found no compelling state interest—criminal or moral—sufficient to infringe on the Native American free exercise claim. The court rejected the state's assertion of a compelling interest to protect Native Americans "from the superstitious 'shackles' of their 'unenlightened' and 'primitive condition.'"[78]

The California Supreme Court also noted the "sacramental equivalent" of peyote to wine in Christian eucharistic services and the fact that "[i]t is the sole means by which defendants are able to experience their religion; without peyote defendants cannot practice their faith."[79] The court found not only constitutional protection but also a richness and worth to be celebrated and preserved:

On the other hand, the right to free religious expression embodies a precious heritage of our history. In a mass society, which presses at every point toward conformity, the protection of a self-expression, however unique, of the individual and the group becomes ever more important. The varying currents of the subcultures that flow into the mainstream of our national life give it depth and beauty. We preserve a greater value than an ancient tradition when we protect the rights of the Indians who honestly practiced an old religion in using peyote one night at a meeting in a desert hogan near Needles, California.[80]

The *Smith* majority, with Justice Scalia writing, went completely in the opposite direction as to the matter of constitutional interpretation, as well as turning from the California Supreme Court's perception of "depth and beauty" to its concern about "courting anarchy."[81] Appreciation had turned into fear. This fear of anarchy appeared to require a revisiting and a significant revision of the compelling state interest test analysis.

The Court could not avoid the compelling state interest test as it did in the *Lyng* case. Alfred Smith and Galen Black, the two respondents in this case, had been *penalized* for their use of peyote as members of the Native American Church. Both had been fired from their jobs as counselors with a private drug rehabilitation organization and were denied state unemployment benefits because they were terminated for "work-related 'misconduct.'"[82] The fact that Smith and Black were penalized for practicing their religion definitely invoked free exercise analysis.

The Court, however, turned a new jurisprudential page. According to this new view, the compelling state interest test, heretofore regarded as the universal black letter test in free exercise cases, was not so universal in its application. The Court announced that it was confined to the unemployment insurance cases that conditioned the availability of benefits upon an applicant's willingness to work under conditions forbidden by his religion and whose application for benefits was subject to *individual* review. This observation was particularly ironic in light of the fact that *Smith* itself was an unemployment insurance case.[83] The Court further noted that previous compelling state interest analysis in the context of a "neutral, generally applicable law" was limited to "hybrid situations" in which additional constitutional protections such as free speech or parental (liberty) rights were involved.[84]

The Court, having successfully isolated the respondents' claim from the compelling state interest analysis, noted that no free exercise claim could "protect" the respondents from a state criminal law of general applicability.[85] To do so, according to Justice Scalia, would create an intolerable burden on the majority to excuse any religiously motivated unwillingness to obey ordinary laws of general applicability. Even for Justice Scalia, however, such a blunt result required some explanation. He wrote that while the "exception" the respondents sought was not "constitutionally required," it may be adopted by any state as a "nondiscriminatory religious-practice exemption."[86] Yet, he also noted the oddity of directing a religious minority away from the courts, usually the branch of government most associated with protecting minority rights, to the legislative branch most often noted for protecting the interests of the majority.[87]

The concurrence of Justice O'Connor and the dissent of Justice Blackmun are interesting in quite contrasting ways. Both opinions contended that the appropriate free exercise analysis was the compelling state interest test, but Justice O'Connor believed the test to be satisfied, and Justice Blackmun reached the opposite conclusion. Their competing views and methodologies are instructive. Justice O'Connor took the large or macro view that there was a compelling state interest within the national policy of the "war on drugs" and Oregon's decision to ban peyote as a controlled substance.[88]

Justice Blackmun reached the opposite conclusion. He applied a more micro analysis about the actual effects of peyote use on members of the Native American Church. This analysis yielded findings that use of peyote by members of the Native American Church actually helped them lead good lives and be productive citizens within the church's ethical framework. Not only does the church's doctrine forbid nonreligious use of peyote but also it advocates self-reliance, family responsibility, and abstinence from alcohol. The Native American Church's "ethical code" has four parts: brotherly love, care of family, self-reliance, and avoidance of alcohol.[89]

Justice Blackmun found that the use of peyote by members of the Native American Church did not promote "lawless and irresponsible use of drugs" but rather "exemplifies values that Oregon's drug laws are presumably intended to foster."[90] The dissent also noted that the use of peyote by members of the Native American Church seemed

> closely analogous to the sacramental use of wine by the Roman Catholic Church. During prohibition, the Federal Government exempted such use of wine from its general law on possession and use of alcohol. See National Prohibition Act, Title II, § 3, 41 Stat. 308. However compelling the Government's then general interest in prohibiting the use of alcohol may have been, it could not plausibly have asserted an interest sufficiently compelling to outweigh Catholics' right to take communion.[91]

As with the Lyng case, there was substantial adverse public reaction by both Indian and non-Indian religious groups across the country. There was also substantial scholarly criticism.[92] Congress reacted to Smith by enacting the Religious Freedom Restoration Act of 1993 (RFRA).[93] In signing RFRA into law, President Clinton commented that "this Act reverses the Supreme Court's decision in Employment Division v. Smith and reestablishes a standard that better protects all Americans of all faiths in the exercise of their religion."[94]

Yet this attempt to reestablish the "compelling state interest" in free exercise cases was also struck down by the Supreme Court. In City of Boerne v. Flores,[95] the Court set aside RFRA's applicability to the states because it impermissibly enlarged individuals' substantive rights under the Fourteenth

Amendment, which is traditionally limited to remediating violations of existing protections.[96]

Although RFRA does not apply to the states because of *City of Boerne*, it does apply to the federal government because of the Court's decision in *Gonzales v. O Centro Espirita Beneficente Uniao Do Vegetal*.[97] O Centro Espirita Beneficente Uniao Do Vegetal (UDV) is a Brazilian-based Christian Spiritualist sect with an American branch of approximately 130 members.[98] Receiving communion through *hoasca* is central to UDV's faith.[99] Hoasca is a sacramental tea made from two plants unique to the Amazon region. One of the plants contains a hallucinogen that is listed in Schedule I of the federal Controlled Substances Act.[100] In 1999, U.S. Customs inspectors intercepted a shipment of three drums of hoasca to the American UDV.[101] The UDV filed suit against the attorney general, alleging, among other things, that applying the Controlled Substances Act to the UDV's sacramental use of hoasca violated RFRA.[102] The result was a unanimous opinion authored by Chief Justice Roberts that upheld the applicability of RFRA against the federal government.

In analyzing the UDV's claim, the Court recognized that an exemption exists for use of peyote, a Schedule I substance, by members of federally recognized tribes. The Court reasoned that there is little, if any, difference between Native American use of peyote and UDV use of hoasca.[103] Furthermore, RFRA allows courts to recognize exceptions to the Controlled Substances Act. For the government to prevail under RFRA, it has to satisfy the strict scrutiny test.[104] The Court found that the government failed to carry its burden by simply invoking the general interests behind enforcing the prohibition of a Schedule I substance.[105]

The *O Centro* opinion is likely to be troubling to the general public because it seems to create different First Amendment standards, depending on whether the prosecution is by the federal government or the state. If a local police department had intercepted the hoasca shipment as a violation of a *state* criminal law of general applicability, the result would be quite different. The test from *Smith* would apply, and the free exercise claim would not prevail. Instead, U.S. Customs inspectors intercepted the shipment, so the UDV was able to bring a successful free exercise claim under RFRA's more exacting strict scrutiny standard.

Such differing standards in the context of the First Amendment are nevertheless justified under principles of federalism. The rule of *O Centro* recognizes a constitutional *floor* that is binding on both the federal and state governments. Although neither sovereign can go below the floor, each sovereign may elevate the ceiling of protection by enacting laws to that effect. RFRA failed to raise the ceiling for states[106] but did raise it for the federal government.

Like *Lyng*, the Supreme Court failed in the *Smith* case to uphold a Native American free exercise claim. The vaunted protection of the free exercise of religion clause in the First Amendment again proved wholly illusory for Native Americans. Only the actions of the public and Congress (partially) mitigated the harshness of Justice Scalia's cold and convoluted jurisprudence. Congress subsequently enacted legislation to extend the federal exception for the use of peyote by members of the Native American church to all states.[107] Regardless of this statutory change, *Smith* reflects a jurisprudence in which the protections of the Free Exercise Clause do *not* reach those who were here first, and it is a most unworthy testament to the alleged universality of the constitutional free exercise of religion protection we like so much to celebrate.

Eagle Feathers

If the sense of sacred place and the sacramental use of peyote are two of the hallmarks of much Native American religion, the third is surely the possession and use of eagle feathers for religious purposes. The Native American possession and use of eagle feathers for religious purposes has also engendered much litigation, but no case has yet been decided by the Supreme Court on this issue. Given the result in the *Lyng* and *Smith* cases, this is probably a good thing.

The nub of the eagle feather cases is usually whether general (criminal) statutes such as the Bald Eagle Protection Act[108] and the Endangered Species Act[109] that ban the acquisition, possession, or sale of any part of bald eagles and golden eagles preclude any religious exception for Native Americans.[110] The statutes themselves do not grant any *express* exemptions, though there is a permit system in effect to allow the taking of eagles by members of federally recognized tribes for Native American religious purposes.[111] The eagle feather cases are often complicated by the claim that the right to take eagles is also a protected treaty right. No treaty makes any express reference to the taking of eagles, but this right is subsumed under a broader treaty authority to hunt and fish on the reservation.

The leading lower court cases include *United States v. Top Sky*,[112] *United States v. Thirty Eight (38) Golden Eagles or Eagle Parts*,[113] *United States v. Hardman*,[114] and *United States v. Antoine*.[115] In *Top Sky*, the defendant Native American's conviction for violation of the Bald Eagle Act was affirmed. The defendant had no standing to raise a free exercise claim in that his sale of eagle parts to non-Indians was strictly commercial in nature.[116] In the *Thirty Eight Golden Eagles* case, the federal government's forfeiture action against the Native American defendant

was upheld upon a finding that his free exercise claim must yield to the compelling government interest of conservation of golden eagles, especially in light of
the fact that the defendant, a member of the Red Lake Band of Chippewa, never
applied for a permit.[117]

In the more recent *Hardman* case, the Tenth Circuit found that pursuant
to the Religious Freedom Restoration Act, the federal government's seizure of
eagle feathers from a Chiricahua Apache, whose tribe was terminated in the
nineteenth century, did violate the Free Exercise Clause.[118] The Tenth Circuit
has recently determined the permit process to be an appropriate "least restrictive alternative."[119] An opposite result was obtained in the Ninth Circuit case of
United States v. Antoine,[120] which involved a Canadian Indian who was not eligible for a federal permit.

One case involving the taking of eagles, which was based solely on a treaty
rights claim and not a free exercise claim, has been decided by the Supreme
Court. This is the case of *United States v. Dion*.[121] In *Dion*, the Court held that
while the Treaty of 1858 with the Yankton Sioux Tribe did contain a general
treaty right to hunt, the treaty was partially abrogated by amendments to the
Eagle Protection Act in 1962.[122]

The focus in *Dion* was not on any free exercise claim but rather on treaty
abrogation and, more specifically, deciding the appropriate standard for the
congressional abrogation of treaty rights. After a review of the Court's past
inconsistent statements and approaches to treaty abrogation, the Court adopted
the following standard:

> What is essential is clear evidence that Congress actually considered
> the conflict between its intended action on one hand and Indian
> treaty rights on the other, and chose to resolve that conflict by
> abrogating the treaty.[123]

The Court found the standard satisfied and upheld Dion's conviction.

Although the possession and use of eagle feathers by Native Americans for
religious purposes remains unresolved by the Supreme Court, the eagle feather
cases (and, to a lesser extent, some lower court peyote cases) raise some additional provocative questions. Kevin Worthen has identified these questions as
whether eagle feather exemptions available to Native Americans can be denied
to non-Indians simply because they are non-Indian and whether the Native
American exemptions can be limited to Native Americans who are members of
federally recognized tribes.[124]

These questions most often come up in the context of the 1962 amendments to the Eagle Protection Act and the regulations governing the permit
process. The 1962 amendments authorized the secretary of the interior to issue

permits allowing the taking, possession, or use of golden and bald eagles and their feathers "for the religious purposes of Indian tribes."[125] The attendant regulations promulgated by the U.S. Fish and Wildlife Services provide that such permits will be issued only to members of federally recognized tribes who are participating in "bona fide tribal religious ceremonies."[126] It is this set of regulations that sets up the questions raised by Worthen.

These problems have not been directly addressed by any of the cases except to note, for example, that the permit system is a legitimate "least restrictive alternative" to meet the twin goals of species conservation and protecting Native American cultures and religions from "extinction."[127] Such an observation, while quite accurate, completely skirts the more difficult questions of the permit system advancing the rights of Native Americans who are members of federally recognized tribes and (potentially) limiting the free exercise rights of other Native Americans who are *not* members of federally recognized tribes, as well as limiting the free exercise rights of non-Indians who are adherents of Native American religions that involve the use of eagle feathers. Such potential results appear contrary to basic notions of equality and equal protection, especially in the context of free exercise claims.

Worthen suggested a way to negotiate this dilemma by proposing an interlocking set of four reasons to justify any apparent inequality and differential treatment: (1) Native American religions were created and exist only here within the United States, (2) these beliefs are often unique and all-encompassing without any sacred-secular distinction, (3) these beliefs often revolve around sacred sites that are found only within the United States, and (4) Native Americans have suffered systematic land dispossession within the United States.[128] Worthen placed particular emphasis on the fourth reason as providing the "extra weight needed to tip the equity scales" in favor of such differential treatment for *some* Native Americans.[129]

Such differential treatment cannot be justified on some free-floating, feel-good grounds relative to Native Americans, but rather as a specific means employed "in remedying the ongoing effects of past or present racial discrimination," where the past discrimination is identified with sufficient particularity[130] and there is a strong basis for concluding that remedial action is still necessary.[131] Although such an analysis is more than constitutionally plausible, the pall of *Lyng* and *Smith* do not inspire much confidence, should such a case and argument reach the bar of the U.S. Supreme Court. This is especially true when the "preference" expressly limits non-Indian and nonenrolled Indian access to *scarce* religious resources such as eagle feathers.[132]

Currently, the circuit courts are divided on whether non-Indians should be allowed to possess eagle feathers. The Eleventh Circuit rejected the claim of a non-Indian in *Gibson v. Babbitt*.[133] The court recognized that the non-Indian's religious practice was substantially burdened because he could not have eagle feathers but held that restricting the possession of eagle feathers to members of federally recognized tribes furthered the compelling governmental interest in fulfilling treaty obligations with Indian tribes in the least restrictive way.[134] The Tenth Circuit took the opposite view in *United States v. Hardman*.[135] The court there acknowledged that restricting eagle feather possession to Native Americans promoted a compelling governmental purpose of preserving Native American cultures and religions, but it held that excluding non-Indians was not the least restrictive means to address the purpose.[136]

The further narrowing of the preference from Native American ancestry to membership in a federally recognized tribe creates another set of problems relative to "preference" *within* Native American populations. In this regard, there is one Supreme Court decision—not in the free exercise area—upholding an employment preference for tribal members within the (federal) Bureau of Indian Affairs against an equal protection challenge brought by non-Indian employees.[137] The Court held that the employment preference was *not* based on race but on political affiliation (i.e., tribal membership); it was thus not subject to equal protection strict scrutiny analysis but rather subject to the lower standard of rational basis analysis.[138] In *Mancari*, the Court found the rational basis standard easily satisfied by viewing the Native American employment preference as a legitimate means to improve federal responsiveness to Native American tribal and governance concerns.[139]

The Supreme Court would probably resist such an extension of *Mancari*-like analysis in the context of a First Amendment free exercise of religion claim as against a limited employment preference within a single federal agency solely concerned with Indian affairs. Any potential limitation—however mild—on the free exercise of religion of a person from the majority or a non-member Indian is unlikely to find favor with the Court. The policy grounds so central in *Mancari* are likely to have little or no force in the matter of free exercise.

In the membership context, it is possible to identify some other distinctions that might justify such a regime, including notions of tribal citizenship, imposition of tribal norms, and verifiability.[140] In this view, tribal membership understood as tribal citizenship sets a conceptual framework for considering the differential treatment of Indians enrolled in federally recognized tribes and Indians not so enrolled. Such a notion of tribal citizenship might provide a basis to support such a distinction in the historical government-to-government relationship.

Such differential treatment thus might also be justified because tribal members "are subject to [tribal] governmentally imposed religious norms and values in ways that other Native Americans are not."[141] This is so because many tribes do not make a major distinction between tribal culture/religion and tribal government. This more direct (potential) link between governance and religion is not legally problematical because the Indian Civil Rights Act of 1968 contains a free exercise clause but not an establishment clause.[142] The absence of an establishment clause in the Indian Civil Rights Act of 1968 does not, of course, permit tribal limitations on free exercise; rather, it simply recognizes a closer nexus between religion and governance in much of Indian country than in the dominant society.

The final element in this set of reasons focuses on the argument that tribal membership may help boost judicial confidence in discerning the essential legitimacy of the claim. Tribal membership potentially opens the door for confirming attestation by the tribe itself and/or tribal members about the basic bona fides of the individual's belief.[143] This element is double-edged, however, in that it privileges one group of Native Americans over another, which might bleed over into other free exercise areas involving sacred sites, prisons, and schools. It also might inadvertently encourage judicial scrutiny into basic tenets of various Indian religious practices and the requirements for such practice.

The validity of the preference, such as it is, for Native American tribal members to obtain permits to take and possess eagle feathers also faces a potential Establishment Clause challenge in that the government's permit system impermissibly "favors" Indian religion. Resolution of this issue will probably turn on the Court's view of whether the permit preference leads to an improper "entanglement"[144] of government with religion or improper government "endorsement"[145] of religion. Neither excessive entanglement nor endorsement appears prevalent in this scheme. It seems to be no more than reasonable accommodation, rather than prohibited establishment.

There is a cruel twist at work here. Native Americans have been denied free exercise protection by the Supreme Court in the context of sacred sites[146] and peyote.[147] Now they face further (potential) religious disenfranchisement through Establishment Clause analysis. This is certainly a disheartening prospect fraught with historical irony. The irony stems from a widespread early practice of government support for Christianizing Indians that was never seriously questioned on Establishment Clause grounds, yet today for Native Americans, there is potential for further limitation on their free exercise rights under Establishment Clause analysis. This is a most unfortunate prospect. In this view, hard to imagine for many, both the Free Exercise Clause and the Establishment Clause work—however inadvertently—to keep Native Americans from vindication and expression of their most deeply held religious beliefs. It is an old saw in a new era: growing constitutional inclusion for most, continued constitutional exclusion for Native Americans.

Incarcerated Native Americans

Native American free exercise claims have also not fared well in the penitentiary context. No case involving a free exercise claim by a Native American inmate has gone to the Supreme Court, but the lower court results have not been encouraging. Many lower courts have denied Native American free exercise claims in prison by focusing on a jurisprudential policy of extreme deference to prison security and discipline concerns.

Particular Native American claims may be grouped into two categories: (1) hair length and headbands and (2) possession of religious objects and access to ceremonies. Most judicial opinions in this area mix significant deference to prison regulations with a lack of empathy and understanding. The backdrop to these cases is, of course, the Christian framework. If you need the Bible and you need to go to church, accommodation and understanding are close at hand. But in the Native American context, the *essentials* are different and include the necessity to *look* a certain way (e.g., hair length, headband), to *possess* certain sacred items (e.g., medicine bundles, sacred pipes), and to have *access* to people (i.e., medicine men) and to ceremonies (i.e., sweat lodge). These requirements greatly reduce the likelihood of free exercise success.

As the Ninth Circuit noted in *Allen v. Toombs*:

> The Supreme Court has made clear that an inmate who is an
> adherent of a minority religion must be afforded "a reasonable
> opportunity of pursuing his faith comparable to the opportunity
> afforded fellow prisoners who adhere to conventional religious
> precepts." *Cruz v. Beto*, 405 U.S. 319, 322 (1971).[148]

Yet the Court also made it clear that *reasonable* does not mean "identical facilities or personnel."[149] In addition, there is the further problem of the "reasonable" and "comparable" test, when it is connected to matters of "internal security and inmate discipline." Thus, the hurdles for free exercise for incarcerated Native Americans, while not insurmountable, are considerable.

The federal court jurisprudence in this area is not, however, uniformly negative. The most favorable cases are usually those that were decided earlier and applied the compelling state interest and least restrictive alternative analysis. These cases include *Teterud v. Gillman*,[150] *Gallahan v. Hollyfield*,[151] and

Weaver v. Jago.[152] These cases inclined to see hair length as an essential religious tenet and the state's interest in cutting it less than compelling.

Subsequent decisions have not been as deferential, and several cases have found that Native American inmates' religious practices "must yield" to legitimate prison official concerns for "internal security and inmate discipline."[153] More recently, a number of cases have applied the "reasonably related" test as articulated by the Supreme Court in such cases as *O'Lone v. Estate of Shabazz*[154] and *Turner v. Safley.*[155] In *Turner,* the Court stated: "When a prison regulation impinges on inmates' constitutional rights, the regulation is valid if it is reasonably related to legitimate penological interests."[156]

In *Standing Deer v. Carlson,*[157] the Ninth Circuit found that a prison regulation banning headgear satisfied the "reasonably related" test relative to safety and security, and in *Iron Eyes v. Henry,*[158] the Eighth Circuit found that the mandatory cutting of a shackled Native American inmate's hair was also permissible under the "reasonably related" test.

The federal courts have also reached decidedly mixed results relative to First Amendment claims asserting access to religious objects and to ceremonies. This includes access to sweat lodges, which "are constructed from willow, are attached to the earth and contain a fire pit in which rocks are heated," as well as access to sacred objects such as pipes, prayer bags, and tobacco ties.[159] In the sweat lodge ceremony, which involves pouring water over heated rocks, participants experience physical and spiritual purification and "feel more in harmony with life, gain increased wisdom, and are better able to follow the good red road."[160]

Despite these benefits, the lower courts have been hesitant at best.[161] For example, in the *Indian Inmates of Nebraska Penitentiary v. Gunter* case, the district court examined a consent decree that sanctioned "access to Indian medicine men and spiritual leaders and to provide facilities for spiritual and religious services, including but not limited to the Native American Church,"[162] and found that such access was subject to legitimate penological interests. It further found such a legitimate penological interest relative to security in denying a Native American inmate access to the sweat lodge when he was placed in the protective custody unit.[163] The Court did find, however, a violation of an inmate's free exercise rights when the institution permitted the access of only a single "official" medicine man, whose practices were contrary to the beliefs of the Native American inmate.[164]

Although there is no doubt that the double tests of "reasonable" but not "identical facilities and personnel" and "reasonably related" to "internal security and inmate security" will continue to set a high bar, the essential quandary and poignancy remain:

That the question of religious freedom in prison is raised in this case by a Native American compounds the lamentable character of cases of this nature, since it cannot be gainsaid that the destruction of American Indian culture and religious life was for many years a conscious policy of this nation.... Moreover, and independent of the special poignancy derived from the fact that this case is brought by Native Americans, it is a terrible comment upon our society that a serious question exists as to whether security of a prison is compromised by permitting inmates to engage in legitimate religious practices.[165]

As in the beginning, Native Americans are welcome to become Christians and have their religious rights fully protected. Yet the norm of actual and potential *constitutional* exclusion of non-Christian Native American free exercise claims remains pervasive and threatening in the context of sacred sites in the public domain, the use of peyote (and other controlled substances), the possession of eagle feathers for religious purposes, and incarceration. Despite some positive statutory and executive branch policy changes, the Constitution has failed to keep up.

This jurisprudence disturbs and repels rather than comforts and attracts. It is a repudiation of the religious liberty at the core of the First Amendment. Instead of empathy, there are mostly such things as Justice O'Connor's irritation in *Lyng* and Justice Scalia's concern with anarchy in *Smith*. There is no sense whatsoever in either of these opinions of how this might feel or look to Native Americans or whether it even matters. The core element of understanding difference is to seek to understand it from the other's point of view, not from one's own. Such an approach guarantees no particular *result* but demonstrates a necessary sense of fairness and engagement. There is also an ethical and analytical shortfall in the sense of the inability of the Court to understand that the various Native American religious practices should possess parity with mainstream religious expression within the Judeo-Christian framework. Without the necessary empathy, understanding, and translation, the First Amendment guarantee of free expression of religion will remain tantalizingly elusive to Native Americans.

PART III

The Modern Encounter

8

Indian Law Jurisprudence in the Modern Era

A Common Law Approach without Constitutional Principle

INDIAN LAW JURISPRUDENCE IN THE MODERN ERA HAS FOCUSED ON THREE major concerns: regulating state authority in Indian country, regulating tribal authority over non-Indians and nonmember Indians in Indian country, and interpreting federal statutes that set benchmarks for tribal and/or state activity in Indian country. The first two major concerns have been routinely decided without constitutional or statutory direction. Most of this jurisprudential activity has taken place on the civil side of the docket because Congress has enacted almost no legislation that sets standards for parsing civil jurisdiction in Indian country.

The major federal statutes in this era have focused on establishing (federal) civil rights guarantees in Indian country,[1] establishing minimum federal standards for the removal of Indian children from their homes,[2] establishing federal standards for Indian gaming activities,[3] and recognizing inherent tribal criminal jurisdiction over nonmember Indians.[4] The Supreme Court has interpreted each of these statutes and has found each statute, with one minor (but significant) exception, to be within Congress's plenary power in Indian affairs. These statutes and cases are analyzed later in this chapter.

On the criminal side of the docket, jurisdiction is, for the most part, apportioned among the three competing sovereigns through the General Crimes Act,[5] the Major Crimes Act,[6] and to a lesser degree, the Assimilative Crime Act.[7] All of these statutes have routinely been held to be within the scope of Congress's lawmaking authority in Indian affairs. You will recall, of course, that the Supreme Court upheld the validity of the Major Crimes Act in *United States v. Kagama*,[8] noting that it was within Congress's ill-defined protective and trust responsibility to Indians. This jurisprudential rationale was developed after the Court expressly rejected the only proffered constitutional text, namely, the Indian Commerce Clause, as an adequate source for Congress's enactment of the statute.[9]

The Supreme Court departed from the plain language of the General Crimes Act when it carved out an exception to federal jurisdiction in crimes involving only non-Indians as both perpetrators and defendants, reasoning that no significant federal interest was implicated and therefore state jurisdiction was appropriate.[10] More notoriously, in the 1978 case of *Oliphant v. Suquamish Indian Tribe*,[11] the Court ruled that tribes have no criminal jurisdiction over non-Indians. The Court did not cite the Constitution or any federal statute to support its decision; rather, it simply pronounced that such authority of tribes was "inconsistent with their status."[12] Arguably, the decision was predicated on some kind of common law interpretation, but if it was, the Court did not bother to say so.

Unfortunately, *Oliphant*-like thinking has come to dominate the Court's approach to analyzing[13] the issue of tribal (civil) judicial and legislative authority over non-Indians. This kind of analysis was less likely to be followed when the Court examined claims of state authority over Indians in Indian country because of the early bulwark against state authority established in the Marshall trilogy.

State assertiveness in the modern era is overwhelmingly focused on the issue of taxation over both Indians and non-Indians. The results—even when favorable to the states—do not oust tribal authority. Dual-taxation options remain. Tribes do not lose any legal power per se. The loss, if any, is economic in nature. Yet even this basic rule has come under stress.[14] But as we will see, when the assertiveness shoe is on the other foot, the loss of tribal sovereignty is considerable.

When the tribe is the assertive sovereign and it loses, then significant regulatory and judicial sovereignty is defaulted to the states, especially when non-Indians are involved.[15] There are no concurrent options in these situations. The results are grossly asymmetrical, and tribal sovereignty is continually at risk. The analytical method employed to achieve these results has been to balkanize the landscape of Indian country, to expand the (legal) categories of individuals living there, and to create a strong presumption in favor of state jurisdiction over non-Indians. This new analytical framework derives from an expansive development of federal *judicial* plenary power that lacks statutory or constitutional authorization.

This jurisprudential metamorphosis completely reverses the historical understanding embodied in the Indian Commerce Clause and treaties, which was first articulated in the *Cherokee Nation* cases.[16] The nature of this reversal is twofold. It reverses the understanding that the states have no authority in

Indian country unless there is express congressional authorization, and it reverses the corollary understanding that without express congressional limitation, tribal authority in Indian country remains unimpaired.[17]

Williams v. Lee to White Mountain Apache Tribe v. Bracker: Keeping the States at Bay

The 1959 case of *Williams v. Lee*[18] has been described as the cornerstone of the modern era of Indian law. As Wilkinson noted:

> Most of the litigation to reach the Court during the twentieth century before 1959 arose out of disputes involving individual Indians or even non-Indians; as a result, the decisions lacked the public law overtones of either the modern era or the nineteenth century....After *Williams* the pace of decisions began to accelerate, with the result that the Court has become more active in Indian law than in fields such as securities, bankruptcy, pollution control, and international law.[19]

The more "public law" approach to Indian law discerned by Wilkinson has also given way to a series of decisions that have splintered the legal landscape of Indian country. In a sense, *Williams v. Lee* was the lull before the storm. The first wave of the storm was the increased attempt by the states (and non-Indians) to secure potential islands of state jurisdiction within Indian country. The second wave was the concerted action of tribes to assert regulatory and adjudicatory authority over non-Indians in Indian country. Sovereignty in theory met challenge in fact. As tribes have increasingly sought to actualize their sovereignty, the Supreme Court has consistently, without constitutional or statutory authority, held tribes in check.

In *Williams*, the respondent *Lee* was a non-Indian who operated a general store on the Navajo Reservation under a license required by federal law.[20] He originally "brought this action in the Superior court of Arizona against petitioners, a Navajo Indian and his wife who lived on the Reservation, to collect for goods sold [to] them there on credit."[21] The Arizona state courts maintained jurisdiction on the theory that because no act of Congress expressly forbade state jurisdiction, state jurisdiction was unimpaired.[22]

The Supreme Court reversed. It noted that the applicable standard with which to review state claims of authority over Indians on the reservation was "whether the state action infringed on the right of reservation Indians to make their own laws and be ruled by them."[23] The Court noted that the Treaty of 1868 with the Navajo preserved the right of self-governance and that the State of

Arizona had failed to avail itself of the option to obtain state jurisdiction under Public Law 280.[24] The Court concluded:

> There can be no doubt that to allow the exercise of state jurisdiction here would undermine the authority of the tribal courts over Reservation affairs and hence would infringe on the right of Indians to govern themselves. It is immaterial that the respondent is not an Indian. He was on the reservation and the transaction with the Indian took place there. The cases in this Court have consistently guarded the authority of Indian governments on their reservations.... If this power is to be taken away from them, it is for Congress to do it.[25]

The *Williams* case gave rise to what is generally referred to as the "infringement test." The decision was not grounded in any particular statute, much less the Constitution itself, but rather in a historical policy to support tribal self-governance that was rooted in the early decision of *Worcester v. Georgia*.[26] The Court also recognized that Congress could change this policy.[27]

Yet the Court might have been more constitutionally direct by noting that legislation enacted pursuant to the Indian Commerce Clause, such as the Indian trader licensing statute, as well as the enactment of "comprehensive statutes in 1834 regulating trade with Indians,"[28] created both constitutional and statutory bars to state authority in this instance. Although the decision was clearly favorable to tribes and generally affirmed tribal self-governance and sovereignty, it wobbled in its unwillingness to rule that the result was constitutionally required. As a result, its precedential force was (and is) weak and, as more recent cases demonstrate, unreliable as well.[29]

In *McClanahan v. Arizona State Tax Commission*,[30] the Court confronted the issue of whether the state of Arizona could assert its state income tax on "a reservation Indian whose entire income derives from reservation sources."[31] The Court ruled that it could not and expressly held "[t]hat by imposing the tax in question on this appellant, the State has interfered with matters which the relevant treaty and statutes leave to the *exclusive* province of the Federal Government and the Indians themselves."[32]

Although the Court cited *Williams* approvingly, it noted that this case was distinguishable because non-Indians were not directly involved. The *McClanahan* Court stated that, in situations involving non-Indians, "both the tribe and the State could fairly claim an interest in asserting their respective jurisdictions. The *Williams* test was designed to resolve this conflict by providing that the State could protect its interest up to the point where tribal self-government would be affected."[33] The Court continued: "The problem posed by the case is completely different. Since appellant is an Indian and since her income is derived wholly from reservation sources, her activity is totally within the sphere which the relevant treaty and statutes leave for the Federal Government and for the Indians themselves."[34]

In the absence of the applicability of the *Williams* test, the Court looked elsewhere for an appropriate analytical framework and found it in the

> trend...away from the idea of inherent Indian sovereignty as a bar to state jurisdiction and toward reliance on federal pre-emption. The modern cases thus tend to avoid reliance on platonic notions of Indian sovereignty and to look instead to the applicable treaties and statutes which define the limits of state power.[35]

In this new formulation, the Indian sovereignty doctrine rooted in *Worcester v. Georgia* was relegated to "a backdrop against which the applicable treaties and federal statutes must be read."[36] In *McClanahan*, this "backdrop" in the Navajo context remained strong, as evidenced by the Treaty of 1868's commitment to Navajo self-governance. In addition, several federal statutes, while not directly on point, strongly evinced an intent to limit state taxation in Indian country. These statutes included the Arizona Enabling Act[37] and the Buck Act,[38] both of which created Indian tax immunities in Indian country. The Court characterized its analysis as focusing on Indian law conceptions of federal pre-emption of state authority. Arizona had also failed to take advantage of the jurisdiction offered by Public Law 280.[39]

All in all, it was a rather straightforward opinion without dissent. Yet, it did little to develop its preemption analysis within a constitutional context. In fact, the Court had already expressly rejected the opportunity to do so:

> Since we hold that this state tax cannot be imposed consistently with federal statutes applicable to Indians on the Navajo Reservation, we find it unnecessary to consider whether the tax is also barred by that part of the Commerce Clause giving Congress the power to regulate commerce with Indian tribes.[40]

Once again, the Court eschewed constitutional analysis and opted for a more flexible, even vague, approach to reviewing claims of state authority over Indians in Indian country. The Court itself realized that clarity and consistency were not the hallmarks of its Indian law jurisprudence, but its *McClanahan* opinion did little to change this assessment.[41]

Subsequent Indian tax cases have hewed to the general rule of *McClanahan* that without express congressional authorization, states may not tax Indians (or Indian tribes) *in* Indian country. Yet, the Court seldom speaks of preemption in this area any longer and, instead, is more likely to speak of a "categorical approach" with its advantages of a "bright line standard" and desired certainty in the area of state taxation.[42] This bright-line limitation does *not* apply to off-reservation situations.[43]

Preemption in Indian law is no more than a shadow or distant cousin to mainstream constitutional preemption doctrine. In general constitutional parlance, preemption refers to the ability of Congress to oust (in whole or in part) state authority to act in certain otherwise legitimate areas. That is, a state may have a general police power to do a particular thing, but Congress under a constitutional grant may have a superior power to occupy the field and displace state action. For example, the Court has struck down a state statute imposing weight limitations on trucks operating under an Interstate Commerce Commission Certificate of Commerce.[44] Federal preemption couples the specific constitutional grant of subject matter authority with the Supremacy Clause of Article VI to displace any conflicting state legislation.[45]

Outside the area of state taxation of Indians, preemption in Indian law is weak to nonexistent. In the context of the ability of the state to tax non-Indian businesses on the reservation, the Court has been much more ambiguous and tended to rely more on a kind of raw economic analysis and balancing test rather than preemption or any straightforward legal analysis. For example, in *White Mountain Apache Tribe v. Bracker*,[46] the Court struck down an attempt by the State of Arizona to impose its motor carrier license tax and fuel use tax against Pinetop, a non-Indian company, doing business with the Fort Apache Timber Company, a tribal enterprise that managed, harvested, and sold timber on the White Mountain Apache Reservation.[47]

The Court in *White Mountain Apache* noted that the *Williams* "infringement test" and the *McClanahan* "preemption test" were "two independent but related barriers to the assertion of state regulation over tribal reservations and members."[48] Yet, the Court later went on to essentially dismantle this statement with its observation that "[m]ore difficult questions arise where, as here, a State asserts authority over the conduct of non-Indians engaging in activity on the reservation."[49] The Court indicated that in such a situation:

> we have examined the language of the relevant federal treaties and
> statutes in terms of both the broad policies that underlie them and
> the notions of sovereignty that have developed from historical
> traditions of tribal independence. This inquiry is not dependent on
> mechanical or absolute conceptions of state or tribal sovereignty, but
> has called for a particularized inquiry into the nature of the state,
> federal, and tribal interests at stake, an inquiry designed to determine

whether, in the specific context, the exercise of state authority would violate federal law.[50]

In the balancing equation, federal-tribal concerns were found predominant because comprehensive federal regulations governed the harvesting of timber on the reservation, petitioner logging company's activities took place exclusively on tribal and Bureau of Indian Affairs roads, and state taxes would threaten the overall federal objective of maximizing tribal profit in its timbering operation.[51] The Court further found that the state performed no regulatory function or service that would justify its assessment of taxes.[52] Such pinpoint balancing, according to the Court, avoided "treacherous" generalizations.[53]

The Court found itself in an even deeper quandary when faced with the issue of whether the state could tax a non-Indian business that was already (legitimately) taxed by the tribe. Was such double taxation permissible? The Court offered no fixed analytical (much less constitutional) guidance. The answer was dependent on the specific facts. For example, in *Washington v. Confederated Tribes of the Colville Indian Reservation*,[54] decided the same month as *Bracker*, the Court held the state could tax cigarette sales to non-Indians (and nonmember Indians) on the reservation, even if the tribe was already taxing such sales.[55]

The core of the Court's holding centered on the twin facts that the tribes were merely seeking to market a competitive tax advantage (that is, no state sales tax on cigarette purchases on the reservation) and that there was no value generated on the reservation. In distinction to the native timber in *Bracker*, the cigarettes in *Colville* were imported onto the reservation. In this context, the likely tribal *economic* loss from such double *taxation* offended neither the "infringement" nor the "preemption" test. Tribal law and self-governance were not impaired by economic competition.[56] Conversely, the Court found the state to have a strong and legitimate taxing interest "when the tax is directed at off-reservation value and when the taxpayer is the recipient of state services."[57] The Court also stated: "Washington's taxes are reasonably designed to prevent the Tribes from marketing their tax exemption to nonmembers who do not receive significant tribal services and who would otherwise purchase their cigarettes outside the reservations."[58]

The Court readily disposed of the claim that the state taxes were barred by the Indian Commerce Clause. The one relevant sentence stated that it could "no longer be seriously argued that the Indian Commerce Clause, of its own force, automatically bars all state taxation of matters significantly touching the economic and political interests of the Tribes."[59] Certainly, more exegesis might have been expected, given the historical roots of the Indian Commerce Clause, to severely restrict, if *not* foreclose, state authority in Indian country, but none was forthcoming. Any notion of a dormant Indian Commerce Clause, analogous to the dormant Interstate Commerce Clause, which would potentially foreclose state taxation of any kind in Indian country, was never considered.[60]

This potential notion of *dual* tribal and state taxing authority over non-Indian commercial activity was further considered in *Cotton Petroleum Corp. v. New Mexico*.[61] In *Cotton Petroleum*, the Court held that despite the presence of the 1938 Indian Mineral Leasing Act, New Mexico's severance tax was not preempted by federal law or precluded by imposition of a tribal tax.[62] In the absence of *express* congressional legislation to the contrary, dual taxation was not impermissible.

Subsequently, the Court ruled for the first time that tribal authority to tax non-Indian business or commerce in Indian country was not a black letter rule. In *Atkinson Trading Co., Inc. v. Shirley*,[63] the Court held that the Navajo Nation did not have authority to tax guests at a non-Indian-owned hotel located on fee simple land within the Navajo Reservation. Chief Justice Rehnquist, writing for a unanimous Court, stated that the Navajo Nation's authority to tax nonmembers "reaches no further than tribal land" unless it can prove one of the *Montana* exceptions.[64]

In sum, the Court has effectively nullified state attempts to regulate and tax Indians on the reservation under "infringement" and "preemption" analysis but has doctrinally equivocated when the state seeks to tax non-Indians or non-Indian businesses for on-reservation activity. Infringement and preemption analysis is paramount when Indians are the target of state authority. When non-Indians are the target of state authority, especially in the tax arena, the focus is on a balancing of interests and economic analysis. The Constitution plays no significant role in the Court's reasoning.

More broadly, these cases represent the Court's attempt to regulate state authority in Indian country, where the state is the assertive sovereign. The default position is always tribal authority. But what of the converse situation when the tribe is the assertive sovereign? What is the appropriate analysis? What is the default position?

Montana v. United States to *Plains Commerce Bank v. Long* Family Land and Cattle Co., Inc.: Keeping the Tribes at Bay

If *Williams* inaugurated the modern era in Indian law, *Montana v. United States*[65] inaugurated a disturbing counter-era whose primary feature is the substantial withering away of tribal sovereignty as it pertains to civil regulatory and judicial authority over non-Indians on fee land within the reservation. In *Montana*, the central issue was whether the Crow Tribe could enact a *comprehensive* hunting and fishing regulatory code effective on all land and over all individuals found within the reservation. The Court answered in the negative.

The rationale of the Court broke new ground in three unique and overlapping ways. Two had previously been introduced into the Court's jurisprudence in slightly different settings. First, in the criminal jurisdiction context, the Court had held in *Oliphant* that tribes lacked criminal jurisdiction over non-Indians because it was "inconsistent with their [dependent] status."[66] The Court did not (and could not) say it was inconsistent with any federal statute or any provision of the Constitution. *Oliphant* did *not* even say that it was a common law decision, although it presumably was.

The Court in *Montana* extended the core of the *Oliphant* analysis into the civil arena but made it a (rebuttable) presumption rather than a black letter rule. It also added its now well-known proviso:

> Though *Oliphant* only determined inherent tribal authority in criminal matters, the principles on which it relied support the general proposition that inherent sovereign powers of an Indian tribe do not extend to the activities of the non-members of the tribe. To be sure, Indian tribes retain inherent sovereign power to exercise some forms of civil jurisdiction over non-Indians on their reservations, even on non-Indian fee lands. A tribe may regulate, through taxation, licensing or other means, the activities of nonmembers who enter consensual relationship with the tribe or its members, through commercial dealing, contracts, leases, or other arrangements. A tribe may also retain inherent power to exercise civil authority over the conduct of non-Indians on fee lands within its reservation when that conduct threatens or has some direct effect on the political integrity, economic security, or the health or welfare of the tribe.[67]

Second, in the tax area, the Supreme Court had already introduced the category of nonmember Indians who were potentially subject to (concurrent) state jurisdiction. In *Montana*, this distinction was extended into the tribal regulatory context, where no concurrent authority was possible. As a result, tribal regulatory authority over nonmember Indians became potentially as limited and attenuated as its authority over non-Indians.

Third and most significant was the new legal ground in *Montana* that created a jurisdictional distinction based on the status of the land *within* the reservation. Prior to *Montana*, Indian law analysis came into play whenever one was on the reservation in accord with 18 U.S.C. § 1151.[68] Distinctions were made based on whether the individual was Indian, non-Indian, or a nonmember Indian—a distinction of *who* not *where*.

Montana began to carve up the landscape and to parse the significance of *where* something took place on the reservation. The Court found the Crow Tribe's attempt to regulate the hunting and fishing of *all* individuals on *any* part of the reservation to exceed its grasp. The Court characterized the issue this way:

> The Court of Appeals held that the Tribe may prohibit nonmembers from hunting or fishing on land belonging to the Tribe or held by the United States in trust for the Tribe, and with this holding we can readily agree. We also agree with the Court of Appeals that if the Tribe permits nonmembers to fish or hunt on such lands, it may condition their entry by charging a fee or establishing bag and creel limits. What remains is the question of the power of the tribe to regulate non-Indian fishing and hunting on reservation land owned in fee by nonmembers of the Tribe.[69]

The Court answered this question in the negative. It rejected the tribe's claim that the requisite authority could be found in either the 1851 or 1868 treaties with the United States or in the tribe's inherent sovereignty.

The Court found that both of these potential sources of tribal authority gave way under the weight of the General Allotment Act and the Crow Allotment Act. These allotment acts ultimately brought non-Indians to the reservation as permanent residents and landholders in a context quite inimical to tribal authority:

> There is simply no suggestion in the legislative history that Congress intended that the non-Indians who would settle upon alienated allotted lands would be subject to tribal authority. Indeed, throughout the congressional debates, allotment of Indian land was consistently equated with the dissolution of tribal affairs and jurisdiction.[70]

This statement was the beginning of the judicial dismantling of the historical presumption in favor of tribal jurisdiction in all of Indian country[71] and its replacement with the requirement of "express congressional delegation":

But exercise of tribal power beyond what is necessary to protect tribal self-government and to control internal relations is inconsistent with the dependent status of the tribes, and so *cannot* survive without express congressional delegation.[72]

The Court's statutory analysis makes no reference to the *text* of either the General Allotment Act or the Crow Allotment Act, because there is no text in either statute that speaks to jurisdiction. Nor is there any mention of jurisdiction involving *non-Indians* in the legislative history of these statutes. All that is cited in *Montana* from the text and history of these statutes are the broadest historical forecasts and projections about the *future* of tribal existence—a future of dissolution that never materialized.

This is not to say that these statutes are completely irrelevant in the jurisdictional context. It is *not* unreasonable, for example, to conclude that these statutes offer some jurisdictional protection to the non-Indian land-holders themselves (and their successors) as an element of their fee *ownership* of the land. Such protection is largely consistent with their status as individual owners of private property. How this individual protection could be extended to the entire *class* of non-Indians (who do not hold title to land) to hunt on land that was *not* theirs, now or then, is anomalous to say the least.[73]

The Court's analysis of the tribe's ability to regulate fishing proceeded on a different track. Tribal authority to regulate the fishing of Indian and non-Indian individuals on nonnavigable bodies of water within the reservation was not diminished. Nevertheless, the tribe's ability to regulate the fishing of non-Indians on navigable streams within the reservation, such as the Big Horn River, was extinguished. The Court ruled that neither the Fort Laramie Treaty of 1851 nor the Fort Laramie Treaty of 1868 was able to displace the presumption in favor of the states that the United States conferred title of the riverbeds of all navigable streams within its territory to a new state upon statehood. This was so despite treaty guarantees that the reservation would be "set apart for the absolute and undisturbed use and occupation of the Indians herein named"[74] and despite the fact that Montana did not even exist as a state at the time of the Fort Laramie Treaty of 1868.

The Court's analysis in the fishing context was bolstered by its finding that fishing was not a central treaty activity of the Crow people and that the Crow Tribe had accommodated itself to pervasive state regulation and stocking of the river.[75] Not surprisingly, the Court ultimately found that its own newly minted presumption in favor of state jurisdiction on fee lands within the reservation was not overcome in the instant case.[76]

Montana created the new jurisdictional standard with which to review tribal claims of authority over non-Indian activity on fee lands within the reservation. The new jurisdictional standard was whether either prong of *Montana*'s well-known proviso was satisfied.[77] Subsequent cases extended the balkanization of the reservation landscape for jurisdictional purposes. Yet before this balkanization would fully develop, the Court decided several other cases that appeared to proceed differently. They were cases in which a tribe was asserting judicial, as opposed to regulatory, authority over non-Indians. In these cases, the Court appeared more deferential to the tribal assessment of its own jurisdiction.

The principal case in this regard is *National Farmers Union Insurance Companies v. Crow Tribe of Montana.*[78] The facts in *National Farmers Union* involved a routine tort action in which the plaintiff in the original tribal court action was an Indian minor who sued the local (state) school for injuries he suffered as a result of a motorcycle accident that took place in the school's parking lot. After a default judgment was rendered against the school in tribal court, the school's insurer challenged the tribal court's jurisdiction in federal court.[79]

The Supreme Court held that any challenge to a tribal court's judicial jurisdiction over non-Indians could be brought only in federal district court after the "[e]xhaustion of tribal court remedies."[80] Exhaustion was required for a diverse set of reasons:

> Our cases have often recognized that Congress is committed to a policy supporting tribal self-government and self-determination. That policy favors a rule that will provide the forum whose jurisdiction is being challenged the first opportunity to evaluate the factual and legal basis for the challenge. Moreover the orderly administration of justice in the federal court will be served by allowing a full record to be developed in the Tribal Court before either the merits or any question concerning appropriate relief is addressed.... Exhaustion of tribal court remedies, moreover, will encourage tribal courts to explain to the parties the precise basis for accepting jurisdiction, and will also provide other courts with the benefit of their expertise in such matters in the event of any further judicial review.[81]

The *National Farmers Union* case is further revealing and significant beyond its enunciation of the exhaustion doctrine. The Court, as it did in *Montana*, rejected any extension of *Oliphant* into the context of assessments of tribal judicial jurisdiction:

Thus, we conclude that the answer to the question of whether a tribal court has the power to exercise civil subject-matter jurisdiction over non-Indians in a case of the kind is not automatically foreclosed, as an extension of *Oliphant* would require. Rather, the existence and extent of a tribal court's jurisdiction will require a careful examination of tribal sovereignty, the extent to which that sovereignty has been altered, divested, or diminished, as well as a detailed study of relevant statutes, Executive Branch policy as embodied in treaties and elsewhere, and administrative or judicial decisions.[82]

In seeking to reconcile *Montana* with *National Farmers Union*, many scholars initially thought that the Court was simply more hospitable to a tribe's judicial jurisdiction as opposed to its regulatory jurisdiction. Such a view was rendered nugatory in the 1997 case of *Strate v. A-1 Contractors*.[83] *Strait* was a run-of-the-mill tort case that involved a car and truck accident that took place on a state highway running through the Fort Berthold Indian Reservation in North Dakota. The plaintiff, Gisela Fredericks, a non-Indian resident of the reservation whose (deceased) husband and children were tribal members, sued the defendants, including the non-Indian driver and owner of the gravel truck, in tribal court as a result of the accident with her vehicle. The defendant non-Indians were nonresidents of the reservation, who were on the reservation doing landscape work pursuant to a contract with a wholly owned tribal corporation.[84]

The defendants raised the now familiar issue of jurisdiction. *Montana* analysis came back to the fore. The Court confronted two doctrinal issues, namely, whether there was an analytical distinction between tribal regulatory and tribal adjudicatory authority and whether *Montana* analysis extended beyond land held in fee by non-Indians. In its unanimous opinion, the court moved swiftly. The Court rejected the claim that there was any difference between a tribe's regulatory and adjudicatory jurisdiction. It prefaced this conclusion with a reminder that exhaustion was prudential, not jurisdictional.[85] It was a matter of comity, not a jurisdictional prerequisite.[86] This hardening of tone, whether intentional or not, signaled a turning away from any likelihood of tribal court jurisdiction.

Montana analysis became the sole occupier of the field:

Regarding activity on non-Indian fee land within a reservation, *Montana* delineated—in a main rule and exceptions—the bounds of the power tribes retain to exercise "forms of civil jurisdiction over non-Indians." As to nonmembers, we hold, a tribe's adjudicative jurisdiction does not exceed its legislative jurisdiction. Absent congressional direction enlarging tribal-court jurisdiction, we adhere to that understanding. Subject to controlling provisions in treaties and statutes, and the two exceptions identified in *Montana*, the civil authority of Indian tribes and their courts with respect to non-Indian fee lands generally "does not extend to the activities of non-members of the tribe."[87]

This language effectively swept away any lingering doubt about the potency of *Montana* as a general rule. *Montana* was much less central in at least two earlier cases involving tribal zoning[88] and tribal authority over land taken by the federal government for a dam on the Missouri River.[89] In *Brendale v. Confederated Tribes and Bands of Yakima Nation*, the zoning case, the Court split with three different opinions, none of which garnered a majority, allowing tribal zoning of fee land in a *closed* area of the reservation, but not in the *open* portion.[90] In *South Dakota v. Bourland*, the federal dam and reservoir case, the key *Montana* analysis occurred only on remand.[91]

Justice Blackmun's partial dissent in *Brendale* had no takers in *Strait*. He, Justice Marshall, and Justice Brennan had all passed away, and no one on the current Court stepped in to carry on their cavil with *Montana*. Justice Blackmun believed *Montana* had gotten its Indian law jurisprudence backward:

> But *Montana* is simply one, and not even the most recent, of a long line of our decisions discussing the nature of inherent tribal sovereignty. These cases, landmarks in 150 years of Indian-law jurisprudence, establish a very different "general principle" governing inherent tribal sovereignty—a principle according to which tribes *retain* their sovereign powers over non-Indians on reservation lands unless the exercise of that sovereignty would be "inconsistent with the overriding interests of the National Government."[92]

Justice Ginsburg's *Strate* opinion continued the trend to balkanize the jurisdictional landscape by extending *Montana* analysis to state highways. This was so, according to the Court, even when the state highway was constructed on tribal trust land pursuant to a tribally granted right of way, which contained no cession of jurisdictional authority by the tribe.[93]

Applying the *general* rule of *Montana* to this new jurisdictional landscape, the Court found that neither of the prongs of the rule's proviso was satisfied. There was no "consensual" agreement. The plaintiff was not a party to the defendant's subcontract with the tribe, and the tribe was a stranger to the accident.[94] In addition, the Court found there was no conduct "that threatens or has some direct effect on the political integrity, the economic security, or the health or welfare of the tribe."[95] In reviewing its precedent in this area, the Court appeared to double back to *Williams v. Lee*: "Neither regulatory nor adjudicatory authority over the state highway accident at issue is needed to preserve 'the right of reservation Indians to make their own laws and be ruled by them.'" The *Montana* rule, therefore, and not its exceptions, applied to this case.[96]

The Court was notably jittery about potentially requiring the non-Indian defendants "to defend against this commonplace state highway accident claim in an *unfamiliar* court."[97] The Court did not bother to explicate what it meant by *unfamiliar*, nor did it dwell on the contract that brought the defendants onto the reservation voluntarily, but rather took comfort that the plaintiff "may pursue her case against A-1 Contractors and Stockert in the state forum open to all who sustain injuries on North Dakota's highway."[98]

Montana was now firmly in place as the "pathmarking case concerning tribal civil authority over nonmembers."[99] All that remained was the question of how much of the remainder of the reservation legal landscape it might swallow. The answer appears to be all of it. The Court applied *Montana* analysis for the first time in the context of a tribal tax in the case of *Atkinson Trading Co., Inc. v. Shirley*.[100] In this case, the Court held that the Navajo Tribe could not assert its hotel occupancy tax against non-Indians staying at a non-Indian hotel located on fee land within the Navajo Reservation.[101]

Chief Justice Rehnquist's unanimous and succinct opinion[102] cut directly to the chase. The appropriate analysis is *Montana* without any special consideration in the area of tribal taxation:

> We therefore do not read *Merrion* to exempt taxation from *Montana*'s general rule that Indian tribes lack civil authority over nonmembers on non-Indian fee land. Accordingly, as in *Strate*, we apply *Montana* straight up. Because Congress has not authorized the Navajo Nation's hotel occupancy tax through treaty or statute, and because the incidence of the tax falls upon nonmembers on non-Indian fee land, it is incumbent upon the Navajo Nation to establish the existence of one of *Montana*'s exceptions.[103]

The Court did not find either of *Montana's* exceptions satisfied. The Court rejected the Navajo Nation's argument that Atkinson Trading Co.'s status as a federally licensed trader was sufficient "consent" for the tribe to tax the Trading Post's guests.[104] Despite the tribal provision of substantial services to Atkinson Trading Co. and the presence of a significant number of Navajo individuals employed at the trading post in an area of mostly tribally owned land, the Court failed to see how the petitioner's "operation of a hotel on non-Indian fee land, 'threatens or has some direct effect in the political integrity, the economic security, or the health or welfare of the tribe.' "[105]

The opinion characterized *Montana* as the "most exhaustively reasoned of our modern cases."[106] Justice Souter's concurrence chimed in with its observation that "if we are to see coherence in the various manifestations of the general law of tribal jurisdiction over non-Indians, the source of doctrine must be *Montana v. United States*."[107] But then a seed of doubt was sown about *Montana*'s landscape specific analysis. Although *Montana*'s "first principle" was essential, it ought not be tethered too rigidly to only *part* of the reservation landscape:

> "[T]he inherent sovereign powers of an Indian tribe do not extend to the activities of the non members of the tribe." That general proposition is, however, the first principle, *regardless of whether the land at issue is fee land, or land owned by, or held in trust for an Indian tribe.*[108]

Justice Souter's concern about the landscape ingredient in *Montana* analysis came to the forefront in *Nevada v. Hicks*.[109] In *Hicks*, a tribal member brought suit in tribal court against state game wardens, tribal officials, and the State of Nevada for harm resulting from two different searches at his residence on trust land within the Fallon Paiute-Shoshone Reservation. Both searches concerned the alleged off-reservation criminal activity of taking and possessing a California bighorn sheep. Search warrants were issued from state court but were backed by tribal court warrants as well.[110] Plaintiff Hicks claimed that his (legal) Rocky Mountain bighorn sheep heads had been damaged and that each search exceeded the bounds of the warrant. The causes of action, asserting violations of both tribal and federal law, were based on trespass to land, abuse of process, unreasonable search and seizure, and violation of civil rights. Various dismissals left the suit to proceed only against state officials in their individual capacities.

Justice Scalia characterized the issue as "whether a tribal court may assert jurisdiction over civil claims against state officials, who entered tribal land to execute a search warrant against a tribe member suspected of having violated state law outside the reservation."[111] The Court's answer was no. The Court relied on both *Montana* and *Strait* as "pathmarking," but first went on to undo the landscape specifics of *Montana*. The Court recharacterized this aspect of *Montana*:

> "To be sure, Indian tribes retain inherent sovereign power to exercise some forms of civil jurisdiction over non-Indians on their reservations, even on non-Indian fee lands,"—clearly implying that the general rule of *Montana* applies to both Indian and non-Indian land.

The ownership status of land, in other words, is only one factor to consider in determining whether regulation of the activities of nonmembers is "necessary to protect tribal self-government or to control internal relations."[112]

"The ownership status of land," once thought to be near dispositive, was now just a backdrop or an ingredient plugged into the analysis. The Court concluded without sustained *Montana* analysis, but rather with echoes of *Williams v. Lee*, "that tribal authority to regulate state officers in executing process related to the violation, off reservation, of state laws is not essential to tribal self-government or internal relations—to 'the right to make laws and be ruled by them.' "[113]

The Court went on to proscribe tribal court jurisdiction over federal causes of action, holding that tribal courts were not courts of "general jurisdiction" because of existing impediments to their jurisdiction.[114] Thus the tribal court could have no jurisdiction over the federal claim premised on 42 U.S.C. §1983 asserted against the state officials.[115] This pronouncement was not accompanied by sustained analysis or citation to any statutory or constitutional principle.

Justice Souter's concurrence pressed further. With *Montana*'s landscape focus in retreat, the core focal point, according to Souter, should be to look

first to human relationships, not land records, and it should make no difference *per se* whether acts committed on a reservation occurred on tribal land or on land owned by a nonmember individual in fee. It is the membership status of the unconsenting party, not the status of real property, that counts as the primary jurisdictional fact.[116]

Whether intended or not, Justice Souter's concurrence suggests the centrality of the legal or "racial" identity of the defendant in the Court's calculations, or perhaps it is more accurate to say that his primary concern is with the likely treatment of such defendants by tribal courts. In fact, Justice Souter is quite specific about this issue of difference, both procedurally and substantively:

The ability of nonmembers to know where tribal jurisdiction begins and ends, it should be stressed, is a matter of real, practical consequence given "the special nature of [Indian] tribunals," which differ from traditional American courts in a number of significant respects.[117]

These differences include the apparent flexibility accorded tribal courts in interpreting the due process and equal protection guarantees of the Indian Civil Rights Act in a less than "jot-for-jot" replication of Supreme Court precedent, the problems of tradition and custom "which would be unusually difficult for an outsider to sort out," separation of powers concerns about the existence of independent tribal judiciaries, and limited federal review.[118] Although these questions were not directly at issue in the case, Justice Souter wrote: "In any event, a presumption against tribal-court civil jurisdiction squares with one of the principal *policy* considerations underlying *Oliphant*, namely, an overriding concern that citizens who are not tribal members be 'protected . . . from unwarranted intrusions on their personal liberty.' "[119] Whatever the merits of Justice Souter's critique, it is grounded in neither the Constitution nor any statute, but rather in "policy considerations" that have grown increasingly attractive and dispositive to the Court in its Indian law jurisprudence, especially when it deals with non-Indians. This rippling subtext is reinforced by Justice Scalia's observation "that we have never held that a tribal court had jurisdiction over a non-member defendant."[120] *Montana* began a process of dividing Indian country where *place* was most significant for jurisdictional *purposes*, but by *Nevada v. Hicks*, place was receding in jurisdictional importance, and personal identity was ascendant.

The 2008 decision in *Plains Commerce Bank v. Long Family Land and Cattle Company, Inc.*[121] did nothing to allay concerns about the trajectory of the Court's Indian law jurisprudence. In that case, the Court held in a five-to-four vote that a tribal court did *not* have jurisdiction over a discrimination claim that grew out of the financial terms set in a contract for the sale of fee land on the reservation by a non-Indian bank to an Indian couple.[122]

Despite the obvious consensual nature of the contract and its nexus to the discrimination claim, the Court, nevertheless, created a new rule that completely departed from the "pathmarking" analysis set forth in *Montana v. United States*.[123] The new rule simply stated that tribal courts lacked jurisdiction over the discrimination claim "because the Tribe lacks civil authority to regulate the Bank's sale of its fee land."[124] Somehow, the sale of fee land was not an "activity" regulated by the well-known *Montana* test. There was neither precedent nor logic for such an assertion.[125] The Court appeared determined to say no to tribal court jurisdiction, and it did. Unstated policy concerns completely displaced legal reasoning.

All of this involves significant extrapolation from *Montana*'s initial concern with the import of the General Allotment Act and Crow Allotment Act on events involving non-Indians that took place on *their* fee land. Yet there is no doubt that this is the crucible of modern Indian law, where tribal sovereignty engages non-Indians on the reservation within a framework of layer upon layer of ad hoc (common law) decision making by the Supreme Court.

Whether by design or by the drift of a miasmic case-by-case determination, the Court (and not Congress) has become the primary gatekeeper in modern

Indian law that regulates the assertiveness of both the state and tribal sovereign in Indian country. It has done this with minimal (to nonexistent) constitutional authority and congressional authorization. In the absence of significant congressional regulation of civil jurisdiction in Indian country, the Court has adopted a mantle of judicial plenary power to chart its own course in Indian law. It has largely departed from the Marshall Court's jurisprudence rooted in the Indian Commerce Clause and treaties foreclosing state authority in Indian country, and it has consistently constrained tribal authority on the reservation, especially in regard to non-Indians. This trend has been noted by a number of scholars who emphasize such themes as subjectivism, common law colonialism, and judicial plenary power.[126]

The Court has developed a most robust activist posture to deal with the nettlesome challenges of modern Indian law. It is an approach almost completely shorn of any concern for constitutional and historical doctrine, the role of a limited judiciary, and respect for those who were here first. Justice Scalia, a self-proclaimed originalist,[127] has made the most frank declaration in this regard. In correspondence with Justice Brennan concerning the case of *Duro v. Reina*,[128] he declared:

> [O]pinions in this field have not posited an original state of affairs
> that can subsequently be altered only by explicit legislation, but
> rather sought to discern *what the current state of affairs ought to be* by
> taking into account all legislation, and the congressional "expecta-
> tions" that it reflects, down to the present day.[129]

In this startling view, modern Indian law before the bar of the Supreme Court becomes wholly a field of "ought," to be filled not by constitutional and statutory dictates, but rather by what the Court thinks is best for all concerned. In a sense, the Court has become the ultimate organ for formulating Indian policy in contemporary Indian law. This raises a quintessential separation of powers issue, with the Court usurping the constitutional role of Congress to make law and formulate policy. This essential problem has largely gone unnoticed by both the Court and Congress. The Court has forged a pattern of judicial activism so brazen that it eludes those branches of government that should be most concerned. Solutions to this quandary will be more fully explored in chapter 10.[130]

The extremely broad use of (federal) common law to demarcate the boundaries of tribal sovereignty bears scrutiny, especially in regard to tribal regulatory and judicial jurisdiction over non-Indians. Although common law plays a recognized role in federal courts jurisprudence in some areas, such as the rights and duties of the federal government, international law, conflicts among the states, and admiralty law, its role in Indian law is seldom noted or analyzed within the federal courts scholarly community.[131]

The Court itself has been less than forthcoming about the role of common law within the contemporary Indian law jurisprudence. In fact, in the key modern cases dealing with tribal civil authority over non-Indians running from *Montana v. United States* through *Plains Commerce Bank v. Long Family Land and Cattle Co., Inc.*,[132] the term is rarely used, despite the fact that it provides the rule of decision for every case. It is expressly mentioned in *National Farmers Union* only in order to provide the necessary ingredient for *federal* jurisdiction pursuant to 28 U.S.C. § 1331.[133]

When ruling on the merits in all the other cited cases, the Court never relies on the Constitution or any federal statute but rather on such constructions as "inconsistent with the dependent status of the tribes"[134] or "beyond what is necessary to control internal relations."[135] Upon inspection, these phrases are mere euphemisms to disguise the Court's policy preferences, and thus perhaps the Court is too embarrassed to dignify its pronouncements with the express mention of the term *common law*. Of course, this style of decision making was partially confronted in *United States v. Lara*,[136] especially by Justice Thomas, when he noted: "*Duro, Oliphant*, and *Wheeler* are classic federal-common law decisions."[137] Justice Thomas's observation was not contested or denied by any other opinion in the case.

All of this slipperiness and denial about the role of federal common law in Indian law is in marked contrast to the knock-down exchange about federal common law in the case of *Sosa v. Alvarez-Machain*,[138] which involved the interpretation of the Alien Tort statute. The key issue was whether respondent Alvarez-Machain could make out any cause of action under the Alien Tort statute based on his illegal abduction in Mexico by federal Drug Enforcement Administration agents. Such an "abduction," according to the Court, was not a "violation of the law of nations" as that term was understood in 1789. The Law of Nations at that time was limited to "violations of safe conduct, infringement of the rights of ambassadors, and piracy and thus no common law cause of action existed."

Justice Scalia's concurrence saw unrestrained federal common law as undermining the democratic process:

> We Americans have a method for making the laws that are over us.
> We elect representatives to two Houses of Congress, each of which
> must enact the new law and present it for the approval of a President,
> whom we also elect. For over two decades now, unelected federal

judges have been usurping this lawmaking by converting what they regard as norms of international law into American law.[139]

Justice Scalia might do well to turn his penetrating gaze concerning the vigor and vitality of the democratic process from the perils of "international norms" to the thinly veiled policy preferences routinely applied by the Court in much contemporary Indian law jurisprudence. According to Justice Scalia, "This Court seems incapable of admitting that some matters—*any* matters—are none of its business."[140] Indian law might be a place for Justice Scalia to begin to practice what he preaches.

Parsing the Entrails of Contemporary Indian Law Jurisprudence

Although the Supreme Court has become increasingly obscure and incoherent (even to itself)[141] in its Indian law jurisprudence, it has finally come clean, albeit quite inadvertently, in the case of *City of Sherrill v. Oneida Indian Nation*.[142] In *City of Sherrill*, the Court, in an eight-to-one decision written by Justice Ginsburg, held that the Oneida Indian Nation's recent purchase of fee land within the original boundaries of its reservation, established by the 1794 Treaty of Canadaigua, was not immune from local property taxes. More specifically, the Court stated:

> We hold that the Tribe cannot unilaterally revive its ancient sover-
> eignty, in whole or in part, over the parcels at issue. The Oneidas
> long ago relinquished the reins of government and cannot recognize
> them through open-market purchases from current titleholders.[143]

The Court noted that the 300,000-acre reservation had dwindled to approximately 17,000 acres, with a 99 percent population of non-Indians within the original reservation area.[144] Such demographic and land tenure patterns are often a death knell for tribes in "diminishment" cases, which are concerned with the intent of Congress in passing statutes that allowed non-Indians to homestead in Indian country. *Sherrill* was not such a diminishment case, according to the Court, but rather an attempt by the Oneida Indian Nation at "rekindling embers of sovereignty that long ago grew cold."[145] The Court itself blew new life into the defenses of laches, impossibility, and acquiescence in order not to disturb the "justifiable expectations" of non-Indians with a "disruptive remedy."[146]

The fear of the Court clearly was that the Oneida Indian Nation was seeking to use its sovereignty "offensively" against non-Indians, and thus it must be struck down. Justice Stevens's lone dissent deftly highlighted this move by the majority. For Justice Stevens, the tribe was not seeking to advance offensive sovereignty against non-Indians but was using its sovereignty "as a *defense* against a state collection proceeding."[147]

Indeed, this is the explanatory key to the majority's opinion. Tribal sovereignty, it appears, may be used only defensively, not offensively. Justice Stevens clearly saw the Court taking extravagant steps to incorrectly convert a case of (permissive) defensive sovereignty into a case of (impermissible) offensive sovereignty:

> In the present case, the Tribe is not attempting to collect damages or eject landowners as a remedy for a wrong that occurred centuries ago; rather, it is invoking an ancient immunity against a city's present day attempt to tax its reservation lands.
>
> Without benefit of relevant briefing of the parties, the Court has ventured into legal territory that belongs to Congress. Its decision today is at war with at least two bedrock principles of Indian law. First, only Congress has the power to diminish or disestablish a tribe's reservation. Second, as a core incident of tribal sovereignty, a tribe enjoys immunity from state and local taxation of its reservation lands, until that immunity is explicitly revoked by Congress. Far from revoking this immunity, Congress has specifically reconfirmed it with respect to the reservation lands of the New York Indians. Ignoring those principles, the Court has done only what Congress may do—it has effectively proclaimed a diminishment of the Tribe's reservation and an abrogation of its elemental right to tax immunity.[148]

Justice Stevens insightfully noted that the majority rests almost all of its opinion on "speculation about what may happen in future litigation over *other* regulatory issues"[149] and "the majority's fear of opening a Pandora's box of tribal powers."[150]

If we take this defensive-offensive use of tribal sovereignty as a potential model, how accurate a predictor of case results is it? The answer is that it is extremely accurate. For example, if we take the early classic cases of the modern era, such as *Williams v. Lee*[151] and *McClanahan v. Arizona Tax Commission*,[152] and recast them as cases involving the use of "defensive" sovereignty *against* state assertions of authority against Indians, tribes should prevail, and they do. This is also true in more recent cases such as *Minnesota v. Mille Lacs Band of Chippewa Indians*.[153]

If we assume the use of "offensive" tribal sovereignty as a basis for asserting tribal authority over non-Indians on nontrust land in such cases as

Montana v. United States,[154] *South Dakota v. Bourland*,[155] *Strate v. A-1 Contractors*,[156] *Alaska v. Village of Venetie*,[157] *Atkinson Trading Co., Inc. v. Shirley*,[158] *Nevada v. Hicks*,[159] and most recently *Plains Commerce Bank v. Long Family Land and Cattle Co., Inc.*,[160] the paradigm accurately predicts tribal losses in every single case. The apparent exceptions of *National Farmers Ins. Cos. v. Crow Tribe of Indians*[161] and *Iowa Mutual Ins. v. LaPlante*[162] were later subsumed into the rule of *Strate v. A-1 Contractors*, which collapsed the distinction between tribal judicial and tribal regulatory jurisdiction and made "exhaustion" of tribal remedies merely prudential, rather than mandatory. The Supreme Court itself has subsequently never held in favor of tribal (judicial or regulatory) jurisdiction over non-Indians. The Court has never expressly fashioned a black letter rule that tribes do not have civil jurisdiction over non-Indians on nontrust land, but then again, it has never held to the contrary in any specific case.[163]

In addition, there is a hybrid set of cases, where the state seeks affirmatively to regulate, primarily through taxation, the activities of non-Indians, rather than Indians, on the reservation. These cases do not directly involve the paradigm because the use of offensive or defensive tribal sovereignty is *not* front and center. Results in these cases are not so readily predictable and are often decided on the (subjective) intricacies of interest balancing. The best examples of such hybrid cases are *Washington v. Confederated Tribes of Colville Indian Reservation*,[164] *White Mountain Apache Tribe v. Bracker*,[165] and *Cotton Petroleum Corp. v. New Mexico*.[166] In *Colville* and *Cotton Petroleum*, the Court permitted dual taxation of non-Indians; in *Bracker*, it denied state taxation of certain non-Indian activity.

The value of the paradigm is not limited to its accuracy in predicting results, but also its revelation of the Court's essential "fear" of "offensive" tribal sovereignty. This is at the heart of what tribes confront in seeking to realize widespread governing authority in Indian country, especially with regard to non-Indians. Tribes must seek to parse and to allay these fears. These fears probably include lingering racial animus; ignorance of what tribes actually do and how they do it; concerns about the potential tribal abuse of power, especially in regard to non-Indians, the absence of direct federal review; and the continuing historical dilemma of how tribes "fit" into the national governing structure. Much of this book develops these themes, particularly within a constitutional framework.

Tribes are *not* responsible for the racial animus that exists or the ignorance of the Court and society at large, but they must nevertheless seek to overcome these obstacles. Certainly, one of the most effective ways in any such endeavor would be for tribes to develop greater transparency in regard to what tribal law is, how it is made, and how it is interpreted by tribal courts. Such increasing transparency would presumably demonstrate a significant symmetry, if not identity, with approaches at both the state and federal level. This transparency would also be likely to foster a stronger basis for identifying legitimate contours to a federal-tribal federalism—a federalism that relies less on raw plenary power and more on respect and understanding of common spheres of mutual activity, and a federalism that might ultimately result in statutory reform and culminate in the necessary constitutional amendment to fully integrate tribal sovereignty within the structure of the U.S. Constitution.

Felix Cohen

No discussion of modern Indian law is complete without consideration and acknowledgment of the seminal contribution of Felix Cohen. Felix Cohen, named after the jurist Felix Frankfurter, a friend of his philosopher father, Morris, was born in New York City in 1907, the son of Jewish parents raised on the Lower East Side of Manhattan. He was educated at the City College of New York; Harvard University, where he received a doctorate in philosophy; and Columbia University, where he received his law degree.

Cohen's academic studies in philosophy and law developed an interest in two areas of thought that significantly influenced his engagement with, and commitment to, the field of Indian law. These twin concepts were legal realism and legal pluralism.[167] Legal realism is a school of jurisprudential thought that largely developed in the 1940s as a "general revolt against formalism and absolutism and engaged in a harsh critique of classical legal thought."[168] Classical legal thought viewed law as an autonomous and logical system, where judicial decisions were the product of internal, coherent reasoning, immune from any social, economic, and political interests.[169] Legal realists considered such views as hermetic, naive, and lacking connection with the real world of judicial decision making. Judges were not mere ciphers of inference and logic, but rather, like the rest of us, products—at least in part—of experience:

> Legal realists argued that law was not an autonomous body of
> abstract axioms from which judges could deduce rules but rather the
> outcome of debatable policy judgments about the social utility of
> diverse activities in a rapidly changing society. Legal realists rejected
> the idea that law was discovered through internal reasoning. They

argued that by depicting law as apolitical, the classicist model obscured the indeterminacy of legal doctrine and the social, economic, and political interests that legal decisions promoted.[170]

Indian law, from its inception in the Marshall trilogy through the "common law" (policy) ramblings of the current Court, would appear to be a veritable gold mine for legal realism excavation. Indeed, it proved to be so for Felix Cohen.

If legal realism was one bookend of Cohen's thought, which was used to describe the law as it worked in the real world, legal pluralism was the other bookend, and it was used to describe what the law ought to be in the real world. In this view, political and legal pluralism, especially as it was formulated in the 1920s, sought to carve out new philosophical and political ground within the boundaries of American liberalism by avoiding the extremes of excessive individualism on one hand and radical collectivism on the other.[171]

Legal pluralism emphasized the importance of group belonging and group action as central vehicles beneficial to both the individual and society as a whole. The primary attributes of such groups were to be autonomy and self-governance. Legal pluralism viewed groups as necessary to mitigate the harshness of the capitalist state and to ameliorate the resulting atomization of the individual. Early pluralistic visions tended to focus on political and economic groups such as labor unions; later ones focused more on cultural and ethnic groups. In Cohen's case, Indian tribes were a prototypical example of the latter.

Despite all of this, Cohen's entrance into the field of Indian law was the result of fortuity, not design. Cohen had not traveled in Indian country and had not practiced Indian law. Yet in 1933, he was asked by Nathan Margold, a friend of the family and the new solicitor of the Department of Interior, to join him for a year to help change federal Indian policy. Cohen accepted the offer and remained at the Department of the Interior for fourteen years.[172]

While at the Department of the Interior, Cohen played a significant role in helping to mold the Indian Reorganization Act, the legislative centerpiece of the energetic Commissioner of Indian Affairs, John Collier, to oversee its implementation, and to prepare the penultimate *Handbook of Federal Indian Law*, which now bears his name.[173] The Indian Reorganization Act, as originally drafted, sought significant reform in Indian Affairs in four important areas, namely, self-government, education, Indians' lands, and law and order.[174] The bill had little support from the Indian groups and the tribes themselves. Congress itself was unenthusiastic, especially because of the bill's very wide scope. Nevertheless, a drastically shortened version of the bill, reduced from forty-eight pages to five, did pass.[175]

The version of the bill that was adopted by Congress was consent-based and included further options for tribes to adopt constitutions and corporate charters for economic development purposes. Although Cohen was hesitant to prepare a model constitution, believing strongly that a constitution had to be the "offspring of Indian hearts and minds," he did prepare a "Basic Memorandum on Drafting Tribal Constitutions," which outlined many of the key provisions that would find their way into most IRA tribal constitutions.[176] This entire process, which was swift, largely uniform, and without significant tribal input, led to significant resentment within many tribes.[177] Despite these not inconsiderable problems, Cohen eloquently noted that "an Indian constitution will exist as long as there remains in human hearts a community of interdependence, of common interests, aspiration, hopes, and fears in realms of art and politics, work and play.[178]

The *Handbook of Federal Indian Law* began in 1938 as a joint project between the Departments of Justice and Interior to survey, categorize, and synthesize the hundreds of scattered sources—federal, state, and tribal—that dealt with Indian law. Cohen headed this project, but his work was often criticized by others, especially at the Department of Justice, as too expansive in its views of tribal authority and power. Despite its rocky history, it was published by the Department of the Interior in 1941. It was a masterly work, vast in scope, that rested on four principles: the political equality of races, tribal self-government, federal (rather than state) sovereignty in Indian affairs, and governmental protection of Indians.[179]

The *Handbook* did not prove popular within government circles. The bureau reprinted a bowdlerized version in 1958 that omitted much that was critical of BIA practices. The original *Handbook* did not appear back in print until it was republished by the University of New Mexico Press in 1973, under the leadership of Robert Bennett. It continues to hold canonical status within the field of Indian law and has been revised in two updated scholarly editions in 1982 and 2005.[180]

In staking a claim for the legitimacy of tribal existence and self-governance, particularly when tribes were at a historical low point, Cohen nevertheless advanced a view of tribal sovereignty that many have come to criticize.[181] His most succinct and often quoted formulation states:

> The whole course of judicial decisions on the nature of Indian
> tribal power is marked by adherence to three fundamental prin-
> ciples: (1) An Indian tribe possesses, in the first instance, all the
> powers of a sovereign state. (2) Conquest renders the tribe subject
> to the legislative power of the United States and, in substance,
> terminates the tribe's external sovereignty, for example, its power

to enter into treaties with foreign nations, but does not by itself affect the tribes' internal sovereignty, that is, its powers of local self-government. (3) These powers are subject to qualification by treaties and express legislation of Congress, but, save as thus expressly qualified, full powers of internal sovereignty are vested in the Indian tribe and in their duly constituted organs of government.[182]

Despite the unfortunate use of the term *conquest* and a concession to extensive (even plenary?) congressional power, Cohen's statement may be seen as a valiant attempt to stanch the view of many at that time "that Indian tribes had withered away under the weight of non-Indian society and that courts should acknowledge the decline of tribes and doctrines such as sovereign immunity."[183]

Tribes are once again under (jurisdictional) assault, and the spirit of Felix Cohen's work suggests that it is both timely and necessary to revisit and reconceptualize tribal sovereignty. Perhaps, at last, so reconsidered, it might rest on the enduring plane of the Constitution.[184] The challenge of his miner's canary remains as potent as ever:

> [l]ike the miner's canary, the Indian marks the shift from fresh air to poison gas in our political atmosphere, and our treatment of Indians, even more than our treatment of other minorities, reflects the rise and fall of our democratic faith.[185]

Supreme Court Statutory Interpretation in the Modern Era of Indian Law

Although Congress has enacted many statutes[186] in the modern era of Indian law, four statutes are the most significant: the Indian Civil Rights Act of 1968,[187] the Indian Child Welfare Act of 1978,[188] the Indian Gaming Regulatory Act of 1988,[189] and the *Duro* override statute.[190] Each has been reviewed and interpreted by the Supreme Court. In each instance, the Court has hewed to the text and intent of Congress, without inserting its own policy preferences.

The Indian Civil Rights Act of 1968

The Indian Civil Rights Act of 1968 (hereinafter "ICRA") was enacted by Congress in the mid-1960s in the context of other notable civil rights legislation dealing with the extension of basic civil rights protection in the field of public accommodations and the right to vote. The need for such legislation in Indian country caught Congress's attention when it was reminded that the basic Bill of Rights protections contained in the Constitution did *not* apply against tribal governments. This was the classic holding of *Talton v. Mayes*,[191] which was decided in 1896.

Talton involved a homicide committed by one Cherokee Indian against another Cherokee Indian on the Cherokee Reservation. The defendant challenged his prosecution in tribal court for its failure to provide grand jury indictment in accord with the Fifth Amendment of the U.S. Constitution.[192] The Court held that the Constitution did not constrain the powers of the Cherokee Nation because the Cherokee Nation's powers of self-government "existed prior to the Constitution."[193] The Court also noted—somewhat paradoxically— that, despite the absence of any *constitutional* limit on tribal power, tribes were nevertheless subject to "the paramount authority of Congress."[194] This paramount authority of Congress was previously addressed in cases like *United States v. Kagama*[195] and subsequently in *Lone Wolf v. Hitchcock*,[196] which ultimately gave birth to Congress's plenary power.

The text of the Indian Civil Rights Act largely replicates the guarantees and protections of the Bill of Rights. There are, however, some notable differences and accommodations. There is no establishment clause, there is no right to free counsel in a criminal case, there is no right to a jury trial in a civil case, criminal trials require only six jurors, there is no right to grand jury indictment, and there is no right to bear arms. There is also an express sanction limitation of one year in jail and a fine of $5,000. The statute expressly provides that:

No Indian tribe in exercising powers of self-government shall—

(1) make or enforce any law prohibiting the free exercise of religion, or abridging the freedom of speech, or of the press, or the right of the people peaceably to assemble and to petition for a redress of grievances;

(2) violate the right of the people to be secure in their persons, houses, papers, and effects against unreasonable search and seizures, nor issue warrants, but upon probable cause, supported by oath or affirmation, and particularly describing the place to be searched and the person or thing to be seized;

(3) subject any person for the same offense to be twice put in jeopardy;

(4) compel any person in any criminal case to be a witness against himself;

(5) take any private property for a public use without just compensation;

(6) deny to any person in a criminal proceeding the right to a speedy and public trial, to be informed of the nature and cause of the accusation, to be confronted with the witnesses against him, to have compulsory process for obtaining witnesses in his favor, and at his own expense to have the assistance of counsel for his defense;

(7) require excessive bail, impose excessive fines, inflict cruel and unusual punishments, and in no event impose for conviction of any one offense any penalty or punishment greater than imprisonment for a term of one year and a fine of $5000, or both;

(8) deny to any person within its jurisdiction the equal protection of its laws or deprive any person of liberty or property without due process of law;

(9) pass any bill of attainder or ex post facto law; or

(10) deny to any person accused of an offense punishable by imprisonment the right, upon request, to a trial by jury of not less than six persons.[197]

The sole express remedy provided by the Indian Civil Rights Act is the writ of habeas corpus.[198]

The landmark case interpreting the Indian Civil Rights Act of 1968 is *Santa Clara Pueblo v. Martinez*.[199] The sole issue in the case was "whether a federal court may pass on the validity of an Indian tribe's ordinance denying membership to the children of certain female tribal members."[200] The facts and the relevant law of Santa Clara Pueblo were remarkably straightforward. Julia Martinez was a full-blooded member of the tribe who resided on the Santa Clara Pueblo Reservation in Northern New Mexico. In 1941, Martinez married a Navajo man. They had several children, all of whom were denied membership in the tribe because they did not meet the requirements of the tribe's 1939 membership ordinance.[201] The membership ordinance expressly barred from membership all children of a female tribal member who married a nontribal member but expressly authorized the membership of all children of a male tribal member who married a nonmember.[202] This differential treatment had obvious legal consequences:

Although the children were raised on the reservation and continue to reside there now that they are adults, as a result of their exclusion from membership they may not vote in tribal elections or hold secular office in the tribe; moreover, they have no right to remain on the reservation in the event of their mother's death, or to inherit their mother's home or her possessory interests in the communal lands.[203]

After failing to persuade the tribe to change its membership rule, Martinez filed directly in federal court an action alleging a violation of the due process and equal protection guarantees of the Indian Civil Rights Act, 25 U.S.C. § 1302 (8), and seeking declaratory and injunctive relief that the Pueblo's membership ordinance violated federal law.[204] The primary defense of the tribe was jurisdictional, in that the Court lacked authority to decide intratribal controversies affecting matters of self-government and sovereignty.[205] Both the District Court and the Tenth Circuit Court of Appeals found jurisdiction based on *an implied cause of action* in the Indian Civil Rights Act and 28 U.S.C. § 1343 (a)(4)[206] and decided the case on the merits. The district court found for the tribe on the merits. It held that membership rules were basic to the tribe's survival as a cultural and economic entity and that the necessary balancing of interests was to be left to the tribe.[207]

The Tenth Circuit reversed because the classification was based on gender and therefore presumptively invalid. This presumptive invalidity was not overcome by any compelling tribal interest. The Court of Appeals found no compelling tribal interest because of the recent vintage of the membership ordinance and because the membership rule did not rationally identify those persons who were emotionally and culturally Santa Claran.[208]

The Supreme Court reversed the Tenth Circuit ruling on jurisdictional grounds and made no finding on the merits. Justice Marshall's[209] opinion focused intently on the text of the statute and the backdrop of tribal sovereignty.[210] It also noted that the basic legislation itself was well within Congress's plenary power in Indian affairs.[211] In looking at the text of the Indian Civil Rights Act, the Court focused on two things: the absence of any waiver of tribal sovereign immunity and the express authorization of only one remedy, namely, the writ of habeas corpus.[212] The Court noted that any congressional waiver of a tribe's sovereign immunity must be express rather than implied, and it found no such express language in the Indian Civil Rights Act of 1968. It therefore held that ICRA suits against the tribe in federal court were barred by its sovereign immunity.[213]

The Court noted, however, that an officer of the Pueblo, Lucario Padilla, a named defendant, was not protected by the tribe's immunity from suit. Therefore, the Court had to analyze whether there was an implied cause of action for declaratory and injunctive relief available against Padilla in his official capacity. Again, the Court answered in the negative.[214] In this part of the Court's analysis, much emphasis was placed on the historical tradition of preserving tribal self-government, especially over its own members. This emphasis was coupled with a review of the statute's structure and legislative history that strongly suggested that "Congress' failure to provide remedies other than habeas corpus was a deliberate one."[215]

The Court went on to describe the statute as involving "[t]wo distinct and competing purposes," namely, "strengthening the position of individual tribal members vis-à-vis the tribe" and promoting "the well established federal 'policy of furthering Indian self-government.' "[216] The Court cautioned that it would be "more than usually hesitant to infer from its [i.e., the statute's] silence a cause of action that, while serving one legislative purpose, will disserve the other."[217] Although the availability of a federal forum might advance compliance with the guarantees of 25 U.S.C. § 1302, it would unduly invade the province of tribal self-government and undermine the authority of tribal forums.[218] The Court concluded:

> Tribal forums are available to vindicate rights created by the ICRA, and § 1302 has the substantial and intended effect of changing the law which those forums are obliged to apply. Tribal courts have repeatedly been recognized as appropriate forums for the exclusive adjudication of disputes affecting important personal and property interests of both Indians and non-Indians.[219]

Although the decision, on its face, is a strong endorsement of tribal sovereignty,[220] there are some other elements to consider. One is the structural shift the decision caused by making tribal courts the premier forum for the resolution of civil rights disputes that involve alleged deprivations by tribal governments. Prior to *Santa Clara Pueblo*, much of this local power resided in tribal councils and tribal executive branches, with little such authority recognized in tribal courts. Most challenges to tribal government abuses under ICRA were initially brought *directly* in federal court on the theory of an *implied* cause of action. Tribal courts therefore gained new power and prominence both *within* tribal government and *vis-à-vis* the federal courts. Tribal courts were now to be the first and often the last forum for the resolution of important civil rights issues involving tribal governments.[221]

The decision has also been, in some quarters, roundly criticized as perpetuating the subordination of women, which was of no consequence to a (then) all-male Supreme Court.[222] A corollary to this issue has been concern over whether the 1939 membership ordinance did, in fact, reflect the tribe's traditional cultural values or whether it reflected a Bureau of Indian Affairs policy designed to limit eligibility for federal Indian benefits, such as health care.[223]

All of this, in turn, loops back to an overarching question in modern Indian law of how much normative space is available to tribes to employ tradition and custom that diverges from, and even trenches on, the dominant canon. *Santa Clara Pueblo* may be understood as a case that maximizes such normative space, at least when tribal members are involved.[224] As we have seen, however, such normative space is severely constricted, often nonexistent, when non-Indians are involved, even in the absence of any statutory or constitutional framework. The question thus remains: What is the Court's justification for such differential treatment of tribal members as compared with nonmembers? Is it tribal sovereignty, "consent" of tribal members, respect for certain kinds of difference, or is it some kind of mixture, including insensitivity and indifference? The Court has yet to really say, nor has it identified whether there are outer limits or borders to this normative space of tribes in dealing with tribal members.

The Indian Child Welfare Act of 1978

If the Indian Civil Rights Act of 1968 is in the mainstream of the national civil rights legislation, the Indian Child Welfare Act of 1978 (hereinafter ICWA) definitely is not. Of course, its subject matter is different, but even in the context of federal Indian law, the ICWA is quite wide-ranging and probably the most significant piece of modern Indian law legislation in its off-reservation cause and effect.

The tribal impetus for such federal legislation was rooted in a harsh empirical reality. Tribes were losing their children to the non-Indian, off-reservation world in disturbing numbers. These losses were occasioned through "a unique and longstanding record of child welfare abuses by federal officials, state court judges, and private adoption agencies that led to widespread removal of Indian children from their homes and communities."[225] Testimony before congressional committees in 1974, 1977, and 1978 documented a pattern of harm that caused much alarm in Indian country. It was a pattern so dire that it threatened tribal survival.[226] As noted in testimony before the House of Representatives: "The wholesale separation of Indian children from their families is perhaps the most tragic and destructive aspect of American Indian life today."[227] The actual numbers were staggering. For example, testimony before Congress revealed:

> The disparity in placement rates for Indian and non-Indian children is shocking. In Minnesota, Indian children are placed in foster care or in adoptive homes at a per capita rate five times greater than non-Indian children. In Montana, the ratio of Indian foster care placement is at least 13 times greater. In South Dakota, 40 percent of all adoptions made by the South Dakota Department of Public Welfare since 1967–1968 are of Indian children, yet Indians make up only 7 percent of the juvenile population. The

number of South Dakota Indian children living in foster care homes is per capita, nearly 16 times greater than the non-Indian rate. In the state of Washington, the Indian adoption rate is 19 times greater and the foster care rate 10 times greater. In Wisconsin, the risk runs by Indian children of being separated from their parents is nearly 1,600 percent greater than it is for non-Indian children....

....

In 16 states surveyed in 1969, approximately 85 percent of all Indian children in foster care were living in non-Indian homes.[228]

Testimony relative to the etiology of these numbers reflected a continuing (and not unfamiliar) schism:

[S]tate child welfare officials were insensitive to traditional Indian approaches to child rearing, in particular the widespread practice of involving members of a child's extended family in significant caregiving. Applying majoritarian middle-class values, state workers often construed such practice as neglect or even abandonment. In addition, high rates of alcoholism and poverty were relied on as justifications for removing Indian children from their communities.[229]

For some, this was not at all new, but rather the latest update that harked back to the era of (federal) boarding schools, when the primary goal, in the words of William Pratt, a leading educator and spokesman, was "to kill the Indian and save the man."[230]

The ICWA focuses on three interlocking structural approaches to these problems. The statute is jurisdictionally stringent in *favor* of tribal court jurisdiction, creates minimum *federal* standards for the removal of Indian children from their homes by the *state*, and establishes strict placement preferences that must be followed by state courts. The ICWA expressly rests on Congress's authority under the Indian Commerce Clause, plenary power, and its "responsibility for the protection and preservation of Indian tribes and their resources."[231]

The jurisdiction scheme of the statute vests exclusive jurisdiction in tribal courts in "child custody proceeding(s)"[232] involving "Indian children,"[233] when the Indian child is a resident or domiciliary of the reservation.[234] When the Indian child is not a resident or domiciliary on the reservation, the state court shall have concurrent jurisdiction and:

in the *absence of good cause to the contrary*, shall transfer such proceeding to the jurisdiction of the tribe, absent objection by either parent, upon the petition of either parent or the Indian custodian of the Indian child's tribe: *Provided*, that such transfer shall be subject to declination by the tribal court of such tribe.[235]

The minimum *federal* standards for the removal of Indian children by state courts include the necessity of expert testimony,[236] the provision of rehabilitative services,[237] and an enhanced burden of proof.[238] The first two standards are not defined in the statute and have generated a good deal of case law without the benefit of Supreme Court interpretation or guidance.[239] The placement preferences are designed to facilitate placement with Indian families and institutions.[240] The preferences are socially and culturally defined[241] and subject to *tribal* revision.

The leading case on the Indian Child Welfare Act is the Supreme Court's decision in *Mississippi Band of Choctaw Indians v. Holyfield*.[242] The case involved the status of out-of-wedlock twins born off the reservation to a mother and father who were both members of the tribe and residents and domiciliaries of the reservation. It was a conscious choice by the parents to have the birth take place some 200 miles from the reservation in order to facilitate the adoption by non-Indians.[243]

The adoption proceeded with alacrity in Mississippi state court. The twins were born on December 29, 1985. Both parents signed consent forms before the Chancery Court of Harrison County on January 10, 1986. The adoptive parents filed a petition for adoption on January 10, 1986, and a final decree of adoption was issued on January 28, 1986, less than a month after the birth of the twins.[244] The final decree made no reference to the Indian Child Welfare Act and waived the normal six-month waiting period to finalize adoptions under Mississippi state law.[245]

Two months later, the tribe filed a motion in state court to vacate the adoption on the grounds that ICWA vested exclusive jurisdiction in the tribal court. The motion was denied by the court, and its one-page opinion noted that the (biological) parents had specifically chosen to give birth off the reservation to facilitate the (state) adoption and that the twins had never been physically on the reservation.[246]

The Mississippi Supreme Court affirmed. It noted that the key issue was the domicile of the twins. If the twins were domiciliaries of the reservation, the tribe would have exclusive jurisdiction. If the twins were not domiciliaries of the reservation, the state court would have concurrent jurisdiction in this (voluntary) proceeding.[247] Despite its own law that the domicile of children followed their parents, the Mississippi Supreme Court found that the twins were "legally abandoned" to the adoptive parents and hence the twins' domicile was that of the non-Indian adoptive parents.[248] The Court therefore concluded that ICWA was not applicable to the case.[249] This was manifestly incorrect as ICWA expressly requires any adoption of an Indian child in *state* court to comply with the statutory order of preference.[250]

The Supreme Court granted review and was again faced with a question of statutory interpretation. The Court framed the core issue as construing "the provisions of the Indian Child Welfare Act that establish exclusive tribal juris-diction over child custody proceedings involving Indian children domiciled on the tribe's reservation."[251] Resolution of the issue turned on the meaning of a single word, namely, *domicile*. ICWA itself contains no definition of the term.

Justice Brennan's opinion indicated that often in such circumstances where a federal statute is silent, it is permissible to borrow a state definition, especially in an area of state expertise such as domestic relations. Yet two sub-stantial reasons counseled against such an approach in interpreting ICWA. First, there was Congress's desire for nationwide *uniformity* in the application of ICWA, which would not be achieved if each state was free to use its own defi-nition of domicile. Second, and more important, was Congress's intent to limit (not expand) state judicial authority in dealing with Indian children.[252] Rejecting the offer to apply Mississippi state law, the Court decided to define *domicile* consistent with generally held principles that the domicile of a minor child born out of wedlock was that of the mother. The Court held this definition to be the one most consistent with the intent of Congress.[253]

Yet the Court was not finished. If the definition it chose was most consis-tent with Congress's intent of how to resolve the tribal-state tension in Indian child custody matters, what about the potential tension between the preference of the Indian parents for state court adjudication and the tribal preference for tribal court jurisdiction? This axis of tension drove the Court back to the text and history of the statute. According to the Court, a "voluntary" choice of an Indian parent to "surrender" an Indian child does not divest the tribe of its interest in that child, especially when the child is domiciled on the reservation.[254]

Congress had expressly found that there was a significant *tribal* interest in the placement of Indian children that was above and beyond the interests of the parents. The Court pointed to Congress's finding that "there is no resource that is more vital to the continued existence and integrity of Indian tribes than their children"[255] and its commitment "to promote the stability and security of Indian tribes."[256] In addition, the Court found "numerous prerogatives accorded the tribes through the ICWA's substantive provisions,"[257] including exclusive juris-diction over reservation domiciliaries, presumptive jurisdiction over nondomi-ciliaries, the right to intervene, notice of state court proceedings, the right to petition for invalidation of state court action, the right to alter presumptive placement priorities applicable to state court action, the right to obtain records, and the authority to make agreements with states. It noted that all of this must "be seen as a means of protecting not only the interests of individual Indian children and families, but also of the tribes themselves."[258] To allow individual tribal parents to avoid tribal exclusive jurisdiction "by the simple expedient of giving birth off the reservation would, to a large extent, nullify the purpose the ICWA was intended to accomplish."[259]

The Court accordingly reversed the decision of the Mississippi Supreme Court and remanded the case. Upon dismissal by the Mississippi Supreme Court, the case was filed in the Mississippi Band of Choctaw Tribal Court. The tribal court permitted the adoption to go forward, and the twins were adopted by the Holyfield family. This result surprised many, but maybe it should not have, for at least two reasons. First, the statutory adoption preferences that favor Indian adoptive parents apply only in state courts. They do not apply in tribal courts.[260] Second, it is presumptuous to believe that tribal court jurisdiction means the Indians always "win" without any consideration for equity and what is in the best interests of an Indian child in a *particular* case.

There are some interesting comparisons to be made between *Holyfield* and *Santa Clara Pueblo v. Martinez*. Both cases involve interpretations of federal statutes that seek to balance competing concerns. The Indian Civil Rights Act constructs a balance between individual civil rights of Indians (indeed of *all* individuals subject to tribal governance) and the collective right of tribal self-governance without federal interference. The Indian Child Welfare Act also strikes a balance between the individual rights of Indian parents and the tribe's collective interest in the status of its members who are children. ICWA also strikes a balance between tribal and state authority involving Indian children who are not reservation residents or domiciliaries.[261] The Indian Gaming Regulatory Act of 1988 (IGRA), despite its subject matter, also involves congressional balancing of competing claims in Indian law. IGRA involves the perceived tension between tribes and the states in matters of gaming.

The Indian Gaming Regulatory Act of 1988

The Indian Gaming Regulatory Act of 1988[262] was passed by Congress in direct response to the Supreme Court's 1987 decision in the case of *California v. Cabazon Band of Mission Indians*.[263] In *Cabazon*, the issue was whether California could regulate high-stakes bingo and various card games taking place on the reservations of the Cabazon and Morango Bands of Mission

Indians in Riverside County. Both tribes carried out these activities pursuant to tribal ordinances approved by the secretary of the interior.[264]

The games were open to the public, who were largely non-Indians who came to the reservation. The gaming activities were a major source of employment for tribal members, and the profits were the tribes' sole source of income. The State of California sought to apply its statute, which required such gaming activities to be operated for and run by charitable organizations whose workers could not be paid, limited prizes to $250 per game, and required profits to be kept in special accounts and used only for charitable purposes, against the tribes.[265] Normally, of course, the state would have no authority to regulate the activities of a tribe on a reservation that took place on tribal trust land.[266] However, there is a 1953 federal statute that granted California (and several other states) civil and criminal jurisdiction over events that transpired anywhere on reservations within those states.[267]

The central issue thus became whether Public Law 280 conferred the requisite authority on the state to regulate Indian gaming on the reservation. The Court said no, based largely on its analysis that the grant of state criminal and civil *jurisdiction* to Public Law 280 states did not include a grant of civil *regulatory* authority over the tribes. The Court noted that although part of the California statutory scheme in gaming involved potential criminal sanctions, there were sufficient exceptions to make the statute impermissibly regulatory, rather than permissibly prohibitory, in Indian country. Because the California gaming statute was deemed civil rather than criminal in nature, it failed to meet the Public Law 280 test for applicability in Indian country.[268]

After *Cabazon*, the specter of unregulated gaming in Indian country drove many states, particularly in the West, to turn to Congress for some relief from this perceived danger. Congress responded with the Indian Gaming Regulatory Act of 1988. The statute attempted to forge a workable compromise between the competing interests of the tribes and the states. In its bluntest form, the tribes wanted to maximize their authority and autonomy, and states wanted to minimize it. Conversely, the states wanted to maximize their authority in Indian gaming, and the tribes wanted to minimize it. The resulting statutory compromise had both supporters and detractors, but it has—despite some glaring stresses—held up so far. This is especially remarkable in light of the stunning growth of Indian gaming.

According to 2004 statistics provided by the National Indian Gaming Commission, the federal agency established by IGRA to regulate Indian gaming, almost half (224 of 562) of all federally recognized tribes engage in gaming. These tribes operate 354 facilities in twenty-eight states. Annual revenues approach $15 billion, almost a quarter of total gaming revenues in the United

States, which include everything from racetracks to state lotteries. Indian casinos have generated more than 400,000 jobs, most of which are held by non-Indians.[269] There is no doubt that Indian gaming has brought significant economic development and revenue to many tribes and nearby non-Indian communities, but it has been rather asymmetrical in its effects. Many tribes and individual Indians remain extremely poor, but this is seldom reported in the mainstream media. For example, four of the ten poorest counties in the United States are located on reservations in South Dakota.[270] Indian gaming has also created issues for successful gaming tribes about such things as the relationship of wealth, both collective and individual, to traditional values such as sharing, consensus, and inclusiveness. A few highly successful gaming tribes have become bitterly divided around issues of tribal enrollment and even disenrollment of members.[271]

The Indian Gaming Regulatory Act itself is complex and detailed. It organizes Indian gaming into three different classes, requires tribal-state compacts before lucrative Class III gaming can begin on any reservation, establishes the Indian Gaming Regulatory Commission to oversee gaming in Indian country, and creates an intricate remedial scheme to promote tribal-state cooperation. The statute, however, unlike the Indian Child Welfare Act, for example, contains no express statement of Congress's authority to enact such legislation.

Class I games include "social games" for prizes with nominal value and traditional tribal gaming. These games are subject solely to the jurisdiction of the tribe.[272] Class II games include bingo, lotto, and card games that are not played against the house. Class II games are subject to state law relative to hours of operation, as well as limitations on the sizes of wagers and pots, but otherwise are subject to independent tribal regulation, with Department of Interior oversight.[273]

Class III games constitute the heart of Indian gaming and include its most lucrative elements, such as slot machines, blackjack, and roulette. In fact, Class III gaming is any gaming not defined as Class I or Class II gaming. Class III gaming requires a tribal-state compact. Class III gaming also requires the desired gaming to be "located in a state that permits such gaming for any purpose by any person, organization, or entity."[274] The tribal-state compact requirement includes a statutory mandate that the state negotiate in "good faith" and provides for a federal cause of action by tribes against states for their failure to negotiate in good faith.[275]

The statute also established the Indian Gaming Regulatory Commission to oversee Indian gaming with such responsibilities as approving tribal gaming ordinances and management contracts, conducting audits, and approving any per-capita distribution of gaming profits.[276] Tribal gaming profits may be expended only for these express purposes:

   (i) to fund tribal government operations or programs;

  (ii) to provide for the general welfare of the Indian tribe and its members;

 (iii) to promote tribal economic development;

 (iv) to donate to charitable organizations; or

  (v) to help fund operations of local government agencies.[277]

The leading case on the interpretation of the Indian Gaming Regulatory Act is *Seminole Tribe of Florida v. Florida*.[278] This case focused on the narrow but critical question of whether the federal cause of action, which permitted a tribe to sue a state in federal court for its alleged failure to negotiate in good faith, violated the state's sovereign immunity under the Eleventh Amendment.

The Court's opinion, authored by Chief Justice Rehnquist, proceeds within the recognized analytical structure for evaluating Eleventh Amendment claims. The inquiry is twofold: whether Congress "unequivocally expressed its intent to abrogate" and, if so, whether Congress acted "pursuant to a valid exercise of power."[279] The Court answered the first question in the affirmative and the second in the negative. The Court upheld the rest of the statute as constitutional.

The Court had little difficulty in discerning Congress's intent to abrogate the states' Eleventh Amendment protection from the face of the act. The numerous references to the "State" in § 2710(d)(7), which authorizes federal district court jurisdiction over suits brought by the tribe to compel good-faith negotiations by the state, "make it indubitable that Congress intended through the Act to abrogate the States' sovereign immunity from suit."[280]

The question of Congress's *authority* to abrogate the states' Eleventh Amendment protection was significantly more difficult. At the outset, the Court noted that there were only two available constitutional sources that could authorize such abrogation, namely, the Interstate Commerce Clause and Section 5 of the Fourteenth Amendment.[281] The Court seized the opportunity to overrule its lone precedent that had authorized Congress to waive a state's Eleventh Amendment immunity under the Interstate Commerce Clause. In overruling *Pennsylvania v. Union Gas Co.*,[282] the Court noted that its plurality opinion in that case was not joined by a majority of the court, was not subsequently cited or embraced by the Court in its Eleventh Amendment jurisprudence, and was a marked departure from the understanding that the principle of sovereign immunity is a constitutional constraint on the judicial power established in Article III.[283]

The Court noted that while the principle of stare decisis and its values of "evenhanded, predictable, and consistent development of legal principles,... reliance on judicial decisions, and...the actual and perceived integrity of the judicial process" counseled against overruling past precedent, stare decisis was a "principle of policy" not an "inexorable command."[284] According to the Court, such an approach is particularly appropriate in matters of constitutional doctrine, which are seldom amenable to legislative correction.[285] The Court went on to point out that the overruling of *Union Gas* also foreclosed the Indian Commerce Clause as a viable source for Congress's authority to waive a state's Eleventh Amendment sovereign immunity against suit in federal court.[286]

Chief Justice Rehnquist's majority opinion in *Seminole Tribe of Florida* was only 29 pages long, whereas the combined dissents of Justices Stevens and Souter run 109 pages.[287] The core of the dissents is a sustained argument that the majority's Eleventh Amendment views depart from the text of the amendment, misconstrue its surrounding history, and eviscerate precedent.

All of this has little to do with Indian law per se, but it does have much to do with the intense Eleventh Amendment debates that have increasingly engulfed the Court.[288] A number of commentators have found the *Seminole* case "remarkable," but most hold to the view that its impact in Indian law will be minimal:

> *Seminole* is probably not of major significance in regard to federal-
> Indian-state relations. It is designed to be, and is, a major decision
> about the meaning of the Eleventh Amendment and about federal-
> state relations, judicial and congressional. The decision does, obvi-
> ously, affect the IGRA. But the scheme that replaces the one held
> unconstitutional in *Seminole* could prove more advantageous to
> Native Americans rather than less.[289]

Although little commented on, perhaps because the statute itself does not expressly rely on it, there is now no doubt that the reach of plenary power in Indian affairs will be curtailed when it conflicts with other *existing constitutional* guarantees and constraints such as the Eleventh Amendment.[290] Plenary power in Indian law remains extensive, even vast, unless it collides with the operation of some other constitutional principle. *Seminole Tribe* is a rare example of such a collision.

As with the Indian Child Welfare Act, despite the basic validity of the statute, many hotly contested issues remain unresolved. With so much money involved, both tribes and states are pushing (sometimes cooperatively, sometimes antagonistically) the envelope concerning the development of *off*-reservation gaming revenue-sharing agreements and the expansion of current facilities. These issues have often spilled beyond tribal-state negotiations into such areas as statewide referenda in states such as Arizona, Nebraska, and California.[291] In California, for example, there was even a successful statewide initiative that amended California's constitution to give tribes the *exclusive* right to conduct

Class III gaming within the state in exchange for a state share of tribal gaming revenue.[292]

The Indian Child Welfare Act of 1978 and the Indian Gaming Regulatory Act of 1988 are the two most significant statutes in the modern era that expressly seek to balance tribal-state spheres of interest. Both statutes involve critical areas, namely, child welfare and economic development. Each statute has been essentially upheld, but most people believe that there is more to come both in Congress and in the courts.

The Duro Override and United States v. Lara

In 1990, the Supreme Court decided *Duro v. Reina*[293] and extended the rationale of *Oliphant v. Suquamish Indian Tribe* by denying tribes criminal jurisdiction over nonmember Indians.[294] As a result of substantial concern raised in Indian country about the likely disinterest or inability of the states or federal government to prosecute such nonmember Indians, Congress passed a statute—in the form of an amendment to the Indian Civil Rights Act of 1968—that effectively overturned the result in *Duro*[295] and closed the resulting "jurisdictional void." The amendment became popularly known as the *Duro* override, and it is the sole example in the modern era in which Congress expressly enacted legislation to overturn a Supreme Court (common law) decision in Indian law.

United States v. Lara[296] upheld the statute, including its express language recognizing the "inherent power" of tribes to possess criminal jurisdiction over nonmember Indians. The majority opinion was written by Justice Breyer, but the opinions of Justice Thomas and Justice Kennedy that concur in the judgment are particularly illuminating about the past (Justice Thomas) and future (Justice Kennedy) of Indian law jurisprudence. In *Lara*, Justice Breyer characterized the issue as "whether Congress has the constitutional power to relax restrictions that the political branches have, over time, placed on the exercise of a tribe's inherent legal authority."[297] The Court answered in the affirmative with both expected and unexpected reasoning.

Billy Jo Lara, an enrolled member of the Turtle Mountain Band of Chippewa Indians, married a member of the Spirit Lake Tribe and resided with his wife and their children at the Spirit Lake Reservation in North Dakota. While there, he was charged with assaulting a Bureau of Indian Affairs law enforcement officer. He pled guilty in the Spirit Lake Tribal Court to the charge of "violence to a policeman" and served a ninety-day sentence.

He was subsequently charged—based on the same facts—in federal court for assaulting a federal officer.[298] This is most routine in Indian country in accord with the black letter rule that Indian tribes are separate sovereigns for purposes of the double jeopardy protection of the Fifth Amendment.[299] Pursuant to the authority of the *Wheeler* case, double jeopardy is *not* a defense to separate tribal and federal prosecutions growing out of the same set of facts.[300]

Despite this black letter rule, interpretation of the *Duro* override statute was confused in the lower courts, particularly within the Eighth Circuit Court of Appeals. The Eighth Circuit decided that despite the clear language of the statute to the contrary, the *Duro* override was not a recognition of tribal "inherent authority" but rather a federal *delegation* of authority to the tribes, and hence double jeopardy did apply.[301]

The Eighth Circuit en banc opinion foundered on its perception that the original *Duro* decision was somehow *constitutional* in its dimensions, rather than a mere common law decision. If *Duro* was a decision grounded in constitutional principles, its result could not be overturned by Congress, but Congress could still *delegate* some of its plenary power to the tribes.[302] The Ninth Circuit understood the *Duro* decision as merely a common law decision subject to the paramount authority of Congress.[303]

The Supreme Court opted for the view of the Ninth Circuit as being more faithful to the text and legislative history of the statute, as well as to the general sweep of Indian law history. The essence of that sweep is that Congress has broad general powers to legislate with respect to Indian tribes and that such powers are "plenary and exclusive."[304] The Court also recited its core mantra that such powers derive from the Indian Commerce Clause and treaty making.

The Court further noted that both the *Oliphant* and *Duro* decisions were *judicial* assessments of the "tribe's retained sovereign status *as of the time* the Court made them. They did not set forth constitutional limits that prohibit Congress from changing the relevant legal circumstances, *i.e.* taking actions that modify or adjust the tribe's status."[305] In other words, the Constitution does not forbid "Congress to change 'judicially made' federal Indian law through this kind of legislation."[306]

Except for the confusion of the Eighth Circuit, this is no more than a routine case about Congress's plenary power, and ordinarily it would not be of very great interest. Yet its interest and importance are to be found in what Justice Breyer wrote that is outside the scope of his plenary power analysis, as well as Justice Thomas's powerful look *back* at the sweep of Indian law jurisprudence and Justice Kennedy's powerful look *forward* to the new issues he foresees.

Justice Breyer's opinion breaks new ground not in its plenary power analysis, but rather in its identification of Congress's "preconstitutional powers" in Indian law—powers heretofore unacknowledged and unarticulated. These powers are "necessarily inherent in any Federal Government, namely powers that this Court has described as 'necessary concomitants of nationality.' "[307] Justice

Breyer did not elaborate, but his citations have an international and colonial flavor, with references to Hawaii, the Northern Marianas Islands, Puerto Rico, and the Philippines.[308] In light of the Court's heretofore unimpeachable record with regard to plenary power, it remains to be seen why it might be necessary to find yet additional congressional power—power that *predates* the Constitution itself. Perhaps Justice Breyer thinks that Congress may soon need its own "inherent" power in Indian law in order not to lose control over the tribes' own "inherent" powers.

JUSTICE THOMAS'S OPINION CONCURRING IN THE JUDGMENT

If Justice Breyer's opinion rests comfortably on the notion of Congress's plenary power, it might be said that Justice Thomas's opinion looks back with incredulity at this most quizzical of "constitutional" doctrines. The opinion (which no one on the Court joined) starts with the recognition of a fundamental incongruity in how "Congress (rather than some other part of the federal government) can regulate virtually every aspect of the tribes without rendering tribal sovereignty a nullity."[309] Or to put it in a slightly different manner, "the tribes either are or are not separate sovereigns, and our federal Indian law cases untenably hold both positions simultaneously."[310]

Justice Thomas's opinion possesses a certain unassailable, even severe, logic. The Indian Commerce Clause and the treaty-making clauses of the Constitution do not confer the plenary authority routinely ascribed to them. In regard to the Indian Commerce Clause, commerce is not an encompassing category that is somehow beyond commerce itself. The opinion expressly recalls the "implausibility of this assertion" from the Court's own words in *United States v. Kagama* that it would be a "very strained" construction of the Indian Commerce Clause to provide the constitutional basis for enacting the Major Crimes Act in 1885.[311]

As to treaty making, Justice Thomas argues that the power is an executive rather than a legislative one in that it is found in Article II (§ 2, cl. 2), which enumerates the president's powers, not in Article I, which describes Congress's powers. And while a specific treaty may confer on Congress a very limited power it does not otherwise have, Indian treaties as a whole cannot "provide Congress with free-floating authority to legislate as it sees fit" in the field of Indian law.[312] Although Justice Thomas cites no scholarship for his overall analysis, it abounds within the field of Indian law, and it is curious that he does not make any reference of it.[313] This is merely an observation, not a complaint, and it does not detract from Justice Thomas's signature, *jurisprudential* effort to hold the plenary power doctrine up to the light of day and expose its many shadows.

Justice Thomas's views about what is to be done about all this are a bit murkier. *If* tribes are *sovereign*, then it is likely that the executive branch—not Congress enacting *domestic* legislation—has the principal authority to deal with Indian tribes.[314] Yet this is rendered practically moot by the termination of Indian treaty making by Congress in 1871.[315] Justice Thomas does suggest, however, that this statute is "constitutionally suspect" because it is *legislation* that attempts to limit the president's *constitutional* power. Justice Thomas seems willing to start over in Indian law. Such a possibility is clearly quite daunting and does not necessarily guarantee any beneficial revision in the constitutional status of tribes.

Although Justice Thomas's opinion does not have the answer to the problem of the doctrinal incoherence of current Indian law jurisprudence, he does seem to be the only justice willing to admit this and to identify the essential questions. As his opinion itself notes, "until we begin to analyze those questions honestly and rigorously, the confusion that I have identified will continue to haunt our cases."[316]

Many, including the tribes themselves, are likely to be chary of Justice Thomas's views. It would be yet another devastating irony in Indian law that the rare "beneficial" use of plenary power by Congress to recognize the "inherent power" of tribes should provide the occasion for in the future cutting back or even scrapping the doctrine entirely. This is especially troubling in the era of the Court's wholesale common law regime that has consistently eroded tribal authority over non-Indians. Is Congress only to be rebuffed when it arises from its slumber to assist tribes to reacquire "inherent" powers extinguished by a most activist court? Certainly, congressional plenary power must remain, at least to *undo* the common law overriding of the Court in the modern era.

Although it is indeed necessary to be concerned about all these potential effects, the *questions* Justice Thomas raised remain insistent and at the core of modern Indian law. In fact, that is the reason for this book and its own tentative response to advance dialogue by looking back and forward to the Constitution itself as a source point of doctrinal hope.[317] As noted, the opinion was not joined by any of Justice Thomas's colleagues, which probably indicates the Court's fervent unwillingness to take up any of the challenges posed by his opinion. Perhaps Justice Thomas is no more than a maverick iconoclast, a lone wolf (of originalism) on the frontier of contemporary Indian law.[318] Only time will tell.

JUSTICE KENNEDY'S OPINION CONCURRING IN THE JUDGMENT

Justice Kennedy's concurring opinion, like Justice Thomas's, had no supporters. He writes much about the likely *future* of Indian law. Justice Kennedy, who authored the Court's opinion in *Duro*, does not pick up the thread of the legitimate contours of tribal sovereignty; rather, he discusses what tribes can or cannot do with their sovereignty.

The essence of Justice Kennedy's concerns are quite broad and derive from a constitutional perspective not (currently) shared by any of his colleagues on the Court. Yet, as he himself admits, this is not the case that truly brings his concerns to the fore.[319] Justice Kennedy's opinion does not really focus on Lara's double jeopardy claim in *federal* court, but rather on the quandary Lara would have faced had he not pled guilty in *tribal* court.

Justice Kennedy's primary horizon of inquiry turns on the basic fact that "Lara, after all, is a citizen of the United States."[320] Tribal sovereignty is no real match against the citizenship of Billy Jo Lara:

> To hold that Congress can subject him, within our domestic borders, to a sovereignty outside the basic structure of the Constitution is a serious step. The Constitution is based on a theory of original, and continuing, consent of the governed. Their consent depends on the understanding that the Constitution has established the federal structure, which grants the citizen the protection of two governments, the Nation and the State. Each sovereign must respect the sphere of the other, for the citizen has rights and duties to both. Here, contrary to this design, the National Government seeks to subject a citizen to the criminal jurisdiction of a third entity to be tried for conduct wholly within the territorial borders of the Nation and one of the States. This is unprecedented.[321]

Such jurisdiction is not problematic for the tribal member because he "*consents* to be subjected to the jurisdiction of his own tribe."[322] Justice Kennedy's formulation of the problem is, in its way, a variant of Justice Thomas's views about the tension of tribal sovereignty within our current constitutional structure. Justice Kennedy's angle of vision, however, does not focus on federal-tribal constitutional tension but rather on the (nonmember) individual-tribal constitutional tension.

In Justice Kennedy's jurisprudential thinking, Congress cannot "yield authority inside the domestic borders over citizens to a third sovereign by using the euphemistic formulation that in amending the ICRA Congress merely *relaxed* restrictions on the tribes. There is no language in the statute, or the legislative history, that justifies this unusual phrase...."[323] The opinion is quite stringent in this regard. The availability, for example, of due process and equal protection in tribal court that stems from the Indian Civil Rights Act[324] does not offset the affront to the integrity of essential "constitutional structure" that vouchsafes individual liberty.[325]

Although Justice Kennedy's rhetoric approaches the grandiose, he correctly identifies—even invites—what will surely come next. When the next Billy Jo Lara pleads not guilty in tribal court, what *constitutional* guarantees, if any, will he be entitled to?[326] Due process, equal protection, the right to counsel at government expense (if the defendant is indigent), and trial by a jury drawn from a cross-section of the community? Perhaps none of these, except to the extent they are replicated in the Indian Civil Rights Act of 1968, which does, for example, include due process and equal protection guarantees, along with the right to counsel (but only at the defendant's own expense, regardless of indigency), but does not expressly require that all reservation residents be eligible for jury service.[327]

In contrast to Justice Thomas's opinion, there is potential that Justice Kennedy's opinion foreshadows a *new* way of thinking in Indian law, a move to "constitutionalize" Indian law not in order to protect and assist Indian tribes or tribal members, but to protect the essential (constitutional) rights of nonmember Indians and non-Indians. This likelihood is not without its own potential for unintended consequences, in that a statute designed to "relax restrictions" might ultimately create more of a legal and financial burden on tribes if they are, for example, required to provide free counsel to indigent nonmember defendants. This irony, of course, does not necessarily tarnish the appropriateness of such new burdens. It just highlights the continuing, unusual nature of Indian law.[328]

Summary

The Supreme Court's interpretation of the quintessential statutes of modern Indian law reveals a not unexpected penchant to uphold them[329] as within Congress's plenary power. The core analysis in each instance was to parse the statute in order to balance and resolve the essential tension between the tribes and the federal government and the tribe and its members (Indian Civil Rights Act of 1968, *Santa Clara Pueblo v. Martinez*), between the tribes and the states and the tribe and its members (Indian Child Welfare Act of 1978, *Mississippi Band of Choctaw v. Holyfield*), between the tribes and the states (Indian Gaming Regulatory Act of 1988, *Seminole Tribe of Florida v. Florida*), and between the tribe and nonmember Indians (*Duro* override, *United States v. Lara*).

Although there remain many substantial disputes involving the Indian Civil Rights Act of 1968, the Indian Child Welfare Act of 1978, and the Indian Gaming Regulatory Act of 1988,[330] the case with the most unsettling implications is *United States v. Lara*. The case brings some of Indian law's oldest and most potent paradoxes into the light of day, as well as virtually ensuring that cases will follow in which such paradoxes will be front and center as the disposi-tive issue, rather than providing mere opportunity for the jurisprudential mus-ings of certain justices. There appears to be yet another constitutional fork in the road of Indian law, but what the Court or Congress will do remains to be seen.

As a result, this is the time to seize the initiative to advance the dialogue, with the primary goal being to ensure tribal sovereignty a place of dignity and respect in any new era, whatever it might be called. This is especially true within a "constitutionalizing" context. In this regard, it is necessary to recall, as earlier portions of this book demonstrate, that Indian tribes had a more *secure* consti-tutional status at the time the Constitution was adopted than they do today. The constitutional trajectory for Indian tribes has been largely to demean and reduce their constitutional status. They are the only group within the United States to be treated with less, rather than more, constitutional dignity with the passage of time—a most sorry tale of constitutional ethnic cleansing. This is wrong but *not* inexorable. Constitutional inclusiveness is not only about indi-viduals but also about the sovereigns who were here first. To be sure, the related problems are complicated and saturated with historical loss and misunder-standing, but they are not insoluble, as later parts of this book hope to demon-strate.[331] The momentum of (modern) tribal sovereignty requires a new model of respect, dignity, and constitutional community.

9

International Law Perspective

A New Model of Indigenous Nation Sovereignty?

INTERNATIONAL LAW HAS EXISTED AS A SIGNIFICANT BODY OF LAW WITHIN THE Western tradition, tracing back as far as the Roman Empire and ancient Greece. And as part of its ancient pedigree, it has played a significant role in Indian law. In the fifteenth to the seventeenth century—though there was debate and dissent—international law served extensively as an instrument to legitimatize European colonization and oppression of indigenous people.

In its origins, the field of international law was deeply rooted in, and focused on, the definition and scope of state sovereignty, which largely foreclosed inquiry into a nation's domestic affairs, including its treatment of indigenous peoples. Finally, in the contemporary era, there has been a distinctive turn in the field of international law to a broad concern with individual human rights and the collective rights of indigenous peoples within nation-states. These newest changes, in turn, have potential to advance domestic Indian law within the United States, as well as in Canada, New Zealand, Australia, Guatemala, and Nicaragua—indeed, in any nation where there are indigenous peoples. Tracing this arc in the development of international law and its relationship to indigenous peoples[1] helps to illuminate much of what has happened, and might yet happen, in Indian law.

International law, broadly understood, constitutes a "universe of authoritative norms and procedures—today linked to international institutions—that are in some measure controlling across jurisdictional boundaries."[2] This expansive understanding focuses more on norms than on narrow rules. This view does *not* fail to make the usual positivist distinctions among treaties, customs, and general principles of law but rather realizes that they must be evaluated and understood "in light of the values that speak *to all of us*, and with attention to the realities of a changing world of diverse contexts in which previously unheard, and unheard of, groups wield increasing influence."[3]

Early Developments in International Law
Relative to Indigenous Peoples

Western exploration and commercial ventures by Christopher Columbus and others dramatically presented the specific issue of the relationship of indigenous peoples to European nations. These first encounters thus required some authoritative assessment about the nature and character of indigenous peoples. These primordial issues engaged a number of important legal philosophers and theologians of the early sixteenth century.

Two of the leading participants in these disputes were the Dominican priests Bartolomé de las Casas (1484–1566) and Francisco de Vitoria (1486–1546). Both de las Casas and Vitoria argued that in accordance with most natural law thinking of the day, indigenous peoples were indeed rational human beings with rights largely equivalent to those of non-Indian people. Yet there were, especially for Vitoria, special conditions attached to this recognition.[4] These special conditions—or responsibilities—included the European right to travel to indigenous lands, to trade with indigenous peoples, and to proselytize in favor of Christianity. Refusal to permit any of these three activities was grounds for a just war.[5]

Related to this inquiry was the complementary assessment of whether indigenous peoples constituted nation-states capable of "enjoying" sovereign rights or whether such rights were available only at the mercy of European settler nations. The basic conclusion of scholars at the time was that indigenous peoples were not nation-states in the eyes of international law because they lacked the defining characteristics of exclusivity of "territorial domain and hierarchical, centralized authority."[6] In addition, there was a pronounced tendency to privilege agricultural societies over hunter-gatherer ones that limited indigenous peoples' property rights and their status as nations under international law.[7]

These rather arbitrary models had a certain self-fulfilling aspect. A social hierarchy was created that conveniently placed its creators at the top and indigenous peoples largely at the bottom. Yet this "pretext" did not go completely unnoticed. Emmerich de Vattel (1714–1767), a leading international law scholar of the time, remarked:

Those ambitious European States which attacked the American Nations and subjected them to their avaricious rule, in order, as they said, to civilize them, and have them instructed in the true religion— those usurpers, I say, justified themselves by a pretext equally unjust and ridiculous.[8]

Early international law theorists—particularly Vattel—sought to build on natural law principles concerning individuals to create a model of what it was to be a state. Vattel conceived of state sovereignty as being the collective ana-logue to free-standing independent and equal individuals and thus possessing the attributes of exclusive jurisdiction, territorial integrity, and the right of non-interference by others.[9] Vattel presumed the state was formed "consensually" and was committed to the best interests of its constituents in matters of indi-vidual fulfillment and collective safety.[10] Such thinking permitted the extension of natural law reasoning into the arena of what it meant to be a state.

These somewhat imprecise notions about the natural law status of indige-nous people and their societies were tested in the fulcrum of on-the-ground reality posed by the early cases of *Johnson v. McIntosh*,[11] *Cherokee Nation v. Georgia*,[12] and *Worcester v. Georgia*[13] before the U.S. Supreme Court.

The Marshall Trilogy and International Law

In the Marshall Trilogy, but especially in *Johnson v. McIntosh*, the Court relied heavily on principles of international law that were themselves undergirded by certain natural (or not so natural) law principles. In *Johnson v. McIntosh*, the central issue was the "power of Indians to give, and of private individuals to receive, a title which can be sustained in the Courts of this country."[14] Chief Justice Marshall, writing for the Court, held that Indians had no such power to convey title of their land to private individuals.

The rule of decision in this case did *not* come from any principle of consti-tutional law, or from any federal statute, or from any precept of (federal) com-mon law, but rather from a doctrine of international law, namely, the doctrine of discovery—a doctrine, it must be pointed out, that was not part of U.S. domestic law through treaty or positive enactment by Congress and was not identified anywhere in the Constitution.

The "doctrine of discovery" contained two parts. The first part—which was the more direct international law piece—held that "discovery gave title to the government by whose subjects, or by whose authority, it was made against all other European governments, which title might be consummated by possession."[15] The second part was more open-ended, and it involved the relations "between the discoverer and the natives, [which] were to be regulated by themselves. The rights thus acquired being exclusive, no other power could interpose between them."[16]

It is in this zone that the conception of indigenous peoples and their societies became acute. What property rights, if any, did tribes hold, and what was the justifying rationale? Chief Justice Marshall moved swiftly to summarize the view that within the European family of nations, the vast extent of the Americas

> offered an ample field to the ambition and enterprise of all; and the character and religion of its inhabitants afforded an apology for considering them as a people over whom the superior genius of Europe might claim an ascendancy. The potentates of the old world found no difficulty in convincing themselves that they made ample compensation to the inhabitants of the new by bestowing on them civilization and Christianity, in exchange for unlimited independence.[17]

This assessment permitted the "discoverer" to claim *title* to Native lands because of the defects of indigenous people, who lacked two of the cardinal prerequisites to holding property, namely, "civilization" and Christianity.[18]

Having extinguished indigenous title, which is the most significant stick in the normal bundle of property rights, there remained the question of whether indigenous people retained *any* property rights in their lands. The Court answered in the affirmative. There was an impairment, but not an eradication, of these property rights:

> [T]he rights of the original inhabitants were, in no instance, entirely disregarded; but were necessarily, to a considerable extent, impaired. They were admitted to be the rightful occupants of the soil, with a legal as well as just claim to retain possession of it, and to use it according to their own discretion; but their rights to complete sovereignty, as independent nations, were necessarily diminished, and their power to dispose of the soil at their own will, to whomsoever they pleased, was denied by the original fundamental principle, that discovery gave exclusive title to those who made it.[19]

What remained for indigenous peoples were the rights of use and occupancy of the land. Their remaining rights might be extinguished by purchase or a just war of conquest.[20] Such were the understandings within the European family in England, France, Spain, and Holland. The United States, despite its own recent revolution against tyranny, nevertheless readily acceded to this tyranny over indigenous peoples.

Chief Justice Marshall was not unaware of this dilemma and contradiction. Yet he appeared to realize that it was both politically and legally impractical to confront this reality:

> Conquest gives a title which the Courts of the conqueror cannot
> deny, whatever the private and speculative opinions of individuals
> may be, respecting the original justice of the claim which has been
> successfully asserted.[21]

Chief Justice Marshall further realized that the doctrine of discovery itself was grandiose and self-serving:

> However extravagant the pretension of converting the discovery of an
> inhabited country into conquest may appear; if the principle has been
> asserted in the first instance, and afterwards sustained; if a country
> has been acquired and held under it; if the property of the great mass
> of the community originates in it, it becomes the law of the land, and
> cannot be questioned. So, too, with respect to the concomitant
> principle, that the Indian inhabitants are to be considered merely as
> occupants, to be protected, indeed, while in peace, in the possession
> of these lands, but to be deemed incapable of transferring the absolute
> title to others. However this restriction *may be opposed to natural right*
> and to the rights of civilized nations, yet, if it be indispensable to that
> system under which the country has been settled, and be adapted to
> the actual condition of the two people, it may, perhaps, be supported
> by reason and certainly cannot be rejected by Courts of Justice.[22]

With those words, Chief Justice Marshall expressly confirmed the Court's departure from those natural law principles that recognized essential human and property rights in all individual beings, including indigenous peoples.[23] Chief Justice Marshall did not embrace this felt necessity with zest, but rather with wistfulness, a rare sentiment for the time.

In the subsequent trilogy cases of *Cherokee Nation v. Georgia* and *Worcester v. Georgia*, which involved issues focusing on the nature of tribal sovereignty and the tribal relationship to the federal (and state) governments, the Court continued to insert reflections on questionable elements of the discovery doctrine. In the *Cherokee Nation* case, Chief Justice Marshall seemed to carve out a niche for Indian law where it is always difficult to know exactly what was what: "But the relation of the Indians to the United States is marked by peculiar and cardinal distinctions which exist nowhere else."[24]

In *Worcester v. Georgia*, Chief Justice Marshall opined further about the rickety nature of the discovery doctrine:

> It is difficult to comprehend the proposition that the inhabitants of either quarter of the globe could have rightful original claims of dominion over the inhabitants of the other, or over the lands they occupied; or that the discovery of either by the other should give the discoverer rights in the country discovered, which annulled the pre-existing rights of its ancient possessors.[25]

Yet he clung to the "reality" that "power, war, conquest, give rights, which, after possession, are conceded by the world; and which can never be controverted by those on whom they descend."[26]

The core of *Cherokee Nation* and *Worcester* was not, however, primarily concerned with discovery, but rather with the nature of tribal sovereignty and its relationship to the federal government. Again, the Court leaned heavily on developing principles of international law, this time finding significant elements of sovereignty and self-government in the tribe's political and treaty relationships with the United States. Yet in so doing, the Court navigated some middle ground, ever mindful of the precarious nature of a tribal sovereignty that seemed to lack precise, constitutional mooring.

In *Cherokee Nation*, the Court expressly found that an Indian tribe was *not* a foreign nation within the American constitutional structure. Instead, it found that the Cherokee Nation, largely as a result of its treaty relationship with the federal government and its demonstrated capacity for self-government, did possess certain elements of sovereignty. This is best demonstrated by the Court's assessment that:

> They may, more correctly, perhaps, be denominated domestic dependent nations. They occupy a territory to which we assert a title independent of their will, which must take effect in point of possession when their right of possession ceases. Meanwhile they are in a state of pupilage. Their relations to the United States resemble that of a ward to his guardian.[27]

This intriguing notion of tribes as "domestic dependent nations" was not elucidated by the Court then and remains elusive to this day.

Justices Johnson and Baldwin concurred largely on the grounds that the Treaty of Hopewell evinced such a level of dependency of the Cherokee Nation on the United States that it precluded a finding of foreign nation status. Justice Johnson extolled the Cherokees as being far above "every petty kraal of Indians, designating themselves as a tribe or nation, and having a few hundred acres of land to hunt."[28] They were not "so low in the grade of organized society as our Indian tribes most generally are,"[29] but rather "under their present form of government; which certainly must be classed among the most approved forms of civil government."[30]

Justice Thompson dissented and found the Cherokee Nation to be a foreign nation. In reaching this conclusion, Justice Thompson drew extensively on the work of the international jurist Emmerich de Vattel. Justice Thompson found that in accordance with Vattel's writings, the Cherokee Nation was made up of free consenting individuals seeking "mutual safety and advantage" and actively engaged in self-governance despite its alliance with a more powerful state for protection from potential enemies.[31] Justice Thompson concluded that "[t]esting the character and condition of the Cherokee Indians by these rules, it is not perceived how it is possible to escape the conclusion that they form a sovereign state."[32] Yet the ultimate question of whether the Cherokee Nation was a "foreign state or not, is a point on which we cannot expect to discover much light from the law of nations."[33]

This final analysis rested on "the practice of our own government, and the light in which the nation has been viewed and treated by it."[34] Justice Thompson concluded that the Cherokees were never conquered, never reduced to subjects of another sovereign, and never lost their capacity for self-governance.[35] Perhaps the most telling observation in the entire *Cherokee Nation* case was Chief Justice Marshall's surprise that it was brought in the first place:

> At the time the constitution was framed, the idea of appealing to an
> American court of justice for an assertion of right or a redress of
> wrong, had perhaps never entered the mind of an Indian or his tribe.
> Their appeal was to the tomahawk, or to the government. This was
> well understood by the statesmen who framed the Constitution of the
> United States....[36]

The original constitution—in this view—envisioned diplomacy and war, not domestic litigation, as the key signposts of the United States–Indian tribe relationship.

In *Worcester*, the Court again found the existence of tribal sovereignty. This time, it found a sovereignty sufficient to prevent state authority in Indian country. This was a sovereignty, at least vis-à-vis the states, that was further enhanced by the treaty relationship between the federal government and the Cherokee Nation. Chief Justice Marshall's opinion expressly noted in accordance with "the settled doctrine of the law of nations that a weaker power does not surrender its independence—its right to self-government, by associating with a stronger, and taking its protection.[37] Vattel is directly quoted: "'Tributary and feudatory states...do not thereby cease to be sovereign and independent states, so long as self-government and sovereign and independent authority are left in the administration of the state.' "[38] Yet, in some ways *Worcester* was an "easier" case than *Cherokee Nation*. The Court has always—though without any express admission or studied reflection—found it easier (when so inclined) to be expansive with regard to tribal sovereignty in the tribal-state context and rather minimal in the tribal-federal context.

In sum, early international law within the family of nations was supple enough to deny indigenous peoples title to their own land yet at the same time also recognize a substantial capacity for self-government. As colonialism proceeded, however, the primary question that came forward was not only the rights of indigenous peoples to engage in self-governance per se but also discerning their rights (if any) against the colonialist state and the duty (if any) of colonialist states to indigenous peoples. This quandary birthed the international law concept of trusteeship.

Trusteeship in Early International Law

As concern with the individual rights of indigenous peoples began to recede from its central role in early international law, it was replaced with a concern for the collective rights of indigenous people to engage in self-governance, which in turn gave way to a focus on the relationship of such self-governance to the colonialist state itself. Within this framework, international law developed to assess and measure these shifting dimensions of power and their attendant legal obligations.

Colonialist states increasingly consolidated political and military power over indigenous peoples, and these moves gathered the attention of the international law community. According to James Anaya:

> As colonizing states and their offspring consolidated power over
> indigenous lands, many such states adopted trusteeship notions akin
> to those proposed earlier by Vitoria as grounds and parameters for
> the nonconsensual exercise of authority over indigenous peoples.[39]

The key elements in this formulation of trusteeship were its nonconsensual nature and its cloak of humanism. Trusteeship thus understood served to posit the colonialist state as the beneficent guardian, freely committed to assisting the deficient beneficiary. Such notions conveniently omitted to disclose that the alleged deficiency of indigenous peoples flowed from the West's own tradition of social and cultural hierarchy and its ongoing exploitation of indigenous peoples. This dynamic of rhetoric and action was often buried under the superficial benevolence invoked by the term *trusteeship*.

Much of the "trusteeship" notion harkened back to the *Johnson v. McIntosh* mission to "civilize" indigenous peoples, except that it was now dressed up in the pedigree of "scientific racism" with its affirmative agenda "to wean native people from their 'backward' ways and to 'civilize' them."[40] Yet, all this ignored the inconvenient reality that the primary goal of colonialist states was not to help anybody but themselves in obtaining indigenous peoples' land and natural resources. Their mission was about wealth and power; it was not about assisting the less fortunate who were increasingly pauperized by the "civilizing" actions of the trustee.

The trusteeship mission was designed to cover up not only divided loyalties and conflicts of interest but also its desire to change indigenous peoples. The perception, especially strong in nineteenth-century England, was essentially double-edged in nature. Part of this impulse was indeed to "civilize"— that is, to assimilate—indigenous people to the colonial ways of the dominant society. This was particularly true in the Christian missionary segments of colonial societies. It was also true, however, that the civilizing agenda had a more practical calculus beyond the "obligations of conscience to impart the blessings we enjoy":

> [w]e have abundant proof that is greatly for our advantage to have
> dealings with civilized men rather than barbarians. Savages are
> dangerous neighbors and unprofitable customers, and if they remain
> as degraded denizens of our colonies they become a burden on the
> state.[41]

National security and profit were thus also part of the "civilizing" ethos embedded in trusteeship. Such an approach was also picked up in the United States, and trusteeship became the cornerstone doctrine for the administration of Indian affairs throughout Indian country. The task was huge, and so was the accompanying despotism of the Bureau of Indian Affairs bureaucracy. Far into the nineteenth century, the chore appeared daunting:

> What, then, is our duty as the guardian of all the Indians under our
> jurisdiction? To outlaw, to pursue, to hunt down like wolves, and
> slay? Must we drive and exterminate them as if void of reason, and
> without souls. Surely, no.
> It is beyond question our most solemn duty to protect and care
> for, to elevate and civilize them.[42]

These attitudes and policies became prevalent around the globe, from the United States to Canada to Australia to Brazil, Venezuela, Argentina, and Africa.[43] All of this was foreshadowed in the *Cherokee Nation v. Georgia* case with its pregnant metaphor that Indians "are in a state of pupilage. Their relation to the United States resembles that of a ward to his guardian."[44]

The concept of trusteeship eventually found its way into express positivist enactments and declarations of international law. As Anaya noted, these ranged from the 1888 Institute of International Law's statement that there was a "duty of watching over the conservation of aboriginal populations, their education, and the amelioration of their moral and material condition"[45] to the 1919 Covenant of the League of Nations' commitment to "undertake to secure the just treatment of the native inhabitants of territories under their control."[46]

All of this "benevolence" should not obscure the fact that indigenous peoples were objects of international law without their consent and without their participation. They were not subjects who possessed agency. They were not actors; they were the acted upon. The positivist construction of trusteeship further eroded the early natural law elements that accorded some dignity to the status of indigenous peoples. Trusteeship protected little and significantly abetted most colonial forms of acquisition and control. It was a minimalist response to maximalist overreaching. At its best, it prevented only the most egregious aggressions of nation-states against indigenous peoples.

Trusteeship was further immunized from any in-depth scrutiny as it was folded into the narrowing international law focus on nation-state sovereignty and its central attributes of territorial integrity, noninterference, and exclusive jurisdiction within its borders. This notion of exclusive jurisdiction effectively foreclosed any attempt within the international law community to establish meaningful standards to measure or evaluate the performance of nation-states in regard to their trusteeship responsibilities to indigenous peoples.

Because the concept of trusteeship was riddled with basic conflicts of interest and often described in the most abstract and formal terms, such isolation from review was particularly unfortunate. An instructive example in this regard is the well-known Indian law case of *Lone Wolf v. Hitchcock*.[47] In *Lone Wolf*, the Supreme Court held that Congress possessed plenary power in Indian affairs sufficient to unilaterally abrogate treaties with Indian tribes, to require individual Indians to receive allotments against their will, and to force tribes to sell their land to the federal government without negotiation or consent. The Court found

[a]n exercise of such power, a mere change in the form of investment of Indian tribal property, the property of those who, as we have held, were in substantial effect the *wards of the government*. We must presume that Congress acted in perfect good faith in the dealings with the Indians of which complaint is made, and that the legislative branch of the government exercised its best judgment in the premises. In any event, as Congress possessed full power in the matter, the judiciary cannot question or inquire into the motives which prompted the enactment of this legislation.[48]

Trusteeship in the United States was not only immune from international scrutiny but also immune from domestic review by its own courts.[49] This irrebuttable presumption of "perfect good faith in dealings with the Indians" was quite specious in light of the federal government's blatant conflict of interest in this matter. It was not protecting Indians but rather advancing its own self-interest to obtain Indian land and open it for non-Indian settlement. This was the reality of the day. When President McKinley made available the resulting 13,000 allotments of 160 acres land at $1.75 per acre, more than 150,000 non-Indians signed up.

    Lone Wolf was paradigmatic in regard to the larger problem of trusteeship. As Anaya noted:

Shaped by Western perspectives and political power, international law developed a complicity with the often brutal forces that wrested lands from indigenous peoples, suppressed their cultures and institutions, and left them among the poorest of the poor.[50]

Trusteeship delivered little and took much from indigenous peoples.

International Law and Indigenous Peoples in the Modern Era

International law—like other areas of the law—has not remained static. And in the modern era, it has begun to move away from its overwhelming concern with the rights of states and toward a growing concern for the rights of indigenous peoples—a concern that on balance is more positive and more respectful. It is a shift—not without its own problems and tensions—that reclaims a moral dimension for international law.

    This new dynamic within international law is firmly rooted in the process of change and progressive evolution, both doctrinally and institutionally. There has been a partial but significant migration away from state-centered positivism and sovereignty and toward concern with the broad issues of world peace and human rights.[51] There has also been a globalization of international law, which has given it truer universality and a resulting expansion of the recognized number of members within the "family of nations." This expanded concept of universality has made international law more inclusive, which in turn has generated more input from, and concern with, nonstate actors and perspectives.[52] These nonstate actors include not only indigenous peoples but other groups such as international organizations, transnational corporations, labor unions, and other nongovernmental organizations.[53]

These developments in turn sparked a renewed international law scholarly inquiry that is more aspirational in nature. This aspirational turn, within the original natural law context, is equally concerned with *what is* and *what ought to be*.[54] Such a line of inquiry naturally unfolds when there is concern about the meaning of world peace and essential human rights. War is often the epitome of what is; peace is the epitome of what ought to be.

This new emerging framework began to take root in the international organizations that sprang up after World War II. The premier institution in this movement was the United Nations. The United Nations Charter reflected both the old and the new. It prominently "embraces substantive statist precepts by including among the organization's founding principles respect for the 'sovereign equality' and 'territorial integrity' of member states and for nonintervention in their domestic affairs." Yet despite this affirmation of traditional state sovereignty principles, the charter also points to the support and promotion of respect for "[e]qual rights and self-determination of peoples";[55] "respect for human rights and for fundamental freedoms for all without distinction as to race, sex, language, or religion";[56] and "conditions of economic and social progress and development."[57]

The realpolitik continued to tilt almost exclusively in favor of state sovereignty, but there were minor structural nuances that created new institutional space for voices of change. Most prominent was the charter's recognition of a process permitting the UN Economic and Social Council, the parent body of the United Nations human rights and social policy organizations, to consult with nongovernmental organizations (NGOs).[58] Such consultation often provided NGOs with an important platform from which to address significant human rights and social justice issues. In the context of Indian law, for example, the NGO status of the International Treaty Council has provided a significant voice for Native American concerns within the United Nations. To be sure, voice alone does not so readily translate into political power, but it is often a necessary predecessor to the acquisition of such power.

Within the charter of the United Nations, it is thus possible to discern a limited return to a concern with the individual's basic "human rights." Although seldom defined with precision, it is clear that such concern was based on humanistic and moral concerns that were different from, and often at odds with, the sovereign goals of states. This was, perhaps, not so surprising in light of the experience of World War II, which clearly demonstrated the tragic inability of some states to protect their own citizens and the brutal ability of other states to persecute and kill their own citizens.

Initially, none of this dealt directly with the *collective* rights of indigenous peoples, but rather more with the *individual* human rights of all people, including indigenous peoples. This development eventually crystallized into a full-scale model dealing with the individual human rights of all. This model also drew on the growing worldwide revolutionary movements to fight colonialism in the name of freedom, individual civil rights, and self-governance. This process of decolonization took root in significant parts of South America, Africa, and Asia.

The first major international document to take up these concerns in an important way was the International Labor Organization (ILO) Convention 107 of 1957.[59] This convention had very little input from indigenous peoples and strongly focused on the issues of assimilation and full citizenship.[60] In this view, nation building was not only a policy to strengthen and protect states from outsiders but also, and perhaps more important, to break down ethnic and cultural differences within the society.[61] Such assimilationist moves, despite their progressive thrust, were often an anathema to preserving the identity and collective integrity of indigenous peoples. "Assimilation" that points the way to nondiscrimination and inclusion is indeed beneficial to indigenous peoples, but these benefits ought not come at the price of the loss of culture, identity, and autonomy. The growing political and scholarly tension between the individual and group within the international framework ultimately resulted in the emergence of a new model with a specific focus on the collective rights of indigenous peoples.

The View of Indigenous Peoples

During the 1960s and the 1970s, dialogue expanded among the growing number of NGOs, human rights organizations, and a new generation of international law scholars. Within this mix, indigenous peoples began to describe a new vision or agenda that pushed beyond the concern with individual rights to "demands for their continued survival as distinct communities with historically-based cultures, political institutions, and entitlements to land."[62] This was not so much a rebuke of individuals' rights concerns, but rather an extension and reconfiguration of these concerns.

This movement was highlighted and largely legitimized as a result of the 1977 International Non-Governmental Organization Conference on Discrimination against Indigenous Populations in the Americas, held in Geneva, Switzerland, which was organized as a project of the NGO Sub-Committee on Racism, Racial Discrimination, Apartheid, and Colonialism. This conference helped to forge the beginning of a movement, to extend its concerns worldwide, and to foster a growing network of communication among indigenous peoples from all over the globe.[63] This work culminated in the UN General Assembly's designation of 1993 as the International Year of the World's Indigenous Peoples and a further extension to an "International Decade" on this theme.[64] This work—at least within United Nations circles—was significantly advanced with the establishment of a Permanent Forum on Indigenous Issues within the United Nations Economic and Social Council, which met for the first time in 2002.[65]

These efforts began to bear fruit with the development of specific international conventions concerning indigenous peoples, such as International Labor Convention (ILO) 169 that was adopted in 1989.[66] Convention 169, a significant revision of Convention 107 of 1957, began to move forcefully beyond the primary assimilationist philosophy of the day. The language of its preamble set a new tone and direction, which recognized "the aspirations of [indigenous] peoples to exercise control over their own institutions, ways of life and economic development and to maintain and develop their identities, languages and religions, within the framework of the states in which they live."[67]

Although the convention contained provisions advancing cultural integrity, land and resource protection, and nondiscrimination, it was not without criticism within the indigenous rights movement because of its supposed failure to press for the broader definition of indigenous peoples as compared with mere populations. The distinction was regarded by many as key because the former term was more comprehensive and directly linked to the complementary notion of *self-determination*.[68]

This linkage with self-determination was potentially more dynamic, active, and collective in its concern with distinct communities than the more static notion of simple populations. This tension over terminology might strike some as semantic niggling, and to a degree it was, but it was more revealing of "an aversion on the part of numerous states to expressly acknowledge a right of self-determination for indigenous groups out of fear that it may imply an effective right of secession."[69] Issues of politics and power are often initially manifested in the parsing of a dictionary's entrails.

Concomitant with positivistic developments such as ILO Convention 169 there were parallel activities with regard to customary international law. A certain synergy took hold, as there was increased discussion about the rights of indigenous peoples within the entire international law community, including states, NGOs, indigenous communities, international forums, and scholars. According to Anaya:

> It is now evident that states and other relevant actors have reached a certain new common ground about minimum standards that should govern behavior toward indigenous peoples, and it is also evident that the standards are already in fact guiding behavior. Under modern theory, such a controlling consensus, following as it does from widely shared values of human dignity, constitutes customary international law.[70]

The concept of customary international-indigenous law has both a procedural component and a substantive component. The procedural component focuses on the notion of "new common ground about minimum standards" for dealing with indigenous peoples.[71] Although not very precise, the best description of this process states:

> Norms of customary international law arise—or to use the now much favored term *crystallize*—when a preponderance of states and other authoritative actors converge on a common understanding of the norms' contents and generally expect future behavior in conformity with those norms.[72]

To be sure, the absence of any procedural *formality* provides any state that is so inclined the opportunity to deny applicability of the norm to its behavior. Without some form of more overt consent, this gap in likely compliance remains extremely wide.

The substantive content of such a customary norm is generally understood to have two elements. One element is that which can be identified from past uniformities of actual state practice—what might be called the "material" or empirical component. The second element is more subjective and focuses on the "oughtness" of such a norm.[73]

This kind of norm making risks irrelevance if it becomes lost in a high level of abstraction without express adherents and supporters. In this regard, the formation in 1982 of the United Nations Working Group on Indigenous Populations was a critical link to legitimacy and sober reality. The working group is an organ of the Sub-Commission on the Promotion and Protection of Human Rights. It is composed of five individuals who rotate in from the subcommission. These individuals do not directly represent nation-states but are independent experts within the field.

The working group's work over the years has steadily increased and culminated in the granting of its request to develop a draft of the Declaration on the Rights of Indigenous Peoples for potential adoption by the United Nations General Assembly. This first draft—subject to significant input from indigenous peoples—was produced in 1988. It has been revised several times and was submitted to the United Nations Commission on Human Rights in 1994.[74] It was adopted by the United Nations General Assembly in September 2007.[75]

All of this work was further supplemented with increasing worldwide discussion at conferences within the scholarly community about the emerging nature of the rights of indigenous peoples, which in turn increased the developing multilateral consensus about these rights. The process is dynamic and ongoing, but it is not without its critics. Some indigenous groups find that the United Nations declaration does not go far enough; a number of nation-states feel that it goes too far. Yet a basic common ground is now present within the international law community.[76]

The Fundamental Principle of Self-Determination

Within the arc of ILO Convention 169 and the United Nations Declaration on the Rights of Indigenous Peoples, a core of articulated norms has emerged. These norms are most often organized around the central principle of self-determination, which is also the very policy that likewise animates the contemporary field of federal Indian law.[77] In this topography, self-determination is a quintessential human right that connects or bridges the distance between indigenous individuals, communities, and the state. It is also a key marker of legitimacy with which to measure the performance of state institutions.

The principle of self-determination is most often grouped around elements described as constitutive and ongoing. The constitutive aspect focuses on the initial participation and consent of the indigenous peoples involved, and the ongoing component focuses on the requirement that the governing political order permit indigenous people to "live and develop freely on a continuous basis."[78]

The principle of self-determination contains *five* components relative to nondiscrimination, cultural integrity, land and natural resources, social welfare and development, and self-government.[79] As is often the case with such norms, precise definitions are lacking; nevertheless, each one does include some broad identifiable contours. The norm of nondiscrimination is perhaps the most precise because it readily lends itself to the well-known individual human right that proscribes any denial of fair treatment and, like the United Nations Charter, calls for "respect for human rights and for fundamental freedom for all without distinction as to race, sex, language or religion."[80]

The norm of cultural integrity is clearly group-focused and advances the precept that indigenous peoples have the right to maintain and to pursue their cultural identities. Although such a norm appears unexceptional, it clearly is critical from the indigenous perspective of wanting to resist certain assimilative pressures in the context of retaining language, religious beliefs, and other cultural practices that differ from the mainstream. Such concerns are favorably related to the norm of nondiscrimination in that decisions to engage in practices relative to cultural integrity cannot result in discrimination against any indigenous individual.

Yet, there is potential tension between these two norms as well. The tension derives from the situation where there is concern that a particular cultural practice is harmful in that it discriminates against certain individuals or groups *within* the community of indigenous people. Such examples usually involve the position of women within certain indigenous communities in regard to their status as women and their treatment by their spouses or other family members in matters of bodily integrity, freedom of expression, and the right to divorce. This tension raises a deeper philosophical question of whether there is such a thing as *universal* human rights that take precedence over certain indigenous cultural practices or whether the concept of *universal* human rights is itself a product of the Western cultural tradition and therefore cannot bind non-Western cultures.

This tension and paradox remain unresolved (perhaps they are inherently unresolvable), but the working pragmatism in this regard has been to create a zone of deference such that

> In any assessment of whether a particular cultural practice is prohibited rather than protected, the cultural group concerned should be accorded a certain margin of deference for its own interpretative and decision-making processes for the application of universal human rights norms, just as states are accorded such deference.[81]

Despite the seeming illogic, the universal must accommodate itself to the particular. Yet this approach does make sense in its hesitancy to potentially repeat Western historical patterns of cultural insensitivity, which were devoid of understanding and respect.

It is also necessary to remember that in most cases this tension is not an issue, and in fact the norm of cultural integrity has indeed benefited indigenous communities on numerous occasions within the international law community. For example, in several cases before the United Nations Human Rights Committee, the committee has relied on Article 27 of the Covenant on Civil and Political Rights and its embodiment of the cultural integrity norm to reach decisions favorable to indigenous people. In the case of Sandra Lovelace,[82] a Canadian Indian tribal member challenged Sec. 12(1)(b) of Canada's Indian Act, which denied Indian status and benefits to any Indian woman who married a non-Indian. Canada's Indian Act did not apply in the same manner to a male Indian who married a non-Indian.

Although the Human Rights Committee found that the application of the Act to Lovelace also constituted sex discrimination, it rested its holding in her favor on the larger grounds of a right to cultural belonging:

> The right of Sandra Lovelace to access her native culture and
> language "in community with the other members" of her group, has
> in fact been, and continues to be interfered with, because there is no
> place outside the Tobique Reserve where such a community exists.[83]

Canada subsequently amended its Indian Act to change this practice of gender discrimination.

The international customary norm for dealing with land and natural resources is the broadest in scope and the one most problematic for nation-states. Because colonialization was primarily concerned with obtaining the riches of indigenous land and natural resources, it is the area most fraught with opposition and resistance by nation-states. Land and natural resources have both a spiritual and an economic nexus within indigenous cultures. In this view, land and natural resources constitute both an essential human right and a property right. This nexus thus requires acknowledgment of, and respect for, traditional patterns of land tenure and usage.

Such a view, of course, must contend with the legacy of the doctrine of discovery that placed title to indigenous lands in most of the world in the hands of the European and Western colonizers. This was the essence, for example, of the 1823 American case of *Johnson v. McIntosh*.[84] The strength of this new norm is not in its ability to completely displace or undo the doctrine of discovery, but rather to mitigate its most jagged contours in the modern era. This includes such things as recognizing contemporary property rights of indigenous peoples when they continue to live on the land, a right to have such lands surveyed and title recorded in their name, a right of consultation before the beginning of any development activities on their lands, and a right *not* to be removed from their lands.

The case of the Mayagna (Sumo) Awas Tingni Community in Nicaragua is an instructive example involving these issues.[85] The Mayagna Awas Tingni is an indigenous community that resides in the Atlantic Coast region of Nicaragua.[86] After repeated unsuccessful attempts within the domestic courts of Nicaragua to obtain cancellations of timber concessions granted by Nicaragua to private companies and to obtain proper demarcation and registration of their title to these lands, the community brought an action against the state of Nicaragua before the Inter-American Human Rights Commission, an organ of the Organization of American States (OAS).[87]

The Inter-American Commission on Human Rights was formally created by an amendment to the OAS Charter that was adopted in 1967.[88] It therefore has authority over all member states, including Nicaragua and the United States. In contrast, jurisdiction of the Inter-American Court of Human Rights rests primarily on a nation-state's ratification of the American Convention on Human Rights.[89] Nicaragua has ratified the convention and accepted the jurisdiction of the court, but the United States has not.[90] In this case, the commission brought suit against the state of Nicaragua in the Inter-American Court of Human Rights after investigating and finding in favor of the Awas Tingni Community complaint filed with the commission.[91]

The thrust of the commission's application against Nicaragua was that it failed to demarcate the communal lands of the Awas Tingni Community and otherwise failed to protect the property rights of the community by granting timber concessions in those lands to various multinational corporations.[92] These failures to perform by the state of Nicaragua constituted alleged violations of Articles 1, 2, and 21 of the American Convention on Human Rights.[93] Articles 1 and 2 establish the right to effective state measures, and Article 21 identifies the basic property rights to be protected.[94]

The court received extensive evidence and held three days of hearings at the court's seat in San José, Costa Rica. The court ruled in favor of the commission's application on behalf of the Awas Tingni Community and against the state of Nicaragua.[95] The court found that Nicaragua violated Articles 1, 2 and 21 of the American Convention on Human Rights.[96] The court also used expansive language, employing what it called an "evolutionary" method of interpretation that was willing to consider international norms both within and without the Inter-American system.[97] The court further stated that such norms had "autonomous" meaning beyond that of domestic law.[98]

The court directed that "Nicaragua should proceed to demarcate and title the lands of the Awas Tingni and other indigenous communities, 'in accordance with their customary land, values, customs and mores.' "[99] The court also ordered limited monetary reparations.[100]

This decision is historic in that it was

the first legally binding decision by an international tribunal to
uphold the collective land and resource rights of indigenous peoples
in the face of a state's failure to do so. It strengthens a contemporary
trend in the processes of international law that helps to empower
indigenous peoples as they press their demand for self-determination
as distinct groups with secure territorial rights.[101]

The principles relative to social welfare and development constitute the
fourth customary norm that helps to elaborate the fundamental principle of
indigenous peoples' right to self-determination. This norm is twined around
the notion of entitlement to health, education, and an adequate standard of living, along with the broader notion, for example, in the United Nations
Declaration on the Right to Development, of development as "an inalienable
human right by virtue of which every human person and *all peoples* are entitled
to participate in, contribute to, and enjoy economic, social, cultural and political development, in which all human rights and fundamental freedoms can be
fully realized."[102]

The primary elements of this norm are directed to reversing the blunt
force of the process of colonialization that often left indigenous peoples as the
poorest of the poor. These communities are often still disenfranchised from
participating in or receiving services from the state, which would help them
move forward in contemporary society. The legitimate thrust of this norm
cannot be denied, but its particulars are often elusive, in that it is quite difficult to quantify what these entitlements exactly mean. Yet despite this flaw,
the existence of the norm itself suggests a consensus that there is at least some
floor in the provision of services below which nation-states are not permitted
to go. Part of this norm thus provides indigenous peoples with a platform
from which they may address their nation-states about the adequacy of essential services.

The final customary norm in the cluster that illuminates the elements of
self-determination is that of self-government. Self-government is understood
to have two prongs, which are essentially complementary but occasionally may
be in tension. These prongs consist of the tuning forks of autonomy and participation. The concept of autonomy covers the recognition of the ability of
indigenous peoples to govern their own communities without outside interference. In a broad way, the notion of autonomy is directed to that aspect of colonialization that routinely eroded, even eviscerated, the ability of indigenous
communities to govern themselves. Thus, indigenous communities seek both
to retain what self-governance remains, while further developing their capacity

to self-govern. The key in this arena often turns on consideration of what is "appropriate to their circumstance."[103]

With the breakup of the Soviet Union, for example, in many quarters there has been a move away from authoritarian models of statehood to more flexible, democratic models that are arguably more conducive to some form of self-governance within indigenous communities. Such thinking has also advanced with the renewed valuation and commitment to national pluralism. As more and more nation-states confront their current population, there is often recognition of greater diversity than ever before. Such cultural pluralism, in turn, advances notions conducive to respect for indigenous peoples' desire to engage in self-governance.[104]

The flip side of autonomy is participation. Participation is understood as the opportunity for indigenous people to participate as full citizens in the dominant society without discrimination or the lack of the full complement of political rights. This view is found in such prominent international documents as the United Nations Declaration on the Rights of Indigenous Peoples and ILO Convention 169. The former affirms the view that "[i]ndigenous peoples have the right to participate in decision-making in matters which would affect their rights."[105] The latter document similarly announces the right of indigenous peoples to possess sufficient means so they "can freely participate...at all levels of decision-making affecting them."[106]

On one level, such declarations are no more than recitals of citizenship that are indeed important, but they contain other elements of participation of particular significance to indigenous peoples. Primary among these are the concepts of consultation and consent. Consultation often is a key, if elusive, ingredient, when the nation-state undertakes development of land or natural resources within the traditional homelands of indigenous peoples. This is particularly important when indigenous peoples do *not* possess any formal recognition of rights to the land or natural resources under the (current) domestic law of the state.[107]

The international right of consultation is analogous to the U.S. domestic concept and constitutional right of due process, with its core ingredients of notice and the opportunity to be heard. Yet there is also a certain catch-22 element at play. If indigenous people possessed recognized rights in their land and natural resources, "consultation" would inhere in the nature of the recognized right itself. It is only when such a right is missing, usually as a result of the process of colonialization, that the shadow or penumbral right of consultation becomes necessary. Without calling itself such, the right of consultation is an often small thread of respect in the large spool of historical forces that have done much to oppress and disenfranchise indigenous peoples in the first instance. A key concern thus remains whether the thread of consultation may be rewoven into a fuller garment that provides warmth and substance when the sun of cooperation threatens to, and often does, dip behind the clouds and obfuscations of the past and present.

In their way, these strands of autonomy and participation argue for a kind of indigenous federalism that recognizes (despite the forces of colonialization) significant legitimate (national) political authority in the states but also recognizes significant reserved powers of local autonomy in indigenous communities. This theory of indigenous federalism further recognizes the full rights of participation by indigenous peoples at both the national and local levels.

In sum, the developing customary international norm of self-determination for indigenous peoples is adumbrated by its five constitutive elements: nondiscrimination, cultural integrity, land and natural resources, social welfare and development, and self-governance. Although all these parts are eminently reasonable and there is a growing (rhetorical) consensus in favor of this norm within various national and international spheres, the potential for on-the-ground implementation is severely limited by the issues of jurisdiction, consent, and remedy.

Jurisdiction, Consent, and Remedy

Nation-states, not surprisingly, guard their sovereignty jealously and are most reluctant to see it reduced or attenuated in any manner. This is particularly true in the international law sphere, where as a general matter, there is not a great deal of pressure from most citizens for their governments to voluntarily embrace international customary norms. There is also a strong international law legacy of noninterference with the sovereignty of nation-states and the exclusive jurisdiction of nation-states over such matters. These elements in combination have made it most difficult to change the behavior of those nation-states that do not want to change their behavior. In this regard, it is relevant to note, as discussed in the case of the Awas Tingni Community, that the state of Nicaragua was subject to the jurisdiction of the Inter-American Human Rights Commission and the Inter-American Court of Human Rights.

Despite its questionable treatment of indigenous peoples, Nicaragua presumably recognized that adherence to its revolutionary ideals of equality and fairness required it to ratify the American Convention on Human Rights and to accept the jurisdiction of the Inter-American Commission and Inter-American Court of Human Rights. Jo Pasqualucci points out:

Every American State has accepted the competence of the Inter-American Commission to consider violations of human rights in its jurisdiction, just by virtue of having ratified the Charter of the Organization of American States, a treaty. Thus, the Dann Sisters, members of the Western Shoshone Peoples of the Southwest United States, could take their case alleging the US government's violation of their land rights before the Inter-American Commission when the US Supreme Court denied them relief. If the State, as is the case with both the United States and Canada, has not also ratified the American Convention on Human Rights (American Convention), the Commission will determine whether the State violated the protections set forth in the American Declaration on the Rights and Duties of Man (American Declaration). For those American States that are also States Parties to the American Convention, the Commission determines whether there have been violations of that Convention. The Commission or the State Party involved then may refer a case to the Inter-American Court of Human Rights if the State has also accepted the jurisdiction of the Court either *ipso facto* for all cases or by special agreement in a particular case. Consequently, some indigenous rights cases, most notably those against the United States, Canada and Belize, were decided solely by the Inter-American Commission, whereas the Inter-American Court also issued judgments in other cases brought against Nicaragua, Colombia, Guatemala and Paraguay.

Although the American Convention, unlike its African counterpart, generally sets forth only individual rights and does not directly address the corresponding rights of peoples, the Inter-American Court of Human Rights and the Inter-American Commission on Human Rights have developed a progressive case law on indigenous peoples' rights. The Inter-American Court has recently decided seminal indigenous rights cases, giving its judicial imprimatur to evolving principles of international indigenous law.[108]

The issue of ratification and jurisdiction is not, however, a simple either-or proposition. In today's complex and media-saturated world, there are many informal pressures, largely in the vein of most nation-states wanting to avoid too much hostile publicity and news coverage, so as not to damage potential commercial ventures with other nations and business entities. Such pressures function, at least at times, to keep some nations' feet to the fire in their treatment of indigenous peoples. Of course, this is not enough, but it is something to acknowledge and build on. In a globalized cyberworld, the dissemination of damaging information and the threat of adverse publicity to a nation-state's economic interests do have credible force and clout.

The element of adverse publicity or obloquy has also taken root within international bodies themselves. For example, several international agencies such as the International Labor Organization (ILO) and the United Nations Working Group on Indigenous Populations regularly issue reports on the status of nation-state compliance with the various norms discussed in this chapter. The research and hearings related to these reports often provide significant opportunities or platforms for the voices of indigenous peoples to have substantial impact on the assessment of nation-state compliance with those important norms. Such processes and reports, while largely voluntary and nonbinding, do form an important bridge between the two ends of the continuum, namely, brute noncompliance and a remedial regime with real enforcement teeth.

This problem surrounding remedies in the international law context is obvious and well known. There is, for example, no way to *enforce* these norms domestically, even when an international agency or court has so ruled. State sovereignty, if it so chooses, trumps the remedial force of such international bodies. The remedial issue is particularly potent and threatening to nation-states because of its unknown scope and potential threat as a vehicle for decolonialization relative, for example, to the return of land and resources to indigenous peoples. Thus there is a sense of extreme caution in this arena:

> Considerations of state sovereignty form a backdrop for the elabora-
> tion of self-determination remedies and influence the degree to
> which remedies may be subject to international scrutiny. The
> limitations of the international doctrine of sovereignty in its modern
> formulation are essentially twofold. First, sovereignty upholds a
> substantive preference for the status quo of political ordering
> through its corollaries protective of state territorial integrity and
> political unity. Second, the doctrine limits the capacity of the interna-
> tional system to regulate matters within the spheres of authority
> asserted by states recognized by the international community. This
> limitation upon international competency is reflected in the United
> Nations Charter's admonition against intervention "in matters which
> are essentially within the domestic jurisdiction of any state."[109]

Despite remedial limitations and the sway of state sovereignty, perceptions of state fallibility and culpability with regard to colonialization, genocide, and worldwide war have significantly tempered the international enthusiasm for untrammeled state sovereignty. Although state sovereignty is a core necessity to create and maintain civil and ordered societies, it is increasingly apparent that it must also promote self-determination for indigenous peoples to retain its legitimacy as a force "to promote a peaceful, stable and humane world."[110]

The Dann Sisters

The case of the heroic and persistent Dann sisters within both the domestic legal system of the United States and the Inter-American Commission is instructive as a pointed illustration of what is and is not possible within these various forums. Mary and Carrie Dann are members of the Western Shoshone Tribe who have valiantly attempted to assert their "individual aboriginal title claims" to certain grazing lands within the original territory of the Western Shoshone.[111]

The lands they were claiming were "public lands" held by the federal government, and the Dann sisters were cited by the Bureau of Land Management for grazing cattle on public lands without a permit. The Dann sisters claimed that this land was in possession of their family since "time immemorial."[112] The Supreme Court held that tribal aboriginal title to these lands was extinguished pursuant to an award of $26 million made to the Tribe by the Indian Claims Commission. The deposit of the money in a trust account for the Tribe was considered final payment.[113]

The Court did not, however, bar the *individual* aboriginal claims of the Dann sisters:

> The Danns also claim to possess individual as well as tribal aborigi-
> nal rights and because only the latter were before the Indian Claims
> Commission, the "final discharge" of § 22(a) does not bar the Danns
> from raising individual aboriginal title as a defense in this action.
> Though we have recognized that individual aboriginal rights may
> exist in certain contexts, this contention has not been addressed by
> the lower courts and, if open, should first be addressed below.[114]

On remand, the Ninth Circuit decided that the Dann sisters—pursuant to the policy of public land settlement at that time—did have the right to occupy one section of land and graze stock on others.[115] Yet that right was extinguished pursuant to the change of public land policy reflected in the 1934 Taylor Grazing Act, which withdrew all unappropriated land from settlement.[116]

For most litigants, the exhaustion of domestic remedies, for better or worse, terminates the legal controversy, but not for the Danns. They decided to go international, by filing a petition with the Inter-American Commission on Human Rights (IACHR) of the Organization of American States (OAS).[117] The gist of their complaint against the United States in the IACHR was that the denial of their aboriginal property rights by the United States violated their human rights as indigenous peoples, which were protected under the American Declaration of the Rights and Duties of Man.

The Inter-American Commission on Human Rights found in favor of the Danns and against the United States because the United States "failed to ensure the Danns' right to property under conditions of equality contrary to Articles II, XVIII and XXIII of the American Declaration."[118] The Commission's "recommendation" was to:

> Provide Mary and Carrie Dann with an effective remedy, which includes adopting the legislative or other measures necessary to ensure respect for the Danns' right of property in accordance with Articles II, XVIII, and XXIII of the American Declaration in connection with their claims to property rights in the Western Shoshone ancestral lands.[119]

The United States informed the Commission that the Danns' property rights had been litigated to finality in its courts and that it "respectfully declines to take any further action to comply with the Commission's recommendations."[120] The United States subsequently seized 225 head of the Danns' cattle on these lands and sold them at auction. It did this despite the Commission's express request to the contrary.[121]

Thus it appears that even when the Danns "won," they lost or, perhaps more accurately, they secured a moral victory without practical vindication. The worth of such moral currency remains unclear. Its value is likely to be found in the eyes of the beholder.[122]

A Comparative Law View

Although the developing international law relative to indigenous peoples provides a valuable perspective from which to view both historical and contemporary developments in American Indian law, comparative views of what other developed nation-states with substantial indigenous populations, such as Canada, New Zealand, and Australia, are doing are equally instructive. The domestic courts of Canada, New Zealand, and Australia, for example, have attempted to confront the legacy of oppressive colonialism and mitigate its contemporary impact. The results have been decidedly mixed, but the tone of openness and reconciliation is unflinchingly candid when compared with the more pinched and frustrated tone of the U.S. Supreme Court in contemporary Indian law. A sketch of the Canadian, New Zealand, and Australian judicial responses in these areas is illuminating.

Canada

Canada has often been in the forefront of the developed world's responses to the plight of indigenous peoples. For example, in 1982, Canada expressly amended its constitution to include a provision on the rights of the aboriginal peoples of Canada. Section 35 expressly provides:

(1) The existing aboriginal and treaty rights of the aboriginal peoples of Canada are hereby recognized and affirmed.
(2) In this Act, "aboriginal peoples of Canada" include the Indian, Inuit and Metis peoples of Canada.
(3) For greater certainty, in subsection (1) "treaty rights" includes rights that now exist by way of land claim agreements or may be so acquired.
(4) Notwithstanding any other provision of this Act, the aboriginal and treaty rights referred to in subsection (1) are guaranteed equally to male and female persons.[123]

The Canadian Supreme Court's decision in the case of *Delgamuukw v. British Columbia*[124] is illustrative of this major breakthrough. In the *Delgamuukw* case, the Court confronted a single issue, namely, the nature and scope of the constitutional protection afforded by Section 35 (1) to common law aboriginal title. In a case of much intricacy and complexity involving 374 days of argument and the presentation of evidence, the Court considered an aboriginal claim to 58,000 square kilometers in British Columbia brought by Gitksan and Wet'suwet'en hereditary chiefs.[125]

The trial court received evidence not only of physical and tangible indicators of these peoples' aboriginal association with the territories but also evidence drawn from other such diverse sources as *adaawk*, which is a collection of sacred oral traditions about their ancestors, histories, and territories, and an *kungax*, which is a spiritual song or dance or performance that ties these individuals to their land. As to this unique evidence, the Court noted that laws of evidence must be "adapted in order that this type of evidence can be accommodated and placed on an equal footing with the types of historical evidence that courts are familiar with, which largely consists of historical documents."[126]

On the legal side, as opposed to the evidentiary side, the Court sought first to comprehensively define aboriginal title, before discussing its constitutional parameters. The court summarized aboriginal title:

> [B]y two propositions: first, that aboriginal title encompasses the right to exclusive use and occupation of the land held pursuant to that title for a variety of purposes, which need not be aspects of those aboriginal practices, customs and traditions which are integral to distinctive aboriginal cultures; and second, that those protected uses must not be irreconcilable with the nature of the group's attachment to the land.[127]

The Court then acknowledged that the effect of Sec. 35.1 was not to create aboriginal rights but to *constitutionalize* those aboriginal rights that existed in 1982. Despite this constitutionalization, such aboriginal rights were nevertheless subject to infringement based on the doctrine of "justification." This "nascent jurisprudence" of justification contained two components:

> First, the infringement of the aboriginal right must be in furtherance of a legislative objective that is compelling and substantial....
>
> The second part of the test of justification requires an assessment of whether the infringement is consistent with the special fiduciary relationship between the Crown and aboriginal peoples.[128]

The concept of justification is understood as part of the process of "reconciliation" that recognizes aboriginal peoples as possessing rights, but that such rights are not superior to those of the Crown and, further, that aboriginal communities are not separate from but part of the broader social, political, and economic community of the nation.[129] An essential element of the doctrine of justification is the duty of consultation, which includes the requirements of good faith, meaningful responses to aboriginal concerns, and if the infringement actually takes place, an award of compensation.[130]

In the end, the Court attempted to further imbue this constitutional norm with a sense of morality, mutual give-and-take, and reconciliation:

> Ultimately, it is through negotiated settlements, with good faith give and take on all sides, reinforced by the judgments of this Court, that we will achieve, what I stated in *Vander Peet* [...] to be a basic purpose of S. 35(1)—"the reconciliation of the pre-existence of aboriginal societies with the sovereignty of the Crown." Let us face it, we are all here to stay.[131]

The approach of the Supreme Court of Canada in the *Delgamuukw* case largely parallels the emerging international customary norms relative to land and nondiscrimination. The Court did not look directly back to right historical wrongs, but rather it looked forward to transforming the past by creating a fair and reasonable future for all. Although the proof is always in the reality of what happens on the ground in actual cases, the synthesis articulated by the Court appears to have achieved a reasonable middle ground. History cannot (and should not) be ignored, but it must aid rather than hinder the process of forging a meaningful future for all. That is its task.

New Zealand

The situation in New Zealand is similar to, yet different from, Canada, Australia, and the United States. It's similar in the sense that the indigenous peoples of New Zealand—made up of different tribes or *iwi* but usually referred to collectively as Maori—were subject to the usual forces of British colonialism that sought to extend the sovereignty of the Crown over the people and their land. What is unique in the situation of New Zealand is that a single treaty—the Treaty of Waitangi—was signed by almost all of the tribes or *iwi* in 1840.[132]

The rub, of course, is in the meaning of the treaty. What did the various iwi chiefs confer, what did they retain, what did the Crown acquire, and what did the Crown recognize as remaining with the iwi? Not surprisingly, the interpretations vary significantly and are further exacerbated by the existence of two different textual versions of the treaty. There is, however, an initial point of convergence or agreement. The iwi did possess sovereignty, at least in sufficient degree to have the (international) capacity to enter into treaties, which in turn acknowledged the existence of essential property rights in the iwi and, by implication, their status as communities with agency in history:

> [T]hat this attributed to them a history, a previous and inherent
> existence, a past, a present and a future. The language of European
> jurisprudence had that effect, and it further attributed to the Treaty
> itself the status of a historical document, a document performing an
> authoritative act in history, to which reference could be made in the
> future by actors who saw it as executing authority in their present
> arising from their past.[133]

The heart of the treaty controversy was whether it merely created a protectorate to permit the Crown to defend its presence in New Zealand against outside competitors or whether it created a civil regime with the authority and capability to regulate (potential) transfers of lands from indigenous occupants to the Crown or its settlers as a kind of preemptive sovereignty to be situated in the Crown.[134] The reality of power and force—as in all other colonizing situations—resolved the issue largely in favor of the colonizing Crown.

Despite this political reality, there remained the ongoing claim of the Maori that the treaty did not mean what the Crown asserted, but rather what the Maori understood the key terms in the Maori language version to mean. This unique fact of an official treaty text in an indigenous language provided the Maori with a strong platform from which to make their case.[135] For the Maori, the key treaty term was *rangatiratanga*. Maori interpret this term not simply to mean some possessory right in the land,

> but "possession according to Maori ways, according to the structures of authority and value inherent in *iwi* society"; the Chiefs had no intention that they or their peoples should become mere subjects of the Crown, whose possession of the land was protected by Crown law indeed, but only by the kind of law the Crown was accustomed to administer.[136]

Such a claim is difficult for many Westerners to comprehend because it not only involves material claims to land and resources but also makes claims relative to culture and identity, which are inseparable in the Maori worldview from the land itself. This perspective manifests itself in a remedial context that seeks "repossession of both land and cultural identity (which are inseparable) where repossession is possible, and to compensation and resources to use in building a new identity where it is not."[137]

The creation of the Waitangi Tribunal in New Zealand approximates the middle ground established in Canada by its constitutionalization of aboriginal rights.[138] The Waitangi Tribunal is a statutorily created judicial body empowered to hear claims by Maori arising out of performance or nonperformance of the treaty's provisions: "[I]ts findings are not binding at law and take the form of recommendations of such authority that courts and parliament do well to give them attention."[139] The Waitangi Tribunal thus functions as an advisory body not to undo history (which is impossible), but rather to rework it in order to fashion (if it can) a mutually acceptable middle way to go forward.

Of course, this is easier said than done in the real world of politics, power, and enmity, but it does establish possibilities, if there is the necessary commitment on both sides. For example, at the tribunal's request, New Zealand's State-Owned Enterprises Act of 1986, which authorizes the transfer of Crown land to state-owned enterprises, was amended to state that "nothing in this Act shall permit the Crown to act in a manner that is inconsistent with the Treaty of Waitangi."[140]

In such a case as *New Zealand Maori Council v. Attorney General*,[141] the court of appeals described the Treaty of Waitangi as "a partnership between races" requiring utmost good faith and fiduciary responsibilities on the part of the Crown,[142] whereas in the *Huakina Development Trust v. Waikato Valley Authority* case,[143] the court characterized the Treaty of Waitangi as part of the "fabric of New Zealand society," and thus it was necessary to consider Maori culture and spiritual values as articulated by the Waitangi Tribunal in the context of a Maori water rights case.[144] These cases both display and represent the attempt within New Zealand jurisprudence to show respect and foster a spirit of cooperation.

To be sure, certain tensions continue, and political backlash has periodically erupted in the dominant society. Yet there remains—at least within most of the judicial system—a willingness to maintain a genuine ethos of thoughtful accommodation. A cruel past that battered the land and culture of indigenous peoples is not so easily undone and often threatens resurgence. Political and moral fortitude must hold their ground. History is not suddenly changed when its error and harm have been established.

Australia

Australia is the third inheritor of the great common law tradition of the English Crown that has taken up the challenge in the modern era to jurisprudentially confront the legacy of colonialism. This endeavor is perhaps most forcefully illustrated in the case of *Mabo v. Queensland [No. 2]*.[145] In *Mabo*, the High Court of Australia confronted the issue of whether the Meriam people of the Murray Islands retained a form of recognized native title to their lands within the common law framework of Australia. The Court held in the affirmative.

In reaching this conclusion, the Court forcefully revisited the common law underpinning of colonialism and the capability of the common law to evolve to a more principled moral ground in accord with the developments of modern international law. The Court began by noting that the common law ratification of universal and absolute Crown ownership of the land of indigenous people is gravely problematic today. In fact, "judged by any civilized standard, such a law is unjust and its claim to be part of the common law to be applied in contemporary Australia must be questioned."[146]

The Court also realized that the stability created by the law of the past cannot in any way be fully disregarded:

> The peace and order of Australian society is built on the legal system.
> It can be modified to bring it into conformity with contemporary
> notions of justice and human rights, but it cannot be destroyed.[147]

If a common law rule rooted in the past offends the contemporary norms of justice and human rights, the issue becomes whether the "particular rule is an essential doctrine of our legal system and whether, if the rule were to be overturned, the disturbance to be apprehended would be disproportionate to the benefit flowing from the overturning."[148]

The Court further apprehended that the common law doctrine of discovery was premised on early international law doctrines, and thus contemporary common law principles must keep abreast of developing international law norms. Contemporary international law, according to the Court, abandoned the colonial principles of conquest, unconsented cession, and occupation of indigenous lands based on the theory of *terra nullius*, and this shift created a significant challenge for Australian common law:

> The common law does not necessarily conform with international
> law, but international law is a legitimate and important influence on
> the development of the common law, especially when international
> law declares the existence of universal human rights. A common law
> doctrine founded on unjust discrimination in the enjoyment of civil
> and political rights demands reconsideration.[149]

The rationales of the past for unequal treatment must therefore fall, but what is to replace them? What was articulated by the Court is a doctrine recognizing significant property rights in native communities. These newly recognized property rights involving native title are by no means absolute. As noted in the jurisprudence of both Canada and New Zealand, they are still subject to ultimate Crown regulation. In *Mabo*, the Court referred to this doctrine as the principle of "extinguishment."[150] This power to extinguish native title was understood to be strictly in the nature of a legislative power outside the common law authority of the courts.

The Court indicated that each case would have to be examined individually within this new framework to determine whether the Crown had exercised its earlier common law right to alienate the land of indigenous peoples; if so, there may be little that can be done about it. But if not, contemporary native title may only be extinguished by a "clear and plain intention to do so" exercised by the legislature or by the executive.[151] Such an act of extinguishment is also constrained by any other appropriate laws that pertain to the exercise of legislative and executive power. The Court finally held that the Crown had not extinguished the native title of the Meriam people of the Murray Islands, and thus significant property rights remained within the Meriam Community. The Court also acknowledged the broader reality that "[a]borigines were dispossessed of their land parcel by parcel, to make way for expanding colonial settlement. Their dispossession underwrote the development of the nation."[152]

In sum, each of the three common law nations, Canada, New Zealand, and Australia, has sought to recognize and temper the legacy of colonialism and the doctrine of discovery in the contemporary era. Canada amended its constitution to "constitutionalize" aboriginal rights. New Zealand created the Waitangi Tribunal to more fully consider Maori Treaty claims, and Australia reworked its common understanding of native rights to accord more fully with developing norms of international law. All of these approaches reflect a moral evolution and a colonial devolution to seek a middle way. Yet these various approaches are not without fault. Each still recognizes ultimate sovereign authority in the state, when dealing with indigenous rights. Canada retains the doctrine of justification, the Waitangi Tribunal's findings are *not* binding on New Zealand's courts, and Australia reserves the right of extinguishment. It remains to be seen whether these exceptions will seldom or often be invoked and whether they represent legitimate provisos to the tempering of the brute force of history or merely colonialism with a civilized face. If these new rules for change continue to be interpreted broadly, and the exceptions narrowly, there is real opportunity for even more improvement with regard to the status and rights of indigenous peoples within their respective countries. It should give everyone pause to note that despite these advances, all three nations voted against the ratification of the United Nations Declaration on the Rights of Indigenous Peoples.

Lessons for Contemporary American Indian Law

Developments in the international law of indigenous peoples and comparative law perspectives provide both insight and challenge to the field of contemporary Indian law. The international law paradigm of self-determination for indigenous peoples is not in any way beyond the pale of what currently exists in Indian law. In fact, the current federal policy in Indian law is also self-determination.[153] Thus, there is a certain convergence between the domestic and the international, but this convergence is also somewhat misleading. The international model with its supporting norms of nondiscrimination, cultural integrity, land and natural resources, social welfare and development, and self-governance would not be denied by any federal Indian law policy maker. Yet the rub is often in the details of federal funding, the execution of the trust relationship, and judicial accountability. The questionable results in these areas to date provide alarming uncertainty and asymmetry between these norms and their meaningful implementation. This is particularly aggravated in domestic Indian law when there is no constitutional (or even statutory) tether from which to discern an enduring national commitment to the program of self-determination. This is further exacerbated in the case of federal Indian law, where the Supreme Court has effectively closed one of the spigots of tribal sovereignty and self-governance, namely, the assertion of tribes to any but the most minimal criminal and civil authority over non-Indians.[154]

Perhaps key in all this is whether there is sufficient belief and commitment to the doctrine of (legal) evolution. Although the evolution—not random but the product of direct human effort—of the international law norm of self-determination for indigenous peoples has clearly moved forward, it remains necessary to consolidate and deepen its progress. The international law paradigm provides a powerful moral and doctrinal model for domestic Indian law. Yet this is not without irony in light of the view of some of the current justices on the Supreme Court that international law has no role to play in domestic courts of the United States[155] These justices fail to recall that the early international law of the doctrine of discovery, which effectively stripped indigenous people of title to their lands, has been with us since at least 1823.[156] Yet, if there is sufficient political and legal will, this amnesia about the past can thus potentially be treated with the balm of emerging international norms that support the rights of indigenous peoples to self-determination.

In the context of the comparative law review of Canada, New Zealand, and Australia, the salient message is essentially twofold. In the jurisprudence of all three countries, there has been an express confrontation with, and acknowledgment of, the historical errors of the past and an attempt, however limited, to fashion a future that both repudiates that past and formulates a mutually beneficial way to go forward in the present. Compare, for example, the High Court of Australia's statement in *Mabo v. Queensland [No. 2]* that:

> The facts as we know them today do not fit the "absence of law" or
> "barbarian" theory underpinning the colonial reception of the
> common law of England. That being so, there is no warrant for
> applying in these times rules of the English common law which were
> the product of that theory. It would be a curious doctrine to propound
> today that, when the benefit of the common law was first extended to
> Her Majesty's indigenous subjects in the Antipodes, its first fruits
> were to strip them of their right to occupy their ancestral lands.[157]

with Justice Rehnquist's statement in *United States v. Sioux Nation* that:

> There were undoubtedly greed, cupidity, and other less-than-admirable tactics employed by the Government during the Black Hills episode in the settlement of the West, but the Indians did not lack their share of villainy either. It seems to me quite unfair to judge by the light of "revisionist" historians on the mores of another era actions that were taken under pressure of time more than a century ago.[158]

This inability to confront the past or even acknowledge its depredations often prevents securing a stable platform from which to move forward. Confronting the past does not mean getting stuck there in some fog of collective guilt but rather to acknowledge error, learn from mistakes, and resolve to move forward. To do so is primarily the work of recategorizing and redrafting—to make a new map whose primary coordinates are respect, reconciliation, and cooperation and to put away the old maps whose primary coordinates were greed, oppression, and intolerance. The colonial maps of old represent a flat world that no longer exists and no longer gets us where we need to go.

The experience of Canada, New Zealand, and Australia is further instructive in that they have not only confronted the past but also attempted to fashion a future that builds on that encounter, whether it involves amending Canada's constitution, establishing the Waitangi Treaty Tribunal in New Zealand, or infusing Australia's common law with contemporary international law norms. None of this has worked perfectly, and there is much work still to do, but it does constitute a legitimate beginning.[159] These moves, however tentative, suggest some roads not yet taken in American Indian law, and they might make all the difference.[160]

IO

Conclusion

Imagination, Translation, and Constitutional Convergence

THE YOKE OF HISTORY DOES NOT PREVENT CHANGE, BUT IT CAN HINDER IT unless confronted and held accountable. Indeed, that is the very point of history, to make it accountable and render it useful in the realization of important values, such as liberation, self-determination, and fair play. Much of this book has confronted the Indian law jurisprudence of the past and present with one eye on the Constitution and the other on the rather consistent doctrinal patterns that have departed from the Constitution and caused great harm to tribal culture and sovereignty, as well as often resulting in significant impairment of individual Indians' rights. It is now time to suggest some ways back to a legitimate constitutional footing in Indian law that accords tribes and individual Indians the appropriate measure of dignity and respect.

Although such full inclusion and respect no doubt require a constitutional amendment, it is not realistic or pragmatic to assume such a constitutional journey can reach its destination without a series of intermediate steps. Such intermediate or bridging steps are necessary to forge the political consensus and social dialogue that can create and sustain movement toward such constitutional change.

This process might be well described as a project to reconstitutionalize Indian law. The main culprits in deconstitutionalizing Indian law have been Congress and the Supreme Court, and initial efforts might begin there. Because both Congress and the Supreme Court have departed from the Constitution to inhabit plenary realms of unbounded authority,[1] the question becomes: How might they be summoned back to the confines of the Constitution? Each branch of this constitutional tree has the authority to curtail its own excesses and those of its neighbor.

The history of Indian law jurisprudence is pocked with periodic concerns by the Court itself about the constitutional and doctrinal footing within the field. As early as the 1830 case of *Cherokee Nation v. Georgia*, Chief Justice Marshall observed that the "relation of the Indians to the United States is marked by peculiar and cardinal distinctions which exist no where else."[2] In *United States v. Kagama*, Justice Miller pointed out that "the relation of Indian tribes living within the borders of the United States, both before and since the Revolution, to the people of the United States has been an anomalous one and of a complex character."[3]

In the modern cases, there is more of a sense of confusion, even irritation, about identifying the doctrinal core of Indian law. In *McClanahan v. Arizona State Tax Commission*, Justice Marshall both acknowledged and sought to clarify the doctrinal confusion:

> The source of federal authority over Indian matters has been the subject of some confusion, but it is now generally understood that the power derives from federal responsibility for regulating commerce with Indian tribes and for treaty making.[4]

More recently, there have been explicit statements about the need for doctrinal coherence. For example, Justice Rehnquist noted in *Washington v. Confederated Tribes of the Colville Indian Reservation* that

> Since early in the last century, this Court has been struggling to develop a coherent doctrine by which to measure with some predictability the scope of Indian immunity from state taxation...I am convinced that a well-defined body of principles is essential in order to end the need for case-by-case litigation which has plagued this area of the law for a number of years.[5]

Justice Souter has made the same observation in a newer context: "If we are to see coherence in the various manifestations of the general law of tribal jurisdiction over non-Indians, the source of doctrine must be *Montana v. United States*."[6]

All of this boiled over again in the 2004 case of *United States v. Lara*.[7] In this case, much discussed elsewhere in this book, the emperor appeared to be losing his clothes. Although the majority relied on the mantra that the "Constitution grants Congress broad general powers to legislation in respect to Indian tribes, powers we have consistently described as 'plenary and exclusive,' "[8] there was significant rumbling from others that this cannot really be so, especially in light of the Court's previous rejection of inherent tribal criminal jurisdiction over nonmember Indians,[9] which Congress had just overturned.

Justice Kennedy found it "a most troubling proposition to say that Congress can relax the restriction on inherent tribal sovereignty in a way that extends that sovereignty beyond those historical limits."[10] Justice Thomas went even further to proclaim: "As this case should make clear, the time has come to reexamine the premise and logic of our tribal sovereignty cases."[11] Justice Thomas identified the Court's source of "confusion" in "two largely incompatible and doubtful assumptions,"[12] namely, Congress's plenary power on one hand and tribal sovereignty on the other. This tension places federal Indian law at "odds with itself,"[13] indeed, makes it "schizophrenic."[14]

Justice Souter quoted the *Kagama* Court "that the relationship of Indian tribes to the National Government is an 'anomalous one and of a complex character' "[15] as a preface to his lament that "confusion, I fear, will be the legacy of today's decision, for our failure to stand by what we have previously said reveals that our conceptualization of sovereignty and dependent sovereignty are largely rhetorical."[16]

This pattern of doctrinal confusion has become more predominant in recent times because the Supreme Court has arrogated to itself a judicial version of plenary power that has muddied the jurisprudential waters of Indian law even further. This judicial plenary power doctrine—which has not been acknowledged by the Court itself—is deeply rooted in the cases of *Oliphant v. Suquamish Indian Tribe*[17] and *Montana v. United States*.[18] In both cases, the Court, without constitutional or statutory authority, sharply reduced tribal sovereignty. In *Oliphant*, the Court established a black-letter rule that tribes lack criminal jurisdiction over non-Indians because it was inconsistent with their dependent status[19] and in *Montana*, similarly fashioned a rule that created a substantial presumption *against* tribal civil jurisdiction over non-Indians on fee land.[20] In subsequent cases, *Montana* became "pathmarking,"[21] but it has created a very confusing path because essentially it is not doctrinally rooted in the Constitution or in any congressional mandate. It is rather a judicially formulated marker, which permits the Court to make policy-driven decisions about what is "best" for non-Indians who might potentially be subject to tribal jurisdiction.

In both these cases, the Court also elided Congress's overarching authority in Indian affairs. In *Oliphant*, the Court claimed it was merely actualizing Congress's (unspoken) assumptions about tribal criminal jurisdiction;[22] in *Montana*, it said its rule might be derived from the (unspoken) assumption surrounding the General Allotment and Crow Allotment Act.[23] Beneath the facile nod to what supposedly "Congress consistently believed"[24] were an invasion of Congress's near-exclusive lawmaking authority in Indian law and the creation of a colonialist-like common law regime.

The Court's own sense of confusion is not rooted in any sense that its assertion of complete authority (absent express congressional enactment to the contrary) is the primary source of that confusion. Yet that is the core of the problem, the failure to perceive that such extensive power, which is largely unbounded, becomes no more than a marker for policy preferences about what tribes should or should not be allowed to do. As a result, such policy preferences abet, not allay, the declared confusion. This doctrinal confusion is also a product of a free-floating normative angst within the Court about what tribes should be *permitted* to do, especially in regard to non-Indians. It is this sense of normative bias that is at the heart of Justice Scalia's 1990 memo to Justice Brennan, in which he stated that the primary guide in Indian law was not precedent but "what the current state of affairs ought to be."[25] Law uncoupled from constitutional principle—especially in regard to those who were here first— holds little promise for dignity, respect, and appropriate limits. On a Court where many claim a fidelity to judicial restraint, it is time to bring such a commitment to bear in the field of Indian law.

Supreme Court and Congressional Reform

The Supreme Court might call itself to task and return to mainstream Indian law jurisprudence, which has always held that in the absence of congressional action to the contrary, tribal authority remained unimpaired. Indeed, this is Felix Cohen's classic formulation, in which he observed that the powers of tribal self-government "are subject to qualification by treaty and express legislation of Congress, but, save those expressly qualified, full powers of internal sovereignty are vested in the Indian tribe and in their duly constitutional organs of government."[26] The Court has strayed far afield in its contemporary Indian law jurisprudence, and it needs to return itself to a more restrained role in Indian law, where both history and the Constitution originally placed it—a role designed to protect tribes from the states, rather than to abet states' aggression into Indian country, as well as to develop a robust "our federalism" in federal-tribal relations that strikes a proper balance between federal and tribal authority in Indian country.

Not only should the Court curb its own common law excesses but also it has the authority, even the duty, to curb the extraconstitutional "plenary" excesses of Congress, despite their longtime acceptance within the penumbra of *Lone Wolf*. The Court does not need to look far for justification to do so; it needs only to extrapolate from some of its own recent Interstate Commerce Clause jurisprudence. In both the *Lopez*[27] and *Morrison*[28] cases, the Court decided that the "plenary" scope of the Interstate Commerce Clause was not infinite, but rather "subject to outer limits."[29] The Court found, in a rather commonsensical manner, that the Interstate Commerce Clause could *not* justify a federal statute that made it a criminal offense for any individual to knowingly possess a firearm within school zones.[30] Chief Justice Rehnquist further noted the overreaching potential of a too broad plenary approach:

> To uphold the Government's contention here, we would have to pile inference upon inference in a manner that would bid fair to convert congressional authority under the Commerce Clause to a general power of the sort retained by the states.[31]

The Court further realized that the "question of Congress' power under the Commerce Clause 'is necessarily one of degree.'"[32] In the context of the principles of enumerated powers and federalism, such analysis and potential restraint is necessary.[33]

Similarly in *Morrison*, the Court struck down the civil remedy portion of the Violence Against Women Act of 1994 as beyond the constitutional limits of both the Interstate Commerce Clause and Section 5 of the Fourteenth Amendment.[34] Chief Justice Rehnquist's opinion noted that "we invalidate a congressional enactment only upon a plain showing that Congress has exceeded its constitutional bounds."[35] Recalling *Lopez*'s core warning "that under our modern, expansive interpretation of the Commerce Clause, Congress' regulatory authority is not without effective bounds,"[36] the Court found that "gender-motivated claims of violence are not, in any sense of the phrase, economic activity."[37]

Without putting too fine a point on it, there is the reasonable argument to be made that such constitutional restraint and boundary setting is also needed with regard to the Indian Commerce Clause. Yet the Court has given no indication of any interest in so doing, except in a rather perverse way. Although the Court in *United States v. Lara*[38] accepted Congress's constitutional authority to adjust the limitations on tribal sovereignty set by other political branches, such as the Court or the Executive Branch, it was quick to point out that there were clearly "limits" to the process. "We are not now faced with a question dealing with constitutional limits on congressional efforts to legislate far more radical changes in tribal status. In particular, the case involves no interference with the power or authority of any state."[39]

The Court was never concerned with "constitutional limits on Congressional efforts" when Congress was eviscerating tribal sovereignty, but it is already on alert concerning future legislation and further "radical changes" to restore tribal sovereignty at the expense of state power in Indian country. Such a view seeks to turn Indian law on its head, using Congress's plenary power and the Indian Commerce Clause as a shield to protect state authority in Indian country and as a sword to further incapacitate tribal sovereignty. This is Indian law without shame.

To be clear, the Court could properly confine congressional "plenary power" to the essential plain meaning parameters of the text of the constitution and the Marshall trilogy; establishing constitutional boundaries that provide dignity and respect to tribes. Congress acting within such boundaries could presumably overturn any of the Court's modern common law decisions that erode tribal sovereignty.

What about the converse problem of Congress setting limits on the Court's judicial plenary power regime? This is not a problem, presumably, because Congress may enact a statute to replace or supplant a common law rule. This is a power that Congress has used quite sparingly to date in Indian law. With the exception of the *Duro* override, Congress has let stand the results of disturbing cases like *Oliphant v. Suquamish Indian Tribe*,[40] *Montana v. United States*,[41] *South Dakota v. Bourland*,[42] *Strate v. A-1 Contractors*,[43] *Alaska v. Native Village of Venetie Tribal Government*,[44] *Atkinson Trading Co. v. Shirley*,[45] *Nevada v. Hicks*,[46] and *Plains Commerce Bank v. Long Family Land and Cattle Co., Inc.*[47] But can it do so unequivocally in Indian law? The Court in *Lara* said yes, but it clearly hedged about whether Congress could or would go further than the slight adjustment of restoring tribal criminal jurisdiction over non-member Indians. For example, could Congress do away with the common law rule of *Oliphant*[48] that tribes have no criminal jurisdiction over non-Indians? Justice Breyer, without much analysis, appeared very doubtful, with his vague notion that states possess some kind of "constitutional" authority in Indian country that cannot be adjusted by Congress.[49] This makes a rather porous mush of both the Constitution and the Marshall trilogy.

Although it has yet to be formally submitted to Congress, there has been at least one tribally initiated legislative proposal relative to curbing the perils of judicial plenary power in Indian law. This legislative proposal has the working title of the Tribal Sovereignty and Economic Enhancement Act, and it is part of a larger nationwide strategy led by the National Congress of American Indians under the name of the Tribal Sovereignty Protection Initiative. The draft bill focuses on three broad principles, namely, the full restoration of inherent territorial sovereignty, except as expressly surrendered by treaty or affirmative congressional action; a return to the "impenetrable barrier" to state authority in Indian country created by the Marshall trilogy; and the creation of enhanced federal review at the circuit court level, particularly of claims stemming from the Indian Civil Rights Act of 1968.[50]

Tribal support for this potential legislation has been modest, if not tepid, to date. Although there is near-unanimous support for the renewed recognition of wide-ranging inherent tribal sovereignty, there has been significant resistance to enhanced federal review as yet another unjustified compromise of tribal sovereignty. The proponents of the legislation regard enhanced federal review as the necessary quid pro quo for congressional support that can withstand and respond to likely non-Indian opposition and state resistance. No consensus from Indian country has yet emerged to push this proposed legislation off the drawing board and into the halls of Congress. This last point is quite salient. It is very unlikely that Congress will attempt to stem or roll back judicial plenary power that has already significantly advanced state authority in Indian country without some legislative trade-offs to curtail vigorous state and non-Indian opposition. In the real world of give-and-take politics, doing the right thing, standing alone, is seldom enough to advance legislative success.

The current Supreme Court created these plenary doctrines and is therefore an unlikely source to disavow them. Congress, for its part, has shown little inclination to get involved. As a result, the foundational principles of Indian law[51] are gravely at risk as both promise and law. In the short run, Congress must be persuaded to use its extensive legislative authority to curb these denigrations of tribal sovereignty that are contrary to the long-standing congressional and executive policy of meaningful self-determination.[52] Yet, in the long run, only a constitutional amendment can truly guarantee and vouchsafe an essential and enduring tribal sovereignty.

There are at least two other things that Congress might do to counter the likely quicksand that underlies *Lara*. One is to pass a (nonbinding) joint congressional resolution that affirms the constitutional status of tribal sovereignty. Such a resolution might synthesize or restate the basic constitutional stature of the Marshall trilogy principles that tribes possess sovereignty sufficient for self-governance on the reservation, states have no inherent authority in Indian country, and the federal government possesses legislative and executive authority to protect and to assist tribes (i.e., trust relationship) but not to otherwise limit and deny tribal sovereignty. Such a resolution might be similar to the resolution that noted and commemorated the contribution of the Iroquois Confederacy to American democratic thought and constitutional governance.[53] Although such resolutions do not possess the force of law, they are significant as public statements of the sentiment of Congress and as such can provide a baseline for future congressional enactments as a matter of law. Once Congress is on record concerning a particular issue, it makes it easier to go forward and more difficult to go backward.

The second and more dramatic approach would be enactment of legislation that pushes beyond the "plenary" status quo but stops short of constitutional amendment, and that seeks to advance and shore up tribal sovereignty in the modern era. This is Alex Tallchief Skibine's model of a self-determination paradigm of (consensual) incorporation in which Congress would enact legislation

> similar to the legislation extending commonwealth status to Puerto Rico. Perhaps it can be termed a "compact of incorporation." The compact would establish a baseline of tribal sovereignty and define the relationship among the tribes, the United States, and the individual states of the Union. After enactment of the compact, each tribe could vote whether to accept incorporation under the terms of the compact. Once the decision to join is made, the terms of incorporation could only be changed through mutual agreement of the parties.[54]

This proposal seeks to advance beyond the dependency models of the past to establish a more vibrant and inclusive "our federalism." Skibine notes the models of the past have both denigrated tribal sovereignty and been constitutionally suspect.

One of the important themes explored by Skibine is the shifting legal perspectives that have developed to explain "how tribes became incorporated into the fabric of the United States political system."[55] This theme of incorporation refers to the process whereby tribes, originally outside the structure and reach of the Constitution, came more and more to be politically and socially absorbed within the republic and Constitution without any constitutional amendment or adjustment to mark, much less authorize, this seismic shift. Skibine identifies three models within this framework: John Marshall's geographical incorporation under a protectorate model, the guardian-ward trusteeship concept of incorporation, and Felix Cohen's plenary power paradigm.[56] Within this dynamic of ever-increasing incorporation, Skibine's proposal—however skeletal its details—is decidedly a positive move to shift the thinking away from the dependency paradigm of Indian law and the suffocating enclosure of unconstitutional "incorporation" and toward an open window of doctrinal fresh air—a fresh view that seeks to enlarge "our federalism" thinking to "incorporate Indian tribes under a third sphere of sovereignty"[57] and ultimately, perhaps, to point to the necessity of constitutional amendment.

Treaty Federalism

Given the materials of previous legal encounters, especially treaties, there is significant opportunity to reestablish a meaningful relationship between the federal government and tribes that is characterized by the classic civic values of dignity and respect. Treaty federalism is the name for this approach. Treaty federalism accepts the reality of incorporation but not its dismal confinement within the iron cage of plenary power.[58]

In this view, treaties are not seen as static artifacts marooned in the present or as romantic talismans to rekindle the past, but as a "form of political recognition and a measure of the consensual distribution of power between tribes and the United States."[59] As such, according to Russell Lawrence Barsh and James Youngblood Henderson, treaties originally represented agreements between existing sovereigns. Yet with increasing incorporation, their core structure came more and more to resemble compacts:

> Compacts differ in origin, nature, and effect. Their object is to restructure the parties and create or enlarge some common, national sovereignty. Treaties are agreements between existing sovereigns; compacts create new sovereigns. Since compacts alter the fabric of government, they require the consent of the people themselves, the same as an internal amendment of either party's constitution. Once ratified by the people, a compact cannot be modified, dissolved or superceded except by the same process. It is not an alliance, but the constitution of an amalgamated body politic.[60]

In the context of treaties as alliances of sovereigns, "the ultimate relief from oppression is exit. In a national compact, the only safety is in the architecture of its constitution and laws."[61] Thus such a compact is a form of political integration, which is premised on consent. The notion of a compact is not completely foreign to the field of Indian law. For example, "The Indian Reorganization Act revitalized it in 1934 with its central focus on *mutual consent*: the consent of the United States manifested in the act, and the consent of participating tribes in referenda called for the purpose of adopting it."[62]

Treaty federalism seeks to guarantee the enduring political security and cultural integrity of tribes and rests on the principles of consent of the governed, democratic representation, and political pluralism. As Felix Cohen observed more than three generations ago:

> In point of form it is immaterial whether the powers of an Indian
> tribe are expressed and exercised through customs handed down by
> word of mouth or through written constitutions and statutes. In
> either case the laws of the Indian tribe owe their force to the will of
> the members of the tribe.[63]

In this view, treaty federalism thus becomes the cornerstone for a constitutional amendment that is necessary to realize the essential bounty of inclusion and respect.

The work of Barsh and Henderson provides a basic text for such an amendment. The foundation of this approach is to treat tribes constitutionally as if they were states. The proposed amendment states in its entirety:

> Section 1. Except as provided by this amendment, Indian Tribes shall
> be deemed "States" for all purposes under this Constitution.
>
> Section 2. All Constitutional powers of State self-government not
> hereafter expressly delegated to the United States by the vote of
> three-fourths of the members of an Indian Tribe are reserved by that
> tribe, and cannot be divested by Congress.
>
> Section 3. The reserved powers of an Indian Tribe shall include,
> but not be limited to, the power to regulate behavior and tax persons
> and property within the exterior boundaries of its territory, concur-
> rent only with the general Constitutional authority of the United
> States.
>
> Section 4. Tribes shall have power to fix criteria for membership
> notwithstanding the second clause of the second section of the
> Fourteenth Amendment.
>
> Section 5. For ten years from the date of ratification of this
> amendment. Congress shall appropriate $500 million to the use and
> for the benefit and economic development of Tribes, which fund shall
> be apportioned on the basis of membership and distributed directly to
> the respective Tribal governments without condition or limitation.
> Nothing in this amendment shall authorize the United States through
> any of its officers or agencies to supervise or regulate the use of this
> fund or the administration of tribal government generally.
>
> Section 6. (a) For purposes of representation in Congress, there
> shall be two assemblies separate and apart from those established by
> Article I of this Constitution. The Tribal Senate Caucus shall consist
> of one Delegate from each Tribe. The Tribal House Caucus shall be
> apportioned by the membership of each Tribe, Tribes to have one
> Delegate for every five thousand members or part thereof.

(b) Delegates shall each serve for four years, one-fourth of the Delegates to be elected each year in such a manner as each Tribe shall respectively provide in its constitution.

(c) From year to year or at such times as each Caucus shall establish by rules, the Tribal Senate Caucus shall send two Senators to the Senate and the Tribal House Caucus shall send two Representatives to the House of Representatives, which Senators and Representatives shall serve and act in every way as any other members of Congress.

(d) The expenses of Delegates and the expenses of the respective Caucuses herein provided shall be paid by the United States.

Section 7. Henceforth no State shall exercise any power over the territory of any Tribe, except by the terms of a Compact approved by Congress, nor shall the resident members of any Tribe have the right of suffrage or election in any State.

Section 8. This amendment shall apply only to those Indian tribes which were incorporated by a constitution of their choosing for five years prior to the date of ratification, and which may consent to its application to them by the vote of two-thirds of their members in a plebiscite convened for that purpose.[64]

While the text is straightforward enough, it is not without flaw. The primary problems involve the problems of tribal jurisdiction over non-Indians and the substantial presence of state-derived institutions such as public schools and counties within reservation boundaries. A potential solution to the first of these problems is embedded within the proposed text itself. In the assumption of statelike status, there is the concurrent necessity to provide all the constitutional guarantees currently incumbent upon the states through the Fourteenth Amendment. Although this is potentially problematic in terms of cost for many tribes, a federal form of reimbursement is a likely cure. As to the second problem, state institutions, such as public schools, would be transferred to tribal control, and state and local governing bodies dissolved. Such problems are certainly complicated but not insurmountable. Some tribes may also lack the political will to provide such guarantees or otherwise be involved, and they may use the consent provision to opt out.

The issue of tribal consent is obviously primary. Without provision for tribal consent, such an amendment, even if otherwise passed by Congress and the states, would lack baseline legitimacy with its target community of beneficiaries. Although some form of tribal consent is absolutely essential, there is the problem with this proposal of developing an asymmetrical result that has some tribes with constitutional status and others without. Such a result would probably be very confusing and untenable.

In addition to these immediate and front-end concerns, there are the wider issues relative to the cost of such a venture and the actual relationship of these newly incorporated sovereigns to the federal government, especially Congress itself. In the financial realm, continued economic development is of the essence. Without it, the constitutional advance of such an amendment will be muted, to say the least. In this regard—despite the very real but quite uneven advances provided by Indian gaming—an Indian country Marshall Plan analogous to European reconstruction after World War II would greatly advance the likelihood of economic growth to support and bolster the proposed constitutional advance. The authors of this proposal include as part of the amendment an unrestrictive congressional appropriation of $500 million annually for the "benefit and economic development of Tribes, which shall be apportioned on the basis of membership and distribution directly to the respective Tribal governments without condition or limitation."[65]

For the proponents of this proposed amendment, a crucial issue would be not only the constitutional recognition of tribal sovereignty but also—as with the states—the issue of tribal representation in the national government.[66] Sections 6 and 7 specifically address this issue.

Section 6 creates both a Tribal Senate Caucus and a Tribal House Caucus. Although these caucuses would be nonvoting, it is likely that they would have a strong and positive influence on any proposed legislation affecting individual Indians or tribes. The right to serve on committees, participate in debate, and have expenses paid would probably advance both the visibility and the quality of discussion involving proposed Indian legislation.

Section 7 is a strongly worded section that would clearly repeal any existent state authority in Indian country, except via any state-tribal compact as ratified by Congress. Equally daring is the complementary provision that resident tribal members would lose any right of franchise to participate in state elections. This appears eminently fair. A member of a constitutionally recognized tribal sovereign should not be able to participate in the electoral politics of a state occupying all or some of the territory of a tribe.

As review of this proposed amendment indicates, there is no doubt that there are significant legal issues relative to extending tribal authority over non-Indians, the loss of state citizenship by individual Indians, and connecting this new tribal status to the project of federalism, especially within Congress, as well as matters relative to tribal consent and the likely cost and long-range economic impact. Yet these difficulties ought not detract or undermine the vitality of the general constitutional endeavor as a whole. It appears that this is a most propitious time to reinvigorate thinking about the status of tribal sovereignty *within* the structure of the Constitution. As tribes move forward to actualize more and more sovereignty in the modern era, the moribund thinking of plenary power—both congressional and judicial—is no more than a doctrine of containment, a domestic branch of continuing colonialism. There is a better way.

The proposed constitutional amendment drafted by Henderson and Barsh, while no doubt comprehensive, is quite unwieldy and even potentially unworkable. It provides too much detail and threatens to collapse under its own weight. Its model of statelike constitutional status also lacks sufficient textual connection to inherent tribal sovereignty. I propose a much simpler version, which emphasizes dignity, essential sovereignty, and durable inclusion.

> *Proposed Amendment to the United States Constitution*
> The inherent sovereignty of Indian tribes within these United States shall not be infringed, except by powers expressly delegated to the United States by the Constitution.
> The Congress shall have power to enforce, by appropriate legislation, the provisions of this Article.

This proposed amendment draws on language from both the Tenth and Fourteenth Amendments. Its goal is to provide respectful and durable constitutional recognition of inherent tribal sovereignty, which harks back to the original text of the Constitution, with a new sense of respect and inclusion; it further recognizes congressional authority to enact (necessary) legislation to enforce its basic guarantees. Such a constitutional amendment would not displace treaties as the cornerstone of tribal sovereignty. Rather, such an amendment would build on that sturdy foundation to create a modern structure that synthesizes the best of the old and the new—to create, as it were, a modern architecture of sovereignty that is best capable of preserving the past and advancing the future.

In the earlier era of modern Indian law, tribes were essentially engaged in deploying a kind of defensive sovereignty, seeking to use treaties and the heft of the Marshall trilogy to keep states at bay. Constitutional status was not key, and tribes were often successful. Yet, as tribes have moved further in the more recent modern era to realize tribal sovereignty on the ground in a mode of offensive sovereignty, especially involving non-Indians, the Supreme Court has been adamant in saying no.[67] Constitutional status is paramount to ward off the notions of dependency and "implied divestiture," which hold tribal sovereignty hostage to the whims and sufferance of a Congress and Supreme Court untethered to the Constitution.

Although some might regard this constitutional project as far-fetched, others might regard it as ill conceived, preferring instead, for example, a return to treaty making as the best way to reestablish meaningful government-to-government relationships.[68] Yet, despite the strong (cultural) attraction for many of returning to a *literal* past of treaty making, such an approach is conceptually and practically problematic for several reasons. Because Indian people are now federal (and state) citizens, there is the basic problem of making a treaty between the citizens of the same country, which trenches on a basic tenet of treaty making: It is an agreement between separate sovereigns, who *each* represent separate and distinct groups of citizens. It is also important to note that a constitutional amendment would not in any way abrogate existing treaties and their mutual obligations.

There is also the statutory bar that has existed since 1871 against treaty making with Indian tribes.[69] Despite the good argument that can be made that the statute is unconstitutional as an improper Article I enactment that violates the Article II powers of the president, the statute is now 137 years old and unlikely to be struck down. A more likely vehicle in this vein might be agreements between the federal government and the tribes. Agreements differ from treaties *legally* (if not culturally) only as to the manner of federal ratification. Treaties must be approved by two thirds of the Senate,[70] whereas agreements require only majority approval by both houses of Congress.[71]

Agreements remain viable even with—perhaps especially with—constitutional amendment, to forge important joint efforts similar to such agreements that exist between the federal government and states. They can supplement, rather than supplant, constitutional amendment. Reliance on treaty making or agreement standing *alone* is especially fraught with difficulty because it would permit the federal government to maintain the status quo by simply failing to achieve agreement or accord with tribes. There is also the sheer magnitude of the challenge of whether the federal government would be able to negotiate (and the Senate ratify) such treaty agreements with more than 500 tribes. It seems a very unlikely prospect, to say the least.

It is also true that to date there has been little or no push from Indian tribes or national Indian organizations for such constitutional reform. The likely reasons include the fact that the pressing issues of day-to-day governance effectively deny sufficient time to thoroughly consider reform beyond focus on the elusive government-to-government relationship, as well as a singular and ongoing commitment to the treaty commitments of the past. Yet, it is worth considering that the "defensive" sovereignty deployed in the past to contain state aggression in Indian country may be an inadequate framework to support the new "offensive" sovereignty, which tribes seek to realize in their attempt to govern all those found within reservation borders.[72] A constitutional amendment is the surest footing to advance and uphold tribal sovereignty in this newest of eras in Indian law. The proposals here are designed to advance discussion about a (potential) way forward. They claim neither finality nor exclusivity.

The Process of Constitutional Amendment Ratification

The ratification process for proposed constitutional amendments is set forth in Article V of the Constitution, which provides:

> The Congress, whenever two thirds of both Houses shall deem it
> necessary, shall propose Amendments to this Constitution, or, on the
> Application of the Legislatures of two thirds of the several States,
> shall call a Convention for proposing Amendments, which, in either
> Case, shall be valid to all Intents and Purposes, as Part of this
> Constitution, when ratified by the Legislatures of three fourths of the
> several States, or by Conventions in three fourths thereof, as the one
> or the other Mode of Ratification may be proposed by the Congress;
> Provided that no Amendment which may be made prior to the Year
> One thousand eight hundred and eight shall in any Manner affect the
> first and fourth Clauses in the Ninth Section of the first Article; and
> that no State, without its Consent, shall be deprived of its equal
> Suffrage in the Senate.

In a nutshell, the most likely route to constitutional amendment would be initial proposal by "two thirds of both Houses" and ratification "by the legislatures of three fourths of the several states." These numbers are large, but they are not insuperable. Presumably, there is a strong moral and legal argument to be made, based on the themes of inclusion and respect. Tribes were here first and were recognized as separate and distinct sovereigns when the Constitution was adopted in 1789. Over time, they were incorporated into the republic involuntarily, without their consent, and without any constitutional adjustment. This gap substantially threatens the Constitution as the core vehicle of this nation's overarching commitment to inclusion and fair play. Without constitutional amendment, there might well have been continued slavery, discrimination, and denial of citizenship to African Americans[73] and discrimination and denial of the franchise to women.[74]

The procedures of the amendment process itself are relatively straightforward. The first step is securing the approval of two thirds of both houses of Congress. In the Senate, that would mean 67 votes (of 100); in the House of Representatives, it would mean 290 (of 435); then it would need approval by three fourths of the state legislatures, that is, 38 states.

If we start with the proposition that states without or with very few federally recognized tribes within their borders would readily support such an amendment, the numbers look like this:

1. States without federally recognized tribes: Arkansas, Delaware, Georgia, Hawaii, Illinois, Kentucky, Maryland, Missouri, New Hampshire, New Jersey, Ohio, Pennsylvania, Tennessee, Vermont, Virginia, and West Virginia.

Total Senators: 32
Total Representatives: 138
Total States: 16

2. States with one or two federally recognized tribes: Alabama, Colorado, Connecticut, Florida, Indiana, Iowa, Massachusetts, Mississippi, North Carolina, Rhode Island, South Carolina, and Wyoming.

Total Senators: 24
Total Representatives: 94
Total States: 12

3. States with three or more federally recognized tribes: Alaska, Arizona, California, Idaho, Kansas, Louisiana, Maine, Michigan, Minnesota, Montana, Nebraska, Nevada, New Mexico, New York, North Dakota, Oklahoma, Oregon, South Dakota, Texas, Utah, Washington, and Wisconsin.

Total Senators: 44
Total Representatives: 203
Total States: 22

These initial totals for states with two federally recognized tribes or less are as follows: 56 members in the Senate, or about 84 percent of the necessary vote, and in the House 232 representatives or about 80 percent of the necessary vote. For final ratification of state legislatures, there are 28 states or 74 percent of those needed for final passage. These very rough percentages indicate that there is much more work to do but that it is by no means a hopeless project.

This threshold appraisal demonstrates that there is a likely foundation of support on which to build.

Promise and Reality

Of course, this rough, political assessment is only part of the picture. The other part of the picture is assessing the potential effect of a campaign to make the case for the amendment on normative and ethical grounds—a case that centers on the constitutional theme of inclusion and on the historical American project to reach out to all its citizens and provide them with equal opportunity and a sense of full participation within the society at large. In this regard, the case for Indian tribes is not identical to what has happened in the past. The inclusions of the past—whether involving African Americans or women—focused on individuals, but the proposed constitutional amendment focuses on Indian *tribes* as cultural and self-governing *sovereigns*, not as mere (oppressed) individuals. The proposed amendment therefore involves reverberations significantly beyond mere individual inclusion and touches the more complex issue of integrating the tribal sovereign within a constitutional structure heretofore only concerned with the federal-state relationship as a matter of constitutional federalism. The proposed amendment would move away from the traditional bilateral view of constitutional federalism toward a trilateral federalism involving the federal government, the states, and the tribes.

The term *sovereignty* has increasingly become a staple of much discourse within the United States (and elsewhere). Such discussions have multiple dimensions that are both external and internal in nature. The external

> focuses on the prerogatives of the United States vis-à-vis other nations—to participate (or not) in new legal institutions such as the International Criminal Court, to join (or not) transnational agreements such as the Convention on the Elimination of All Forms of Discrimination Against Women (EDAW), to use (or not) opinions of other nations' courts in the development of domestic legal norms, to engage (or not) in dialogues through adjudication to articulate international norms. External sovereignty is about the literal and legal power of the United States in its relationship to other nations and the world community.[75]

The internal dimension concerns the

relationship among governments *within* this country's borders. This "internal sovereignty" talk arises when states claim prerogatives of lawmaking free from "interference" by federal law and when Indian tribes seek release from constraints imposed by either state or the federal government.[76]

This internal discourse involving the relationship of the federal government to states has increasingly focused on the concept of state "dignity," especially in the Court's Eleventh Amendment jurisprudence. "For example, in 2002, a majority of the Supreme Court proclaimed that '[t]he preeminent purpose of state sovereign immunity is to accord states the dignity that is consistent with their status as sovereign entities.'"[77]

As Resnik and Suk noted, this "invigoration" of state sovereignty has been accompanied by a diminishment of tribal sovereignty.[78] This process of diminishing tribal sovereignty is unlikely to be significantly reversed until there is a broad return to a similar concern with tribal dignity. Such dignity is most likely to fully emerge with an appropriate constitutional amendment. State "dignity" is deeply embedded in its constitutional status. Tribal sovereignty and dignity must be similarly situated to provide a legitimate and attractive horizon for the future.

The constitutional recognition and status of Native peoples is not without precedent within the law of other nations. For example, the Constitution of Canada expressly provides that "the existing aboriginal and treaty rights of the aboriginal people of Canada are hereby recognized and affirmed."[79] Other nations that include constitutional recognition of Native sovereignty and international norms include Nicaragua,[80] Argentina,[81] Brazil,[82] Honduras,[83] Colombia,[84] Mexico,[85] and Russia.[86] Much of this constitutional activity has developed in recent years in order "to broadly affirm indigenous peoples' rights in a way consistent with developing international norms."[87] These reforms, however attenuated in practice, are often accorded "the highest level of respect within the domestic realm" of law and "may substantially motivate the implementation of the norms in concrete settings."[88]

This challenge is not without obstacle and is by no means an easy task. It will take much tribal wisdom, lawyerly craft, and political acumen to succeed.[89] Yet in seeking a secure and vital future for tribal sovereignty, it makes sense to appeal to the aspiration and tradition of a *living* constitution to truly become all that it can be for those who were here first[90]—a living constitution that imagines the future, translates the past, and forges a remarkable convergence of promise and reality.

Notes

CHAPTER ONE

1. A word about terminology is in order. Most often the term *Indian tribe* is used to refer to the federally recognized entity made up of indigenous people with a recognized territory and the capacity of self-governance. This is the primary term used within the field of Indian law. There are many synonyms, such as Indian Nations, First Nations, First Peoples, and Indigenous Peoples. Individual Indians (again the primary federal legal term) are also referred to by their individual tribal affiliation (e.g., Navajo, Sioux, Apache) and such other terms as Native American, Native person, and Indigenous person. In the western part of the Plains where I have my greatest experience, Indian people are most likely to refer to themselves by tribal affiliation (e.g., Rosebud Sioux, Crow, Navajo) or as an Indian person. The various terms are used interchangeably throughout the text.

2. See the treaty-making clause at Art. II, Sec. 2; the Indian Commerce Clause at Art. I, Sec. 8; and the Indians not taxed provision at Art. I, Sec. 2. These provisions are discussed throughout this book, but with especially significant detail in chapters 3, 4 and 7.

3. 187 U.S. 553 (1903). See in-depth analysis in chapter 5.

4. See, e.g., the Thirteenth (1865), Fourteenth (1869), and Fifteenth (1870) Amendments enacted after the Civil War to end slavery, confer citizenship, and grant the right to vote to African Americans. See also the Nineteenth Amendment (1920) guaranteeing women the right to vote.

5. 187 U.S. 553 (1903).

6. Although some commentators have noted the veritable exponential growth in constitutional scholarship, there has been no such increase in scholarship that deals with tribal sovereignty and the Constitution. Professor Tribe's insightful and summary observation in this regard makes no mention of the existence or need for such scholarship:

An embarrassment of riches confronts anyone interested in constitutional law; there has been a veritable cascade of writing on constitutional issues— scholarship that one cannot afford to ignore, but that is too abundant to fully assimilate. It is nonetheless true that the constitutional canon—the collection of materials generally deemed to be worth studying—continues to be truncated in artificial and arguably unfortunate ways.

Laurence H. Tribe, *American Constitutional Law*, 3rd ed., vol. 1 (Foundation Press, 2000), 2. In note 2, Professor Tribe also notes the vernacular version, "Honk if you are tired of constitutional theory," citing Rebecca I. Brown, "Accountability, Liberty, and the Constitution," 98 *Colum. L. Rev.* 531 (1998). I have not seen (or heard) any such honking in Indian country.

7. Frank Pommersheim, *Braid of Feathers: American Indian Law and Contemporary Tribal Life* (University of California Press, 1995).

8. See, e.g., Charles Mann, *1491: New Revelations of the Americas before Columbus* (Alfred A. Knopf, 2005).

9. See, e.g., the discussion in Gordon Wood, "Apologies to the Iroquois," *New York Review of Books*, April 6, 2006, at 50:

During the past thirty years or so the Indians have become increasingly central to early American historical scholarship, especially to the period of the late eighteenth and early nineteenth centuries.

10. Akhil Reed Amar, *America's Constitution: A Biography* (Random House, 2005), 270. The complete text of this observation ironically (or not) makes no reference to Indians:

It was the promise of land that lured many of the first Europeans to the New World and that kept them coming in the ensuing centuries. In a sense the continent itself structured a giant footrace for real estate between England (and later America), France and Spain. Among the English-speaking, different views about the disposition of Western land would initially pit colonist against Crown, then "landed" states against "landless" ones, and ultimately North against South.

CHAPTER TWO

1. Francis Jennings, *The Invasion of America: Indians, Colonialism, and the Cant of Conquest* (W. W. Norton, 1975), 39.

2. See ibid.,105. For example, Christopher Columbus's "function was to find wealth" (ibid., 34). Crowns were also eager to extend their rule: "It was not Indians as such that Louis XIV or William and Mary befriended; it was Indians claimed as subjects" (ibid., 36).

3. Ibid., 39–40.

4. The Western rule of law tradition requires that nation-states act within recognized legal parameters, however artificial or formalistic the legal categories might

be. See, e.g., Stuart Banner, *How the Indians Lost Their Land* (Belknap Press of Harvard University Press, 2005).

5. See Jennings, *The Invasion of America*, 106.

6. See, e.g., the discussion in Banner, *How the Indians Lost Their Land*, 1–6.

7. Benjamin Friedman, *The Moral Consequence of Economic Growth* (Alfred A. Knopf, 2005), 41–42:

> Smith's central point in the WEALTH OF NATIONS, which Bernard Mandeville had anticipated more than sixty years earlier in his FABLE OF THE BEES, was that when economic activity is guided by commerce, the public interest is advanced not despite but *because of* individuals' self-interest. (p. 40; emphasis in original)

8. Ibid., 42.

9. Ibid.

10. Ibid., 43.

11. Ibid., 30. Native America was infinitely more complex than these sentiments suggest. See, e.g., Charles Mann, *1491: New Revelations of the Americas before Columbus* (Alfred A. Knopf, 2005).

12. Friedman, *The Moral Consequence*, 31.

13. Daniel K. Richter, *Facing East from Indian Country: A Native History of North America* (Harvard University Press, 2001), 2–3.

14. Ibid., 8.

15. Ibid.

16. Ibid., 43–44.

17. Ibid., 44.

18. Ibid., 45.

19. Stephen Cornell, *The Return of the Native: American Indian Political Resurgence* (Oxford University Press, 1988), 15–18.

20. Ibid.

21. Richter, *Facing East*, 40.

22. Ibid., 52.

23. Ibid., 53.

24. Ibid., 53–54.

25. Ibid., 54–55.

26. Ibid., 57–58.

27. William Cronon, *Changes in the Land: Indians, Colonists, and the Ecology of New England* (Hill and Wang, 1983), 15.

28. Ibid., 12.

29. Ibid., 12–15.

30. Ibid., 170.

31. When westward expansion began in the mid-nineteenth century, at least forty million buffalo roamed the plains. Toward the end of the century, only about twenty animals were spared under the protection of the new Yellowstone National Park. See Tina S. Boradinsky, "Conflicting Values: The Religious Killing of Federally Protected

Wildlife," 30 *Nat. Resources J.* 709, 712–13 (Summer 1990). Some estimates conclude that five million buffalo were killed each year in the early 1870s (719, n. 19).

32. Cronon, *Changes in the Land*, 170.

33. See, e.g., Mann, *1491*, 98–100.

34. Richter, *Facing East*, 64.

35. Ibid., 178–79. Indians nevertheless continued, in part, to be important constituents to missionaries, to traders (despite the general decline of trade), and to royal officials as a source of intercultural alliances against other imperial rivals (182).

36. Ibid., 184.

37. 21 U.S. (8 Wheat.) 543 (1823). See the extended discussion in chapter 5.

38. Cronon, *Changes in the Land*, 56.

39. Ibid., 56.

40. Ibid., 57.

41. Ibid., 63–65.

42. Ibid., 67–68.

43. In basic property terms, Indians were not transferring their complete "bundle of sticks," including title and occupancy, but a lesser bundle that included only the usufructuary right to use. Such a view was also in accord with a general Native American conception of property as a living being that could not be "owned."

44. Cronon, *Changes in the Land*, 68–72. The doctrine of "discovery" eventually became the primary legal rationale for placing title to Indian land initially in European nations and subsequently in the United States. See the detailed discussion in chapter 4.

45. In *The War That Made America: A Short History of the French and Indian War* (Penguin Books, 2005), Fred Anderson writes:

> In bringing to an end the French empire in North America, the French and Indian War undermined, and ultimately destroyed, the ability of native peoples to resist the expansion of Anglo-American settlement. The war's violence and brutality, moreover, encouraged whites—particularly those on the frontier—to hate Indians with undiscriminating fury....The widespread Indian-hating that the French and Indian War engendered would be reinforced by the War of Independence and contribute to the formation of American cultural identity, sanctioning the removal or annihilation of native peoples as necessary to the advance of civilization. (vii–viii)

> Anderson also notes that "The coming of the Seven Years' War in America (that is, the French and Indian War, 1754–1760) is a story often told in terms of the struggle of two great, fundamentally different empires for preeminence on the continent."(xxiii)

46. Richter, *Facing East*, 187.

47. Banner, *How the Indians Lost Their Land*, 92.

48. Ibid., 93–94.

49. Ibid., 104–5. See the detailed discussion of treaties in chapter 3. The Non-Intercourse Act remains the law of the land and may be found at 25 U.S.C. § 177 (2006).

50. 21 U.S. (8 Wheat.) 543 (1823). See the detailed discussion in chapter 4. And even *Johnson v. McIntosh* did not answer all the questions.

51. Cronon, *Changes in the Land*, 66–68.

52. 21 U.S. (8 Wheat) 543. See the in-depth discussion in chapter 4.

53. Banner, *How the Indians Lost Their Land*, 4.

54. Ibid.

55. Ibid. Banner notes that

there are two parallel stories to tell: one about how Indians actually lost their land, and another about the law that in principle governed how the Indians were to lose their lands. Neither story can be understood without the other. (5)

This dialectic of law and power is at the heart of this book and the entire field of Indian law as a whole.

56. Jennings, *The Invasion of America*, 107–8.

57. Ibid., 109.

58. Ibid., 110.

59. Ibid., 111.

60. Ibid.

61. 384 F.Supp. 312, 355 (W.D. Wash. 1974), aff'd 520 F.2d 676 (9th Cir. 1975), cert. denied, 423 U.S. 1086 (1976).

62. Jennings, *The Invasion of America*, 81.

63. Ibid., 74.

64. Ibid.

65. Ibid.

66. See, e.g., Mann, *1491*, 250–51:

Rather than domesticate animals for meat, Indians retooled ecosystems to encourage elk, deer, and bear. Constant burning of undergrowth increased the number of herbivores, the predators that fed on them, and the people who ate them both.... [T]he great eastern forest was a kaleidoscope of garden plots, blackberry rambles, pine barrens, and spacious groves of chestnut, hickory, and oak.

67. Robert A. Williams Jr., *The American Indian in Western Legal Thought: The Discourses of Conquest* (Oxford University Press, 1990), 78–81.

The first Spanish bull, *Inter caetera divinai*, issued in May 1493, simply declared that whereas Christopher Columbus had come upon a people "undiscovered by others...well disposed to embrace the Christian faith," all the lands discovered or to be discovered in the name of the Spanish Crown in the region belonged legally to Ferdinand and Isabella. By this bull, medieval Church colonizing doctrine was inelegantly stretched to incorporate a new proposition better suited to a world in which previously unknown, distant lands and peoples were rapidly being revealed to Europeans. The pope could place non-Christian peoples under the tutelage and guardianship of the first Christian nation discovering their lands as long as these peoples were reported by the discovering Christian nation to be "well disposed to embrace the Christian faith." It will be recalled that Innocentian doctrine had originally permitted military conquest of non-Christian societies *not* well disposed to accept Christianity—that is, those peoples who idolatrously believed in their own opposed deity or who refused rights of entry to Christian missionaries, and who therefore violated Christocentrically understood natural law. Alexander's first *Inter caetera* thus significantly extended the aggrandizing sweep of Christian legal doctrine on pagan rights and status. Spain's lawyers, who drafted the Crown's proposed bulls, had convinced Rome that random discovery of peaceful non-Christians not in apparent gross violation of natural law permitted the pope to exercise his guardianship responsibilities by placing such peoples under the tutelage and direction of the discovering Christian prince. (80, footnotes omitted)

68. See, e.g., *Johnson v. McIntosh*, 21 U.S. (8 Wheat.) 543, 573–82 (1823), discussed in detail in chapter 4.

69. For example:

Native Americans appear in the foreground, and Europeans enter from distant shores. North America becomes the "old world" and Western Europe the "new," Cahokia becomes the Center and Plymouth Rock the periphery, and themes rooted in Indian country rather than across the Atlantic begin to shape a larger story. The continent becomes a place where diverse peoples had long struggled against and sometimes worked with one another, where societies and political systems had long risen and fallen, and where these ancient trends continued right through the period of colonization. The process by which one particular group composed of newcomers from Europe and their descendants—themselves a diverse and contentious lot—came to dominate the others becomes a much more complicated, much more interesting, much more revealing, if no less tragic, tale. (Richter, *Facing East*, 8)

70. See ibid., 85–104.

71. Cronon, *Changes in the Land*, 79–80 (footnotes omitted).

72. As noted by Jennings (*The Invasion of America*, 41):

Indians, like Europeans, could make certain choices about the direction of change, and individual Indians did choose a wide variety of adjustments and experiments in their behavior, but the one choice never within their power was to stay exactly the same.

73. This trilogy of cases was *Johnson v. McIntosh*, 21 U.S. (8 Wheat.) 543 (1823), *Cherokee Nation v. Georgia*, 30 U.S. (3 Pet.) 1 (1831), and *Worcester v. Georgia*, 31 U.S. (6 Pet.) 515 (1832). See the detailed discussion in chapter 4.

74. Richter, *Facing East*, 12.

75. Gordon S. Wood, "Apologies to the Iroquois," *New York Review of Books*, Apr. 6, 2006, at 50. More specifically:

Through the efforts of dozens of historians, the Indians have made their presence in early America felt, not as foils in the whites' efforts at self-examination but as historical participants in their own right, integrally involved in the making of the nation. During the fifteen years between 1959 and 1973, the principal journal of early American history, *The William and Mary Quarterly*, published only four articles on Indians; in the fifteen years between 1974 and 1988 it published twenty. Since 1988 the number of contributions to what is often now referred to as "ethnohistory" has increased even faster. Indeed, as the historian Ian Steele pointed out a decade ago, the "field of ethnohistory...is developing so quickly that any attempt at accessible synthesis is bound to be premature and incomplete." Some of the best historians in the U.S. have turned to the Indians as a topic of research, and books on Indians in early America are now winning prestigious prizes.

Much of this new scholarship is contested as exaggerated:

The best of the recent historians of the Indians, including Alan Taylor, do not have to make such exaggerated claims to justify the importance of the Indians in histories of early America. They now know only too well that the Indians were present everywhere in early America. Not only did the native peoples dominate nearly all of the trans-Appalachian West in the eighteenth century, but at the time of the Revolution they were also essential to the life of the eastern seaboard—as traders, as farmers, laborers, as hunters, as guides, even as sailors. Both Thomas Jefferson in Virginia and John Adams in Massachusetts grew up knowing Indians who lived near their homes.

76. Cronon, *Changes in the Land*, 80–81.

77. This phrase only came later with the drafting and ratification of the Constitution in 1789. U.S. CONST. pmbl.:

We the people of the United States, in order to form a more perfect union, establish justice, insure domestic tranquility, provide for the common defense, promote general welfare, and secure the blessings of liberty to ourselves and our posterity, do ordain and establish this Constitution for the United States of America.

78. Akhil Reed Amar, *America's Constitution: A Biography* (Random House, 2003), 25 (quoting *Journals of the Continental Congress* 5:425, 431).

79. Ibid.

80. Even during the drafting debates, the bloom of national unity was threatened by the noxious weed of disunity:

Historian Jack Rakove has observed that during debates over the drafting of the proposed Articles—debates after the Declaration of Independence— "threats of disunion flowed freely. James Wilson warned that Pennsylvania would never confederate if Virginia clung to its western claims. The Virginia delegates replied that...their constituents would never accept a confederation that required their sacrifice." South Carolina's Thomas Lynch, Jr., sternly advised his fellow congressman on July 30, 1776 that "if it is debated, whether…slaves are [our] property, there is an end of the confederation." (Ibid., 26, quoting Jack Rakove, *The Beginnings of National Politics* (Alfred A. Knopf, 1979), 218).

81. Amar, *America's Constitution*, 25.

82. Ibid., 26.

83. Ibid.

84. Articles of Confederation, art. V.

85. Ibid., art. IX.

86. Ibid.

87. Ibid.

88. See ibid.

89. Ibid.

90. 31 U.S. (6 Pet.) 515 (1832). See the detailed discussion in chapter 4.

91. Ibid., 559.

92. Ibid.

93. The full title of the Articles of Confederation is "The Articles of Confederation and Perpetual Union."

94. Robert Clinton, "There Is No Federal Supremacy Clause for Indian Tribes," 34 *Ariz. St. L. J.* 113, 128 (Spring 2002).

95. The Avalon Project at Yale Law School, *Journals of the Continental Congress, Speech to the Six Nations; July 13, 1775* at http://avalon.law.yale.edu/18th_century/contcong_07–13–75.asp (last visited 9/2/2008).

96. The Avalon Project at Yale Law School, *Journals of the Continental Congress, Franklin's Articles of Confederation; July 21, 1775 art. X*, at http://avalon.law.yale.edu/18th_century/contcong_07–21–75.asp (last visited 9/2/2008).

97. Ibid.

98. Ibid.

99. Ibid., art. XI.

100. Ibid.

101. Ibid.

102. The thirteen states were united in their struggle to wrest control of the West from England, but they often held conflicting and clashing views about this territory. Various landed states claimed much of this western territory, which threatened a potential imbalance of wealth and power. The articles said nothing about this contentious matter, but landless Maryland refused to ratify the articles until New York and Virginia finally took steps to cede their western claims. Amar, *America's Constitution*, 271.

CHAPTER THREE

1. Bernard Bailyn, *The Ideological Origins of the American Revolution* (Harvard University Press, 1967), 160–229.

2. Ibid., 173–74 (quoting various authors including Blackstone, J. W. Gough, and Charles H. McIlwan).

3. Ibid., 183 (quoting Samuel Cooke, Charles Turner, and Peter Whitney) (emphasis in original).

4. Ibid., 188.

5. Ibid.

6. Ibid., 200.

7. Duties in American Colonies Act, 1765, 5 Geo. 3, ch. 12, § 57 (Eng.). The act imposed duties on American colonies as a means of raising revenue. It was repealed by statute, 1766, 6 Geo. 3, ch. 11 (Eng.), after riots in opposition to the act occurred in the colonies.

8. See the discussion in chapter 2.

9. Charles C. Mann, *1491: New Revelations of the Americas before Columbus* (Random House, 2005), 331. Note that the Tuscarora joined the alliance in about 1720.

10. Ibid.

11. Ibid., 332.

12. Ibid.

13. Ibid.

14. Ibid., 334.

15. See discussion in chapter 2.

16. Mann, *1491*, 334. Quotes are from frontiersman Robert Rogers and the French explorer Nicholas Perrot.

17. Ibid., 333 (alteration in the original):

But the Indians of the eastern seaboard institutionalized their liberty to an unusual extent—the Haudenosaunee especially, but many others, too. ("Their whole constitution breathes nothing but liberty," said colonist James Adair of the Tsalagi [Cherokee].) Important historically, these were the free people encountered by France and Britain—personifications of democratic self-government so vivid that some historians and activists have argued that the Great Law of Peace directly inspired the U.S. Constitution.

> Taken literally, this assertion seems implausible. With its grant of authority to the federal government to supersede state law, its dependence on rule by the majority rather than consensus, its bicameral legislature (members of one branch being simultaneously elected), and its denial of suffrage to women, slaves, and the unpropertied, the Constitution as originally enacted was sharply different from the Great Law. In addition, the Constitution's emphasis on protecting private property runs contrary to Haudenosaunee traditions of communal ownership. But in a larger sense, the claim is correct. The framers of the Constitution, like most colonists in what would become the United States, were pervaded by Indian ideals and images of liberty.

Congress adopted a resolution in 1988 that acknowledged the contribution of the Six Nations of the Iroquois Confederacy to the forming of the United States although Congress did not mention the Great Law of Peace by name. *See* A concurrent resolution to acknowledge the contribution of the Iroquois Confederacy of Nations to the development of the United States Constitution and to reaffirm the continuing government-to-government relationship between Indian tribes and the United States established in the Constitution, H. Con. Res. 331, 100th Cong., 134 Cong. Rec. S 15323 (1988) (enacted) (stating that the original republic of the United States "was explicitly modeled upon the Iroquois Confederacy as were many of the democratic principles which were incorporated into the Constitution itself").

18. Ibid.

19. See Francis Jennings, *The Invasion of America: Indians, Colonialism, and the Cant of Conquest* (W. W. Norton, 1975), 107–8.

20. John J. Patrick, ed., *Founding the Republic: A Documentary History* (Greenwood, 1995), 113.

21. See The Federalist Nos. 22, 23 (Alexander Hamilton).

22. U.S. Const. art. I, § 8, cl. 3.

23. 22 U.S. (9 Wheat.) 1 (1824).

24. Act of Feb. 18, 1793, Ch. 8, 1 Stat., 305 (1793).

25. *Gibbons*, 22 U.S. at 238–40.

26. Ibid. at 194.

27. Ibid. at 195.

28. Ibid.

29. Laurence H. Tribe, *American Constitutional Law* (Foundation Press, 3rd ed. 2000), § 6–3, at 1044.

30. Ibid., § 6.3, at 1045.

31. See ibid., §§ 6–2 to–3, at 1032–43. For example, Justice Scalia has criticized the dormant Commerce Clause concept and insists that the Commerce Clause itself "is nothing more than a grant of power to Congress, not the courts; and that grant to Congress cannot be read as being exclusive of the States." Ibid. at 1032 (quoting *Northwest Central Pipeline Corp. v. State Corp. Comm'n of Kansas*, 489 U.S. 493, 526 (1989)). He has also stated that the dormant Commerce Clause " 'is [supposedly] an inference' from the language and history of the Clause, rather than an explicit textual command." Ibid. at 1037 (alteration in original) (quoting *Wyoming v. Oklahoma*, 502 U.S. 437, 469 (1992) (Scalia, J., dissenting)).

32. Ibid., § 6.2, at 1029.

33. Ibid. at 1031 (citing *Wyoming*, 502 U.S. at 454–55).

34. Ibid. § 6.2, at 1032.

35. Ibid. at 1030.

36. *Gibbons*, 22 U.S. at 197.

37. The Supreme Court has often called the power in the Indian Commerce Clause "plenary" as well. See Tribe, *American Constitutional Law*, § 5–4, at 807 n. 1.

38. John E. Nowak and Ronald D. Rotunda, *Constitutional Law* (West, 7th ed. 2004), § 4.4 at 166 (quoting Felix Frankfurter, *The Commerce Clause under Marshall, Taney and Waite* (University of North Carolina Press, 1937), 40):

> Marshall not merely rejected the Tenth Amendment as an active principle of limitation; he countered with his famous characterization of the powers of Congress, and of the commerce power in particular, as the possession of the unqualified authority of a unitary sovereign. He threw the full weight of his authority against the idea that, apart from specific

restrictions in the Constitution, the very existence of the states operates as such a limitation.

39. 514 U.S. 549 (1995).

40. Ibid. at 552.

41. Tribe, *American Constitutional Law*, § 5–4, at 818.

42. Ibid.

43. See ibid. at 824.

44. 529 U.S. 598 (2000) (holding 42 U.S.C. § 13981's remedial scheme unconstitutional as beyond Congress's powers under both the Interstate Commerce Clause and §5 of the Fourteenth Amendment).

45. Ibid., at 613.

46. Ibid., at 640 (Souter, J., dissenting).

47. 545 U.S. 1 (2005).

48. 21 U.S.C. §§ 811–814 (2000).

49. Cal. Health & Safety Code § 11362.5 (West 2006).

50. *Raich*, 545 U.S. at 9. The production and distribution of marijuana is a quintessential interstate economic activity. Ibid., at 33.

51. Ibid. at 23–26.

52. See Tribe, *American Constitutional Law*, § 5–4, at 807 n. 1 (stating "the Court's reliance on the authority conferred by the [Indian] Commerce Clause waxed and waned over the years"), but also noting: "Although the Supreme Court's identification of the source of Congress' power over Indian tribes has changed, the Court's construction of the scope of that power has been remarkably consistent, the Court has found the power to be extremely broad (often calling the power 'plenary')."

53. Charles Alan Wright, *Law of Federal Courts* (Foundation Press, 9th ed. 1994), 2 (quoting 1 Farrand, *The Records of the Federal Convention*, 104, rev. ed. 1937).

54. Ibid.

55. An Act to Establish the Judicial Courts of the United States, Ch. 20, 1 Stat. 73 (enacted Sept. 24, 1789).

56. U.S. Const. art. VI, cl. 2.

57. See, e.g., *Howlett v. Rose*, 496 U.S. 356 (1990).

58. Tribe, *American Constitutional Law*, § 5–11 at 863–64.

59. Ibid., § 6–28, at 1172.

60. Ibid., § 6–28, at 1172–73.

61. Ibid., § 6–31, at 1206–7.

62. Ibid., § 6–31, at 1210.

63. Ibid., § 6–31, at 1210–11.

64. U.S. Const. art. VI, cl. 2 (emphasis added).

65. In such an unlikely event, Congress's "plenary" power is no doubt available to fill any constitutional void.

66. 435 U.S. 313 (1978).

67. Ibid. at 323.

68. Ibid.

69. Robert Clinton, "There Is No Federal Supremacy Clause for Indian Tribes," 34 *Ariz. St. L. J.* 113 (2002).

70. See, e.g., Frank Pommersheim, *Braid of Feathers: American Indian Law and Contemporary Tribal Life* (University of California Press, 1995), 38–41.

71. See, e.g., *United States v. Wheeler*, 435 U.S. 313 (1978).

72. U.S. Const. Amend. X.

73. Tribe, *American Constitutional Law,* § 5–11, at 861 (quoting *Hopkins Federal Savings and Loan Assoc. v. Cleary,* 296 U.S. 315, 337 (1935)).

74. 259 U.S. 20 (1922).

75. See Tribe, *American Constitutional Law,* § 5–11, at 862 n. 16.

76. *New York v. United States,* 505 U.S. 144, 159 (1993).

77. 78 U.S. (11 Wall.) 113 (1870).

78. Ibid. at 127.

79. *Ableman v. Booth,* 62 U.S. (21 How.) 506, 516 (1859).

80. *Collector,* 78 U.S. at 124.

81. 306 U.S. 466 (1939).

82. 312 U.S. 100 (1941).

83. Ibid. at 124.

84. 505 U.S. 144 (1992) (holding that a clause of the Low-Level Radioactive Waste Policy Amendments Act of 1985 violated the Tenth Amendment because it was not an exercise of congressional power enumerated in the Constitution).

85. 521 U.S. 898 (1997) (striking down interim provisions of the Brady Act that directed state law enforcement officers to participate in administering a federally enacted regulatory scheme because Congress cannot compel states to enact or enforce a federal regulatory program).

86. *New York,* 505 U.S. at 188.

87. Tribe, *American Constitutional Law,* § 5–12, at 903–5.

88. See ibid., § 3–25, at 519–36.

89. 2 U.S. (2 Dall.) 419 (1793).

90. Article III of the Constitution appeared to allow such actions to be brought directly in the Supreme Court under the diversity provision:

> Section 2. [1] The judicial Power shall extend to all Cases, in Law and Equity, arising under this Constitution, the Laws of the United States, and Treaties made, or which shall be made, under their Authority;—to all Cases affecting Ambassadors, other public Ministers and Consuls;—to all Cases of admiralty and maritime Jurisdiction;—to Controversies to which the United States shall be a Party;—to Controversies between two or more States;—between a State and Citizens of another State;—between Citizens of different States;—between Citizens of the same State claiming Lands under Grants of different States, and between a State, or the Citizens thereof, and foreign States, Citizens or Subjects.

91. Tribe, *American Constitutional Law,* § 3–25, at 521.

92. Ibid., 522.

93. *Blatchford v. Native Village of Noatak and Circle Village,* 501 U.S. 775, 779 (1991).

94. 134 U.S. 1 (1890).

95. Tribe, *American Constitutional Law*, § 3–25, at 524–25.

96. 501 U.S. 775 (1991) (holding that an Indian tribe was barred from bringing an action against the State of Alaska because the state was immune and the Eleventh Amendment protected the state from a lawsuit).

97. 517 U.S. 44 (1996) (holding that the Eleventh Amendment prohibited Congress from making the State of Florida capable of being sued by a tribe in federal court).

98. 521 U.S. 261 (1997) (prohibiting a lawsuit by an Indian tribe against the State of Idaho under the Eleventh Amendment because Idaho's sovereign interest in its lands and waters would be affected in a degree fully as intrusive as in almost any action against it for funds if the tribe was to prevail).

99. 527 U.S. 627 (1999) (holding that Congress's waiver of states' sovereign immunity from claims of patent infringement in the Patent Remedy Act was improper under the Eleventh Amendment).

100. 527 U.S. 706 (1999) (holding that Congress had no constitutional authority to force Maine courts to hear a Fair Labor Standards Act suit by workers employed by the State of Maine, even though that suit was based on a federal right that Congress had authority to confer upon the workers).

101. *Blatchford*, 501 U.S. at 779 (citations omitted).

102. 491 U.S. 1 (1989).

103. *Seminole Tribe*, 517 U.S. at 76.

104. Without the ability to sue the states for not acting in good faith, tribes were left with little recourse when states refused to enter into tribal-state gaming components with tribes. (See generally ibid.) Subsequently, the Bureau of Indian Affairs has adopted regulations that permit the Secretary of the Interior to approve Indian gaming when a tribe and state are unable to negotiate an appropriate compact. See 25 C.F.R. §§ 291.1—291.15 (2007).

105. *Coeur d'Alene*, 521 U.S. at 281.

106. The legal contours of the trust relationship are discussed in chapter 4.

107. Indeed, much of the response to the *Seminole* decision in law reviews identified the effect it had on bankruptcy law and employment law, as well as other areas of law, not Indian law. See, e.g., Troy A. McKenzie, Note, "Eleventh Amendment Immunity in Bankruptcy: Breaking the Seminole Tribe Barrier," 75 *N.Y.U. L. Rev.* 199 (2000).

108. Article IV also contained the privileges and immunities clause and the fugitive from justice clause. Articles of Confederation, Art. IV (1781).

109. See U.S. Const. art. IV, §§ 1–2; Tribe, *American Constitutional Law*, § 6–1, at 1026 (3d ed. 2000) ("the Privileges and Immunities and Full Faith and Credit Clauses of Article IV centrally delineate both the relationship of the states to one another and the treatment that one state must accord the citizens of another...[w]ithout these provisions, the Union as we know it could not exist.").

110. *Toomer v. Witsell*, 334 U.S. 385, 395 (1948).

111. U.S. Const. art. IV, § 1.

112. 28 U.S.C. § 1738 (2000).

113. *Americana of Puerto Rico, Inc. v. Kaplus*, 368 F.2d 431, 439 (3rd Cir. 1966).

114. See *Huron Holding Corporation v. Lincoln Mine Operating Co.*, 312 U.S. 183, 194 (1941).

115. See *Stoll v. Gottlieb*, 305 U.S. 165, 173 (1938).

116. Robert A. Leflar et al., *American Conflicts Law* (Aspen Pub,, 4th ed., 1986), § 74 at 217–21.

117. 159 U.S. 113 (1895) (finding a French court's full and fair adjudication of an action brought by a French partnership to recover money from its U.S. trading partners not entitled to full comity for want of reciprocity, as such foreign judgments would be reexaminable in the courts of France).

118. See, e.g., Peter D. Trooboft, "Foreign Judgments," *Nat'l. L. J.*, Oct. 17, 2005, at A-5.

119. Fort Laramie Treaty of 1868, art. I, 15 Stat. 635, 635 (1868).

120. See, e.g., the discussion in Robert N. Clinton, "Comity and Colonialism: The Federal Courts' Frustration of Tribal-Federal Cooperation," 36 *Ariz. St. L. J.* 1 (2004).

121. 59 U.S. (18 How.) 100 (1855).

122. Ibid. at 104.

123. 28 U.S.C. § 1738 (2000) (emphasis added).

124. 25 U.S.C. § 1911(d) (2000).

125. 18 U.S.C. § 2265(a) (2000).

126. 28 U.S.C. § 1738B (2000).

127. See 25 U.S.C. § 2207 (2000).

128. See 25 U.S.C. § 3106 (c) (2000).

129. See 25 U.S.C. § 3713 (c) (2000).

130. See 25 U.S.C. § 1725 (g) (2000).

131. David H. Getches et al., *Cases and Material on Federal Indian Law* (West Group, 4th ed., 1998), 649–53.

132. *Wilson v. Marchington*, 127 F.3d 805 (9th Cir. 1997).

133. *John v. Baker*, 982 P.2d 738, 762–63 (Alaska 1999).

134. *Mexican v. Circle Bear*, 370 N.W.2d 737 (S.D. 1985). This judicially created rule was subsequently replaced by a more restrictive comity statute. See SDCL § 1–1–25 (2006).

135. *Jim v. CIT Financial Services*, 533 P.2d 751 (N.M. 1975).

136. *In re Adoption of Buehl*, 555 P.2d 1334 (Wash. 1976).

137. Wyo. Stat. Ann. § 5–1–111 (Michie 2006).

138. Ariz. Rev. Stat. § 12–1702 (2006).

139. Alaska Stat. § 09.30.110 (Michie 2006).

140. N.D. Cent. Code § 27–01–09 (2006).

141. 2001 CROW 13¶; 39; Civ. App. Dkt. No. 98–16(II), slip op. at 39 (Crow Ct. App., Dec. 18, 2001).

142. South Dakota is one; see SDCL § 1–1–25 (2000). See also, e.g., Ho-Chunk Nation R. Civ. P. 73(A); Blackfeet Tribal Law and Order Code, Ordinance 81, § 1 (1999).

143. 370 N.W.2d 737 (S.D. 1985).

144. 159 U.S. 113 (1895).

145. SDCL § 1–1–25 provides in full:

No order or judgment of a tribal court in the state of South Dakota may be recognized as a matter of comity in the state courts of South Dakota, except under the following terms and conditions:

(1) Before a state court may consider recognizing a tribal court order or judgment the party seeking recognition shall establish by clear and convincing evidence that:

(a) The tribal court had jurisdiction over both the subject matter and the parties;

(b) The order or judgment was not fraudulently obtained;

(c) The order or judgment was obtained by a process that assures the requisites of an impartial administration of justice including but not limited to due notice and a hearing;

(d) The order or judgment complies with the laws, ordinances and regulations of the jurisdiction from which it was obtained; and

(e) The order or judgment does not contravene the public policy of the state of South Dakota.

(2) If a court is satisfied that all of the foregoing conditions exist, the court may recognize the tribal court or judgment in any of the following circumstances:

(a) In any child custody or domestic relations case; or

(b) In any case in which the jurisdiction issuing the order or judgment also grants comity to orders and judgments of the South Dakota courts; or

(c) In other cases if exceptional circumstances warrant it; or

(d) Any order required or authorized to be recognized pursuant to 25 U.S.C. § 1911(d) or 25 U.S.C. § 1919.

146. See, e.g., Robert Laurence, "The Off-Reservation Garnishment of an On-Reservation Debt and Related Issues in the Cross-Boundary Enforcement of Money Judgments," 22 *Am. Indian L. Rev.* 355, 361–362 (1998). See also Clinton, "Comity and Colonialism."

147. U.S. Const. art. I, § 8, cl. 3.

148. Articles of Confederation, art. IX.

149. The Federalist No. 42, at 334 (James Madison) (John C. Hamilton ed., 1892).

150. U.S. Const. art. I, §§ 8, 10.

151. 187 U.S. 553 (1903). See in-depth discussion in chapter 5.

152. 25 U.S.C. § 177 (2000).

153. 411 U.S. 164 (1973).

154. Ibid. at 175, 177–78.

155. 450 U.S. 662 (1981).

156. Ibid. at 665–66, 671.

157. 358 U.S. 217 (1959).

158. Ibid. at 220.

159. Robert N. Clinton, "The Dormant Indian Commerce Clause," 27 *Conn. L. Rev.* 1105, 1186 (1995).

160. Francis Paul Prucha, *The Great Father: The United States Government and American Indians* (abridged ed., University of Nebraska Press, 1986), 31.

161. Trade and Intercourse Act of 1790, ch. 33, § 4, 1 Stat. 137, 138 (codified as amended in part at 25 U.S.C. § 177 (2000)).

162. The Trade and Intercourse were carried forward with the Act of Mar. 1, 1793, ch. 19, 1 Stat. 329; the Act of May 19, 1796, ch. 30, 1 Stat. 469; the Act of Mar. 3, 1799, ch. 46, 1 Stat. 743; the Act of Mar. 30, 1802, ch. 13, 2 Stat. 139; the Act of May 6, 1822, ch. 58, 3 Stat. 682; and the Act of June 30, 1834, ch. 161, 4 Stat. 729. The acts are now codified as amended at 18 U.S.C. §§ 1152, 1154, 1160, 1165 (2000), and at 25 U.S.C. §§ 177, 179–80, 193–94, 201, 229–30, 251, 263–64 (2000).

163. Prucha, *The Great Father*, 32.

164. 30 U.S. (5 Pet.) 1 (1831). See the detailed discussion in chapter 4.

165. 31 U.S. (6 Pet.) 515 (1832). See the detailed discussion in chapter 4.

166. 118 U.S. 375 (1886). See the detailed discussion in chapter 5.

167. Ibid. at 378–79.

168. Ibid. at 383–84.

169. See 187 U.S. 553 (1903).

170. *Kagama*, 118 U.S. at 381.

171. 411 U.S. 164 (1973).

172. Ibid. at 172 n. 7 (emphasis added).

173. 541 U.S. 193 (2004). The case is discussed in more detail in chapter 8. The case, however, unintentionally validates the undertaking of this book to develop a legitimate constitutional perspective in the field of Indian law.

174. Ibid. at 224 (Thomas, J., concurring) (citations omitted). It is interesting to note Justice Thomas's cite to the *Morrison* and *Lopez* cases. These cases, as noted previously, revisit the scope of Congress's "plenary" authority under the "interstate" commerce clause.

175. U.S. Const. art. II, § 2, cl. 2.

176. Getches et al., *Cases and Materials*, 281–82.

177. 25 U.S.C. § 71 (102 Stat. 3641) (2006).

Section 2079 of the Revised Statutes (25 U.S.C. § 71) is amended by adding at the end thereof the following new sentence: "Such treaties, and any Executive orders and Acts of Congress under which the rights of any Indian tribe to fish are secured, shall be construed to prohibit (in addition to any other prohibition) the imposition under any law of a State or political subdivision thereof of any tax on any income derived from the exercise of rights to fish secured by such treaty, Executive order, or Act of Congress if section 7873 of Title 26 [the Internal Revenue Code of 1986] does not permit a like Federal tax to be imposed on such income.

178. See, e.g., Great Sioux Agreement of 1889, 25 Stat. 888 (1889), establishing six reservations in South Dakota within the original boundaries of the Great Sioux Nation.

179. See *Antoine v. Washington*, 420 U.S. 194, 202–204 (1975); Nell Jessup Newton et al., eds., *Felix Cohen's Handbook of Federal Indian Law* (LexisNexis, 2005 ed.), § 1.04.

180. The one exception appears to be Justice Thomas's concurrence in *United States v. Lara*, 541 U.S. 193, 218 (2004) (Thomas, J., concurring). No casebook in Indian law, including Felix Cohen's *Classic Treatise on Federal Indian Law* and its 1982 revision, describes the possibility. See also Clinton, "There Is No Federal Supremacy Clause in Indian Law," for a brief discussion of this issue.

181. See Tribe, *American Constitutional Law*, §§ 5–1 to 5–2, at 789–98.

182. See the previous discussion of the Supremacy Clause.

183. *Foster v. Neilson*, 27 U.S. (2 Pet.) 253, 314 (1829).

184. U.S. Const. art. VI, cl. 2.

185. Tribe, *American Constitutional Law*, § 4–4, at 645.

186. See generally *Chae Chan Ping v. United States*, 130 U.S. 581 (1889).

187. *Holden v. Joy*, 84 U.S. (17 Wall.) 211, 242 (1872); *Worcester v. Georgia*, 31 U.S. (6 Pet.) 515, 558 (1832).

188. See generally *The New York Indians*, 72 U.S. (5 Wall.) 761 (1867).

189. *De Geofroy v. Riggs*, 133 U.S. 258, 267 (1890). As noted before, this includes Indian tribes.

190. Ibid. See also *The Cherokee Tobacco Case*, 78 U.S. (11 Wall.) 616, 620 (1870), in which Justice Swayne wrote, "[a] treaty cannot change the Constitution or be held valid if it be in violation of that instrument." See also *Worcester v. Georgia*, 31 U.S. (6 Pet.) 515 (1832) (treaty recognition of tribal self-governance within state boundaries held valid).

191. 354 U.S. 1, 16 (1957) (finding that an executive agreement between the United States and Great Britain permitting U.S. military courts, which do not provide for trial by jury or other Bill of Rights protections, to exercise exclusive jurisdiction over offenses committed by the civilian dependents of American servicemen may not be applied, as treaties must comply with the provisions of the Constitution).

192. 198 U.S. 371 (1905).

193. Ibid. at 380.

194. Ibid.

195. Ibid. at 381.

196. Ibid. at 377–78.

197. 207 U.S. 564 (1908).

198. The Court has also recognized a reserved right of tribal members to hunt and fish on the reservation, even if no such right is expressly mentioned in a treaty. See, e.g., *United States v. Dion*, 476 U.S. 734 (1986). See also *Menominee Tribe v. United States*, 391 U.S. 404 (1968) (concluding that the Menominee Termination Act did not terminate the tribe's hunting and fishing rights and emphasizing that the act must be read *in pari materia* with an act passed in the same Congress that preserved the hunting and fishing rights of all other tribes subject to Public Law 280).

199. 450 U.S. 544 (1981).

200. Second Treaty of Fort Laramie, May 7, 1868, Art. II, 15 Stat. 650.

201. *Montana*, 450 U.S. at 566.

202. Ibid. at 564–65 (internal citations and footnote omitted). Of course, the *Montana* proviso remains, but the Supreme Court has yet to find it satisfied in a single case. See the detailed discussion in chapter 8.

203. See, e.g., *Strate v. A-1 Contractors,* 520 U.S. 438 (1997).

204. 187 U.S. 553 (1903).

205. 476 U.S. 734 (1986).

206. 130 U.S. 581 (1889). *Lone Wolf* is described in its full range of implications in chapter 5.

207. General Allotment Act, Ch. 114, 24 Stat. 388 (1887).

208. *Chae Chan Ping,* 130 U.S. at 600.

209. *Lone Wolf,* 187 U.S. at 568.

210. Ibid.

211. Id. See the discussion of wardship and the trust relationship in chapter 2.

212. Ibid.

213. These canons of construction include these three: the duty to construe treaties liberally, the duty to interpret the terms of a treaty as Indians would have understood them, and the duty to resolve ambiguities favorably to Indians. These canons have been applied unevenly. See, e.g., Charles F. Wilkinson and John M. Volkman, "Judicial Review of Indian Treaty Abrogation: 'As Long as Water Flows or Grass Grows upon the Earth,' How Long a Time Is That?" 63 *Cal. L. Rev.* 601, 607–08 (1975).

214. 430 U.S. 73 (1977).

215. 448 U.S. 371 (1980).

216. *Weeks,* 430 U.S. at 85 (alteration in original).

217. "The district courts shall have original jurisdiction of all civil actions arising under the Constitution, laws, or treaties of the United States."

218. "Except as otherwise provided by Act of Congress, the district courts shall have original jurisdiction of all civil actions, suits or proceedings commenced by the United States, or by any agency or officer thereof expressly authorized to sue by Act of Congress." 28 U.S.C. § 1345 (1948).

219. 28 U.S.C. § 1491 (2000).

220. 25 U.S.C. § 70 (2000).

221. 25 U.S.C. § 177 (2000).

222. A lawsuit to establish a party's title to real property against anyone and everyone.

223. An act in violation of a party's duty to manage property for another's benefit. See the discussion in chapter 4.

224. Nor Congress itself for that matter. In 1946, Congress enacted legislation forming the Indian Claims Commission. The purpose of the Indian Claims Commission Act was to settle historic claims of tribes. The commission was charged with adjudicating these claims, specifically, claims originating before 1946. The act exempted such claims from laches and statute of limitations defenses. The commission operated until 1978, when its pending claims were transferred to the Court of Claims. For a detailed description of the Indian Claims Commission See Newton et al., eds., *Felix Cohen's Handbook,* at § 5.06.

225. Wilkinson and Volkman, "Judicial Review of Indian Treaty Abrogation," 619.

226. Ibid.

227. Ibid.

228. See ibid. at 608–23. See also the discussion of the trust relationship in chapter 4.

229. Ibid.

230. *Jones v. Meehan*, 175 U.S. 1, 11 (1899).

231. Wilkinson and Volkman, "Judicial Review of Indian Treaty Abrogation," 611.

232. See Fort Laramie Treaty, April 29, 1868, 15 Stat. 635.

233. Wilkinson and Volkman, "Judicial Review of Indian Treaty Abrogation," 618.

234. 420 U.S. 425 (1975).

235. Ibid. at 447. Scholars have suggested that in cases such as *Montana v. United States*, "courts have simply ignored the Indian law canons." Newton et al., eds., *Felix Cohen's Handbook*, § 2.02, at 125.

236. 198 U.S. 371 (1905).

237. See, e.g., *Shoshone Tribe v. United States*, 304 U.S. 111 (1938).

238. 526 U.S. 172 (1999).

239. The equal footing doctrine provides that new states entering the union are on equal footing with the original thirteen states with respect to rank, the exercise of sovereign powers, and the restrictions placed on all alike by the federal Constitution. See 81A C.J.S. *States* § 8 (2006).

240. 526 U.S. at 196.

241. The litmus test in these cases is supposedly congressional intent, but the reality is that the outcomes are result-driven, especially by current demographics and land tenure patterns in the affected areas. If current demographics and land tenure patterns greatly favor non-Indians, the likelihood of finding diminishment is extremely high. This empirical predictor is more reliable than any analytical or doctrinal rubric. Although the Court is not unaware of the problems presented by such an unorthodox approach, it regards it as a necessary expedient. Frank Pommersheim, "'Our Federalism' in the Context of Federal Courts and Tribal Courts: An Open Letter to the Federal Courts' Teaching and Scholarly Community," 71 *U. Colo. L. Rev.* 123, 135–136 (2000).

242. *Solem v. Bartlett*, 465 U.S. 463, 472 n. 13 (1984).

243. Getches et al., *Cases and Materials*, 449.

244. *United States v. Sioux Nation*, 448 U.S. 371 (1980).

245. Ibid. at 422.

246. Ibid. at 413 n. 28:

For this reason, the Government does not here press *Lone Wolf* to its logical limits, arguing instead that its "strict rule" that the management and disposal of tribal lands is a political question, "has been relaxed in recent years to allow review under the Fifth Amendment rational-basis test." Brief for United States 55, n.46. The Government relies on *Delaware Tribal Business Comm. v. Weeks*, 430 U.S. 73, at 84–85 (1977) and *Morton v. Mancari*, 417 U.S. 535, 555 (1974), as establishing a rational-basis test for determining whether Congress, in any given instance, confiscated Indian property or engaged merely in its power to manage and dispose of tribal lands in the Indians' best interests. But those cases, which establish a standard of review for judging the constitutionality of Indian legislation under the Due Process Clause of the Fifth Amendment, do not provide an apt analogy for resolution of the issue presented here—whether Congress' disposition of tribal property was an exercise of its power of eminent domain or its power of guardianship. As noted earlier . . . the Sioux concede the constitutionality of Congress' unilateral abrogation of the Fort Laramie Treaty. They seek only a holding that the Black Hills "were appropriated by the United States in circumstances which involved an implied undertaking by it to make just compensation to the tribe." *United States v. Creek Nation*, 295 U.S. 103, 111 (1935). The rational-basis test proffered by the Government would be ill-suited for use in determining whether such circumstances were presented by the events culminating in the passage of the 1877 Act.

247. See ibid. (stating that the taking of the Black Hills "implied an obligation on the part of the Government to make just compensation"). Throughout the entire *Sioux Nation* opinion, the Court repeatedly stated that tribes must allow Congress to act on their behalf. See, e.g., ibid. at 415 (noting "that tribal lands are subject to Congress' power to control and manage the tribe's affairs"). See also *County of Oneida v. Oneida Indian Nation*, 470 U.S. 226, 232 (1985): "We agree that this litigation makes abundantly clear the necessity for congressional action."

248. *Fed. Power Comm'n v. Tuscarora Indian Nation*, 362 U.S. 99, 120 (1960).

249. *Seneca Nation of Indians v. Brunker*, 262 F.2d 27, 27 (D.C. Cir. 1958), *cert denied* 360 U.S. 909 (1959).

250. *Menominee Tribe of Indians v. United States*, 391 U.S. 404, 413 (1968).

251. 476 U.S. 734 (1986).

252. Ibid. at 739 (citations omitted).

253. Ibid. at 739–740.

254. The Court stated that evidence of Congressional intent to abrogate treaty rights to hunt bald eagles and golden eagles was "strongly suggested" on the face of the Eagle Protection Act. Ibid. at 740. When determining whether congressional action abrogates a treaty right, the Court looks for "clear evidence that Congress actually considered the conflict between its intended action on the one hand and Indian treaty rights on the other, and chose to resolve that conflict by abrogating the treaty." Ibid.

255. *Fed. Power Comm'n*, 362 U.S. at 142 (Black, J., dissenting).

256. See, e.g., Pommersheim, *Braid of Feathers*, 11–36.

257. See generally Robert A. Williams Jr., *Linking Arms Together: American Treaty Visions of Law and Peace 1600–1800* (Oxford University Press, 1997).

258. See ibid., 62–85.

259. Ibid.

260. Jennings, *The Invasion of America*, 111–120.

261. Ibid. See also additional discussion in chapter 2.

262. Peter John Powell, "The Sacred Treaty," quoted in Roxanne Dunbar Ortiz, *The Great Sioux Nation* (Random House, 1977), 106.

263. Pommersheim, *Braid of Feathers*, 40–41.

264. See, e.g., Joseph Epes Brown, ed., *The Sacred Pipe: Black Elk's Pursuit of the Seven Rites of the Oglala Sioux* (University of Oklahoma Press, 1989).

265. Daniel K. Richter, *Facing East from Indian Country: A Native History of Early America* (Harvard University Press, 2001), 135–37 (internal footnotes omitted).

266. Ibid., 139.

267. Williams, *Linking Arms Together*, 103–13.

268. Ibid., 103 (quoting Bruce G. Trigger, vol. ed., 15 *Handbook of North American Indians: Northeast* (1978), 631–32).

269. Ibid. (quoting W.C. Vanderwerth ed., *Indian Oratory: Famous Speeches by Noted Indian Chieftains* (University of Oklahoma Press, 1971), 64–65.

270. Ibid., 115.

271. Russel Lawrence Barsh and James Youngblood Henderson, *The Road: Indian Tribes and Political Liberty* (University of California Press, 1980), 271.

272. Ibid., 270–82. There is further exploration of this idea in chapter 10.

273. Treaty with the Delawares, Sept. 17, 1778, art. III (Fort Pitt Treaty), 7 Stat. 13 (emphasis added). See also the discussion in Clinton, "The Dormant Indian Commerce Clause," 1190.

274. Ibid., art. IV.

275. See the in-depth discussion in chapter 10. There is also the cruel irony that the Delaware or Lenni Lenape hold none of their aboriginal lands, were removed to the Oklahoma territory, and lost much of their national identity until they were (re) recognized by the federal government in 1996. Clinton, "The Dormant Indian Commerce Clause," 1124–25.

276. Treaty with the Cherokee, Dec. 29, 1835, 7 Stat. 478 (emphasis added).

277. Ezra Rosser, "The Nature of Representation: The Cherokee Right to a Congressional Delegate," 15 *B. U. Pub. Int. L. J.* 91, 92–94 (2005).

278. Ibid., 130. The right to a (nonvoting) delegate has been realized for Puerto Rico, the District of Columbia, Guam, the Virgin Islands, and American Samoa.

Location of Non-Voting Delegate	(a) Year Congress established/ authorized	(b) Population near Time of Authorization	(c) Current Population
Puerto Rico	1900	953,243	3,808,610
District of Columbia	1970	756,510	572,059
Guam	1972	86,000 (1970)	154,805
The Virgin Islands	1972	63,000 (1970)	108,612
American Samoa	1978	32,000 (1980)	57,291
Cherokee People	1835	16,000+	280,000

279. Clinton, "There is No Federal Supremacy Clause for Indian Tribes," 126–27 (footnotes omitted). According to John Locke, a government's power is limited to the rights the members agree to grant the sovereign. Locke's "social compact" theory is

premised on the notion that the relation between the government and the individual "justified government as arising out of the agreement of the members of society to submit to being governed." Ibid., 127 n. 35.

280. See, e.g., *McClanahan v. Arizona State Tax Commission*, 411 U.S. 164, 172 (1973):

> Finally, the trend has been away from the idea of inherent Indian sovereignty as a bar to state jurisdiction and toward reliance on federal pre-emption. See *Mescalero Apache Tribe v. Jones*, 411 U.S. 145. The modern cases thus tend to avoid reliance on platonic notions of Indian sovereignty and to look instead to the applicable treaties and statutes which define the limits of state power. Compare, *e.g., United States v. Kagama*, 118 U.S. 375 (1886), with *Kennerly v. District Court*, 400 U.S. 423 (1971).

Note that there is no discussion in the case concerning the limits on *federal* power.

CHAPTER FOUR

1. 21 U.S. (8 Wheat.) 543 (1823).
2. 30 U.S. (5 Pet.) 1 (1831).
3. 31 U.S. (6 Pet.) 515 (1832).
4. The Non-Intercourse Act, 25 U.S.C. § 177 (2000), prohibits any land transaction by private individuals or the states with Indians that is not expressly ratified by the federal government. Other amendments to the Non-Intercourse Act regulated trade with Indians, including such things as licensing traders and prohibiting the introduction of liquor into Indian country. The Non-Intercourse Act and its various amendments are sometimes referred to as the Trade and Intercourse Acts.
5. See, e.g., the discussion later in this chapter.
6. See, e.g., *Oneida Indian Nation v. New York*, 860 F.2d 1145 (2nd Cir. 1988).
7. This section provided:

> The United States in Congress assembled shall also have the sole and exclusive right and power of . . . regulating the trade and managing all affairs with the Indians, not members of any of the States provided that the legislative right of any State within its own limits be not infringed or violated. . . . (Articles of Confederation, art. IX)

See also the discussion in chapter 2.

8. David H. Getches et al., *Cases and Materials on Federal Indian Law* (Thomson West, 5th ed. 2005), 61–62; see generally Nell Jessup Newton et al., *Felix Cohen's Handbook of Federal Indian Law* (LexisNexis, 2005 ed.), 23–25; Robert N. Clinton et al., *American Indian Law: Native Nations and the Federal System* (LexisNexis, 5th ed. 2007), 21–22.
9. Northwest Ordinance of 1787, Art. III, 1 Stat. 50, 52 (1789).
10. *Johnson*, 21 U.S. at 562.
11. Ibid. at 572.

12. Ibid. at 604–5. Yet this was not really the issue at all. The real issue was not the capacity of the Indians to sell, but the capacity of the non-Indian buyers to purchase under the Proclamation of 1763. See the discussion later in this chapter.

13. Ibid. at 573.

14. Ibid. at 572–73.

15. Ibid. at 574 ("The history of America, from its discovery to the present day, proves, we think, the universal recognition of these principles").

16. In this early period, international law consisted largely of the unwritten customary practices within the European (including the United States) family of nations.

17. *Johnson*, 21 U.S. at 573. Justice Marshall opined:

The United States, then, have unequivocably acceded to that great and broad rule by which its civilized inhabitants now hold this country. They hold, and assert in themselves, the title by which it was acquired. They maintain, as all others have maintained, that discovery gave an exclusive right to extinguish the Indian title of occupancy, either by purchase or by conquest; and gave also a right to such a degree of sovereignty as the circumstances of the people would allow them to exercise. (Ibid. at 587)

18. Ibid. at 590.

19. Ibid.

20. See, e.g., Charles C. Mann, *1491: New Revelations of the Americas before Columbus* (Alfred A. Knopf, 2005). The essential thesis of this well-documented work is that the Americas were more complex, populous, clean, and diverse than anything that existed in Europe at the time. There is also a cautionary note to be made about "presentism," which distinguishes between judgments of the past based on present moral and ethical standards and judgments based on the standards of the day. See generally ibid.

21. *Johnson*, 21 U.S. at 588.

22. Ibid. at 589.

23. Ibid. at 587.

24. Ibid. at 593–94. Such purchases were already proscribed by the Non-Intercourse Act of 1796. More accurately, the Court struck down the ability of any non-Indian purchaser of Indian land to ever sue in *federal* court for redress:

The person who purchases land from the Indians within their territory, incorporates himself with them, so far as respects the property purchased; holds their title under their protection, and subject to their laws. If they annul the grant, we know of no tribunal which can revise and set aside the proceeding. (Ibid. at 593)

25. Ibid. at 591–92. Notice that the hinge of "natural law," so central to much of Chief Justice Marshall's thinking about individual rights, was foreclosed to Indians. According to White:

The message of *Johnson v. McIntosh*, then, was that the natural rights of human beings to dispose of property that they held by virtue of possession did not apply to Indians in America. While Marshall had intimated that the circumscription of the rights of conquered peoples was a prerogative of conquest, he had not suggested that such a circumscription would have occurred if the conquered persons had been other than "fierce savages," incapable of being "incorporated with the victorious nation" and thereby retaining "unimpaired" their rights to property. The special principles of Indian-white property rights were a function of the "character and habits" of the Indians. (G. Edward White, *The Marshall Court and Cultural Change, 1815–1835* (Abridged ed., Oxford University Press, 1991), 710)

26. *Johnson*, 21 U.S. at 587.

27. Felix S. Cohen, "Original Indian Land Title," 32 *Minn. L. Rev.* 28, 48 (1947).

28. Getches et al., *Cases and Materials*, 68–69; see also Clinton et al., *American Indian Law*, 55–56; Newton et al., eds., *Felix Cohen's Handbook*, 970–74.

29. See, e.g., Frank Pommersheim, *Braid of Feathers: American Indian Law and Contemporary Tribal Life* (University of California Press, 1995), 42–43. See also the discussion later concerning other legal concerns and the attempted retreat from the doctrine of discovery.

30. This section draws extensively on the work of Robert Williams and Robert Miller. See, e.g., Robert A. Williams, *The American Indian in Western Legal Thought: The Discourses of Conquest* (Oxford University Press, 1990), 325–28; Robert J. Miller, "The Doctrine of Discovery in American Indian Law," 42 *Idaho L. Rev.* 1 (2005). See also Robert J. Miller, *Native America Discovered and Conquered: Thomas Jefferson, Lewis & Clark, and Manifest Destiny* (Praeger, 2006).

31. Miller, "Doctrine of Discovery," 3.

32. Ibid., 8–9.

33. Williams, *The American Indian*, 93–108; Miller, "Doctrine of Discovery," 8–9.

34. Miller, "Doctrine of Discovery," 12.

35. Williams, *The American Indian*, 96–101; Miller, "Doctrine of Discovery," 14.

36. Ibid.

37. Miller, "Doctrine of Discovery," 16.

38. Ibid., 23 (citing W. Keith Kavenagh, ed., *Foundations of Colonial America: A Documentary History* (1973), 1267–68).

39. Ibid., 22–24.

40. See ibid., 23–27.

41. See ibid., 27–30.

42. Ibid., 79.

43. Ibid., 83 n. 395 (quoting Letter from Thomas Jefferson to the United States Senate (Jan. 15, 1803), reprinted in James A. Richardson, ed., *Compilation of Messages and Papers of the Presidents* (1910), 190, 422).

44. Ibid., 88. Jefferson's desire to establish discovery claims in the northwest is evidenced in the vast amount of gifts Lewis and Clark bestowed upon delegations of Indians, in the name of the president. These gifts were more than diplomacy—they signaled expansion.

Colonial experience taught that fruitful diplomacy and peaceful relations with native people required the exchange of gifts at each meeting. French and English forest diplomats learned that lesson early and did their best to offer goods of substance and quality....

Lewis knew the gift-giving tradition and early in 1803 made note of funds to be set aside for presents for the Indians. In his initial tally of expedition costs, Lewis allocated $696 for trade goods....

All of the gifts stowed in the expedition's luggage for transport to St. Louis had a purpose beyond diplomatic protocol. Those items, everything from ivory combs to calico shirts, represented what the United States offered to potential trading partners. As Jefferson repeated to every delegation of western Indians, Americans sought commerce, not land.... Although Jefferson and his explorers honestly pursued intertribal peace as a requisite to trade, arming friends seems equally reasonable. What all those gifts represented was, in fact, the fundamental element in Jefferson's western Indian policy. Trade and diplomacy, commerce and sovereignty were all parts of the engine that drove American expansion and guided the Lewis and Clark expedition. (James P. Ronda, *Lewis and Clark among the Indians* (University of Nebraska Press, 1989), 8–9)

Indian presents clearly would consume more of his initial funds than any other class of supplies. The gifts were not bribes, but unconditional statements, in the Indians' minds, of goodwill and friendship. So down went itemized notations about blue beads and brass buttons, favored as ornaments by the natives; kettles, knives, awls, rings, and burning (magnifying) glasses; tobacco, cloth, and sewing needles; ear trinkets, vermilion, and strips of copper and sheets of tin that could be converted into adornments. He also planned to take along three hand-turned mills for grinding corn, a first step in the civilizing process. Plus several peace and friendship medals of varying sizes and designs, to be passed out to deserving chiefs as tokens of esteem from President Jefferson. The more powerful the chief, the bigger the medal. (David Lavender, *The Way to the Western Sea* (Harper and Row, 1988), 25)

45. Interestingly, the Court in *Johnson v. McIntosh* appeared to recognize the Indian right to sell, but a disgruntled purchaser could find no recourse in state or federal court:

The person who purchases land from the Indians, within their territory, incorporates himself with them, so far as respects the property purchased; hold their title under their protection, and subject to their laws. If they annul the grant, we know of no tribunal which can revise and set aside the proceeding. (543 U.S. at 593)

46. See, e.g., Getches et al., *Cases and Materials*, 174. Federal government ownership of Indian land remains an essential element of the trust relationship. Despite its more positive elements of judicial protection and management of tribal

resources, it flatly contradicts true tribal sovereignty. See also Pommersheim, *Braid of Feathers*, 45. See further discussion in chapter 5.

47. See, e.g., Lindsay G. Robertson, *Conquest by Law: How the Discovery of America Dispossessed Indigenous Peoples of Their Lands* (Oxford University Press, 2005).

48. Ibid., xi.

49. Ibid., 6.

50. Ibid., 14–44.

51. Stuart Banner, *How Indians Lost Their Land* (Harvard University Press, 2003), 179–80.

52. Robertson, *Conquest by Law*, 46. Harper was a well-known southern attorney who was hired by the Illinois and Wabash Land Companies to manage their claims. He adopted a strategy similar to the one he used successfully in other land disputes. In this instance, he located a friendly federal district court in the new state of Illinois, which was admitted to the union in 1818. The benefits of this court were substantial: part of the land purchases from the Illinois and Piankeshaw Indians was located there, the court was authorized to hear civil claims without the presence of a circuit-riding supreme court justice (because of its distance from the capital), and direct appeals to the U.S. Supreme Court from its decision were also permitted.

Harper recruited a compliant defendant, McIntosh, probably looking to enhance the potential value of his property and exact a certain revenge against his enemies. Diversity jurisdiction was created because McIntosh was a citizen of Illinois and Johnson was a citizen of Maryland. Judge Nathaniel Pope was also compliant. He accepted a plea in ejectment on a stipulated set of facts (errors of fact could not be appealed to the Supreme Court in 1823) and identified a single legal issue, namely, the validity of the Proclamation of 1763. Judge Pope agreed to issue a pro forma ruling without an opinion in favor of the Defendant McIntosh. Ibid., 41–59.

53. Ibid., xi.

54. Ibid., 101.

55. Ibid., 86–89.

56. Chief Justice Marshall stated:

It has never been doubted, that either the United States, or the *several States*, had clear title to all lands within the boundary lines described in the Treaty [1763 Treaty of Paris ending the Revolutionary War], subject only to the Indian right of occupancy, and that the exclusive power to extinguish that right, was vested in that government which might constitutionally exercise it. (*Johnson*, 21 U.S. at 584–85,emphasis added)

57. Robertson, *Conquest by Law*, 92. Kentucky, however, was not persuaded and refused to recognize the Virginia grants to its militia veterans. In 1830—pursuant to a request of the Virginia legislature—Congress voted to allow these individuals to exchange their militia "land warrants" for federal public lands in Ohio, Indiana, and Illinois. (Ibid., 117–18)

58. 31 U.S. (6 Pet.) 515 (1832). In *Worcester*, Chief Justice Marshall admits the doctrine of discovery was wrong. Robertson, *Conquest by Law*, 133. Chief Justice Marshall stated in *Worcester*:

America, separated from Europe by a wide ocean, was inhabited by a distinct people, divided into separate nations, independent of each other and of the rest of the world, having institutions of their own, and governing themselves by their own laws. It is difficult to comprehend the proposition that the inhabitants of either quarter of the globe could have rightful original claims of dominion over the inhabitants of the other, or over the lands they occupied; or that the discovery of either by the other should give the discoverer rights in the country discovered, which annulled the pre-existing rights of its ancient possessors. (*Worcester*, 31 U.S. at 542–43)

59. Obviously, this was self-contradictory. Yet that is what the opinion said. See note 57, at 152. How could title to Indian lands be in both the original states and federal government? Treaties were made between tribes and the federal government, not the states. In fact, the 1786 Hopewell Treaty with the Chickasaw dealt with these very lands.

60. Given its importance, it is not surprising that *Johnson v. McIntosh* has generated a plethora of commentary. See, e.g., Richard J. Ansson Jr., "The United States Supreme Court and American Indian Tribal Sovereignty," 23 *Am. Indian L. Rev.* 465 (1999); David J. Bloch, "Colonizing the Last Frontier," 29 *Am. Indian L. Rev.* 1 (2005); Steven Paul Sloy, "Revisiting the 'Courts of the Conqueror': American Indian Claims against the United States," 44 *Am. U. L. Rev.* 537 (1994).

61. See generally Melanie McGrath, *The Long Exile: A Tale of Inuit Betrayal and Survival in the High Arctic* (Alfred A. Knopf, 2007). See also Robert Miller, "A 'New World' to Claim—the Arctic," *Indian Country Today* (April 25, 2007), A3.

62. McGrath, *The Long Exile*, 61.

Ellesmere is the world's ninth largest island, an area about the same size as Great Britain. It is also the most mountainous of the Arctic islands, home to the highest and longest alpine ranges in the eastern North American continent. Three-quarters of Ellesmere Island is an impenetrable mass of frozen crags, deep fiords and terrible, green-ice valleys topped in the northern interior by forbidding age-old ice caps up to a half-mile deep. Combined, Ellesmere's glaciers cover 40 per cent of its surface area. (Ibid., 130–31)

63. Ibid., 69. "The Arctic seemed to spawn bad ideas in white men, of which relocation of Inukjuamiut was only the latest" (ibid., 124–25).

64. Ibid., 238.

65. Ibid., 258–59.

66. Ibid., 259.

67. 30 U.S. (5 Pet.) 1 (1831).

68. 31 U.S. (6 Pet.) 515 (1832).

69. Getches et al., *Cases and Materials*, 95.

70. This issue was created by the fact that European land grants to the original colonies extended their western borders all the way to the "sea." See, e.g., Paul W. Gates, *History of Public Land Law Development* (Zenger, 1968), 49.

71. See, e.g., Treaty of Hopewell, 7 Stat. 18 (1785). This was well before *Lone Wolf v. Hitchcock*, 187 U.S. 553 (1903), and therefore treaty abrogation was *not* so readily available.

72. Francis Paul Prucha, *The Great Father* (University of Nebraska Press, 1984), 196.

73. Wilson Lumpkin, *The Removal of the Cherokee Indians from Georgia* (Arno, 1969), 83.

74. Ch. 148, 4 Stat. 411–12 (1830) (quoted in Getches et al., *Cases and Materials*, 97–98).

75. Getches et al., *Cases and Materials*, 97–98 (quoting Allen Guttman, *State's Rights and Indian Removal: The Cherokee Nation v. Georgia* (D. C. Heath, 1965), 58).

76. Ibid., 100–101. The removal bill had passed narrowly, and controversy continued between President Jackson and Congress:

> The Indians could not hold out forever. Those who wished to stay were given small reservations where they were. The rest were moved to the West, amidst inevitable hardships, which have been repeatedly retold. (Ibid., 101, quoting Francis Paul Prucha, *American Indian Policy in the Formative Years: Indian Trade and Intercourse Acts, 1790–1834* (University of Nebraska Press, 1962, 247–48)

77. U.S. Const. art. III, § 2, cl. 2. The reference to "all the other cases before mentioned" includes controversies "between a state, or the citizens thereof, and *foreign states*." U.S. Const. art. III, § 2, cl. 1 (emphasis added).

78. *Cherokee Nation v. Georgia*, 30 U.S. (5 Pet.) 1, 10–11 (1831).

79. Ibid. at 5.

80. Ibid. at 16.

81. Ibid.

82. The text of the Commerce Clause in its entirety states that "Congress shall have the power To regulate Commerce with foreign Nations, and among the several States, and with the Indian Tribes." U.S. Const. art. I, § 8, cl. 3.

83. *Cherokee Nation*, 30 U.S. at 19. The Court also noted that the text of the Indian Commerce Clause as it appears in the Constitution is a revision that "omitted those qualifications which embarrassed the exercise of it as granted in the Confederation." See chapter 2 for a discussion of matters of Indian commerce in the Articles of Confederation.

84. Ibid. at 20.

85. Ibid. at 15.

86. Ibid. at 17.

87. Ibid.

88. See the detailed discussion in chapter 8.

89. See the detailed discussion in chapter 8.

90. *Cherokee Nation*, 30 U.S. at 18.

91. See the discussion in chapter 2.

92. *Cherokee Nation*, 30 U.S. at 25 (Johnson, J., concurring).

93. Ibid. at 28–30 (Johnson, J., concurring).

94. Ibid. at 32 (Baldwin, J., concurring).

95. Ibid. at 49–50 (Baldwin, J., concurring).

96. Ibid. at 49–50 (Baldwin, J., concurring).

97. Ibid. at 53 (Thompson, J., dissenting).

98. Ibid. at 60–61 (Thompson, J., dissenting).

99. Ibid. at 53 (Thompson, J., dissenting). See also discussion of Vattel's importance in international law concerning indigenous peoples in chapter 9.

100. Ibid. (Thompson, J., dissenting).

101. Ibid. at 55 (Thompson, J., dissenting).

102. 5 U.S. (1 Cranch) 137 (1803).

103. 31 U.S. (6 Pet.) 515 (1832).

104. The relevant state statute was enacted in 1830 and provided as follows:

> Sec. 7. And be it further enacted by the authority aforesaid, that all white persons residing within the limits of the Cherokee nation, on the 1st day of March next, or at any time thereafter, without a license or permit from his excellency the governor, or from such agent as his excellency the governor shall authorise to grant such permit or license, and who shall not have taken the oath hereinafter required, shall be guilty of a high misdemeanour, and, upon conviction thereof, shall be punished by confinement to the penitentiary at hard labour for a term not less than four years: provided, that the provisions of this section shall not be so construed as to extend to any authorised agent or agents of the government of the United States or of this state, or to any person or persons who may rent any of those improvements which have been abandoned by Indians who have emigrated west of the Mississippi: provided, nothing contained in this section shall be so construed as to extend to white females, and all male children under twenty-one years of age.
>
> Sec. 8. And be it further enacted by the authority aforesaid, that all white persons, citizens of the state of Georgia, who have procured a license in writing from his excellency the governor, or from such agent as his excellency the governor shall authorise to grant such permit or license, to reside within the limits of the Cherokee nation, and who have taken the following oath, viz. "I, A.B., do solemnly swear (or affirm, as the case may be) that I will support and defend the constitution and laws of the state of Georgia, and uprightly demean myself as a citizen thereof, so help me God," shall be, and the same are hereby declared, exempt and free from the operation of the seventh section of this act. (Ibid. at 523)

105. Ibid. at 541.

106. Ibid. at 543. See also the previous discussion of this "revisionary" approach.

107. Ibid.

108. Ibid. at 544–45.

109. Ibid. at 554.

110. Ibid. at 556.

111. Ibid. at 556–57 (emphasis added).

112. Ibid. at 559. Notice how this language affirming the "natural rights" of the Cherokee contrasts sharply with the language in *Johnson v. McIntosh* denying tribes access to the benefits of natural law:

> So, too, with respect to the concomitant principle, that the Indian inhabitants are to be considered merely as occupants, to be protected, indeed, while in peace, in the possession of their lands, but to be deemed incapable of transferring the absolute title to others. However this restriction may be opposed to natural right, and to the usages of civilized nations, yet, if it be indispensable to that system under which the country has been settled, and be adapted to the actual condition of the two people, it may, perhaps, be supported by reason, and certainly cannot be rejected by Courts of justice. (*Johnson*, 21 U.S. at 591)

113. *Worcester*, 31 U.S. at 521.

114. Ibid. The Court also noted the essential beneficence and federal approval of Rev. Worcester's activities:

> [H]e entered the aforesaid Cherokee nation in the capacity of a duly authorized missionary of the American Board of Commissioners for foreign missions, under the authority of the president of the United States, and has not since been required by him to leave it: that he was, at the time of his arrest, engaged in preaching the gospel to the Cherokee Indians, and translating the sacred Scriptures into their language, with the permission and approval of said Cherokee nation, and in accordance with the humane policy of the government of the United States, for the civilization and improvement of the Indians.... (Ibid. at 529)

115. Ibid. at 568 (M'Lean, J., concurring).

116. Ibid. at 583. Also note that Justice Baldwin dissented on the same grounds he articulated in the *Cherokee Nation* case. Ibid. at 596.

117. Clinton et al., *American Indian Law*, 66; Newton et al., eds., *Felix Cohen's Handbook*, 49; Getches et al., *Cases and Materials*, 95–127.

118. Getches et al., *Cases and Materials*, 104; see also Newton et al., eds., *Felix Cohen's Handbook*, 49.

119. The absence of such deference and allegiance doomed the efforts of the Articles of Confederation to form an enduring union. See the discussion in chapter 2.

120. Clinton et al., *American Indian Law*, 83; Getches et al., *Cases and Materials*, 122.

121. Clinton et al., *American Indian Law*, 82; Newton et al., eds., *Felix Cohen's Handbook*, 50; Getches, et al., *Cases and Materials*, 122. For discussion of the aftermath of the *Worcester* decision, see Horace Greeley, *The American Conflict* (Hartford, 1864), 106; Marquis James, *The Life of Andrew Jackson* (Bobs-Merrill, 1938), 603–24; Joseph C. Burke, "The Cherokee Cases: A Study in Law, Politics, and Morality," 21 *Stan. L. Rev.* 500 (1969)

122. Clinton et al., *American Indian Law*, 82; Getches et al., *Cases and Materials*, 122.

123. Ibid.

124. See the detailed discussion in chapter 8.

125. See Monroe E. Price and Robert N. Clinton, *Law and the American Indian* (2nd ed., Michie, 1983), 165–76.

126. *Worcester v. Georgia*, 31 U.S. (6 Pet.) 515, 518 (1832) (stating "Protection does not imply the destruction of the protected").

127. See the discussion in chapter 2.

128. 187 U.S. 553 (1903).

129. See, e.g., the detailed discussion of *Lone Wolf v. Hitchcock* and its legacy in chapter 5.

130. See, e.g., *Lone Wolf v. Hitchcock*, 187 U.S. 553 (1905) and the ensuing discussion in chapter 5.

131. One such reform allows the tribe to contract with the BIA for the delivery of BIA services such as law enforcement, natural resources, and education. See, e.g., Newton et al., eds., *Felix Cohen's Handbook*, §§ 22.03[2], 22.07[1][B].

132. For a detailed explanation of the management of the trust responsibility, see ibid. § 5.

133. *McClanahan v. Arizona State Tax Commission*, 411 U.S. 164, 171 (1973) (emphasis added). The Court noted that the "modern cases thus tend to avoid reliance on platonic notions of Indian sovereignty and to look instead to the applicable treaties and statutes which define the limits of state power" (ibid. at 172).

134. See, e.g., Charles Wilkinson, *American Indians, Time and the Law* (Yale University Press, 1987).

135. John Lewis Gaddis, *The Landscape of History* (Oxford University Press, 2002), 32–33.

136. Ibid., 33.

137. Ibid.

138. Ibid., 34.

139. *United States v. Great Sioux Nation*, 448 U.S. 371 (1980).

140. As quoted in Gaddis, *The Landscape of History*, 127.

141. *Sioux Nation*, 448 U.S. at 386.

142. The Supreme Court affirmed the decision of the Court of Claims that payment of $13.5 million plus interest was due to the Great Sioux Nation for an uncompensated taking. In 1980, the amount totaled $102 million. The judgment has yet to be paid, not because of the unwillingness of the United States to pay, but the unwillingness of the Great Sioux Nation to accept payment (now more than $650 million) because of its steadfastness to not accept the judgment unless it is coupled with the land return of the approximately 1.3 million acres still held by the federal government. The impasse continues. See, e.g., John P. LaVelle, "Rescuing Paha Sapa," 5 *Great Plains Nat. Res. J.* 40, 63–65 (2001). The basic "taking" and abrogation of the Fort Laramie Treaty of 1868 was rationalized in accordance with *Lone Wolf v. Hitchcock*. Ibid. at 424. *Lone Wolf* is discussed in chapter 5.

143. *Sioux Nation*, 448 U.S. at 388.

144. Ibid. at 435 (Rehnquist, J., dissenting).

145. 347 U.S. 483 (1954) (holding "separate but equal" schools for black and white students unconstitutional as violative of the constitutional guarantee of equal protection).

146. *Sioux Nation*, 448 U.S. at 435 (Rehnquist, J., dissenting).

147. *Sioux Nation*, 448 U.S. at 435–437 (Rehnquist, J., dissenting). Much of the following draws from a paper written by Daniel Brendtro (University of South Dakota School of Law Class of 2004) for my Indian Law class in Fall 2003 (copy on file with the author).

148. Ibid. at 435 (Rehnquist, J., dissenting).

149. Ibid. at 422, n. 32.

150. Ibid. at 380.

151. Ibid. at 436 (Rehnquist, J., dissenting).

152. The language which Rehnquist quoted was as follows:

Three centuries of bitter Indian warfare reached a tragic climax on the plains and mountains of America's Far West. Since the early seventeenth century, when Chief Opechancanough rallied his Powhatan tribesmen against the Virginia intruders on their lands, each advance of the frontier had been met with stubborn resistance. At times this conflict flamed into open warfare: in King Phillip's rebellion against the Massachusetts Puritans, during the French and Indian wars of the eighteenth century, in Chief Pontiac's assault on his new British overlords in 1763, in Chief Tecumseh's vain efforts to hold back the advancing pioneers of 1812, and in the Black Hawk war....

...In three tragic decades, between 1860 and 1890, the Indians suffered the humiliating defeats that forced them to walk the white man's road toward civilization. Few conquered people in the history of mankind have paid so dearly for their defense of a way of life that the march of progress had outmoded.

This epic struggle left its landmarks behind, as monuments to the brave men, Indian and white, who fought and died that their manner of living might endure. (*Soldier and Brave* (Harper and Row, 1963), xiii–xiv)

153. *Soldier and Brave* (United States Department of the Interior, National Park Service, 1971).

154. See ibid., 33.

155. Ibid. (emphasis added).

156. *Sioux Nation*, 448 U.S. at 437 (Rehnquist, J., dissenting).

157. *Soldier and Brave* (1971), 307.

158. See Luther Standing Bear, *Land of the Spotted Eagle* (University of Nebraska Press, 1978), 160 (recounting common Sioux proverbs, including "No one likes a borrower," "There is a hole at the end of the thief's path," "The lazy person gets into mischief"); ibid. at 161 (noting that "Any position gained by an individual in his own band was due solely to his own abilities and efforts"); ibid. at 169 ("It was not tribal practice, nor was it a rule of their warfare, for the Lakota to torture their enemies"); Ella C. Deloria, *Speaking of Indians* (Dakota Press, 1979), 46–47 (discussing the nature

of Lakota economics, and noting that for long periods between giveaways, people enjoyed what they had and could acquire).

159. *Sioux Nation*, 448 U.S. at 436 (Rehnquist, J., dissenting).

160. Samuel Eliot Morison, *The Oxford History of the American People* (Oxford University Press, 1965), 540 (quoted ibid. at 437).

161. See, e.g., the discussion in chapter 2.

162. *Sioux Nation*, 448 U.S. at 437 (Rehnquist, J., dissenting). That much Indian law history is more within the lawmaking sphere of Congress is true but does not negate the inevitability of such encounters within the U.S. Supreme Court.

163. The judiciary's task, of course, is to interpret the law that exists, not to make new law. Yet interpretation that completely ignores changing times—especially in Indian law, where contested events often have taken place more than a century ago—risks irrelevancy and insensitive formalism. Acknowledgment of such changing circumstances is the first step in the process of change.

164. Gaddis, *The Landscape of History*, 124.

165. *Sioux Nation*, 448 U.S. at 384.

166. See *City of Sherrill v. Oneida Indian Nation of New York*, 544 U.S. 197 (2005). At issue in *City of Sherrill* was a 1794 treaty between the Oneida Nation and the United States. The treaty reserved to the Oneida 300,000 acres in upstate New York. Despite the treaty, the State of New York bought large tracts of land from the tribe, and the federal government removed much of the tribe to Wisconsin. By 2000, 99 percent of the population in the original New York town was non-Indian. In the late 1990s, the tribe began to purchase lands within the original reservation and claimed that the land was exempt from property taxes. After the City of Sherrill brought an eviction suit, a federal district court and appeals court both ruled for the tribe. The Supreme Court, however, held that because of the long lapse in time and change in the demographics of the area, giving the tribe sovereignty over land purchased on the open market would have disruptive consequences. See generally ibid. For a more in-depth explanation of the diminishment issue, see Pommersheim, *Braid of Feathers*, 23–25. See also the additional discussion of the *Sherrill* case in chapter 8.

167. *Mabo v. Queensland* [No. 2] (1992) 175 CLR 1, 30. See the in-depth discussion in chapter 9.

168. *Mabo*, 175 CLR at 30. (The Court ultimately held that the common law recognized native title, and it was not extinguished in this instance.)

169. Gaddis, *The Landscape of History*, 128. "Good historians take the past on its own terms first, and only then, impose their own" (ibid., 140).

170. This is known as the fallacy of presentism. David Hackett Fischer, *Historians' Fallacies: Toward a Logic of Historians' Thought* (Harper Perennial, 1970), 135–40. Presentism has been described as:

> [A] complex anachronism, in which the antecedent in a narrative series is falsified by being defined or interpreted in terms of the consequent. Sometimes called the fallacy of *nunc pro tunc*, it is the mistaken idea that the proper way to do history is to prune away the dead branches of the past, and

to preserve the green buds and twigs which have grown into the dark forest of our contemporary world. (See ibid., 135)

171. Gaddis, *The Landscape of History*, 140.

172. See ibid., 149.

173. Declan Kiberd, *Inventing Ireland* (Harvard University Press, 1995), 614.

174. Ibid.

175. Brian Friel, *Translations* (Faber and Faber, 1981).

176. Kiberd, *Inventing Ireland*, 616 (quoting program note to *Translations*, Field Day 1980).

177. Ibid.

178. Ibid., 628.

179. Ibid., 619. To note the specific colonial convergence of the Irish and Native American experience, there is this statement by the English character Teddy in Brian Friel's play *Faith Healer*:

> That night in the Ballybeg pub and then hanging about [in rural Ireland] for the trial of those bloody Irish Apaches and nobody in the courtroom understands a word I'm saying—they had to get an interpreter to explain to the judge in English what the only proper Englishman in the place was saying! God!

180. Ibid., 620.

181. Ibid., 621.

182. Meron Benvenisti, *Sacred Landscape* (Maxine Kaufman–Lacustra trans., University of California Press, 2000), 16 (emphasis added).

183. Ibid., 43.

184. Ibid., 14–15.

185. Ibid., 13 (quoting J. B. Harley and David Woodward, *History of Cartography* (University of Chicago Press, 1987), 506).

186. See generally Wilbur E. Garrett, ed., National Geographic Society, *Historical Atlas of the United States* (1988). In South Dakota, for example, no current map refers to the sacred Black Hills as *Paha Sapa* or to Bear Butte as *Mato Paha*.

187. Kiberd, *Inventing Ireland*, 629.

188. Benvenisti, *Sacred Landscape*, 259. The speaker quoted is Mahoud Darwish, a Palestinian poet.

189. Ibid., 9. "I cannot envisage my homeland without Arabs, and perhaps my late father, who taught me to read maps and study history, was right in his naïve belief that there is enough space, physical and historical, for Jews and Arabs in their shared homeland" (ibid.).

190. There are other provocative notions of history, including, for example, that of the South Africa satirist, Evita Bezuidenhout, who has remarked, "The future is certain, it is the past that is unpredictable." This seemingly counterintuitive claim nevertheless is quite insightful in its realization "that our perception of the past often changes to suit the political and emotional needs of the present." According to such an analysis, a society's view of the past is as much a reflection of that past as a reflection

of where that society is going in the present. Such a process is probably what so disturbed Justice Rehnquist. Yet his solution to merely accept the past can only perpetuate certain injustices. "History can therefore operate as society's mirror, reflecting the obsessions and concerns of that society through the lens of past events."

Thomas McGrath, the great poet of the Dakotas, also observed in his masterwork, *Letter to an Imaginary Friend*, that "the work of the poem is to *create* a past in order to *rescue* the future that has been stolen from us" (emphasis added).

Most recently, the novelist Philip Roth has stated: "History claims everybody whether they know it or not, and whether they like it or not...[T]he relentless unforeseen was what we schoolchildren studied as 'History,' harmless history where everything unexpected in its own time is chronicled on the page as inevitable. The terror of the unforeseen is what the science of history hides, turning a disaster into an epic" (*New York Times Book Review*, Sept. 19, 2004).

CHAPTER FIVE

1. 187 U.S. 553 (1903).

2. See *Sioux Nation of Indians v. United States*, 601 F.2d 1157, 1173 (Ct. Cl. 1979) (Nichols, J., concurring; stating, "The day *Lone Wolf* was handed down, January 5, 1903, might be called one of the blackest days in the history of the American Indian, the Indians' *Dred Scott* decision"). As noted by a leading Indian law scholar:

> *Dred Scott* is notorious because of its racism—its inhuman conceptualization of African-Americans—and because of its troubling aftermath—it greased the slide into the Civil War. *Lone Wolf* is similarly shocking. It, too, reeks of racism—its treatment of Indians as subjugated, backward peoples under the unconstrained rule of Congress—and had a troubling aftermath—the breakup of many Indian reservations, the disintegration of many tribal governments, and the forced assimilation of many Indians. (Philip P. Frickey, "Doctrine, Context, Institutional Relationships, and Commentary: The Malaise of Federal Indian Law through the Lens of Lone Wolf," 38 *Tulsa L. Rev.* 5, 5 (2002))

See generally the collection of essays on *Lone Wolf* in 38 *Tulsa L. Rev.* 1–157 (2002).

3. David M. Getches et al., *Cases and Materials on Federal Indian Law* (Thomson West, 5th ed., 2005), 165.

4. Ibid., 167 (citing Delos Sacket Otis, History of the Allotment Policy, Hearings on H.R. 7902 Before the House Comm. on Indian Affairs, 73rd Cong., 2d Sess., pt. 9, at 428–85).

5. Ibid. (alteration in original).

6. Ibid. at 167 (citing *Annual Report on Indian Lands*, BIA Office of Trust Responsibilities, Sept. 30, 1985).

7. Ibid., 168 (citing Delos Sacket Otis, History of the Allotment Policy, Hearings on H.R. 7902 Before the House Comm. on Indian Affairs, 73rd Cong., 2d Sess., pt. 9, at 428–85).

8. Ibid.

9. Ibid., 168–69.

10. Ibid., 169.

11. Peter Nabokov, *Native American Testimony: A Chronicle of Indian-White Relations from Prophecy to the Present, 1492–1992* (expanded ed., Viking, 1991), 242.

12. Ibid.

13. Ibid., 247 (first alteration in original).

14. Francis Paul Prucha, *The Great Father: The United States Government and the American Indians* (abridged ed., University of Nebraska Press, 1986), 224.

15. Ibid., 226.

16. Ibid., 232. The consent requirement was changed by the result in the *Lone Wolf* case.

17. Getches et al., *Cases and Materials*, 170 (citing Delos Sacket Otis, History of the Allotment Policy, Hearings on H.R. 7902 Before the House Comm. on Indian Affairs, 73rd Cong., 2d Sess., pt. 9, at 428–85).

18. Wilkinson, *American Indians*, 20.

19. Two federal statutory attempts at reform have been declared unconstitutional as uncompensated takings in violation of the Fifth Amendment. See, e.g., *Hodel v. Irving*, 481 U.S. 704 (1987) and *Babbitt v. Youpee*, 519 U.S. 234 (1997).

20. Charles F. Wilkinson, *American Indians, Time, and the Law* (Yale University Press, 1987), 19 (citing S. Tyler, *A History of Indian Policy* (1973), 104).

21. Frickey, "Doctrine, Context," 6 (quoting Professor Joe Sax). The reference to eminent domain is either unduly charitable or misplaced. Eminent domain as a rationale for "taking" Indian land was not mentioned in any Supreme Court case until 1980. See, e.g., *United States v. Sioux Nation of Indians*, 448 U.S. 371 (1980). The Court has never expounded this rationale in any subsequent case.

22. *Lone Wolf v. Hitchcock*, 187 U.S. 553 (1903).

23. Blue Clark, Lone Wolf v. Hitchcock, *Treaty Rights and Indian Law at the End of the Nineteenth Century* (University of Nebraska Press, 1994), 40.

24. Ibid., 41.

25. Ibid.

26. Ibid., 42.

27. Ibid.

28. Ibid.

29. Ibid., 45.

30. Ibid.

31. Ibid.

32. Ibid., 46.

33. Ibid.

34. Ibid., 47.

35. Ibid., 48.

36. Ibid., 49.

37. Ibid.

38. Ibid., 48–49.

39. Ibid., 52.

40. Ibid., 53.

41. Ibid., 53–54.

42. Ibid., 55.

43. Ibid. (citing *Washington Post*, Oct. 20, 1902).

44. Ibid.

45. Ibid., 59.

46. Getches et al., *Cases and Materials*, 182 (quoting Ann Laquer Estin, "*Lone Wolf v. Hitchcock*: The Long Shadow," in *The Aggressions of Civilization: Federal Indian Policy since the 1880's* (Sandra L. Cadwalader and Vine Deloria Jr., eds. 1984), 215, 216–34.

47. Clark, Lone Wolf v. Hitchcock, 63 (citing Decree of the Court of Appeals of the District of Columbia, no. 1109, March 4, 1902).

48. Ibid., 66.

49. See ibid.

50. This pattern was repeated throughout much of Indian country, including Montana and the Dakotas.

51. Clark, Lone Wolf v. Hitchcock, 67.

52. Ibid., 70.

53. *Lone Wolf*, 187 U.S. at 564.

54. Ibid.

55. See the earlier discussion in this chapter.

56. *Lone Wolf*, 187 U.S. at 565.

57. Ibid. at 568.

58. *Chae Chan Ping v. United States*, 130 U.S. 581 (1889).

59. Ibid. at 589.

60. Ibid. at 595. Part of this characterization reflects a racial animus and the use of negative stereotypes not unlike those used to describe Indians. For example, Justice Field wrote, "[The Chinese were] residing apart by themselves, and adhering to the customs and usages of their own country. It seemed impossible for them to assimilate with our people, or to make any change in their habits or modes of living."

61. Ibid. at 597.

62. Ibid. at 599–600.

63. See ibid. at 602–4.

64. *Lone Wolf*, 187 U.S. at 568.

65. See *Delaware Tribal Business Committee v. Weeks*, 430 U.S. 73 (1978), and *United States v. Sioux Nation*, 448 U.S. 371 (1980), discussed previously, indicating the relaxation of political question doctrine in Indian land questions. The Court has also struggled to identify an appropriate test with which to determine Congress's intent to abrogate a treaty. In the case of *United States v. Dion*, 476 U.S. 734 (1986), the Court—after noting its own inconsistency in this area—identified the appropriate test: "What is essential is clear evidence that Congress actually considered the conflict between its intended action on the one hand and Indian treaty rights on the other, and chose to resolve that conflict by abrogating the treaty." Ibid. at 739–40.

66. 118 U.S. 375 (1886).

67. Ibid. at 378–79.

68. Ibid. at 383–84.

69. *Lone Wolf*, 187 U.S. at 567.

70. 118 U.S. at 381.

71. See the discussion in chapter 8.

72. The point is not to suggest that these formulations in the leading Indian law casebooks are wrong but rather that they are so heavily weighted in favor of congressional policy that they inadvertently deflect attention from the powerful role of the Supreme Court in setting the overarching doctrines within which Congress acts. See, e.g., Getches et al., *Cases and Materials*, 73–128, 141–255:

> The Federal-Tribal Treaty Relationship. The Formative Years (1789–1871)
> Allotments and Assimilation (1871–1928)
> The Period of Indian Reorganization (1928–1945)
> The Termination Period (1945–1961)
> The Era of Self-Determination (1961-Present).

In each of these eras, prominence is given to the work of Congress. In addition, see Clinton et al., *American Indian Law Cases and Materials* (Michie, 3d ed., 1991), 138–64:

> The Colonial Period (1492–1776)
> The Confederation Period (1776–1789)
> The Trade and Intersource Act Era (1789–1835)
> The Removal Period (1835–1861)
> The Reservation Policy (1861–1867)
> The Allotment Period and Forced Assimilation (1871–1934)
> The Indian Reorganization Act Period (1934–1940)
> The Termination Era (1940–1962)
> The Self-Determination Era (1962–Present).

Similarly, in each of the enumerated eras, primary attention is given to the work of Congress.

73. *Lone Wolf,* 187 U.S. at 566.

74. The Marshall trilogy refers to the three foundational Indian law cases decided by the Supreme Court under the leadership of Chief Justice Marshall: *Johnson v. McIntosh,* 21 U.S. 543 (1823) (holding that title to Indian land is held by the "discoverer" European nation with a remaining right of use and occupancy held by the tribe); *Cherokee Nation v. Georgia,* 30 U.S. 1 (1831) (denominating tribes as neither foreign nations nor states within Article III of the Constitution, but rather "domestic dependent nations"); and *Worcester v. Georgia,* 31 U.S. 515 (1832) (finding that Georgia state law has no force and effect in the Cherokee Nation or elsewhere in Indian country as Indian nations are "distinct, independent political communities"). The cases are discussed in depth in chapter 4.

75. This is best seen, for example, in the various (federal) Non-Intercourse Acts enacted from 1790 through 1834. This line of demarcation was itself fraught with tension:

> The goal of American statesmen was the orderly advance of the frontier. To maintain the desired order and tranquility[,] it was necessary to place restrictions on the contacts between the whites and the Indians. The

intercourse acts were thus restrictive and prohibitory in nature—aimed largely at restraining the actions of the whites and providing justice to the Indians as the means of preventing hostility. But if the goal was an *orderly* advance, it was nevertheless [an] *advance* of the frontier, and in the process of reconciling the two elements, conflict and injustice were often the result. (Francis Paul Prucha, *American Indian Policy in the Formative Years: The Indian Trade and Intercourse Acts, 1790–1834* (Bison Books, 1970), 3)

76. See, e.g., An act for the admission of the state of California into the Union, 9 Stat 452 (1850), (providing for the admission of California into the union); 1876 Executive Proclamation no. 6, 19 Stat. 665 (1876) (admitting Colorado to the union); An act to provide for the admission of the state of Idaho into the Union, Ch. 656, 26 Stat. 215 (1890) (providing for Idaho's admission into the union); An act for the admission of Kansas into the Union, Ch. 20, 12 Stat. 126 (1861) (admitting Kansas into the union); An act for the admission of the state of Nebraska into the Union, Ch. 36, 14 Stat. 391 (1867) (admitting Nebraska into the union); 1864 Presidential Executive Proclamation no. 21, 13 Stat. 749 (1864) (admitting Nevada into the union); An act to provide for the division into two states and to enable the people of North Dakota, South Dakota, Montana, and Washington to form constitutions and state governments and to be admitted into the Union on an equal footing with the original states, and to make donations of public lands to such states, Ch. 180, 25 Stat. 676 (1889) (providing for the admission of Montana, Washington, North Dakota, and South Dakota into the union); An act for the admission of Oregon into the Union, Ch. 33, 11 Stat. 383 (1859) (providing for the admission of Oregon); An act to extend the Laws of the United States over the state of Texas, and for other purposes, Ch. 1, 9 Stat. 1 (1845) (extending the laws of the United States to Texas); 1896 Presidential Proclamation no. 9, 29 Stat. 876 (1896) (providing for Utah's admission into the union); An act to provide for the admission of the state of Wyoming into the Union, and for other purposes, Ch. 664, 26 Stat. 222 (1890) (providing for the admission of Wyoming into the union).

77. This is one of the devastating effects set in motion by the allotment policy as authorized by the General Allotment Act (Dawes Severalty Act) 24 Stat. 388 (1887) (codified as amended at scattered sections of chapter 25 of the United States Code at 25 U.S.C. § 348 (2000)). See also the previous discussion.

An enormous loss of Indian land followed, with total Indian landholdings falling from 138 million acres in 1887 to 52 million acres in 1934. More than 26 million acres of allotted land was transferred out of Indian hands after it passed out of trust. Some of this individual allotted land was sold by arms-length transactions and some of it was lost by fraud, sharp dealing, mortgage foreclosures, and tax sales.... In addition, great chunks were carved out of many reservations when surplus lands were opened for homesteading. Sixty million of the 86 million acres lost to Indians by the allotment regime were due to the surplus lands facet of the 1887 act. (Wilkinson, *American Indians*, 20, endnotes omitted)

78. See, e.g., Frank Pommersheim, "Tribal Courts and the Federal Judiciary: Opportunities and Challenges for a Constitutional Democracy," 58 *Mont. L. Rev.* 313, 318–321 (1997); Frank Pommersheim, "Coyote Paradox: Some Indian Law Reflections from the Edge of the Prairie," 31 *Ariz. St. L. J.* 439, 473 (1999). That all of this was colonialist and against the will of the tribes goes without saying. The point is what are the possibilities *now*? The impetus of this book is to suggest a possibility—a possibility, incidentally, that is not meant to exclude other (complementary) possibilities. (See, e.g., the legislative proposal discussed in Tex Hall, Kelsey Begaye, John E. Echohawk, and Susan M. Williams, "Tribal Governance and Economic Enhancement Initiative," *Indian Country Today*, Oct. 11, 2002, A5.)

79. By this, it is meant that the primary federal concern was to regulate—sometimes through the mutuality of treaties, sometimes through congressional legislation—the process of exchange (including, on occasion, appropriation) of goods, land, natural resources, and separation of the governments and their respective peoples rather than interfering very much with how tribes exercised sovereignty and self-government within the reservation.

80. 118 U.S. 375, 384 (1886) (reasoning that Congress's enactment of the Major Crimes Act, while not sustainable within the text of the Constitution itself, was nevertheless permissible because of Indian tribe "weakness and helplessness" and the corresponding federal "duty of protection, and with it the power").

81. Ibid. at 375.

82. See ibid. at 384. This dependency concept drew some vitality from the trust relationship as a doctrine to protect tribes from the exercise of state power on the reservation. See the earlier discussion in this chapter.

83. Ibid. at 384–85.

84. The plenary power doctrine is the subject of extensive scholarly criticism and commentary. Judith Resnik cites the following authorities:

> *See* [Milner S.]Ball, [*Constitution, Court, Indian Tribes,*] 1987 AM. B. FOUND. RES. J. [1,] 46–59; Nell Jessup Newton, *Federal Power over Indians: Its Sources, Scope, and Limitations*, 132 U. PA. L. REV. 195, 197–98, 207–28, 236 ("plenary power" doctrine has been narrowed since the 1930s, but limits on congressional power still unclear); *Inherent Indian Sovereignty*, 4 AM. INDIAN L. REV. 311, 316–20 (1976) (Comment by Jessie D. Green and Susan Work). For debate about the utility for Indian tribes of Congressional "plenary power," *see* Robert Laurence, *Learning to Live with the Plenary Power of Congress over the Indian Nations*, 30 ARIZ. L. REV. 413 (1988) (replying to [Robert A.] Williams, [Jr.] [*The Algebra of Federal Indian Law: The Hard Trail of Decolonizing and Americanizing the White Man's Indian Jurisprudence,*] 1986 WIS. L. REV. 219; Robert A. Williams Jr., *Learning Not to Live with Eurocentric Myopia: A Reply to Professor Laurence*, 30 ARIZ. L. REV. 439 (1988); Robert Laurence, *On Eurocentric Myopia, the Designated Hitter Rule and "The Actual State of Things,"* 30 ARIZ. L. REV. 459 (1988)). (Judith Resnik, "Dependent Sovereigns: Indian Tribes, States and the Federal Courts," 56 *U. Chi. L. Rev.* 671, 693 n. 99 (1989))

In addition, see the critique and sources cited by Robert N. Clinton, "Tribal Courts and the Federal Union," 26 *Willamette L. Rev.* 841, 847 (1990); Robert N. Clinton, "There Is No Federal Supremacy Clause for Indians," 34 *Ariz. St. L. J.* 113 (2002).

85. Such constitutional "incorporation"—at least in my thinking—would have to proceed on a consent model. See, e.g., Russell L. Barsh and James Y. Henderson, *The Road: Indian Tribes and Political Liberty* (University of California Press, 1980), 270–82; Frank Pommersheim, "Is There a (Little or Not So Little) Constitutional Crisis Developing in Indian Law? A Brief Essay," 5 *U. Pa. J. Const. L.* 271 (2003). See also the detailed discussion in chapter 10.

86. An act to provide for the allotment of Indian lands in severalty to Indians on various reservations and to extend the protection of the laws of the United States and Territories over Indians, and for other purposes, Ch. 114, 24 Stat. 388 (1887).

87. The General Allotment Act provided potential federal citizenship for Indian allottees who held fee patents on their allotments. See, e.g., 25 U.S.C. § 348 (2000) (enacted as part of 24 Stat. 388). All Native people became federal citizens pursuant to the Citizenship Act of 1924, 8 U.S.C. § 1401(b) (2000). The issue of citizenship is also significant as a force to vitiate any claim that plenary power in regard to tribes and tribal people is somehow analogous to the "plenary" power of national sovereigns under international law to deal with the immigration of "foreigners." Obviously, it was (and is) a tortured analogy to compare foreigners to indigenous people, but such were (and are) the problems of colonization and the rule of law. See, e.g., Philip P. Frickey, "Domesticating Federal Indian Law," 81 *Minn. L. Rev.* 31 (1996). The issue of citizenship itself, both federal and state, is *not* without controversy. See, e.g., Clinton, "No Federal Supremacy," 246–52; Pommersheim, "Coyote Paradox," 472–75. See also the detailed discussion in chapter 6.

88. 435 U.S. 191 (1978) (holding that tribes have no criminal jurisdiction over non-Indians).

89. 450 U.S. 544, 565–66 (1981) (stating tribes have no civil jurisdiction over non-Indians on fee land within the reservation unless there is a "consensual relationship with the tribe or its members" or the non-Indian conduct "has some direct effect on the political integrity, the economic security, or health or welfare of the tribe"). These exceptions have almost never been satisfied when scrutinized by the Supreme Court. The fee land aspect of the *Montana* landscape has been expanded to include land taken by the federal government to build a dam, *South Dakota v. Bourland*, 508 U.S. 679 (1993); a state highway running through a reservation pursuant to a right of way granted by the tribe, *Strate v. A-1 Contractors*, 520 U.S. 438 (1997); and ultimately to all land on the reservation regardless of its nature or ownership, *Nevada v. Hicks*, 533 U.S. 353 (2001). See also *Atkinson Trading Co. v. Shirley*, 532 U. S. 645 (2001) (holding that the Navajo Tribe may not assert hotel use tax on non-Indian customers staying at a non-Indian motel located on fee land within the reservation).

90. 128 S.Ct. 2709 (2008) (concluding that *Montana* analysis does not apply to the sale of fee land within the reservation by a non-Indian to an Indian).

91. The manipulation is to treat *Montana*, a case described in its own terms as involving statutory construction of the General Allotment Act, to stand for a free-floating proposition creating a presumption against tribal jurisdiction over

non-Indians anyplace on the reservation. See *Montana*, 450 U.S. at 559 n. 9 (stating, "There is simply no suggestion in the legislative history that Congress intended that non-Indians who would settle upon *alienated allotted lands* would be subject to tribal regulatory authority") (emphasis added). See generally *Brendale v. Confederated Yakima Indian Nation*, 492 U.S. 408, 422 (1989) (stating, "We analyzed the effect of the General Allotment Act on an Indian tribe's rights to regulate activities of nonmembers on the land in *Montana v. United States*").

92. David H. Getches, "Conquering the Cultural Frontier: The New Subjectivism of the Supreme Court in Indian Law," 84 *Cal. L. Rev.* 1573 (1996). Getches detects increasing "subjectivism" in Supreme Court Indian law jurisprudence premised on judicial considerations—of "what ought to be"—and he wisely counsels against this trend:

> The foundation principles of Indian law demand resistance to the temptation of judicial activism. A return to foundation principles, furthermore, would spare tribes the subjective judgments of courts by requiring congressional action, with the scrutiny of the political process and the tribes' full participation, before modifying their rights as sovereigns. Indian rights do not depend on sympathy for the plight or historical mistreatment of Native Americans. Self-determination for tribes is rooted in ancient laws and treaties, and is protected against incursions except those that Congress deliberately allows. Well-meaning judicial attempts to balance and accommodate interests of Indians and non-Indians not only are inconsistent with the limited role of courts, as sanctioned by the foundation principles of Indian law, but are inevitably culturally charged. (Ibid., 1654–55)

93. Philip P. Frickey, "A Common Law for Our Age of Colonialism: The Judicial Divestiture of Indian Tribal Authority over Nonmembers," 109 *Yale L. J.* 1 (1999). Frickey discerns a seismic self-aggrandizing shift in the role of the Supreme Court in Indian law:

> In establishing the plenary power of Congress over Indian affairs, the Court performed the perhaps disappointing, but nonetheless unsurprising, role of the "court of the conqueror" reflected in *Johnson v. McIntosh*: It deferred to established patterns and practices designed to centralize the colonial power in the political branches. When it, in effect, arrogated to itself a judicially enforceable "dormant" aspect of this power, however, the Court has become an actor imposing its own set of colonial values, not merely an agent of congressional choices. This second step seems remarkable, even given the realities of a colonial society. The Court has transformed itself from the court of the conqueror into the court as the conqueror. (Ibid., 73, footnote omitted)

94. Pommersheim, "Tribal Courts." I have also identified this metastasis of plenary power:

> The plenary power doctrine can now be seen as coming in two distinct vintages. There is the classic doctrine of congressional plenary power as established in *Lone Wolf*. Yet even if Congress has not acted—where one

would normally presuppose an unimpaired tribal sovereignty—the Court now recognizes a judicial plenary power to parse the limits of tribal court authority based on federal common law. A federal common law that at least heretofore has not been equated with any notion of implied divestiture of tribal authority. (Ibid., 328, footnote omitted)

95. Ibid. This is the beginning, if it is a beginning, of long, arduous legal and political struggle. It would be naive to think otherwise, but then again, every journey must somehow begin. See generally Barsh and Henderson, *The Road*. Also see the in-depth discussion in chapter 10.

96. Sarah H. Cleveland, "Powers Inherent in Sovereignty: Indians, Aliens, Territories, and the Nineteenth Century Origins of Plenary Power over Foreign Affairs," 81 *Texas L. Rev.* 1 (2002). This exceptional article (284 pages, 1,841 footnotes!) is the source of much of what is discussed in this section.

97. Ibid., 95.

98. Ibid., 96.

Finally, the Act's opponents rejected the suggestion that the Constitution did not protect aliens. The mere fact that aliens were not parties to the Constitution, Madison argued, did not establish that Congress had absolute power over them, since "[t]he parties to the Constitution may have granted, or retained, or modified, the [international law] power over aliens, without regard to that particular consideration." (Ibid., quoting Madison's Report at 556)

99. 92 U.S. 259 (1875).

100. Ibid. at 270.

101. Cleveland, "Powers Inherent," 110.

102. *Edye v. Robertson*, 112 U.S. 580 (1884) (holding that treaties with foreign nations were subject to acts passed by Congress for the treaties' enforcement, modification, and repeal).

103. Ibid. at 600.

104. Ibid.

105. 130 U.S. 581 (1889) (holding that treaties are of no greater legal obligation than an act of Congress and affirming the denial of entry of a Chinese laborer because the U.S. government has the right to exclude Chinese laborers as part of the sovereign powers delegated by the Constitution).

106. *Chae Chan Ping*, 130 U.S. at 606–7.

107. Ibid. at 604.

108. *Kagama*, 118 U.S. at 384–85.

109. *Lone Wolf*, 187 U.S. at 566.

110. Cleveland, "Powers Inherent," 158. See, e.g., *Yick Wo v. Hopkins*, 118 U.S. 356 (1886); *Wong Wing v. United States*, 103 U.S. 228 (1896); *United States v. Wong Kim Ark*, 169 U.S. 649 (1898).

111. Cleveland, "Powers Inherent," 158.

112. See Articles of Confederation, Art. XI ("Canada acceding to this confederation, and adjoining in the measures of the United States, shall be admitted into, and

entitled to all the advantages of this Union; but no other colony shall be admitted into the same, unless such admission be agreed to by nine States").

113. U.S. Const. art. IV, § 3, cl. 2. Clause 1 provides for the admission of new states:

> New States may be admitted by the Congress into this Union; but no new State shall be formed or erected within the Jurisdiction of any other State; nor any State be formed by the Junction of two or more States, or Parts of States, without the Consent of the Legislatures of the States concerned as well as of the Congress.

114. Cleveland, "Powers Inherent," 168–69.

115. Ibid., 164 (citations omitted).

116. Ibid., 169.

117. Ibid., 171 (quoting Paul Ford, ed., *The Writings of Thomas Jefferson* (1892), 244).

118. Ibid., 177–78 (quoting Letter from Thomas Jefferson to DeWitt Clinton (Dec. 2, 1803) in *The Writings of Thomas Jefferson*, 283).

119. Ibid., 179.

120. Ibid.

121. Ibid., 182.

122. *Scott v. Sandford*, 60 U.S. (19 How.) 393 (1857).

123. Ibid. at 401.

124. U.S. Const. Amend. XIII (abolishing slavery); U.S. Const. Amend. XIV (equal protection of the laws); U.S. Const. Amend XV (voting rights for emancipated men).

125. The Fourteenth Amendment provides:

> Section 1. All persons born or naturalized in the United States, and subject to the jurisdiction thereof, are citizens of the United States and of the State wherein they reside. No State shall make or enforce any law which shall abridge the privileges or immunities of citizens of the United States; nor shall any State deprive any person of life, liberty, or property, without due process of law; nor deny to any person within its jurisdiction the equal protection of the laws.

126. Cleveland, "Powers Inherent," 196–97. *Elk v. Wilkins*, 112 U.S. 94 (1884). See the detailed discussion in chapter 6.

127. 101 U.S. 129 (1879).

128. Ibid.; Cleveland, "Powers Inherent," 199.

129. Ibid. at 133 (alteration in original) (emphasis added).

130. 114 U.S. 15 (1885).

131. 136 U.S. 1 (1890).

132. Cleveland, "Powers Inherent," 201 (citations omitted).

133. See the earlier discussion of *Kagama v. United States*, 118 U.S. 375 (1886), where extensive federal power is invoked to protect tribes against the states, their "deadliest enemies."

134. Cleveland, "Powers Inherent," 208.

135. Ibid., 212.

136. See, e.g., *Armstrong v. United States*, 182 U.S. 243 (1901); *DeLima v. Bidwell*, 182 U.S. 1 (1901); *Dooley v. United States*, 182 U.S. 222 (1901) (holding that the taxation of imports from New York into Puerto Rico after cession of the island to the United States was improper as Puerto Rico ceased to be a foreign country); *Downes v. Bidwell*, 182 U.S. 244 (1901) (holding that Puerto Rico is territory appurtenant and belonging to the United States, but not part of the United States); *Fourteen Diamond Rings v. United States*, 182 U.S. 176 (1901) (finding that the Philippine Islands did not qualify as a foreign country within the meaning of certain tariff laws requiring duties on imported items); *Goetze v. United States*, 182 U.S. 221 (1901); *Huus v. New York & Porto Rico S.S. Co.*, 182 U.S. 392 (1901); *Hawaii v. Mankichi*, 190 U.S. 197 (1903) (finding that certain constitutional jury provisions were inapplicable to Hawaii after its annexation); *Dorr v. United States*, 195 U.S. 138 (1904) (holding that the right to trial by jury is not constitutionally required in the Philippines); *Kepner v. United States*, 195 U.S. 100 (1905) (finding that the prohibition against double jeopardy applies in the Philippines because of congressional legislation, not through application of the Constitution); *Rasmussen v. United States*, 197 U.S. 516 (1905) (holding that grand jury and jury trial rights are applicable in Alaska because Alaska is an incorporated territory).

137. *Downes v. Bidwell*, 182 U.S. 244, 302–4 (1901) (White, J., concurring).

138. Cited by the United States in its brief in *Bidwell* for the proposition that the United States enjoyed plenary authority over territorial inhabitants. Cleveland, "Powers Inherent," 219.

139. Ibid., 212.

140. *United States v. Wheeler*, 435 U.S. 313, 323 (holding that Indian tribes are separate sovereigns for purposes of the Double Jeopardy Clause). See also *Talton v. Mayes*, 163 U.S. 376 (1890) (constraints of Constitution do not apply against the tribes because their powers are preconstitutional, but they are nevertheless subject to the paramount legislative authority of the United States).

141. 541 U.S. 193 (2004). This case is discussed extensively in chapter 8.

142. *Lara*, 541 U.S. at 225.

CHAPTER SIX

1. U.S. Const., art. I, § 2, cl. 3, *amended by* U.S. Const. Amend. XIV, § 2 (emphasis added).

2. The identical language of Article I, Section 2, Clause 3, is *repeated* in the Fourteenth Amendment, which does excise reference to the three-fifths rule.

3. See, e.g., the power of Congress to confer citizenship through the process of naturalization. U.S. Const., art. I, § 8, cl. 4.

4. Any treaty negotiated by the president has to be ratified by a two-thirds vote of the Senate. U.S. Const., art. II, § 2, cl. 2.

5. Indian Citizenship Act, 43 Stat. 253 (1924).

6. See, e.g., the later discussion in this chapter.

7. Treaty with the Cherokees, July 8, 1817, art. 8, 7 Stat. 156, 159 (emphasis added). A formal removal statute was enacted by Congress in 1830, 4 Stat. 411.

8. Treaty with the Choctaws, Sept. 27, 1830, 7 Stat. 333, 333, 335 (emphasis added). The Choctaws who remained behind in Mississippi were eventually recognized as a federally recognized tribe, known as the Mississippi Band of Choctaw Indians. *See United States v. John*, 437 U.S. 634 (1978).

9. Treaty between the United States of America and the Senecas, mixed Senecas and Shawnees, Quapaws, Confederated, Peorias, Kaskaskias, Weas; and Piankeshaws, Ottawas of Blanchard's Fork and Roche de Boeuf, and certain Wyandotts. Feb. 27, 1867, 15 Stat. 513.

10. Ibid. at art. XVII (emphasis added).

11. Treaty with the Wyandotts, Jan. 31, 1855, art. 1, 10 Stat. 1159, 1159 (emphasis added).

12. Treaty with the Delawares, July 4, 1866, art. IX, 14 Stat. 793, 796 (emphasis added). Article IX also required the acceptance of a fee patent and termination of tribal membership.

13. The issuance of a fee patent lifted restrictions against alienability and taxation.

14. Treaty with the Sioux Indians, Apr. 29, 1868, art. VI, 15 Stat. 635, 637 (emphasis added).

15. *United States v. Lucero*, 1 N.M. 422 (1869); Treaty with the Republic of Mexico, Feb. 2, 1848, 9 Stat. 922. This precise issue was avoided by the U.S. Supreme Court in *United States v. Sandoval*, 231 U.S. 28, 48 (1913) with its curt observation: "As before stated, whether they are citizens is an open question, and we need not determine it now."

16. See the general discussion of allotment in chapter 5.

17. 24 Stat. 388 (1887).

18. 24 Stat. 388, 390. Note the inclusion of nonallotted Indians who have taken up residence "separate and apart" from their tribe and adopted "the habits of civilized life."

19. Ibid.

20. See, e.g., *United States v. Celestine*, 215 U.S. 278, 291 (1909) (stating "Congress, in granting full rights of citizenship to Indians, believed that it had been hasty").

21. 25 U.S.C. § 349 (2000); see also 34 Stat. 182 (1906).

22. Matthew Spalding, "Making Citizens: The Case for Patriotic Assimilation," *First Principles Series No. 3* (Heritage Foundation, 2006), 7.

23. 25 U.S.C. § 182 (1888).

24. An Act Granting citizenship to certain Indians, Pub. L. No. 66–75, 41 Stat. 350 (Nov. 6, 1919).

25. 8 USC § 1401 (a)(2) (2000). Note the language that expressly prohibits conditioning U.S. citizenship on tribal status or affiliation.

26. 112 U.S. 94 (1884).

27. U.S. Const. Amend. XIV, § 1.

28. U.S. Const. Amend. XV, § 1.

29. *Elk*, 112 U.S. at 98.

30. Ibid. at 99.

31. U.S. Const., art. I, § 2, cl. 3.

32. U.S. Const. Amend. XIV (emphasis added).

33. *Elk*, 112 U.S. at 102.

34. Ibid.

35. Ibid. at 103. Interestingly, such a construction was about to buckle with the enactment of the Major Crimes Act, 18 USC § 1153, in 1885, in which the United States asserted direct federal jurisdiction over major crimes committed by Indians in Indian country, regardless of their tribal affiliation.

36. *Elk*, 112 U.S. at 103 (quoting 14 Stat. 27–30).

37. An Act making Appropriations for the current and contingent Expenses of the Indian Department and for fulfilling treaty stipulations with various Indian Tribes for the Year ending June thirty, eighteen hundred and seventy-one, and for other Purposes, July 15, 1870, 16 Stat. 335.

38. An Act to abolish the tribal relations of the Miami Indians and for other purposes, Mar. 8, 1873, 17 Stat. 631.

39. *Elk*, 112 U.S. at 104–5 (citing 16 Stat. 361).

40. Ibid. at 106–7.

41. Civil Rights Act of 1866, Apr. 9, 1866, 14 Stat. 27, 27.

42. *Elk*, 112 U.S. at 112–13 (Harlan, J., dissenting).

43. Ibid. at 115 (Harlan, J., dissenting).

44. Ibid. at 122–23 (Harlan, J., dissenting).

45. *United States ex rel. Standing Bear v. Crook*, 25 F. Cas. 695, 697 (D. Neb. 1879) (No. 14,891). The Court ruled against Standing Bear on the merits.

46. See *In re Heff*, 197 U.S. 488 (1905).

47. See the discussion in chapters 3 and 4 concerning the trust relationship as a source of federal authority in Indian affairs and its partial grounding in cultural condescension and racial animus.

48. *In re Heff*, 197 U.S. at 499.

49. Ibid. at 502–3. Note that this was before the Burke Act of 1907, which delayed citizenship until a fee patent, as opposed to a trust patent, was issued.

50. Ibid. at 504. Many states did not agree. See the later discussion in this chapter.

51. Ibid. at 505.

52. Ibid. at 507.

53. 241 U.S. 591 (1916).

54. Ibid. at 601.

55. Ibid.

56. Ibid. at 598.

57. 187 U.S. 553 (1903).

58. *Ex parte Greer*, 123 F.2d 862 (2d Cir. 1941); Robert Porter, "The Demise of the Ongwehoweh and the Rise of Native Americans: Redressing the Genocidal Act of Forcing American Citizenship upon Indigenous Peoples," 15 *Harv. BlackLetter L. J.* 107 (1999).

59. 143 U.S. 135 (1892).

60. Ibid. at 170.

61. See ibid. at 161–64.

62. *Dred Scott v.Sanford*, 60 U.S. 393, 403–4 (1856).

63. Idaho Const. art. VI, § 3 (1890) (emphasis added). The Idaho constitution also cites the state constitutions of Washington and Wyoming as sources for this provision.

64. Idaho Const. art. VI, § 3 (1950). The constitution was amended again in 1982 to remove the remaining offensive language.

65. Minn. Const., art. VII, § 1 (1857) (emphasis added).

66. Ibid. The constitution was generally revised in 1974.

67. N.M. Const., art. VII, § 1 (1911) (emphasis added).

68. N.M. Const., art. VII, § 1 (1967).

69. N.D. Const., art. V, § 121 (1889) (emphasis added).

70. See N.D. Const., art. V, § 121 (1922).

71. Wash. Const., art. VI, § 1 (1889).

72. Wash. Const., art. VI, § 1 (1974).

73. No. 1350 (D.N.M. Aug. 11, 1948). *Trujillo* was unreported.

74. Jeanette Wolfley, "Jim Crow, Indian Style: The Disenfranchisement of Native Americans," 16 *Am. Indian L. Rev.* 167, 185–86 (1991) (quoting *Trujillo*, No. 1350 (D.N.M. Aug. 11, 1948).

75. Ibid. at 185.

76. 271 P. 411 (Ariz. 1928).

77. Ibid. at 414.

78. Ibid. at 416.

79. 196 P.2d 456 (Ariz. 1948).

80. Ibid. at 461.

81. Ibid. at 463.

82. *Osphal v. Johnson*, 163 N.W. 988, 989 (Minn. 1917) (quoting Minn. Const., art. VII, § 1 (1857)).

83. Ibid. at 990.

84. Ibid. at 991.

85. Ibid. at 989.

86. Ibid. (emphasis added) (quoting *Bem-Way-Bin-Ness v. Eshelby*, 91 N.W. 291, 292 (Minn. 1902).

87. Ibid. at 991.

88. Utah Code Ann. § 20–2–14 (1953).

89. 305 P.2d 490 (Utah 1956).

90. Ibid. at 491.

91. Ibid. at 492.

92. Ibid. at 495.

93. 372 P.2d 387 (N.M. 1962).

94. Ibid. at 395.

95. *Prince v. Board of Education*, 543 P.2d 1176 (N.M. 1975).

96. 42 U.S.C. § 1973 (2000).

97. Voting Rights Act Amendments of 1975, 41 Fed. Reg. 784 (Jan. 5, 1976). The preclearance provisions require prior approval of the U.S. Attorney General of any

proposed state legislation dealing with voting and the establishment of voting districts at any level within the state.

98. Laughlin McDonald, "The Voting Rights Act in Indian Country: South Dakota, a Case Study," 29 *Am. Ind. L. Rev.* 43 (2005). Janklow's quotations may be found in 1977 S.D. Op. Att'y Gen. 175 (1977) available at 1977 WL 36011.

99. 383 U.S. 301 (1966).

100. Ibid. at 360 (Black, J., dissenting). The S.D. Attorney General's Opinion quotes Justice Black's language directly but cites H.R. Doc. No. 94–196, 94th Cong. 1st Sess. 73 (1975) as its source.

101. 1977 S.D. Op. Att'y Gen. 175 (1977) at 8, available at 1977 WL 36011.

102. McDonald, "The Voting Rights Act," 44. The state never obtained relief under the statute's "bail out" provision and remains subject to the preclearance requirements.

103. Ibid., 54.

104. Ibid., 59.

105. Ibid., 54–65. "Some of the most compelling testimony in the *Bone Shirt* case [the Rosebud–Pine Ridge litigation], and which was credited by the district court, came from tribal members who recounted 'numerous incidents of being mistreated, embarrassed or humiliated by whites.'" Ibid., 63.

106. John Wildermuth, "Parties Anticipate Close Election; Observers Mobilize for Big Day, Lawyers Prepare for Fallout," *San Francisco Chronicle*, Sept. 18, 2004, at A1.

107. See ibid.

108. John-John Williams IV, "Voter Registration Charges Dropped," *Sioux Falls Argus Leader*, January 29, 2004, at A1.

109. S.D. Codified Laws § 12–18–6.1 (2006) provides:

Voters Required to provide identification before voting.
    When the voter is requesting a ballot, the voter shall present a valid form of personal identification. The personal identification that may be presented shall be either:
    A South Dakota driver's license or nondriver identification card;
    A passport or an identification card, including a picture, issued by an agency of the United States government;
    A tribal identification card, including a picture; or
    A current student identification card, including a picture, issued by a high school, an accredited institution of higher education, including a university, college, or technical school, located within the State of South Dakota.

The constitutionality of photo identification requirements was upheld by the U.S. Supreme Court in the 2008 case of *Crawford v. Marion County Election Board*, 128 S.Ct. 1610 (2008).

110. SDCL § 12–18–6.2 (2006) provides:

Affidavit in lieu of personal identification.
    If a voter is not able to present a form of personal identification as required by § 12–18–6.1, the voter may complete an affidavit in lieu of the

personal identification. The State Board of Elections shall promulgate rules, pursuant to chapter 1–26, prescribing the form of the affidavit. The affidavit shall require the voter to provide his or her name and address. The voter shall sign the affidavit under penalty of perjury.

Yet it remains unclear how well this exception is known to the Native American public and how vigorously it will be made available to them at the polls. Without photo identification, many Native Americans are probably not even going to attempt to vote.

111. 42 U.S.C. § 1973(c). The preclearance provisions expressly apply to Todd and Shannon counties. In the consent decree in the *Blackmoon* case, Charles Mix County voluntarily agreed to be subject to the preclearance requirement.

112. Letter from Grace Chung Becker, Acting Assistant Attorney General, Civil Rights Division, United States Department of Justice (February 11, 2008) (copy on file with author).

> The timing of the adoption of the proposed change to a five member commission raises concerns of a discriminatory purpose. The first petitioner signed the referendum petition to increase the size of the commission on April 3, 2006. Only 46 people signed the initial circulation prior to June 2006. At the June 2006 Democratic Primary election, Ms. Drapeau won, and she would become the first Native American County Commissioner in Charles Mix County because there was no opponent in the general election. Immediately after the primary election, an article about changing the number of county commissioners appeared in *The Lake Andes Wave*. Momentum for the petition then built, and one thousand signatures were obtained to put the referendum on the ballot. The referendum was held in November 2006, and the measure passed.
>
> Elected officials supported the increase in the number of county commissioners. In particular, the Sheriff and his deputies, actively circulated the petition. According to our contacts in the county, the Sheriff and deputies collected signatures in uniform.
>
> Depositions in *Blackmoon* reveal that one commissioner admitted that the commissioners decided not to redistrict in 2000 despite the fact that they knew that the districts did not provide Native Americans the voting strength to elect a candidate of choice. Various community members, including Native Americans and non-Native Americans, also have informed the Section that county commissioners have made comments that evidence a racially discriminatory intent.

113. See the discussion in chapter 5.

114. For example, the State of Washington entered into the Washington Centennial Accord with the state's sovereign tribes in 1989. Accords of this nature provide for mutual respect between the state and tribes that can lead to meaningful problem solving. Frank Pommersheim, *Braid of Feathers: American Indian Law and Contemporary Tribal Life* (University of California Press, 1995), 154.

CHAPTER SEVEN

1. The First Amendment of the U.S. Constitution states in relevant part:

Congress shall make no law respecting an establishment of religion, or prohibiting the free exercise thereof; or abridging the freedom of speech, or of the press; or the right of the people peaceably to assemble, and to petition the Government for a redress of grievances.

Its two central components recognize, on one hand, the *free exercise* right of the individual, and on the other, a prohibition against governmental *establishment* of any religion.

2. 163 U.S. 376 (1896).

3. 25 U.S.C. §§ 1301–1303 (2000). Section 1302 provides:

No Indian tribe in exercising powers of self-government shall—

(1) make or enforce any law prohibiting the free exercise of religion, or abridging the freedom of speech, or of the press, or the right of the people peaceably to assemble and to petition for a redress of grievances;

(2) violate the right of the people to be secure in their persons, houses, papers, and effects against unreasonable search and seizures, nor issue warrants, but upon probable cause, supported by oath or affirmation, and particularly describing the place to be searched and the person or thing to be seized;

(3) subject any person for the same offense to be twice put in jeopardy;

(4) compel any person in any criminal case to be a witness against himself;

(5) take any private property for a public use without just compensation;

(6) deny to any person in a criminal proceeding the right to a speedy and public trial, to be informed of the nature and cause of the accusation, to be confronted with the witnesses against him, to have compulsory process for obtaining witnesses in his favor, and at his own expense to have the assistance of counsel for his defense;

(7) require excessive bail, impose excessive fines, inflict cruel and unusual punishments, and in no event impose for conviction of any one offense any penalty or punishment greater than imprisonment for a term of one year and a fine of $5,000, or both;

(8) deny to any person within its jurisdiction the equal protection of its laws or deprive any person of liberty or property without due process of law;

(9) pass any bill of attainder or ex post facto law; or

(10) deny to any person accused of an offense punishable by imprisonment the right, upon request, to a trial by jury of not less than six persons.

4. The lack of an establishment clause ban in the ICRA of 1968 was largely the result of a congressional commitment to protect those tribes, mainly the Southwestern Pueblos, who do *not* readily recognize any distinction between their religious and secular governance.

5. See, e.g., Rosebud Sioux Tribe Const. art. X, § 1 ("All members of the tribe and all Indians on the reservation shall enjoy without hindrance freedom of religion… conscience and association"); Miss. Band of Choctaw Indians Const. art. X, § 1(a) ("The Mississippi Band of Choctaw Indians, in exercising powers of self-government shall not make or enforce any law prohibiting the free exercise of religion…").

6. Recent scholarly articles discussing tribal court jurisprudence have not mentioned any free exercise cases. See, e.g., L. M. Fletcher, "Toward a Theory of Intertribal and Intratribal Common Law," 43 *Hous. L. Rev.* 701 (2006).

7. 21 U.S. 543 (1823). See a full discussion in chapter 4.

8. Allison M. Dussias, "Ghost Dance and Holy Ghost: The Echoes of Nineteenth-Century Christianization Policy in Twentieth-Century Native American Free Exercise Cases," 49 *Stan. L. Rev.* 773, 774–75 (1997).

9. Ibid., 777.

10. Ibid., 777–78.

11. Ibid., 778–79.

12. Ibid., 781.

13. Ibid., 784.

14. Ibid.

15. Ibid.

16. Ibid., 785.

17. 210 U.S. 50 (1908).

18. Ibid. at 60.

19. Ibid. at 82 (quoting the opinion of the Court of Appeals).

20. 35 Stat. 781 (1909).

21. 1883 Secretary of Interior, Ann. Rep. at X, as quoted in Dussias, "Ghost Dance," 788.

22. Dussias, "Ghost Dance," 788–89.

23. Office of Indian Affairs, Circular No. 1665, April 26, 1921, quoted in Felix Cohen, *Handbook of Federal Indian Law* (University of New Mexico Press, 1942 ed.), 175 n. 347 (second alteration in original).

24. Dussias, "Ghost Dance," 789–90.

25. Dee Brown, *Bury My Heart at Wounded Knee: An Indian History of the American West* (Holt, 1970), 435 (quoting Wovoka, the Nevada Paiute Indian who received the core vision that animated the Ghost Dance religion). As quoted in Dussias, "Ghost Dance, 794. See also James Mooney, *The Ghost Dance Religion and the Sioux Outbreak of 1890* (1896), 782, describing the moral core of the Ghost Dance religion "as pure and comprehensive in its simplicity as anything found in religious systems from the days of Gautama Buddha to the time of Jesus Christ."

26. Dussias, "Ghost Dance," 795.

27. Ibid., 796–97.

28. Ibid., 799.

29. Ibid., 800. The regulation provided as follows:

The "sun dance" and all other similar dances and so-called religious ceremonies, shall be considered "Indian offenses," and any Indian found guilty of being a participant in any one or more of those offenses shall...be punished by withholding from him his rations for a period of not exceeding ten days; and if found guilty of any subsequent offense under this rule, shall be punished by withholding his rations for a period of not less than fifteen days nor more than thirty days, or by incarceration in the agency prison for a period not exceeding thirty days." (Secretary of Interior, Regulations of the Indian Office (1904) at 102–3, quoted in Walter R. Echo-Hawk, "Native American Religious Liberty: Five Hundred Years after Columbus," *Am. Indian Culture & Res. J.* 33, 37 (1993))

The dance ban was not lifted until 1934. Ibid. at 37. Quoted in Dussias, "Ghost Dance," 800 n. 198.

30. Dussias, "Ghost Dance," 802.

31. Ibid., 801.

32. Ibid.

33. Ibid., 800–801. The "give away" ceremony is particularly instructive. In such ceremonies, Indian people distributed much personal property as a way to "honor" people who had helped their children and families. The irony is patent. Such generosity would seem most Christian with its ethos to share and share alike. Yet it must yield, apparently, to the vessel of accumulation on the altar of capitalism.

34. Ibid., 804. Previous regulations had required attendance at church and Sunday school by all Indian students at government boarding schools (803).

35. 620 F.2d 1159 (6th Cir. 1980), *cert. denied*, 449 U.S. 953 (1980).

36. Ibid. at 1164.

37. Ibid. (citations omitted).

38. 638 F.2d 172 (10th Cir. 1980), *cert. denied*, 452 U.S. 954 (1981).

39. Ibid. at 176.

40. Ibid. at 176–77.

41. Ibid. at 178–79. *See also Wilson v. Block*, 708 F.2d 735 (D.C. Cir. 1983) (the D.C. Circuit court similarly held that the federal government's management and improvement of the Snow Bowl ski area did *not* impair the Navajo and Hopi ability to practice their religion because there was government consultation with the tribes and there would still be access to the area for religious purposes).

42. See, e.g., *Sherbert v. Verner*, 374 U.S. 398 (1963); *Wisconsin v. Yoder*, 406 U.S. 205 (1972). In both of these cases, minority religion plaintiffs prevailed. In *Sherbert*, the context was eligibility for state unemployment benefits, and in *Yoder* the claim involved resistance to mandatory school attendance.

43. 485 U.S. 439 (1988). The case also involved a number of environmental group plaintiffs who claimed the proposed project violated several federal environmental statutes, including the Federal Water Pollution Control Act, 86 Stat. 896, and the National Environmental Policy Act (NEPA) of 1969, 83 Stat. 852. There was also an additional Native American claim that the proposed project violated the federal government's trust relationship with Native Americans.

44. Ibid. at 442.

45. Ibid.

46. Ibid.
47. Ibid. at 443.
48. Ibid. at 444–45.
49. Ibid. at 441–42.
50. Ibid. at 449 (emphasis in the original).
51. Ibid. at 451.
52. Ibid. at 450.
53. Ibid. at 452.
54. Ibid. at 453 (emphasis in the original).
55. Ibid. at 454.
56. Ibid. at 460 (Brennan, J., dissenting).
57. Ibid. at 460–61 (Brennan, J., dissenting).
58. Ibid. at 477 (Brennan, J., dissenting).
59. Ibid. at 465 (Brennan, J., dissenting).
60. Ibid. at 465–66 (Brennan, J., dissenting) (emphasis added).
61. Ibid. at 472 (Brennan, J., dissenting).
62. Ibid. at 473 (Brennan, J., dissenting).
63. Ibid. (Brennan, J., dissenting).
64. This "stress point" involves "the longstanding conflict between two disparate cultures—the dominant Western culture, which views land in terms of ownership and use, and that of Native-Americans, in which such concepts are not only alien, but contrary to a belief system that holds land sacred." Ibid. (Brennan, J., dissenting).
65. Ibid. (Brennan, J., dissenting).

Such an abdication is more than merely indefensible, as an institutional matter: by defining respondents' injury as "non-constitutional" the Court has effectively bestowed on one party to this conflict the unilateral authority to resolve all future disputes in its favor, subject only to the Court's toothless exhortation to be "sensitive" to affected religions. In my view, however, Native Americans deserve—and the Constitution demands—more than this. (Ibid., Brennan, J., dissenting).

66. Ibid. at 477 (Brennan, J., dissenting).
67. Ibid. at 475 (Brennan, J., dissenting).
68. 42 U.S.C. § 1996. Section 2 of the Act provided as follows:

The President shall direct the various Federal departments, agencies, and other instrumentalities responsible for administering relevant laws to evaluate their policies and procedures in consultation with native traditional religious leaders in order to determine appropriate changes necessary to protect and preserve Native American religious cultural rights and practices. Twelve months after approval of this resolution, the President shall report back to the Congress the results of this evaluation, including any changes which were made in administrative policies; and procedures, and any recommendations he may have for legislative actions. (Pub. L. No. 95–341, § 2, 92 Stat. 470)

Even this statute was rather hollow, as the *Lyng* case held that "[n]owhere in the law is there so much as a hint of any intent to create a cause of action or any judicially enforceable individual rights." 485 U.S. at 455.

69. 16 U.S.C. § 460bbb (2000).

70. 16 U.S.C. § 470 *et seq.* (2000).

71. 61 Fed. Reg. 26,771 (May 24, 1996).

72. This is the official (non-Indian) legal name. Native Americans prefer the name Bear Lodge. Joel Brady, "'Land Is Itself a Sacred Living Being': Native American Sacred Site Protection on Federal Public Land amidst the Shadows of Bear Lodge," 24 *Am. Indian L. Rev.* 153, 155 (2000).

73. *Bear Lodge Multiple Use Ass'n v. Babbitt* (No. 96-CV-063 D (D. Wyo., June 8, 1996)).

74. *Bear Lodge Multiple Use Ass'n v. Babbitt*, 2 F. Supp. 2d 1448 (D. Wyo. 1998), *aff'd*, 175 F.3d 814 (10th Cir. 1999), *cert. denied* 529 U.S. 1037 (2000). The District Court noted that "governmental action does not offend the Establishment Clause if it (1) has a secular purpose, (2) does not have the principal or primary effect of advancing or inhibiting religion, and (3) does not foster excessive entanglement with religion." Ibid. at 1454 (citing *Lemon v. Kurtzman*, 403 U.S. 602, 612–13 (1971)). The "voluntary ban" was permissible accommodation, not impermissible establishment. In addition, the government action did not reflect any impermissible "endorsement" of religion.

75. David H. Getches et al., *Cases and Materials on Federal Indian Law* (Thomson West, 5th ed., 2005), 756.

76. *Employment Div., Dep't of Human Res. of Or. v. Smith*, 494 U.S. 872 (1990).

77. 394 P.2d 813 (Cal. 1964).

78. Ibid. at 818–19. See also in this vein *State v. Big Sheep*, 243 P. 1067 (Mont. 1926), upholding the conviction of a Native American's possession of peyote while noting the absence of any mention of peyote in the Bible. Ibid. at 1073.

79. *Woody*, 394 P.2d at 820. This language eerily presages the almost identical observation in the *Lyng* case, but with a dramatically different interpretation and result.

80. Ibid. at 812–22. *People v. Woody* was followed in *State v. Whittingham*, 504 P.2d 950 (Ariz. Ct. App. 1973), *cert. denied*, 417 U.S. 946 (1974) and *Whitehorn v. State*, 561 P.2d 539 (Ok. Crim. App. 1977), but rejected in *State v. Soto*, 537 P.2d 142 (Or. Ct. App. 1975), *cert. denied*, 424 U.S. 955 (1976).

81. *Smith*, 494 U.S. at 888.

82. Ibid. at 874. Respondents were also subject to potential criminal prosecution under the laws of the State of Oregon, which classified peyote as a "controlled substance" and did not recognize any exemption for members of the Native American Church. No such prosecution, however, was ever initiated. This anomaly is particularly odd in that the Court refused to treat the case for what it was—an unemployment insurance case—and, instead, treated it for what it was *not*, a criminal case involving a controlled substance. This inversion definitely worked to the detriment of the respondents and, by extension, all members of the Native American Church.

83. Ibid. at 876. See, e.g., *Hobbie v. Unemployment Appeals Comm'n of Fla.*, 480 U.S. 136 (1987); *Thomas v. Review Bd. of Ind. Employment Sec. Div.*, 450 U.S. 707 (1981); *Sherbert v. Verner*, 374 U.S. 398 (1963).

84. Ibid. at 881–82. See, e.g., *Wisconsin v. Yoder*, 406 U.S. 205, 92 (1972); *Follett v. McCormick*, 321 U.S. 573 (1944); *Murdock v. Pennsylvania*, 319 U.S. 105 (1943); *Cantwell v. Connecticut*, 310 U.S. 296 (1940); *Pierce v. Society of Sisters*, 268 U.S. 510 (1925).

85. Ibid. Any criminal statute that specifically targeted members of the Native American Church would, of course, violate the equal protection guarantees of the Fifth and Fourteenth Amendments.

86. Ibid. at 890. Justice Scalia noted that there already was such a congressionally enacted federal exception and state exception in twenty-three states. Oregon did *not* have such an exception.

87. Ibid.

88. Ibid. at 904 (O'Connor, J., concurring in the judgment).

89. Ibid. at 914 (Blackmun, J., dissenting, internal citations omitted).

90. Ibid. at 915–16.

91. Ibid. at 913, n. 6.

92. One constitutional law scholar suggests that the Court's decision to leave accommodation of religious practices to the political process abdicates a traditionally perceived purpose of judicial review of legislative actions, which is to protect minority rights from majoritarian tyranny. See Jesse H. Choper, "The Rise and Decline of the Constitutional Protection of Religious Liberty," 70 *Neb. L. Rev.* 651, 685–88 (1991). Other commentators have been equally harsh in their criticism of the decision. See Frank S. Ravitch, "A Funny Thing Happened on the Way to Neutrality: Broad Principles, Formalism, and the Establishment Clause," 38 *Ga. L. Rev.* 489 (2004); Craig J. Dorsay and Lea Ann Easton, "*Employment Division v. Smith*: Just Say 'No' to the Free Exercise Clause," 59 *UMKC L. Rev.* 555 (1991); Douglas Laycock, "The Remnants of Free Exercise," 1990 *Sup. Ct. Rev.* 1, 2, 29–44, 55–56; and Ira C. Lupu, "Reconstructing the Establishment Clause: The Case against Discretionary Accommodation of Religion," 140 *U. Pa. L. Rev.* 555, 572 n. 56 (1991). See also Robert N. Clinton et al., *American Indian Law: Native Nations and the Federal System* (LexisNexis, 5th ed., 2007), 1135; Nell Jessup Newton et al., *Felix Cohen's Handbook of Federal Indian Law* (LexisNexis, 2005 ed.), 939; and Getches et al., *Cases and Materials*, 763.

93. "Government shall not substantially burden a person's exercise of religion even if the burden results from a rule of general applicability," unless it can be demonstrated that "application of the burden to the person: (1) is in furtherance of a compelling governmental interest; and (2) is the least restrictive means of furthering that compelling governmental interest." 42 U.S.C. §§ 2000bb–2000bb-4. See also Getches et al., *Cases and Materials*, 763.

94. Religious Freedom Restoration Act Signing Ceremony, Fed. News Service (Nov. 16, 1993).

95. 521 U.S. 507 (1997).

96. Ibid. at 529–36.

97. 546 U.S. 418 (2006).

98. Ibid. at 425.

99. Ibid.

100. Ibid.

101. Ibid. at 425–26.

102. Ibid. at 433.

103. Ibid. at 434.

104. Ibid. at 439.

105. Ibid. at 1221, 1226.

106. States, of course, as a matter of state constitutional law, may raise the ceiling to provide enhanced First Amendment protection.

107. American Indian Religious Freedom Act Amendments of 1994, 42 U.S.C. § 1996a. This statutory exception does not apply in the military or prison context.

108. 16 U.S.C. § 668a (2000). The secretary of the interior may grant permits for the taking of bald and golden eagles "for the religious purposes of Indian tribes." See also 50 C.F.R. § 22.22 (2007).

109. 16 U.S.C. § 1531 (2000), *et. seq.* The bald eagle is no longer on the (federal) endangered species list. U.S. Department of Fish and Wildlife press release (June 28, 2007).

110. Recall that this precise issue was expressly avoided in the case of *United States v. Dion*, 476 U.S. 734 (1986), discussed in chapter 3.

111. A person wishing to take, possess, or transport within the United States or transport into or out of the United States lawfully acquired bald or golden eagles, or their parts, nests, or eggs for Indian religious use must comply with the provisions of 50 C.F.R. § 22.22 (2007) when requesting a permit. An interested person must submit an application, attach a certificate of enrollment from a federally recognized tribe, and adhere to several conditions. Once issued, the permit can be valid anywhere from 180 days to the applicant's lifetime, depending on the type of permit.

112. 547 F.2d 483 (9th Cir. 1976).

113. 649 F.Supp. 269 (D. Nev. 1986), *aff'd*, 829 F.2d 41 (9th Cir. 1987).

114. 297 F.3d 1116 (10th Cir. 2002).

115. 318 F.3d 919 (9th Cir. 2003).

116. 547 F.2d at 485.

117. 649 F.Supp. at 274–78.

118. *Hardman*, 297 F.3d at 1135. The case was remanded on the issue of whether the permit system was the least restrictive alternative to accomplish the government's conservation, trust, and accommodation responsibilities.

119. *United States v. Friday*, 525 F.3d 938 (10th Cir. 2008).

120. 318 F.3d 919 (9th Cir. 2003).

121. 476 U.S. 734 (1986).

122. Ibid. at 745.

123. Ibid. at 739–40. Treaty abrogation, as you will recall, is part of the regime created by *Lone Wolf v. Hitchcock*, 187 U.S. 553 (1903). See the discussion in chapter 4.

124. Kevin J. Worthen, "Eagle Feathers and Equality: Lessons on Religious Exceptions from the Native American Experience," 76 *U. Colo. L. Rev.* 989 (2005).

125. 16 U.S.C. § 668a (2000). As noted by Professor Worthen,

The 1940 Act already authorized exceptions for "scientific or exhibition purposes of public museums, scientific societies or zoological parks" or when "it is necessary to permit the taking of such eagles for the protection of wildlife or of agricultural or other interests in any particular locality...." Bald Eagle Protection Act, ch. 278, 54 Stat. 250, 251 (1940) (codified as amended at 16 U.S.C. § 668 (2000)). In addition to the Native American religious use exception, the 1962 Act authorized "the taking of golden eagles for the purpose of seasonally protecting domesticated flocks and herds...." 16 U.S.C. § 668a (2000). The current version also authorizes an exception for falconry purposes. *See id.* All exceptions are subject to the requirement that the permitted activity be "compatible with the preservation" of the species. (Worthen, "Eagle Feathers and Equality," 991 n. 9)

126. 50 C.F.R. § 22.22 (2007).

127. *Hardman,* 297 F.3d at 1128.

128. Worthen, "Eagle Feathers and Equality," 1007.

129. Ibid.

130. *Shaw v. Hunt,* 517 U.S. 899 (1996).

131. Ibid. at 909. Worthen, "Eagle Feathers and Equality," 1007–8.

132. Worthen, "Eagle Feathers and Equality," 997. The permit process, it could be argued, divides access to this important religious resource based on *ancestry* and then even more narrowly on *membership* grounds.

133. 223 F.3d 1256 (11th Cir. 2000).

134. Ibid. at 1258–59. This, however, is not universally applicable because many federally recognized tribes are not parties to treaties with the United States. Newton et al., *Felix Cohen's Handbook,* 944–47.

135. 297 F.3d 1116 (10th Cir. 2002).

136. Ibid. at 1133–34. The case also involved a non-enrolled Indian.

137. *Morton v. Mancari,* 417 U.S. 535 (1974).

138. Ibid. at 555.

139. Ibid.

140. Worthen, "Eagle Feathers and Equality," 1012–14.

141. Ibid., 1012.

142. 25 U.S.C. § 1302(1). The reason that the statute does not contain an establishment clause is for this very reason. Many tribes such as the Pueblos of the Southwest do not separate religion from tribal governance. Another example may also be found in the Hopi Tribal Constitution:

The Hopi Tribal Constitution, for example, grants special powers to traditional religious leaders known as Kikmongwi, who must certify village representatives to the tribal council, HOPI TRIBAL CONST., art. IV, § 4, and who have the power to call for an election on proposed village constitutions, *Id.* at art. III, § 4. Moreover, until otherwise organized, villages are to be governed "under the traditional Hopi organizations, and the Kikmongwi of such village shall be recognized as its leader." *Id.* at art. III, § 3.

In recognition of the intimate connection between the government and religion in some tribes, when Congress enacted the Indian Civil Rights Act ("ICRA"), which statutorily imposed many of the restrictions in the Bill of Rights on Indian tribes, it excluded a prohibition against the establishment of a religion. (Donald L. Burnett, Jr., "An Historical Analysis of the 1968 'Indian Civil Rights' Act," 9 *Harv. J. on Legis.* 557, 591–92 (1972) (Worthen, "Eagle Feathers and Equality," 1012 n. 108)

Recall, of course, that the Bill of Rights does *not* apply to tribal governments. See *Talton v. Mayes*, 163 U.S. 376 (1896).

143. Worthen, "Eagle Feathers and Equality," 1013–14.

144. See, e.g., *Lemon v. Kurtzman*, 403 U.S. 602, 612–613 (1971). "First, the statute must have a secular legislative purpose; second, its principal or primary effect must be one that neither advances not inhibits religion; finally, the statute must not 'foster an excessive government entanglement with religion'" (citations omitted).

145. See, e.g., *Lynch v. Donnelly*, 465 U.S. 668, 687–88, 691 (1984) (O'Connor, J., concurring).

The Establishment Clause prohibits government from making adherence to a religion relevant in any way to a person's standing in the political community. Government can run afoul of that prohibition...[by] endorsement or disapproval of religion. Endorsement sends a message to nonadherents that they are outsiders, not full members of the political community, and an accompanying message to adherents that they are insiders, favored members of the political community.

....

...The proper inquiry...is whether the government intends to convey a message of endorsement or disapproval of religion. (citations omitted)

146. Recall, of course, the limited executive adjustment effectuated by President Clinton's Executive Order discussed previously.

147. Recall, of course, the congressional action after *Smith*. Congress amended the American Indian Religious Freedom Act (AIRFA) to protect the sacramental use of peyote. 42 U.S.C. § 1996a (2000).

148. *Allen v. Toombs*, 827 F.2d 563, 568 (9th Cir. 1987).

149. Ibid.

150. 385 F. Supp. 153 (S.D. Iowa 1974), *aff'd sub nom., Teterud v. Burns*, 522 F.2d 357 (8th Cir. 1975).

151. 516 F.Supp. 1004 (E.D. Va. 1981), *aff'd*, 670 F.2d 1345 (4th Cir. 1982).

152. 675 F.2d 116 (6th Cir. 1982).

153. *Pollock v. Marshall*, 656 F.Supp 957, 962 (S.D. Ohio 1987), *aff'd*, 845 F.2d 656 (6th Cir. 1987). See also *Capoeman v. Reed*, 754 F.2d 1512 (9th Cir. 1985); *Griffin v. Dugger*, contained in Appendix 1 of *Shabazz v. Barnauskas*, 600 F.Supp 712 (M.D. Fla. 1985).

154. 482 U.S. 342 (1987) (upholding regulations that made it impossible for Muslim inmates to participate in Jumu'ah, a Muslim service held on Friday afternoons, because the regulations were made for the appropriate use of resources, safety, and rehabilitative concerns).

155. 482 U.S. 78 (1987) (applying the reasonable relationship test to uphold a regulation that prohibited correspondence between inmates in different prisons and to strike down a regulation that permitted inmates to marry only with permission of the prison superintendent).

156. Ibid. at 89.

157. 831 F.2d 1525 (9th Cir. 1987).

158. 907 F.2d 810 (8th Cir. 1990).

159. *Indian Inmates of Neb. Penitentiary v. Gunter*, 660 F. Supp. 394, 395 (D. Neb. 1987), *aff'd sub nom.*, *SapaNajin v. Gunter*, 857 F.2d 463 (8th Cir. 1988). See also *Allen v. Toombs*, 827 F.2d 563 (9th Cir. 1987); *Kemp v. Moore*, 946 F.2d 588 (8th Cir. 1991); *Bear v. Nix*, 977 F.2d 1291 (8th Cir. 1992).

160. *Indian Inmates of Neb. Penitentiary*, 660 F. Supp. at 395. In the pipe ceremony:

the Pipe Holder and other participants purify themselves and the pipe by burning sage or sweet grass. The Pipe Holder then fills the pipe with tobacco, praying to various spirits. . . . The Pipe Bearer lights the pipe and passes it to the other participants. When the bowl is empty, the Pipe Bearer cleans it and takes apart the pipe, thereby ending the ceremony. (827 F.2d at 565 n. 4)

161. See, e.g., *Indian Inmates of Neb. Penitentiary* and *Sample v. Borg*, 675 F.Supp. 574 (E.D. Col. 1987).

162. Ibid. at 397–98. The decree was subsequently amended to specifically include the provision of a sweat lodge.

163. Ibid. at 399–400.

164. Ibid. at 400.

165. *Sample*, 675 F.Supp. at 575.

CHAPTER EIGHT

1. Indian Civil Rights Act, 25 U.S.C. §§ 1301–1302 (2000) (extending much of the Bill of Rights to Indian country).

2. See ibid. §§ 1901–1963 (Indian Child Welfare Act).

3. Ibid. §§ 2701–2721 (Indian Gaming Regulatory Act).

4. Ibid. § 1301(2) (often referred to as the *Duro* fix or *Duro* override).

5. 18 U.S.C. § 1152 (2000). The text of the statute reads:

Except as otherwise expressly provided by law, the general laws of the United States as to the punishment of offenses committed in any place within the sole and exclusive jurisdiction of the United States, except the District of Columbia, shall extend to the Indian country.

This section shall not extend to offenses committed by one Indian against the person or property of another Indian, nor to any Indian committing any offense in the Indian country who has been punished by the local law of the tribe, or to any case where, by treaty stipulations, the exclusive jurisdiction over such offenses is or may be secured to the Indian tribes respectively.

6. Ibid. § 1153. The Major Crimes Act currently states:

(a) Any Indian who commits against the person or property of another Indian or other person any of the following offenses, namely, murder, manslaughter, kidnapping, maiming, a felony under chapter 109A, incest, assault with intent to commit murder, assault with a dangerous weapon, assault resulting in serious bodily injury (as defined in section 1365 of this title), an assault against an individual who has not attained the age of 16 years, felony child abuse or neglect, arson, burglary, robbery, and a felony under section 661 of this title within the Indian country, shall be subject to the same law and penalties as all other persons committing any of the above offenses, within the exclusive jurisdiction of the United States.

(b) Any offense referred to in subsection (a) of this section that is not defined and punished by Federal law in force within the exclusive jurisdiction of the United States shall be defined and punished in accordance with the laws of the State in which such offense was committed as are in force at the time of such offense.

Tribes retain criminal jurisdiction over all Indians for tribally defined offenses committed within Indian country. The Indian Civil Rights Act limits the maximum sanction for the conviction of any tribal offense to one year in jail or a $5,000 fine or both. 25 U.S.C. § 1302(7). This limitation severely constrains the ability of tribes to prosecute serious felonies. There is no double jeopardy issue in the context of a federal and tribal prosecution. *United States v. Wheeler*, 435 U.S. 313 (1978). States have no criminal jurisdiction over Indians in Indian country, except in states that have P.L. 280 jurisdiction or some other applicable federal statute.

7. Ibid. § 13. The Assimilative Crime Act fills the gap in federal enclaves (including Indian country) by applying state criminal law when there is no identification or definition of federal criminal law and provides in pertinent part:

(a) Whoever within or upon any of the places now existing or hereafter reserved or acquired as provided in section 7 of this title, or on, above, or below any portion of the territorial sea of the United States not within the jurisdiction of any State, Commonwealth, territory, possession, or district is guilty of any act or omission which, although not made punishable by any enactment of Congress, would be punishable if committed or omitted within the jurisdiction of the State, Territory, Possession, or District in which such place is situated, by the laws thereof in force at the time of such act or omission, shall be guilty of a like offense and subject to a like punishment.

8. 118 U.S. 375 (1886).

9. Ibid. at 378–79. *Kagama* set the stage for the full-blown emergence of the plenary power doctrine seven years later in *Lone Wolf v. Hitchcock*, 187 U.S. 553 (1903). See the discussion in chapter 5.

10. *United States v. McBratney*, 104 U.S. 621, 624 (1881).

11. 435 U.S. 191 (1978).

12. Ibid. at 208.

13. But was the Court really "analyzing" anything or merely making a policy-driven decision about what it thought tribes should and shouldn't be allowed to do? At best, this is a most curious jurisprudence. At worst, it is colonialism and a marked departure from the rule of law. See the later discussion in this chapter.

14. See, e.g., *Atkinson Trading Co., Inc. v. Shirley*, 532 U.S. 645 (2001) (Navajo Nation may not tax non-Indian guest at a non-Indian-owned hotel located on fee land within the Navajo Reservation).

15. Increasing tribal loss at the bar of the Supreme Court is the current trend. See, e.g., David H. Getches et al., *Cases and Materials on Federal Indian Law* (Thomson West, 5th ed., 2005), 456–475; David H. Getches, "Conquering the Cultural Frontier: The New Subjectivism of the Supreme Court in Indian Law," 84 *Cal. L. Rev.* 1573 (1996).

16. See the discussion in chapter 4.

17. This, of course, concedes the existence (if not legitimacy) of a congressional plenary power that is problematic in its own right. See the discussion in chapter 5.

18. 358 U.S. 217 (1959).

19. Charles Wilkinson, *American Indians, Time, and the Law* (Yale University Press, 1987), 1–2 (citation omitted).

20. See 25 U.S.C. § 262 (2000), which provides:

> Any person desiring to trade with Indians on any Indian reservation shall, upon establishing the fact, to the satisfaction of the Commissioner of Indian Affairs, that he is a proper person to engage in such trade, be permitted to do so under such rules and regulations as the Commissioner of Indian Affairs may prescribe for the protection of said Indians.

The regulations are found at 25 C.F.R. §§ 140.1–140.26 (2005).

21. *Williams*, 358 U.S. at 217–18.

22. Ibid. at 218.

23. Ibid. at 220.

24. Ibid. at 220–21. Public Law 280 provided the states with an option to obtain criminal and/or civil jurisdiction in Indian country if they enacted appropriate legislation and, when necessary, amended their constitution. In 1968, Public Law 280 was amended to require a tribal referendum as a condition precedent to any state attempt to secure jurisdiction pursuant to Public Law 280. See 25 U.S.C. § 1323 (2000).

25. Ibid. at 223 (citations omitted).

26. 31 U.S. 515 (1832); see ibid. at 221.

27. *Williams*, 358 U.S. at 222.

28. Ibid. at 220.

29. See the later discussion in this chapter.

30. 411 U.S. 164 (1973).

31. Ibid. at 165. The amount of tax liability in controversy was $16.20 (ibid. at 166).

32. Ibid. at 165 (emphasis added).

33. Ibid. at 179.

34. Ibid. at 179–80.

35. Ibid. at 172 (citations omitted). The Court also stated, "This is not to say that Indian sovereignty doctrine, with its concomitant jurisdictional limit on the reach of state law, has remained static during the 141 years since *Worcester* was decided. Not surprisingly, the doctrine has undergone considerable evolution in response to changed circumstances" (ibid. at 171).

36. Ibid. at 172.

37. 36 Stat. 570 (1910) ("nothing herein, or in the ordinance herein provided for, shall preclude the said State from taxing as other lands and other property are taxed *outside of an Indian reservation* owned or held by any Indian") (emphasis added).

38. 4 U.S.C. §§ 104–110 (2000). Section 109 states: "Nothing in sections 105 and 106 of this title shall be deemed to authorize the levy or collection of any tax on or from any Indian not otherwise taxed."

39. *McClanahan*, 411 U.S. at 177–78.

40. *Warren Trading Post Co. v. Arizona State Tax Commission*, 380 U.S. 685, 686 (1965).

41. *McClanahan*, 411 U.S. at 172 n. 7 (stating, "[t]he source of federal authority over Indian matters has been the subject of some *confusion*, but it is now generally recognized that the power derives from federal responsibility for regulating commerce with Indian tribes and for treaty making" (emphasis added)). See U.S. Const. art. I, § 8, cl. 3; art. II, § 2, cl. 2.

42. See *Oklahoma Tax Commission v. Chickasaw Nation*, 515 U.S. 450 (1995) (employing a bright-line "legal incidence" test, the Court held that Oklahoma may not apply its motor fuels tax to fuel sold by the tribe in Indian country, as the legal incident of the tax rests on the tribe).

43. See, e.g., *Mescalero Apache Tribe v. Jones*, 411 U.S. 145 (1973) (tribe was subject to state tax on its ski resort located outside the reservation). See also *Oklahoma Tax Commission v. Chickasaw Nation*, 515 U.S. 450 (1995) (holding that Indians living off the reservation are subject to state income tax for income earned on the reservation).

44. See generally *Castle v. Hayes Freight Lines, Inc.*, 348 U.S. 61 (1954).

45. See generally Laurence H. Tribe, *American Constitutional Law* (Foundation Press, 3d ed., Vol. 1, 2000), 1172–1220. See also Robert N. Clinton et al., *American Indian Law: Native Nations and the Federal System* (LexisNexis, 5th ed., 2007), 779–81; Nell Jessup Newton et al., eds., *Felix Cohen's Handbook of Federal Indian Law* (LexisNexis, 2005 ed.), 399–401; Getches et al., *Cases and Materials*, 561–65.

46. 448 U.S. 136 (1980).

47. Ibid. at 152–53.

48. Ibid. at 142.

49. Ibid. at 144.

50. Ibid. at 144–45.

51. Ibid. at 148–49.

52. Ibid. at 148.

53. Ibid. at 141 (quoting *Mescalero Apache Tribe v. Jones*, 411 U.S. 145, 148 (1973)).

54. 447 U.S. 134 (1980).

55. Ibid. at 135–36.

56. Ibid. at 157.

57. Ibid.

58. Ibid.

59. Ibid. The citation supporting this proposition is footnote 17 in *Moe v. Salish & Kootenai Tribes*, 425 U.S. 463, 481 (1976), which is mostly concerned with the jurisdictional elements for convening a three-judge court under 28 U.S.C. § 2281.

60. See the discussion in chapter 3.

61. 490 U.S. 163 (1989).

62. Ibid. at 165.

63. 532 U.S. 645 (2001).

64. Ibid. at 645–46. Neither *Montana* exception was satisfied. See the *Montana* discussion later.

65. 450 U.S. 544 (1981).

66. *Oliphant v. Suquamish Indian Tribe*, 435 U.S. 191, 208 (1978) (citing *Oliphant v. Schlie*, 544 F.2d 1007, 1009 (9th Cir. 1976)).

67. *Montana*, 450 U.S. at 565–66 (citations omitted).

68. 18 U.S.C. § 1151 (2000) provides:

Except as otherwise provided in sections 1154 and 1156 of this title, the term "Indian country," as used in this chapter, means (a) all land within the limits of any Indian reservation under the jurisdiction of the United States Government, notwithstanding the issuance of any patent, and, including rights-of-way running through the reservation, (b) all dependent Indian communities within the borders of the United States whether within the original or subsequently acquired territory thereof, and whether within or without the limits of a state, and (c) all Indian allotments, the Indian titles to which have not been extinguished, including rights-of-way running through the same.

69. *Montana*, 450 U.S. at 557 (citations omitted).

70. Ibid. at 559 n. 9.

71. This presumption could obviously be overcome by any *federal statute* expressly directed to such jurisdictional matters.

72. Ibid. at 564 (emphasis added).

73. The Court itself seems to recognize the appropriateness of this more pinpoint characterization:

It defies common sense to suppose that Congress would intend that non-Indians purchasing allotted lands would become subject to tribal jurisdiction when an avowed purpose of the allotment policy was the ultimate destruction of tribal government. And it is hardly likely that Congress could have imagined that the purpose of peaceful assimilation could be advanced if feeholders could be excluded from fishing or hunting on their acquired property. (*Montana*, 450 U.S. at 560 n. 9)

74. Treaty with the Crow Indians, May 7, 1868, art. II, 15 Stat. 650.

75. *Montana*, 450 U.S. at 566.

76. Ibid. at 566–67.

77. Ibid.

78. 471 U.S. 845 (1985).

79. Ibid. at 847–48.

80. Ibid. at 857.

81. Ibid. at 856–57 (citations omitted).

82. Ibid. at 855–56. It is also most anomalous that the Court did *not* even cite, much less discuss, *Montana* in this regard, as *Montana* is arguably the case most on point.

83. 520 U.S. 438 (1997).

84. Ibid. at 443.

85. Ibid. at 451.

86. Ibid.

87. Ibid. at 453 (citations omitted).

88. See *Brendale v. Confederated Tribes & Bands of the Yakima Indian Nation*, 492 U.S. 408 (1989).

89. See *South Dakota v. Bourland*, 508 U.S. 679 (1993).

90. See *Brendale*, 492 U.S. at 422–32. The "closed" area was mostly tribal land not open to the general public. The "open" area was open to the general public, and about half of it was owned by non-Indians.

91. *Bourland*, 508 U.S. at 695–96. On remand, it was held that the Cheyenne River Sioux Tribe did *not* have jurisdiction, and the State of South Dakota did, on land taken by the federal government to build a dam and reservoir. See *South Dakota v. Bourland*, 39 F.3d 368 (8th Cir, 1994).

92. *Brendale*, 492 U.S. at 450 (Blackmun, J., dissenting).

93. Ibid. at 454–55. Also see the authorizing statute for tribally granted rights of way at 25 U.S.C. §§ 323–328 (2000).

94. *Strate*, 523 U.S. at 457.

95. Ibid. quoting *Montana* 450 U.S. 544, 566 (1981) (the second prong of the *Montana* proviso).

96. *Strate*, 523 U.S. at 459 (citations omitted).

97. Ibid. (emphasis added). The Court cites to 28 U.S.C. § 1441, which is the general removal statute that permits nonresident defendants sued in *state* court to remove their cases to federal court. 28 U.S.C. § 1441 does not address removal from a *tribal* court.

98. *Strate*, 520 U.S. at 459.

99. Ibid. at 445.

100. 532 U.S. 645 (2001).

101. Ibid. at 659. As a result, the legal incidence of the tax falls directly on the guests, but the owner or operator of the hotel must collect and remit it to the Navajo Tax Commission. Ibid. at 648.

102. The Chief Justice's opinion is twelve pages in length. See ibid. at 647–59.

103. Ibid. at 654.

104. Ibid. at 656. "A nonmember's consensual relationship in one area thus does not trigger tribal civil authority in another—it is not 'in for a penny, in for a Pound.'"

105. Ibid. at 657.

106. Ibid. at 650.

107. Ibid. at 659 (Souter, J., concurring).

108. Ibid. at 659–60 (Souter, J., concurring) (citing *Montana v. United States*, 450 U.S. 544, 565 (1981) (citations omitted; emphasis added).

109. 533 U.S. 353 (2001).

110. Ibid. at 355–56.

111. Ibid. at 355.

112. Ibid. at 360 (quoting *Montana*, 450 U.S. 544, 565 (1980)).

113. Ibid. at 364 (quoting *Williams v. Lee*, 358 U.S. 217, 220 (1939)).

114. Ibid. at 367. Justice Stevens dissented to this part of the decision, arguing that it was both unnecessary and incorrect. See ibid. at 401–3. He contended that the question of whether a tribal court was a court of general jurisdiction was "fundamentally one of tribal law." Ibid. at 402 (Stevens, J., concurring).

115. Ibid. at 317. It remains unclear whether this is a general rule or a particular rule, which only applies when there is no tribal court jurisdiction over any tribal cause of action.

116. Ibid. at 381–82 (Souter, J., concurring).

117. Ibid. at 383 (citation omitted; alteration in original) (Souter, J., concurring).

118. Ibid. at 383–85 (Souter, J., concurring).

119. Ibid. at 384 (emphasis added).

120. Ibid. at 358 n. 2. This is somewhat misleading in the context of the partial holding in *Brendale v. Confederated Tribes and Bands of Yakima Indian Nation*, 492 U.S. 408 (1989), that the tribe did have zoning authority over a certain parcel of non-Indian land. Perhaps the distinction is that *Brendale* involved regulatory, not judicial, jurisdiction. However, that would be odd given *Strait*'s collapse of the distinction. Some lower courts have upheld tribal judicial jurisdiction over non-Indians. See, e.g., *Superior Oil Co. v. United States*, 605 F.Supp. 674 (D. Utah 1985) (holding that tribal court jurisdiction was proper when a non-Indian entered into a consensual relationship with the Navajo Tribe by becoming a party to an oil-and-gas lease and voluntarily subjected itself to the inherent sovereignty of the tribe to regulate the lease). *Lyon v. Amoco Production Co.*, 923 P.2d 350 (Colo. Ct. App. 1996) (recognizing tribal court jurisdiction over non-Indians when the relevant activity occurred on Indian trust lands within the reservation. The Court also found that the conduct of the non-Indians on fee lands within the reservation threatened or had some direct effect on the political integrity, economic security, or health and welfare of the tribe).

121. 128 S.Ct. 2709 (2008).

122. Ibid. at 2720.

123. 450 U.S. 544 (1981).

124. *Plains Commerce Bank*, at 2720.

125. Justice Ginsburg pointed out in her dissent: "Sales of land—and related conduct—are surely 'activities' within the ordinary sense of the word." Ibid. at 2729–30 (Ginsburg, J., dissenting).

126. David Getches detects increasing "subjectivism" in Supreme Court Indian law jurisprudence premised on judicial considerations of "what the current state of affairs ought to be," and he wisely counsels against this trend:

> The foundation principles of Indian law demand resistance to the temptation of judicial activism. A return to foundation principles, furthermore, would spare tribes the subjective judgments of courts by requiring congressional action, with the scrutiny of the political process and the tribes' full participation, before modifying their rights as sovereigns. Indian rights do not depend on sympathy for the plight of historical mistreatment of Native Americans. Self-determination for tribes is rooted in ancient laws and treaties, and is protected against incursions except those that Congress deliberately allows. Well-meaning judicial attempts to balance and accommodate interests of Indians and non-Indians not only are inconsistent with the limited role of courts, as sanctioned by the foundation principles of Indian law, but are inevitably culturally charged. (David H. Getches, "Conquering the Cultural Frontier: The New Subjectivism of the Supreme Court in Indian Law," 84 *Cal. L. Rev.* 1573, 1654–55 (1996).)

Philip Frickey discerns a seismic self-aggrandizing shift in the role of the Supreme Court in Indian law:

> In the final analysis, in federal Indian law the Court has given the Congress much more legislative power than the text of the Constitution suggests, then bootstrapped that into a judicially enforceable power to clean up those areas of Indian affairs that Congress has not yet addressed. In establishing the plenary power of Congress over Indian affairs, the Court performed the perhaps disappointing, but nonetheless unsurprising, role of the "court of the conqueror" reflected in *Johnson v. M'Intosh*—it deferred to established patterns and practices designed to centralize the colonial power in the political branches. In aggrandizing to itself a judicially enforceable "dormant" aspect of this power, however, the Court has become an actor imposing its own set of colonial values, not merely an agent of congressional choices. This second step seems remarkable, even given the realities of a colonial society. The Court has transformed itself from the court of the conqueror into the court as the conqueror. (Philip P. Frickey, "A Common Law for Our Age of Colonialism: The Judicial Divestiture of Indian Tribal Authority over Non-Members," 109 *Yale L. J.* 1, 72 (1999))

I have also identified this metastasis of plenary power:

> The plenary power doctrine can not be seen as coming in two distinct vintages. There is the classic doctrine of congressional plenary power as

established in *Lone Wolf.* Yet even if Congress has not acted—where one
would normally presuppose an unimpaired tribal sovereignty—the Court
now recognizes a judicial plenary power to parse the limits of tribal court
authority based on federal common law. A federal common law that at least
heretofore has not been equated with any notion of implied divestiture of
tribal sovereignty. (Frank Pommersheim, "Tribal Courts and the Federal
Judiciary: Opportunities and Challenges for a Constitutional Democracy,"
58 *Mont. L. Rev.* 313 (1997))

127. Originalism is a judicial philosophy that holds that constitutional interpretation is limited by the text of the Constitution and its original understanding by the
founders. It is a static, nonevolving approach to what the Constitution means in
contemporary circumstances. See *Black's Law Dictionary* (7th ed., 1999), 1126.
   128. 495 U.S. 676 (1990).
   129. Memorandum from Justice Antonin Scalia to Justice William J. Brennan Jr.
(Apr. 4, 1990) (emphasis added) (*Duro v. Reina*, No. 88–6546), in Papers of Justice
Thurgood Marshall (reproduced from the Collections of the Manuscript Division,
Library of Congress). These remarkable papers were opened to researchers after
Justice Thurgood Marshall's death, and Justice William Brennan's papers also have
been selectively opened to serious scholars. This memorandum was first cited in
Getches, "Conquering the Cultural Frontier," 1573, 1575.
   130. See the discussion in chapter 10.
   131. Erwin Chemerinsky, *Federal Jurisdiction* (Aspen, 4th ed., 2003), 355.
Chemerinsky also notes that despite "a strong presumption against the federal courts
fashioning common law to decide cases, federal courts have fashioned common law in
limited circumstances throughout American history" (354–55). It is a product of the
"necessity" to fill "gaps" in statutory and constitutional law (355–56). It also raises
separation of powers and federalism issues. Does federal common law unfairly
encroach on the legislative powers of Congress or improperly displace state law, thus
usurping state prerogatives? (357–58). Apparently, there is no reliable answer: "neither
value provides any clear guidance as to when federal courts should create or refrain
from creating federal common law" (358). There is no mention of the role of common
law decisionmaking in Indian law jurisprudence.
   132. See, e.g., *Montana v. United States*, 450 U.S. 544 (1981); *National Farmers
Union Insurance Co. v. Crow Tribe*, 471 U.S. 845 (1985); *Iowa Mutual Ins. v. LaPlante*,
480 U.S. 9 (1987); *South Dakota v. Bourland*, 508 U.S. 679 (1993); *Strate v. A-1
Contractors*, 520 U.S. 438 (1997); *Atkinson Trading Co., Inc. v. Shirley*, 532 U.S. 645
(2001); *Nevada v. Hicks*, 533 U.S. 353 (2001); and *Plains Commerce Bank v. Long Family
Land and Cattle Co., Inc.* 128 S.Ct. 2709 (2008).
   133. "It is well settled that this statutory grant of 'jurisdiction will support claims
founded upon federal common law as well as those of a statutory origin.' Federal
common law as articulated in rules that are fashioned in court decisions are 'laws' as
that term is used in § 1331." *National Farmers Union*, 471 U.S. at 850. Note, however,
that there is also discussion of federal common law in *United States v. Lara*, 541 U.S.
193 (2004). This is somewhat odd because *Lara* is a case about statutory construction.

134. "But exercise of tribal power beyond what is necessary to protect tribal self-government or to control internal relations is inconsistent with the dependent status of the tribes, and so cannot survive without express congressional delegation." *Montana*, 450 U.S. at 564.

135. *Strate*, 520 U.S. at 459. Justice Ginsburg's opinion also refers to the Court's opinion in *Montana* as "pathmarking." Ibid. at 445.

136. 541 U.S. 193 (2004).

137. Ibid. at 220 (Thomas, J., concurring in judgment).

138. 542 U.S. 692 (2004).

139. Ibid. at 750.

140. Ibid. (emphasis in the original).

141. See, e.g., the many contradictory viewpoints articulated in *United States v. Lara*, 541 U.S. 193 (2004) and discussed later.

142. 544 U.S. 197 (2005).

143. Ibid. at 202–3.

144. Ibid.

145. Ibid. at 214.

146. Ibid. at 215–19.

147. Ibid. at 255 (Stevens, J., dissenting) (emphasis added).

148. Ibid. at 223–25 (internal footnote omitted) (Stevens, J., dissenting).

149. Ibid. at 226 (emphasis added).

150. Ibid., n. 6. It is interesting to note that the tribe expressly disclaimed "the right to tax or exercise other regulatory authority over reservation land owned by non-Indians."

151. 358 U.S. 217 (1959) (holding that the Arizona courts do not have jurisdiction in an action brought by a non-Indian owner of a store located on the Navajo Reservation to collect for goods sold on credit to Indian individuals).

152. 411 U.S. 164 (1993) (holding that Arizona does not have jurisdiction to impose a personal income tax on Navajo Indians residing on the Navajo Reservation whose income is wholly derived from reservation sources).

153. 526 U.S. 172 (1999) (Tribe retains off-reservation usufructuary rights against state regulation). See also *California v. Cabazon Band of Mission Indians*, 480 U.S. 202 (1987); *Oklahoma Tax Commission v. Chickasaw Nation*, 515 U.S. 450 (1995); and *Kiowa Tribe of Oklahoma v. Manufacturing Technology, Inc.*, 523 U.S. 759 (1998).

154. 450 U.S. 544 (1981) (holding that the Crow Tribe of Montana does not have the authority to prohibit all hunting and fishing by nonmembers of the tribe on non-Indian property within reservation borders).

155. 508 U.S. 679 (1993) (holding that inherent sovereignty did not enable the Cheyenne River Sioux Tribe to regulate non-Indian hunting and fishing in an area of the reservation taken by the federal government for a dam project).

156. 520 U.S. 438 (1997) (holding that the tribal court lacked jurisdiction to adjudicate tort claims arising out of a car accident involving a non-Indian on a portion of a state highway that runs through the reservation but was built on trust land pursuant to a right-of-way granted to the state).

157. 522 U.S. 520 (1998) (holding that the tribe lacked authority to impose a business activities tax on a contractor hired to construct a school on land set aside for the tribe under the Alaska Native Claims Settlement Act but not actually within Indian country as defined at 18 U.S.C. § 1151).

158. 532 U.S. 645 (2001) (holding that the Navajo Tribe lacked jurisdiction to tax nonmember guests of a hotel located on fee land within the boundaries of the reservation).

159. 533 U.S. 353 (2001) (holding that the tribal court lacked jurisdiction over a civil rights and tort action filed by a tribal member against state officials arising from the execution of a search warrant on trust land within the reservation).

160. 128 S.Ct. 2709 (2008) (tribal court has no jurisdiction over a discrimination claim growing out of a contract for the sale of fee land by a non-Indian bank to an Indian couple).

161. 471 U.S. 845 (1985) (holding that the tribal court must have the full opportunity to assess its jurisdiction in a personal injury action against a non-Indian before the matter may be challenged in federal district court).

162. 480 U.S. 9 (1987) (holding that exhaustion of tribal court remedies, including tribal appellate court review, is required before a federal court may consider the issue of the tribal court's subject matter jurisdiction).

163. The lone exception, if it be one, is the plurality opinion that tribes may have zoning jurisdictions over non-Indians in the "closed" part of a reservation. *Brendale v. Confederated Tribes and Bands of Yakima Indian Nation*, 492 U.S. 408 (1989). Of course, non-Indian activities on *trust* land are generally subject to tribal taxing and regulatory authority.

164. 447 U.S. 134 (1980) (holding that Washington's imposition of cigarette and sales tax on on-reservation purchases by nonmembers was valid, but that Washington's motor vehicle and mobile home, camper, and trailer taxes could not properly be imposed upon tribal members' vehicles).

165. 448 U.S. 136 (1980) (holding that the state could not assert a fuel tax on a non-Indian company that engaged in logging activities solely on the reservation, as the imposition of the tax would undermine the federal policy of assuring that the profits from timber sales would inure to the tribe's benefit).

166. 490 U.S. 163 (1989) (holding that the state could validly impose a severance tax on a non-Indian oil and gas producer whose operations are located on the Indian reservation, even though the same operation is subject to a severance tax by the tribe).

167. See, e.g., Dalia Tsuk Mitchell, *Architect of Justice: Felix S. Cohen and the Founding of American Legal Pluralism* (Cornell University Press, 2007).

168. Ibid., 37.

169. Ibid.

170. Ibid., 38.

171. Ibid., 56.

172. Ibid., 63–64.

173. Ibid., 80.

174. Ibid., 84–89.

175. Ibid., 94–99.

176. Ibid., 106–7. The bureaucratic pressure within the Bureau of Indian Affairs for tribes to swiftly adopt constitutions also facilitated this process.

177. Ibid., 110–11. Although much of this resentment has abated over time, it remains alive on some reservations yet today.

178. Ibid., 137.

179. Ibid., 166–72.

180. Ibid. Felix Cohen, *Handbook of Federal Indian Law* (Michie, 1982 ed.); Newton et al., *Felix Cohen's Handbook.* I am a contributor to the 2005 edition.

181. Ibid., 176. See also Frank Pommersheim, *Braid of Feathers: American Indian Law and Contemporary Tribal Life* (University of California Press, 2005), 51–54.

182. Felix Cohen, *Handbook of Federal Indian Law* (University of New Mexico Press, 1942 ed.), 123.

183. David Getches and Charles Wilkinson, *Cases and Materials on Federal Indian Law* (2d ed., 1986, West), 279.

184. Pommersheim, *Braid of Feathers,* 55–56. See also the proposal set out in chapter 10.

185. Ibid., 51 (quoting Felix Cohen).

186. Approximately 300 statutes in Indian law have been enacted by Congress since 1960.

187. See 25 U.S.C. §§ 1301–1303 (2000).

188. See 25 U.S.C. §§ 1901–1963 (2000).

189. See 25 U.S.C. §§ 2701–2721 (2000).

190. See 25 U.S.C. § 1301(2) (2000).

191. 163 U.S. 376 (1896).

192. Ibid. at 379. Note that despite the existence of the Major Crimes Act, 28 U.S.C. § 1153, tribal jurisdiction over its members was reserved to the Cherokee nation by the 1835 Treaty of Hopewell. Ibid. at 380.

193. Ibid. at 384.

194. Ibid. at 382.

195. 118 U.S. 375 (1886).

196. 187 U.S. 553 (1903).

197. 25 U.S.C. § 1302 (2000). These guarantees do not negate, but rather complement, tribal constitutional or statutory protections where they exist. In addition, those guarantees apply to any person (not just Indians) who is subject to tribal governmental authority.

198. 25 U.S.C. § 1303 (2000).

199. 436 U.S. 49 (1978).

200. Ibid. at 51.

201. Ibid. at 52.

202. Ibid. at 52 n. 2.

203. Ibid. at 52–53.

204. Ibid. at 53. Note that this case was decided before the exhaustion of tribal court remedies rule was formulated in the 1985 case of *National Farmer's Union Ins. Co. v. Crow Tribe,* 471 U.S. 845 (1985).

205. Ibid. at 53.

206. Ibid. at 54–55. 28 U.S.C. § 1343 (a)(4) (2000) provides:

(4) To recover damages or to secure equitable or other relief under any Act of Congress providing for the protection of civil rights, including the right to vote.

207. *Santa Clara Pueblo*, 436 U.S. at 54.

208. Ibid. at 55.

209. Thurgood not John; Associate not Chief! See ibid. at 51.

210. Ibid. at 60 (citing *McClanahan v. Arizona Tax Commission*, 411 U.S. 164, 172 (1973)).

211. Ibid. at 56.

212. Ibid. at 56–59.

213. Ibid. at 59.

214. Ibid. The theory of such lawsuits flow from the case of *Ex parte Young*, 209 U.S. 123 (1908), which held that (state) officers did not enjoy the benefits of the state's sovereign immunity when they were acting unconstitutionally.

215. Ibid. at 61.

216. Id. at 62 (quoting *Morton v. Mancari*, 417 U.S. 535 (1974)).

217. Ibid. at 64.

218. Ibid. at 65.

219. Ibid.

220. This is so at least in the context of affirmative congressional legislation that establishes *federal* standards that may be enforced in federal court *in limited* circumstances so as to accord full respect to tribal sovereign immunity.

221. Federal review is limited to habeas relief, which is available only when an individual is *detained* or restrained by government authority. Most civil rights claims do not involve such detention or restraint.

222. Getches et al., *Cases and Materials*, 400–401. Justices O'Connor and Ginsburg were not on the Court in 1978.

223. See generally Judith Resnik, "Dependent Sovereigns: Indian Tribes, States and the Federal Courts," 56 *U. Chi. L. Rev.* 671 (1989). There is also the critique of the white feminist criteria as gender essentialist and racially insensitive. See generally Angela P. Harris, "Race and Essentialism in Feminist Legal Theory," 42 *Stan. L. Rev.* 581 (1990).

224. See Bethany R. Berger, "Indian Policy and the Imagined Indian Woman," 14 *Kan. J. L. & Pub. Pol'y* 103, 114 (2004) (noting that the movement within the Pueblo to change the membership ordinance has not yet succeeded).

225. Barbara Ann Atwood, "Flashpoints under the Indian Child Welfare Act: Toward a New Understanding of State Court Resistance," 51 *Emory L. J.* 587, 601 (2002).

226. See ibid. 601–5.

227. H.R. Rep. No. 95–1386, at 9 (1978), reprinted in 1978 U.S.C.C.A.N. 7530, 7531.

228. U.S. Senate Rep., 93rd Cong. (2d Sess. 1974). 1978 U.S. Code Cong. at Ad News 7530–31 (Statement of William Byler, Executive Director of American

Association of Indian Affairs). See also Manuel P. Guerrero, "Indian Child Welfare Act of 1978: A Response to the Threat to Indian Culture Caused by Foster and Adoptive Placements of Indian Children," 7 *Am. Indian L. Rev.* 51, 57 (1979). There is a blistering critique of this data and the Indian Child Welfare Act in general in Randall Kennedy's book, *Interracial Intimacies: Sex, Marriage, Identity, and Adoption* (Pantheon, 2003).

229. Atwood, "Flashpoints," 603–4.

230. Ibid., 605 n. 73.

231. 25 U.S.C. § 1901(2) (2000).

232. 25 U.S.C. § 1903 defines "child custody proceeding" to include:

(i) "Foster care placement" which shall mean any action removing an Indian child from its parent or Indian custodian for temporary placement in a foster home or institution or the home of a guardian or conservator where the parent or Indian custodian cannot have the child returned upon demand, but where parental rights have not been terminated;

(ii) "termination of parental rights" shall mean any action resulting in the termination of the parent-child relationship;

(iii) "preadoptive placement" which shall mean the temporary placement of an Indian child in a foster home or institution after the termination of parental rights, but prior to or in lieu of adoptive placement; and

(iv) "adoptive placement" which shall mean the permanent placement of an Indian child for adoption, including any action resulting in a final decree of adoption.

Such term or terms shall not include a placement based upon an act which, if committed by an adult, would be deemed a crime or upon an award, in a divorce proceeding, of custody to one of the parents.

233. 25 U.S.C. § 1903(4) defines an "Indian child" as "any unmarried person who is under age eighteen and is either (a) a member of an Indian tribe or (b) is eligible for membership in an Indian tribe and is the biological child of a member of an Indian tribe."

234. 25 U.S.C. § 1911 states:

Exclusive jurisdiction. An Indian tribe shall have jurisdiction exclusive as to any State over any child custody proceeding involving an Indian child who resides or is domiciled within the reservation of such tribe, except where such jurisdiction is otherwise vested in the State by existing Federal law. Where an Indian child is a ward of a tribal court, the Indian tribe shall retain exclusive jurisdiction, notwithstanding the residence or domicile of the child.

235. 25 U.S.C. § 1911(b) (emphasis added). There is much (heated) case law about the meaning of "good cause to the contrary," but the issue has not been resolved by the Supreme Court.

236. 25 U.S.C. § 1912 (f) provides:

Parental rights termination orders; evidence; determination of damage to child. No termination of parental rights may be ordered in such proceeding in the absence of a determination, supported by evidence beyond a reasonable doubt, including testimony of qualified expert witnesses that the continued custody of the child by the parent or Indian custodian is likely to result in serious emotional or physical damage to the child.

237. 25 U.S.C. § 1912(d) provides:

Remedial services and rehabilitative programs; preventive measures. Any party seeking to effect a foster care placement of, or termination of parental rights to, an Indian child under State law shall satisfy the court that active efforts have been made to provide remedial services and rehabilitative programs designed to prevent the breakup of the Indian family and that these efforts have proved unsuccessful.

238. 25 U.S.C. § 1912(e) provides:

Foster care placement orders; evidence; determination of damage to child. No foster care placement may be ordered in such proceeding in the absence of a determination, supported by clear and convincing evidence, including testimony of qualified expert witnesses, that the continued custody of the child by the parent or Indian custodian is likely to result in serious emotional or physical damage to the child.

See also 25 U.S.C. § 1912(f), which requires "evidence beyond a reasonable doubt" for the termination of parental rights.

239. See, e.g., *Matter of K.H. and K.L.E.*, 981 P.2d 1190, 1193 (Mont. 1993) (noting that experts must "have expertise in, and substantial knowledge of, Native-American families and their childrearing practices" in order to satisfy the qualified expert requirement of ICWA); cf. *In re M.J.J.*, 69 P.3d 1226, 1228 (Okla. Civ. App. 2003) (finding that an expert with substantial education and experience need not have special knowledge of Indian life so long as he or she testifies on matters not implicating cultural bias). See also *C.J. v. State Dept. of Health and Social Services*, 18 P.3d 1214, 1219 (Alaska 2001) (specifying that ICWA's requirement that the state engage in active efforts to provide remedial and rehabilitative services is minimally satisfied where a caseworker takes a parent through each step in a plan for reunification of the family); *People ex. rel. D.B.*, 670 N.W.2d 67, 73 (S.D. 2003) (finding that the state had satisfied the remedial and rehabilitative services requirement, in part, by assisting the mother in entering chemical dependency inpatient treatment, by arranging for parental counseling, and by funding the purchase of a stroller and crib for the child).

240. 25 U.S.C. § 1915(a) provides:

Adoptive placements; preferences. In any adoptive placement of an Indian child under State law, a preference shall be given, in the absence of good cause to the contrary, to a placement with
    (1) a member of the child's extended family;

(2) other members of the Indian child's tribe; or

(3) other Indian families.

25 U.S.C. § 1915(b) provides:

> Foster care or preadoptive placements; criteria; preferences. Any child
> accepted for foster care or preadoptive placement shall be placed in the least
> restrictive setting which most approximates a family and in which his special
> needs, if any, may be met. The child shall also be placed within reasonable
> proximity to his or her home, taking into account any special needs of the
> child. In any foster care or preadoptive placement, a preference shall be
> given, in the absence of good cause to the contrary, to a placement with—
> a member of the Indian child's extended family;
> a foster home licensed, approved, or specified by the Indian child's tribe;
> an Indian foster home licensed or approved by an authorized non-
> Indian licensing authority; or
> an institution for children approved by an Indian tribe or operated by an
> Indian organization which has a program suitable to meet the Indian child's
> needs.

Again, the sticky issue regarding the meaning of "good cause to the contrary" remains
unresolved by the Supreme Court. Atwood, "Flashpoints," 669.

241 25 U.S.C. § 1915(d) provides:

> Social and cultural standards applicable. The standards to be applied in
> meeting the preference requirements of this section shall be the prevailing
> social and cultural standards of the Indian community in which the parent or
> extended family resides or with which the parent or extended family
> members maintain social and cultural ties.

242. 490 U.S. 30 (1989).

243. Ibid. at 38–39.

244. Ibid. at 38.

245. Ibid.

246. Ibid. at 39. The tribe has standing to intervene at any time in a state
proceeding involving the placement of Indian children except in divorce or juvenile
delinquency proceedings. See 25 U.S.C. § 1911(c) (2000).

247. Ibid. at 39–40.

248. Ibid.

249. Ibid.

250. Ibid., n. 13.

251. Ibid. at 32.

252. Ibid. at 44–46.

253. Ibid. at 48–49.

254. Ibid. at 52–53.

255. 25 U.S.C. § 1901(3).

256. 25 U.S.C. § 1902.

257. *Holyfield*, 490 U.S. at 49.

258. Ibid.

259. Ibid. at 52. Justice Stevens wrote a dissent that criticized the majority for its distortion of the "delicate balance between individual rights and group rights recognized by the ICWA." Ibid. at 55 (Stevens, J., dissenting).

260. See 25 U.S.C. § 1915.

261. This tension is far from settled in repose. Both sides want ICWA to be amended. The states favor statutory amendments relative to the meaning of "good cause to the contrary" in sections 1911 and 1915, as do the tribes, but with different proposals. Tribes also favor an expanded definition of "notice" and abolition of the judicially created "existing Indian family" exception to tribal jurisdiction. To date, no amendments have been passed by Congress. Some have even argued that ICWA is unconstitutional because it violates the Tenth Amendment by improperly limiting state authority involving Indian children *off* the reservation; however, the few courts that have ruled on such a claim have always struck it down as within Congress's plenary power. See, e.g., *In re Baby Boy L.*, 103 P.3d 1099 (Okla. 2004).

262. 25 U.S.C. §§ 2701–2721 (2000).

263. 480 U.S. 202 (1987).

264. Id. at 204–5.

265. Id. at 205.

266. See, e.g., the previous discussion in this chapter.

267. *Cabazon*, 480 U.S. at 207.

> In Pub. L. 280, Congress expressly granted six states, including California, jurisdiction over specific areas of Indian country within the States and provided for the assumption of jurisdiction by other States. In § 2, California was granted broad criminal jurisdiction over offenses committed by or against Indians within all Indian country within the state. Section 4's grant of civil jurisdiction was more limited. (Ibid., citations omitted)

268. Ibid. at 210–12.

269. See, e.g., 2004 National Indian Gaming Commission Annual Report at http://www.nigc.gov/Default.aspx?tabid=118.

270. More specifically, the poorest county in the United States is Shannon County, the second poorest is Buffalo County, the fifth poorest is Ziebach County, and the eighth poorest is Todd County. Bureau of the Census, U.S. Dep't of Commerce, Prd #9, Capital, 1979 County per Capita Income Figures Released by Census Bureau from the 1980 Census 2 (1983).

271. See, e.g., Kristen Carpenter and Roy Halbritter, "Beyond the Ethnic Umbrella and the Buffalo: Some Thoughts on American Indian Tribes and Gaming," 5 *Gaming L. Rev.* 311 (2001); "Symposium: Indian Gaming," 29 *Ariz. St. L. J.* 1 (1997).

272. 25 U.S.C. § 2703(6).

273. 25 U.S.C. §§ 2703(7), 2710(b).

274. 25 U.S.C. § 2710(d)(B).

275. 25 U.S.C. § 2710(d). Parts of this section were struck down by the Supreme Court in *Seminole Tribe of Florida v. Florida*, 517 U.S. 44 (1996).

276. 25 U.S.C. § 2710(b).

277. 25 U.S.C. § 2710(b)(2)(B).

278. 517 U.S. 44 (1996).

279. Ibid. at 55 (quoting *Green v. Mansour*, 474 U.S. 64, 68 (1985)).

280. Ibid. at 57.

281. Ibid. at 59.

282. 491 U.S. 1 (1989) (holding that the language of Comprehensive Environmental Response, Compensation and Liability Act, as amended by the Superfund Amendments and Reauthorization Act, clearly evinces intent to hold states liable in damages in federal court, and the Eleventh Amendment did not proscribe enforcement of the Act).

283. *Seminole Tribe of Florida*, 517 U.S. at 63–68 (citing *Pennhurst State School and Hospital v. Halderman*, 465 U.S. 89, 98 (1984)).

284. Ibid. at 63 (quoting *Payne v. Tennessee*, 501 U.S. 808, 827 (1991)) and *Helvering v. Hallock*, 309 U.S. 106, 119 (1940)).

285. Ibid. at 63.

286. Ibid. at 62. It goes without saying that Section 5 of the Fourteenth Amendment, with its focus on equal protection and combating racial discrimination by states, was not a viable constitutional source to waive state sovereign immunity in the context of Indian gaming.

287. See generally ibid. at 44–185 (Justices Stevens and Souter dissents).

288. See, e.g., *Kimel v. Fla. Bd. of Regents*, 528 U.S. 62 (2000).

289. Martha Field, "The Seminole Case, Federalism, and the Indian Commerce Clause," 29 Ariz. St. L. J. 3, 304 (1997). The "new" remedial scheme refers to the authority of the secretary of interior to resolve such tribal-state impasses. See, e.g., 25 C.F.R. § 291.1–219.15 (2005).

290. In this regard, it might be mentioned that while the Supreme Court has been traditionally hesitant to strike down federal statutes on Tenth Amendment grounds, it has become somewhat less so and might well revisit the Indian Child Welfare Act on such grounds.

291. See generally Getches et al., *Cases and Materials*, 733–37.

292. See generally K. Alexa Koenig, "Gambling on Proposition 1-A: The California Self-Reliance Amendment," 36 *U.S.F. L. Rev.* 1033 (2002).

293. 495 U.S. 676 (1990).

294. Nonmember Indians are individuals who are (legally) recognized as Indians but are not tribal members of the tribe where the alleged (criminal) activity took place.

295. The added language appears at 25 U.S.C. § 1301(2) (2001). "'[P]owers of self-government' means and includes all governmental powers possessed by an Indian tribe...and means the inherent power of Indian tribes, hereby recognized, to exercise criminal jurisdiction of *all* Indians."

296. 541 U.S. 193 (2004).

297. Ibid. at 196.

298. Ibid. at 197.

299. See generally *United States v. Wheeler*, 435 U.S. 313 (1978). Tribal authority is *pre*-constitutional. It is *not* rooted in the Constitution.

300. *Lara*, 541 U.S. at 197.

301. Ibid. at 198.

302. *United States v. Lara*, 324 F.3d 635 (8th Cir., 2003) (en banc).

303. *United States v. Enas*, 255 F.3d 662 (9th Cir., 2001).

304. *United States v. Lara*, 541 U.S. at 200.

305. Ibid. at 205.

306. Ibid. at 207.

307. Ibid. at 201.

308. See ibid. at 201–4. Justice Breyer cites L. Henkin's international treatise *Foreign Affairs and the U.S. Constitution* (2d ed., 1990), 72, and such cases as *Missouri v. Holland*, 252 U.S. 416, 433 (1920) and *United States v. Curtiss-Wright Export Corp.*, 299 U.S. 304, 315–322 (1936). See also Justice Thomas's pointed rejoinder at 541 U.S. at 224–26.

309. *United States v. Lara*, 541 U.S. at 215 (Thomas, J., concurring).

310. Ibid. (Thomas, J., concurring).

311. Ibid. at 224 (Thomas, J., concurring). A more detailed analysis of *United States v. Kagama*, 118 U.S. 375 (1886), and its tilt toward plenary power grounded in the trust relationship is in chapter 5. Justice Thomas also cites *United States v. Morrison*, 529 U.S. 598 (2000) and *United States v. Lopez*, 514 U.S. 549 (1995) for his willingness to "revisit the question" of the Indian Commerce Clause, as well as the "plenary" nature of the Interstate Commerce Clause. Recall that in these cases the Supreme Court set limits to the reach of the Interstate Commerce Clause.

312. Ibid. at 225 (Thomas, J., concurring).

313. See the earlier discussion in this chapter.

314. Ibid. at 226 (Thomas, J., concurring).

315. 25 U.S.C. § 71 (2000); 16 Stat. 566 (1871). "No Indian nation or tribe within the territory of the United States shall be acknowledged or recognized as an independent nation, tribe, or power with whom the United States may contract by treaty...." Yet bilateral agreements ratified by both houses of Congress would still be a possibility. See, e.g., Great Sioux Agreement of 1889, 25 Stat. 888 (1889).

316. *Lara*, 541 U.S. at 226 (Thomas, J., concurring).

317. See the discussion in chapter 10.

318. There is a condescending fondness to often characterize Justice Thomas as Justice Scalia's mere acolyte, but that is certainly not the case in Indian law jurisprudence.

319. Ibid. at 214 (Kennedy, J., concurring).

320. Ibid. at 212 (Kennedy, J., concurring).

321. Ibid. (Kennedy, J., concurring) (citation omitted).

322. Ibid. (Kennedy, J., concurring) (emphasis added).

323. Ibid. at 213 (Kennedy, J., concurring) (citations omitted) (emphasis added).

324. 25 U.S.C. § 1302 (8).

325. *Lara*, 541 U.S. at 214 (Kennedy, J., concurring).

326. See, e.g., *Means v. Navajo Nation*, 432 F.3d 924, 931 (8th Cir. 2005).

327. 25 U.S.C. § 1302 (6) (stating "and at his own expense to have the assistance of counsel for his defense"); 25 U.S.C. 25 § 1302(10) (stating that there is a right to trial

in criminal cases "by jury of not less than six persons"). There is no statutory language about the makeup of a tribal jury and whether nonmembers (even non-Indians) must be eligible for jury service. To date, this is strictly a question of tribal law in which some tribes do, but most do not, allow nonmember Indians and non-Indians to serve on tribal juries.

328. Justice Souter's dissent is premised on the notion that *Oliphant* and *Duro* were constitutional in nature and thus not subject to legislative adjustment. He also bemoans the legacy of "confusion" and "rhetorical" conceptions of "sovereignty and dependent sovereignty" embedded in the majority's decision. *Lara*, 541 U.S. at 226–31 (Souter, J. dissenting).

329. The noted exception is, of course, the Eleventh Amendment knocking out the tribe's direct action against states in federal court for their failure to negotiate in good faith with tribes to achieve a compact relative to Class III gaming under the Indian Gaming Regulatory Act. See, e.g., *Seminole Tribe of Florida v. Florida*, 517 U.S. 44 (1996).

330. See, e.g., the discussion in chapter 7.

331. See chapter 10 for a more complete discussion of an approach to some of these problems.

CHAPTER NINE

1. Much of the material in parts of this chapter draws on the fine work of S. James Anaya in his book *Indigenous Peoples in International Law* (Oxford University Press, 2d ed., 2004). The term *indigenous peoples* itself is not without complexity and controversy. Anaya's definition is detailed and most helpful:

> Today, the term *indigenous* refers broadly to the living descendants of preinvasion inhabitants of lands now dominated by others. Indigenous peoples, nations, or communities are culturally distinctive groups that find themselves engulfed by settler societies born of the forces of empire and conquest. The diverse surviving Indian communities and nations of the Western Hemisphere, the Inuit and Aleut of the Arctic, the Aboriginal people of Australia, the Maori of Aotearoa (New Zealand), Native Hawaiians and other Pacific Islanders, the Saami of the European Far North, and many of the minority or nondominant tribal peoples of Africa and Asia are generally regarded, and regard themselves, as indigenous. They are *indigenous* because their ancestral roots are embedded in the lands in which they live, or would like to live, much more deeply than the roots of more powerful sectors of society living on the same lands or in close proximity. Furthermore, they are *peoples* to the extent they comprise distinct communities with a continuity of existence and identity that links them to the communities, tribes, or nations of their ancestral past. (3)

2. Ibid., 4.

3. Ibid., 5–6 (emphasis in original).

4. Ibid., 16. Natural law thinking perceived "a normative order independent of and higher than the positive law or decisions of temporal authority." The source of such natural law was thought to stem either from God or as part of what the philosopher Grotius called the "dictate of right reason" (Ibid., 16–17).

5. Ibid., 18.

6. Ibid., 22.

7. Ibid., 23. Such assessments were not always grounded in reality, as any number of indigenous societies possessed more variegated and complex agriculture than that of European settlers. See, e.g., Charles C. Mann, *1491: New Revelations of the Americas before Columbus* (Alfred A. Knopf, 2005), 4, 34.

8. Emmerich de Vattel, *The Law of Nations or the Principles of Natural Law* (Classics of International Law Series, 1916) (Charles G. Ferwick trans. of 1758 ed.), 116, quoted ibid. at 22.

9. Anaya, *Indigenous Peoples*, 21. This despite Vattel's own general observation to the contrary in *The Law of Nations*. A certain ambivalence and contradiction was always present in Vattel's thought.

10. Ibid., 21–22. Needless to say, this is a rather idealized conception of the nation-state in the eighteenth century.

11. 21 U.S. (8 Wheat.) 543 (1823). See a full discussion of the Marshall trilogy in chapter 4.

12. 30 U.S. (5 Pet.) 1 (1831).

13. 31 U.S. (6 Pet.) 515 (1832).

14. *Johnson*, 21 U.S. at 572.

15. Ibid. at 573. "The exclusion of all other Europeans, necessarily gave to the nation making the discovery the sole right of acquiring the soil from the natives, and establishing settlements upon. It was a right in which no Europeans could interfere. It was a right which all asserted for themselves, and to the assertion of which, by others, all assented."

16. Ibid.

17. Ibid. at 572–73.

18. This doctrine, of course, was remarkably self-serving and couched in invidious comparisons and metaphors. Yet it was put forward in good faith, supported by substantial legal and philosophical authority.

19. *Johnson*, 21 U.S. at 574.

20. Ibid. at 587.

21. Ibid. at 588. It is well to remember the fragility of the Supreme Court in 1823. It was the weakest of the three branches of government, and its ability to confront acts by either the legislative or the executive branch was not well-established.

22. Ibid. at 591–92 (emphasis added).

23. This withholding of natural law rights to Indians also characterized the Marshall Court's jurisprudence in regards to African American slaves. See, e.g., G. Edward White, *History of the Supreme Court of the United States: Volumes III–IV The Marshall Court and Cultural Change, 1815–1835* (Oxford University Press, 1988), 680–81:

> The reconstituted natural law argument, on its face, seemed particularly germane to cases affecting two racial minorities in the early American

republic, black slaves and Indians. Black slaves were persons unquestionably deprived of liberty in a nation that had declared itself to be committed to liberty as a natural right; Indians were persons being dispossessed of property, because of their status, in a nation whose founders had taken the right to hold property to be inalienable. That these commitments had not been embodied in positive laws giving unqualified protection to the liberty and property rights of black slaves or Indians was not necessarily decisive, given the respectability of unwritten maxims of natural justice and common humanity as sources of early American law. Indeed, the stature of the natural law argument and the contradictions between natural law precepts and the treatment of slaves and Indians created pressure on positive law itself.

But the reconstituted natural law argument was not to prevail in cases involving discriminatory treatment of blacks and Indians. Those minorities remained outside the circle of groups whose rights were recognized and expanded in early-nineteenth-century America. And not only did the enslavement of blacks and the dispossession of Indians coexist with an expanded recognition of the liberty and property rights of white males, the natural law argument was itself tempered and eventually undermined in racial minority cases.

See also discussion in chapter 4.

24. 30 U.S. (5 Pet.) 1, 16 (1831).

25. 31 U.S. (6 Pet.) 515, 543 (1832).

26. Ibid.

27. *Cherokee Nation*, 30 U.S. at 17.

28. Ibid. at 25. Justice Johnson believed that the Cherokees did not really possess any territory and hence "[t]heir condition is something like that of the Israelites, when inhabiting the deserts." Ibid. at 27.

29. Ibid. at 21.

30. Ibid.

31. Ibid. at 53 (Thompson, J., dissenting. Dissent joined by Justice Story). Justice Thompson's dissent cited Vattel's *Law of Nations* as its sole authority for these principles of international law.

32. Ibid.

33. Ibid. at 54.

34. Ibid.

35. Ibid.

36. Ibid. at 18.

37. *Worcester*, 31 U.S. at 560–61.

38. Ibid. at 561.

39. Anaya, *Indigenous Peoples*, 31.

40. Ibid.

41. House of Commons, Select Committee on Aboriginal Tribes, Report (1837) at 86, as quoted ibid. at 32.

42. Indian Commissioner Nathaniel G. Taylor writing on the question "Shall our Indians be civilized?" in the Annual Report of the Commissioner of Indian Affairs, November 23, 1868, reprinted in *Documents of United States Policy* 123, 126 (Francis Paul Prucha, 2d ed., 1990), quoted in Anaya, *Indigenous Peoples*, 32.

43. Anaya, *Indigenous Peoples*, 33.

44. *Cherokee Nation*, 30 U.S. at 17.

45. Anaya, *Indigenous Peoples*, 33 (quoting 10 Institut de Droit International, *Annuaire* (1888–89), 203 (translation from Alpheus Snow, *The Question of the Aborigines in the Law and Practice of Nations* (Metro Books, 1972 ed.), 174–75.

46. Ibid., 33 (quoting Covenant of the League of Nations art. 23(a)).

47. 187 U.S. 553 (1903). The case is discussed in extensive detail in chapter 5.

48. Ibid. at 568 (emphasis added).

49. This absence of judicial review in the context of the trust relationship was subsequently modified by such cases as *Delaware Tribal Business Comm. v. Weeks*, 430 U.S. 73 (1977) and *United States v. Sioux Nation of Indians*, 448 U.S. 371 (1980). In the modern era, the trust relationship in Indian law has developed to provide a potential cause of action against the United States if a tribe can demonstrate that there is a bona fide trust involving "control and supervision" of tribal assets rather than a "bare" trust. See, e.g., *United States v. Mitchell (Mitchell I)*, 445 U.S. 535 (1980), and *United States v. Mitchell (Mitchell II)*, 463 U.S. 206 (1983).

50. Anaya, *Indigenous Peoples*, 49.

51. Ibid.

52. Ibid., 50.

53. Ibid.

54. Ibid.

55. United Nations Charter art. 1, para. 2.

56. Ibid. at art. 1(3); see also art. 55(c).

57. Ibid. at art. 55(a).

58. Ibid. at art. 71.

59. ILO Convention (No. 107) Concerning the Protection and Integration of Indigenous and Other Tribal and Semi-Tribal Populations in Independent Countries, June 26, 1957, 328 U.N.T.S. 247.

60. Anaya, *Indigenous Peoples*, 55. The International Labor Organization (ILO) is a specialized agency predating but now affiliated with the United Nations. The United Nations developed Convention 107 following a series of studies and meetings of experts that revealed the particular vulnerability of indigenous workers. Ibid., 54.

61. Ibid.

62. Ibid., 56.

63. Ibid., 57.

64. Ibid., 58.

65. Ibid.

66. International Labor Organization Convention (No. 169) Concerning the Indigenous and Tribal Peoples in Independent Countries, June 27, 1989 [hereinafter ILO Convention No. 169].

67. Ibid. at preamble.

68. Anaya, *Indigenous Peoples*, 60.

69. Ibid.

70. Ibid., 61.

71. Ibid.

72. Ibid.

73. Ibid.

74. Ibid., 63.

75. United Nations Declaration on the Rights of Indigenous Peoples, G.A. Res. 61/295, U.N. Doc. A/RES/61/295 (Sept. 13, 2007). The entire text of the Declaration can be found at http://www.un.org/esa/socdev/unpfii/en/declaration.html (last visited October 8, 2008).

76. Note also that the lone four votes in *opposition* came from the United States, Canada, Australia, and New Zealand, Western countries with significant populations of indigenous peoples within their borders. A statement issued jointly by the four dissenting nations explained their vote by noting that "in order for a declaration to provide states and indigenous peoples with a blueprint for harmonious and constructive relationships, it must be clear, transparent, and capable of implementation. Unfortunately, the text before us fails on all three counts." American Society of International Law, "United States Joins Australia, Canada and New Zealand in Criticizing Declaration on Indigenous Peoples' Rights," 101 *Am. J. Int'l L.* 211, 212 (2007). This is particularly ironic in the case of the United States, which readily embraced international law in the earliest days of the republic as a means of gaining title to Indian land. *See Johnson v. McIntosh*, 21 U.S. 543 (1803), and the in-depth discussion in chapter 4. Yet it seems quite unwilling to accede to international law in the twenty-first century, when that law seeks to provide minimal protections to indigenous peoples; this move does little to suggest that the United States is interested in changing its historical commitment to injustice with regard to Native peoples. See also Ezra Rosser, "Rethinking International Law and Indigenous Peoples," *Indian Country Today* (October 10, 2007), A-2. Despite the U.S. opposition, the state of Maine's General Assembly passed a resolution in support of the declaration. Gale Courey Toensing, "Maine Embraces United Nations Declaration on the Rights of Indigenous Peoples," *Indian Country Today* (April 23, 2008), 4. Canada's Parliament has also endorsed the Declaration. Ibid., 1.

77. This policy of self-determination in contemporary federal Indian law is rife with contradiction and misdirection. See generally the discussion in chapter 8; see also David Getches et al., *Cases and Materials on Federal Indian Law* (Thomson West, 5th ed., 2005), 216–57.

78. Anaya, *Indigenous Peoples*, 104–5.

79. Ibid., 129.

80. Ibid. (quoting the United Nations Charter art 1(3)).

81. Ibid., 133.

82. *Lovelace v. Canada*, Communication No. 24/1977, Report of the Human Rights Committee, U.N.G.A.O.R., 36th Sess., Supp. No. 40, at 166, U.N. Doc. A/36/46 Annex 18 (1977) (view adopted July 30, 1981).

83. Ibid. at 173 (quoting art. 27).

84. 21 U.S. (8 Wheat) 543 (1823).

85. *Case of Mayagna (Sumo) Awas Tingni Community v. Nicaragua*, Inter-Am. Ct. H.R. (Ser. C) No. 79 (Judgment on the merits and reparations of August 31, 2001) [hereinafter *Awas Tingni* case]. The case is also published in an abridged version in 19 *Ariz. J. Int'l & Comp. L.* 395 (2002).

86. The people of Awas Tingni prefer the name Mayagna as to the more commonly used term Sumo. They regard the latter as a name imposed by outsiders. The Atlantic Coast region of Nicaragua is generally understood to include roughly the eastern third of the country. This region is home to the Miskito, Mayagna (Sumo), and Rama Indians and to a substantial Black Creole population. The area is geographically isolated, and its inhabitants possess unique history and culture. S. James Anaya and Claudio Grossman, "The Case of Awas Tingni v. Nicaragua: A New Step in the International Law of Indigenous Peoples," 19 *Ariz. J. Int'l & Comp. L.* 1 (2002). The Awas Tingni Community consists of about 600 individuals occupying approximately 40,000 hectares in the region. Complaint of the Inter-American Commission of Human Rights, ibid. at 23.

87. *Awas Tingni* case, para. 6.

88. Charter of the Organization of American States art. 106, 119 U.N.T.S. 3 (entered into force Dec. 13, 1951).

89. See Inter-Am. Ct. H.R. Rules of Procedure, art. 27.

90. See American Convention on Human Rights, July 18, 1978, 1144 U.N.T.S. 123.

91. *Awas Tingni* case.

92. Ibid. at para. 2.

93. Ibid.

94. Ibid.

95. Ibid. at para. 173.

96. Ibid.

97. Ibid. at para. 148.

98. Ibid. at para. 146.

99. Ibid. at para. 164.

100. Ibid. at para. 167.

101. Anaya, *Indigenous Peoples*, 2. As of August 2007, Nicaragua has not carried out the court's mandate. See, e.g., Leonardo J. Alvarado, "Prospects and Challenges in the Implementation of Indigenous Peoples' Human Rights in International Law: Lessons from the Case of *Awas Tingni v. Nicaragua*," 24 *Ariz. J. Int'l & Comp. L.* 609 (2007). According to Dean Claudio Grossman of American University Washington College of Law, Nicaragua finally complied with the court's direction to properly demarcate the lands of the Awas Tingni people in the latter part of 2008.

102. Declaration on the Right to Development, G.A. Res 41/128, Dec. 4, 1986, art. 1(1) (emphasis added).

103. Anaya, *Indigenous Peoples*, 152.

104. Ibid., 151.

105. U.N. Declaration, at art. 18.

106. ILO Convention No. 169, art. 6.1(b).

107. Anaya, *Indigenous Peoples,* 154; see Jo M. Pasqualucci, "The Evolution of International Indigenous Rights in the Inter-American Human Rights System," 6 *Hmn. Rts. L. Rev.* 281 (2006) (providing examples of consultation in the Inter-American system).

108. Pasqualucci, "The Evolution," 282–83.

109. Anaya, *Indigenous Peoples,* 109 (internal citations omitted) (quoting U.N. Charter art. 2(4)).

110. Ibid.

111. *United States v. Dann,* 470 U.S. 39 (1985).

112. Ibid. at 43.

113. Ibid. at 50.

114. Ibid. (footnotes omitted).

115. *United States v. Dann,* 865 F.2d 1528 (9th Cir. 1989).

116. Ibid. at 1536.

117. *Case of Mary and Carrie Dann v. United States* (Case # 11.140) InterAm. C.H.R. No. 75/02 (December 27, 2002).

118. Ibid. at para. 5.

119. Ibid. at para. 173(1).

120. Ibid.

121. Getches et al., *Cases and Materials,* 294–95.

122. The Danns secured a similar moral "victory" when the United Nations Committee on the Elimination of Racial Discrimination (CERD) expressed "concern" over the Danns' situation and recommended that the United States "should ensure effective participation by indigenous communities in decisions affecting them, including those on their land rights." Ibid at 295.

123. The Constitution Act (1982), Pt. II, Sec. 35. Section 52 of the Constitution Act of 1982 declares the Constitution as "the supreme law of Canada."

124. [1997] 3 S.C.R. 1010.

125. Ibid. at 1029.

126. Ibid. at 1069. The trial court decision was, in fact, reversed for its failure to properly consider this evidence.

127. Ibid. at 1083.

128. Ibid. at 1107–8.

129. Ibid.

130. Ibid. at 1113–14.

131. Ibid. at 1123–24.

132. J. G. A. Pocock, "Law, Sovereignty, and History in a Divided Culture: The Case of New Zealand and the Treaty of Waitangi," Iredell Memorial Lecture, Lancaster University, 20–23, 10 October 1991, as excerpted in Getches et al., *Cases and Materials,* 979.

133. Ibid. at 980. The treaty negotiations were conducted bilingually and texts were prepared in both English and Maori, but no final agreed upon text ever emerged (981). Only 39 chiefs signed the English version, whereas 512 chiefs signed the Maori version (984). The original population of Maori at the time of initial contact with Europeans was about 125,000. There was a steady decline of Maori population

through most of the nineteenth and early twentieth century. Today the Maori compromise approximately 15 percent of New Zealand's population of three million.

134. Ibid.

135. The Treaty of Waitangi is one of the very few, if not the only, treaty with indigenous peoples that is bilingual, with separate texts in both English and the indigenous language.

136. Pocock, "Law. Sovereignty, and History," 982.

137. Ibid.

138. See the previous discussion of Canada.

139. Pocock, "Law, Sovereignty, and History," 983.

140. Getches et al., *Cases and Materials*, 985.

141. [1987] 1 N.Z.L.R. 641.

142. Ibid. at 664.

143. [1987] 2 N.Z.L.R. 188.

144. Ibid. at 210. Specifically the Court noted:

> The expertise of the Waitangi Tribunal lies in its understanding of Maori values in the context of the Treaty of Waitangi as the Tribunal interprets that Treaty. A moment's reflection upon the provisions of the Treaty of Waitangi Act, its extremely important statutory functions, the constitution of the Waitangi Tribunal and its reported findings must lead to the conclusion that it is an expert source within its field for instruction in Maori values. While, so far as the present case is concerned, no report of that Tribunal is in any way binding on this Court, its considered opinions, within the area of its expert functions, ought to be accorded due weight in this Court. The way in which the Waitangi Tribunal has dealt with the concept of Maori spiritual values in regard to water establishes, sufficiently for the determination of this branch of the appellant's case, that those values cannot be dismissed in a general sort of way by referring to them as personal to the individual or as something which the community at large may trample upon, at least not in the context of the indigenous population of this country which places great value upon the principles of the Treaty of Waitangi. Nor should the benefit of all New Zealanders be given a degree of absolute emphasis so as to exclude, in a branch of the law which has an affinity with the Treaty, Maori spiritual values. (Ibid. at 223)

145. [1992] 175 C.L.R. 1.

146. Ibid. at 29.

147. Ibid. at 30.

148. Ibid.

149. Ibid. at 42.

150. Ibid. at 63. One of the cases cited for this principle was *Tee-Hit-Ton Indians v. United States*, 348 U.S. 272 (1955), which held that Alaskan natives had no recognized property rights in their land because Congress had not conferred the status of recognized Indian title on them.

151. Ibid. at 64.

152. Ibid. at 69.

153. Getches et al., *Cases and Materials*, 216–57.

154. Tribes have no criminal jurisdiction over non-Indians. See, e.g., *Oliphant v. Suquamish Indian Tribe*, 435 U.S. 191 (1978) and *Nevada v. Hicks*, 533 U.S. 353 (2001), where Justice Scalia observed: "We have never held that a tribal court had jurisdiction over a nonmember defendant." *Hicks*, 533 U.S. at 358 n. 2.

155. See, e.g., the discussion of federal common law in the case of *Sosa v. Alvarez-Machain*, 542 U.S. 692 (2004), in chapter 8.

156. See, e.g., *Johnson v. McIntosh*, 21 U.S. (8 Wheat.) 543 (1823).

157. [1992] 175 C.L.R. 1, 39.

158. 443 U.S. 371, 435 (1980) (Rehnquist, J., dissenting). Justice Blackmun writing for majority, which found that federal government took 7.7 million acres of Sioux land in the Black Hills of South Dakota without paying just compensation and thus violated the Fifth Amendment, did not confront Justice Rehnquist's dissent but characterized the episode as "a colorful and in many respects tragic, chapter in the history of the Nation's past." Ibid. at 374. See detailed discussion in chapter 4.

159. See, e.g., Getches et al., *Cases and Materials*, 1029 n. 3.

160. See, e.g., Robert Frost's poem "The Road Not Taken," in Paul Negri, *Great Short Poems* (Courier Dove, 2000), 44.

CHAPTER TEN

1. Congress assumed plenary power in 1903 with its decision in *Lone Wolf v. Hitchcock*, 187 U.S. 553 (1903). See the detailed discussion in chapter 5. The Supreme Court has assumed, without acknowledgment, its own version of judicial plenary power in the modern era, starting with *Oliphant v. Suquamish Indian Tribe*, 435 U.S. 191 (1978) and *Montana v. United States*, 450 U.S. 549 (1981). See the detailed discussion in chapter 8.

2. 30 U.S. (5 Pet.) 1, 16 (1830).

3. 118 U.S. 375, 381 (1886).

4. 411 U.S. 164, 172 n.7 (1973).

5. 447 U.S. 134, 176 (1979) (Rehnquist, J., concurring and dissenting).

6. *Atkinson Trading Co. v. Shirley*, 532 U.S. 645, 659 (2001) (Souter, J., dissenting).

7. 541 U.S. 193 (2004); see the detailed description in chapter 8.

8. Ibid. at 200.

9. See *Duro v. Reina*, 495 U.S. 676 (1990) and the congressional overturning of this result at 25 U.S.C. § 1301 (2).

10. *Lara*, 541 U.S. at 212 (Kennedy, J., concurring in judgment).

11. Ibid. at 214 (Thomas, J., concurring in judgment).

12. Ibid. at 215.

13. Ibid. at 225.

14. Ibid. at 219.

15. Ibid. at 226 (Souter, J., dissenting).

16. Ibid. at 230.

17. 435 U.S. 191 (1978).

18. 450 U.S. 544 (1981).

19. *Oliphant*, 435 U.S. at 208.

20. *Montana*, 450 U.S. at 564. This rule has subsequently been expanded to include all land on the reservation. *Nevada v. Hicks*, 533 U.S. 353 (2001).

21. See, e.g., *Strate v. A-1 Contractors*, 520 U.S. 438, 445 (1997).

22. *Oliphant*, 435 U.S. at 204.

23. *Montana*, 450 U.S. at 559–60, n. 9. The Court did not heed its own words, but subsequently expanded *Montana* analysis to *all* land on the reservation. *Nevada v. Hicks*, 533 U.S. 353 (2001). See also Frank Pommersheim, *Braid of Feathers: American Indian Law and Contemporary Tribal Life* (University of California Press, 1995), 151.

24. *Oliphant*, 435 U.S. at 204.

25. David Getches, "Conquering the Cultural Frontier: The New Subjectivism of the Supreme Court in Indian Law," 84 *Cal. L. Rev.* 1573, 1575 (1996), more specifically:

> [O]pinions in this field have not posited an original state of affairs that can subsequently be altered only by explicit legislation, but have rather sought to discern what the current state of affairs ought to be by taking into account all legislation, and the congressional "expectations" that it reflects, down to the present day. (quoting memorandum from Justice Antonin Scalia to Justice William J. Brennan Jr., Apr. 4, 1990 (*Duro v. Reina*, No. 88–6546)) (footnote omitted)

26. Dalia Tsuk Mitchell, *Architect of Justice* (Cornell University Press, 2007), 166.

27. 514 U.S. 549 (1995).

28. 529 U.S. 598 (2000).

29. *Lopez*, 514 U.S. at 557.

30. Ibid. Note the eerie similarity to the Court's thinking about the Major Crimes Act and the Indian Commerce Clause in *United States v. Kagama*, 118 U.S. 375 (1886). The Court in *Lopez* might have cited *Kagama*, but it did not. See Justice Thomas to this effect in *United States v. Lara*, 541 U.S. 193 (2004).

31. Ibid. at 567.

32. Ibid. at 568.

33. Ibid. at 567–68.

34. *Morrison*, 529 U.S. at 627.

35. Ibid. at 607.

36. Ibid. at 608.

37. Ibid. at 613.

38. 541 U.S. 193 (2004).

39. Ibid. at 205.

40. 435 U.S. 191 (1978) (holding that tribes do not have criminal jurisdiction over non-Indians).

41. 450 U.S. 544, 566 (1981) (holding that tribes do not have civil regulatory authority over non-Indians on fee land within the reservation unless there is a consensual relationship or the conduct of non-Indians "threatens or has some direct effect on the political integrity, the economic security or the health or welfare of the tribe").

42. 508 U.S. 679 (1993) (holding that the Cheyenne River Sioux Tribe does not have regulatory jurisdiction over non-Indians on federal "taking land" for Oahe Dam).

43. 520 U.S. 438 (1997) (holding that tribal courts do not have jurisdiction over car accidents involving non-Indians that take place on state highways running through a reservation).

44. 522 U.S. 520 (1998) (holding that Alaska Native villages are not "dependent Indian communities" within the meaning of the Indian country statute, 18 U.S.C. § 1151, and therefore do not possess any governmental authority over non-Indians).

45. 532 U.S. 645 (2001) (holding that tribes may not assert a room tax on a non-Indian staying at a motel owned by a non-Indian and located on fee land within the reservation).

46. 533 U.S. 353 (2001) (holding that the *Montana* test applies to events that take place on trust land as well as fee land within the reservation, and tribal courts do not have jurisdiction over 42 U.S.C. § 1983 lawsuits).

47. 128 S.Ct. 2709 (2008) (tribal courts do not have jurisdiction over a discrimination claim arising from the sale of fee land on the reservation by a non-Indian bank to an Indian couple).

48. 435 U.S. 191 (1978). No doubt there would be significant resistance to such a move by many states, particularly in the West. Yet what if the trade-off for overturning *Oliphant* would be increased federal review of tribal court criminal cases under the substantive guarantees of the Indian Civil Rights Act of 1968?

49. See, e.g., *Lara*, 541 U.S. at 284–85.

50. N. Bruce Duthu, *American Indians and the Law* (Viking, 2008), 207–10.

51. David H. Getches, "Beyond Indian Law: The Rehnquist Court's Pursuit of State's Rights, Color-Blind Justice and Mainstream Values," 86 *Minn. L. Rev.* 267, 280 (2001).

52. See, for example, the legislative proposal discussed in Duthu, *American Indians and the Law*.

53. Iroquois Confederacy and Indian Nations—Recognizing Contributions to the United States:

> Whereas the original framers of the Constitution, including, most notably George Washington and Benjamin Franklin, are known to have greatly admired the concepts of the Six Nations of the Iroquois Confederacy;
>
> Whereas the confederation of the original Thirteen Colonies into one republic was influenced by the political system developed by the Iroquois Confederacy as were many of the democratic principles which were incorporated into the Constitution itself; and,
>
> Whereas, since the formation of the United States, the Congress has recognized the sovereign status of Indian tribes and has, through the exercise of powers reserved to the Federal Government in the Commerce Clause of the Constitution (art. I, s.2, cl. 3), dealt with Indian tribes on a government-to-government basis and has, through the treaty clause (art. II, s.2, cl. 2) entered into three hundred and seventy treaties with Indian tribal Nations;

Whereas, from the first treaty entered into with an Indian Nation, the treaty with the Delaware Indians of September 17, 1778, the Congress has assumed a trust responsibility and obligation to Indian tribes and their members;

Whereas this trust responsibility calls for Congress to "exercise the utmost good faith in dealings with Indians" as provided for in the Northwest Ordinance of 1787, (1 Stat. 50);

Whereas, the judicial system of the United States has consistently recognized and reaffirmed this special relationship: Now, therefore, be it

Resolved by the House of Representatives (the Senate concurring),
That–

the Congress, on the occasion of the two hundredth anniversary of the signing of the United States Constitution, acknowledges the contribution made by the Iroquois Confederacy and other Indian Nations to the formation and development of the United States;

the Congress also hereby reaffirms the constitutionally recognized government-to-government relationship with Indian tribes which has been the cornerstone of this Nation's official Indian policy;

the Congress specifically acknowledges and reaffirms the trust responsibility and obligation of the United States Government to Indian tribes, including Alaska Natives, for their preservation, protection, and enhancement, including the provision of health, education, social, and economic assistance programs as necessary, and including the duty to assist tribes in their performance of governmental responsibility to provide for the social and economic well-being of their members and to preserve tribal cultural identity and heritage; and

the Congress also acknowledges the need to exercise the utmost good faith in upholding its treaties with the various tribes, as the tribes understood them to be, and the duty of a great Nation to uphold its legal and moral obligations for the benefit of all of its citizens so that they and their posterity may also continue to enjoy the rights they have enshrined in the United States Constitution for time immemorial. (H. Con. Res. 331 (Oct. 21, 1988))

54. Alex Tallchief Skibine, "Redefining the State of Indian Tribes within "Our Federalism": Beyond the Dependency Paradigm," 38 *Conn. L. Rev.* 667, 692 (2006).

55. Ibid., 669.

56. Ibid., 670–677.

57. Ibid., 667.

58. Russel Lawrence Barsh and James Youngblood Henderson, *The Road: Indian Tribes and Political Liberty* (University of California Press, 1980), 274:

Regardless of their [i.e., treaties] original intent, they have resulted in a completely political and economic integration of tribes into the federal system. Separation is practically impossible.

See also Oren Lyons et al., *Exiled in the Land of the Free: Democracy, Indian Nations, and the U.S. Constitution* (Clear Light Publishers, 1992). There is also a rich, new vein of

Indian law scholarship discussing models of tribal governance. See, e.g., Angela Riley, "Good (Native) Governance," 107 *Col. L. Rev.* 1049 (2007); "(Tribal) Sovereignty and Illiberalism," 95 *Cal. L. Rev.* 799 (2007); Bethany Berger, "Liberalism and Republicanism in Federal Indian Law," 38 *Conn. L. Rev.* 813 (2006); Kevin Washburn, "Tribal Self-Determination at the Crossroads," 38 *Conn. L. Rev.* 777 (2006); Sarah Krakoff, "The Virtues and Vices of Sovereignty," 38 *Conn. L. Rev.* 797 (2006); and Justin Richland, *Arguing with Tradition: The Language of Law in Hopi Tribal Court* (University of Chicago Press, 2008).

59. Barsh and Henderson, *The Road*, 270.

60. Ibid., 271.

61. Ibid., 275.

62. Ibid., 276 (emphasis added).

63. Felix Cohen, *Handbook of Federal Indian Law* (University of New Mexico Press, 1942), 122.

64. Barsh and Henderson, *The Road*, 280–82.

65. Ibid., 281 (Sec. 5 of the proposed amendment).

66. Ibid.

67. See the in-depth discussion in chapter 8.

68. See, e.g., Robert Clinton, "There Is No Federal Supremacy Clause for Indian Tribes," 34 *Ariz. St. L. J.* 113 (2002).

69. 25 U.S.C. § 71.

70. Art. II, Sec. 2(2).

71. See, e.g., the Great Sioux Agreement of 1889, 25 Stat. 888 (1889).

72. See the discussion in chapter 8.

73. See, e.g., the Thirteenth, Fourteenth, and Fifteenth Amendments to the U.S. Constitution.

74. See, e.g., the Nineteenth Amendment to the U.S. Constitution.

75. Judith Resnik and Julie Chi-hye Suk, "Adding Insult to Injury: Questioning the Role of Dignity in Conceptions of Sovereignty," 55 *Stan. L. Rev.* 1921–22 (2003) (footnotes omitted).

76. Ibid., 1922.

77. Ibid., 1923, quoting "*Fed. Mar. Comm'n v. S.C. State Ports Auth.*, 535 U.S. 743, 760 (2002) (holding that sovereign immunity protected states from adjudication by a federal agency responding to a private party's complaint of a violation of a federal statute regulating shipping); see also *Alden v. Maine*, 527 U.S. 706, 715 (1999) (commenting that "[t]he generation that designed and adopted our federal system considered immunity from private suits central to sovereign dignity"); *Idaho v. Coeur d'Alene Tribe*, 521 U.S. 261, 268 (1997) (stating that "the dignity and respect afforded a State, which the immunity is designed to protect, are placed in jeopardy" by private suits in federal courts, regardless of the basis of federal courts' jurisdiction); *Seminole Tribe*, 517 U.S. at 58 (suggesting that a purpose of the Eleventh Amendment, in addition to protecting state treasuries, is to prevent states from the indignity of being subject to private suits); *P.R. Aqueduct & Sewer Auth. v. Metcalf & Eddy, Inc.*, 506 U.S. 139, 146 (1993) (permitting states to appeal the denial of sovereign immunity defenses to ensure "that the States' dignitary interests can be fully vindicated"). Ibid., n. 9.

78. Ibid., n. 8:

Compare Nevada v. Hicks, 533 U.S. 353 (2001) (holding that tribal courts lacked authority to adjudicate a tribal member's claim that state officials had wrongfully entered the Shoshone reservation to conduct a search and that they were not courts of general jurisdiction), *and Strate v. A-1 Contractors*, 520 U.S. 438 (1997) (holding that tribal jurisdiction did not reach a civil dispute of members with nonmembers), *with Iowa Mut. Ins. Co v. LaPlante*, 480 U.S. 9, 18 (1987) (recognizing tribal jurisdiction as a matter of comity and stating that alleged incompetence of tribal court is not among exceptions to exhaustion of remedies requirement), and *Nat'l Farmers Union Ins. Cos. v. Crow Tribe of Indians*, 471 U.S. 845 (1985) (recognizing the exercise of federal jurisdiction as potentially impairing tribal court authority).

79. Constitution of Canada, § 35 (1982).

80. James Anaya, *Indigenous Peoples in International Law* (Oxford University Press, 2d ed., 2004), 145.

81. Ibid., 206.

82. Ibid.

83. Ibid.

84. Ibid.

85. Ibid., 207.

86. Ibid.

87. Ibid., 194.

88. Ibid.

89. For example, Article V of the Constitution requires ratification of amendments by the "Legislatures of three fourths of the several States." Yet national constitutions elsewhere have been successfully amended. See, e.g., Constitution of Canada, §35 (1982).

90. Such an understanding no doubt will require a certain constitutional "faith":

The point of this constitutional "faith" is to identify a fruitful path in the evolving relationship of tribal courts and federal courts. This path begins in the past with an understanding of mutuality grounded in principles of treaty federalism, then moves to sweep aside the plenary brambles, and finally clears the way to complete a constitutional journey. In other words, this emerging "faith" seeks a way that respects both the aspirations of tribal courts to flourish and a national jurisprudence that regards arbitrary power as constitutionally indefensible. Without such "faith" and conscientious effort, there is little hope for meaningful growth and stability but only the likelihood of a kind of blind and erratic development that potentially exposes tribal courts (and tribes in general) to the "decisive operations of merciless power." The presence of such a "faith" is needed to provide both confident institutional grounding and principled constitutional assurance. (Frank Pommersheim, "Tribal Courts and the Federal Judiciary: Opportunities and

Challenges for a Constitutional Democracy," 58 *Mont. L. Rev.* 313, 330–31
(1997) (footnote omitted))

There is not only the matter of constitutional "faith," but also the periodic need for
constitutional "refounding":

> For it is one thing to frame a Constitution. It is quite another to give it a
> grounding that will secure the place of its authority. At a critical moment in
> American history, when the nation was divided over the issue of slavery,
> Abraham Lincoln realized that the Constitution needed to be rescued by
> those who, in coming to the rescue, would decide the fate of its authority. He
> realized, in other words, that the nation's founding scripture was in need of a
> refounding that the scripture itself could not provide. (Robert Pogue
> Harrison, *The Dominion of the Dead* (University of Chicago Press, 2003), 27.)

Index

Alaska v. Native Village of Venetie Tribal Government, 233, 300
Alden v. Maine, 50
Allen v. Merrell, 176
Allen v. Toombs, 206
Allotment, 126
  background, 126–30
  fractionalization, 130
  General Allotment Act (Dawes Severalty Act), 126, 129, 159–60, 168
Amar, Akhil Reed, 314 n. 10, 320 n. 102
American Convention on Human Rights, 277, 280–81
American Indian Religious Freedom Act, 195, 369 n. 107, 371 n. 147
Amish, 190
Anaya, James, 266, 268–69, 273, 391 n. 1
Anderson, Fred, 316 n. 45
Anthropology, 7, 90, 115
Arizona Enabling Act, 215
Articles of Confederation, 5, 26, 27–34, 36, 39–40, 43, 46, 51, 57–58, 88, 95, 112, 145
  amendment process, 28, 33
  Article IX (Indians), 29, 30, 58, 88
  background, 27–29
  Benjamin Franklin's draft, 31–32
  Canada (Art. VI), 325 n. 109

failure, 33, 36, 40
ratification, 28
Assimilative Crime Act, 211
Atkinson Trading Co., Inc. v. Shirley, 218, 225, 233, 300
Australia, 119, 259, 268, 284, 287, 289–93
Axtell, James, 27

Badoni v. Higginson, 190
Bailey v. Drexel Furniture Company, 47
Bailyn, Bernard, 34
Bald Eagle Protection Act, 201
Banner, Stuart, 317 n. 55
Barsh, Russell Lawrence, 303–4, 307, 402 n. 58
Bear Lodge Multiple Use Association v. Babbitt, 367 n. 72, 367 n. 74
Bear, Chief Hollow Horn, 128
Benvenisti, Meron, 346 n. 182, 346 n. 188
Bezuidenhout, Evita, 346 n. 190
Bible, 189, 193, 206
Billington, Ray, 117
Black Hills case, *see United States v. Sioux Nation of Indians*
Blackmoon v. Charles Mix County, 179
Blackstone, 35
Blatchford v. Native Village of Noatak and Circle Village, 50
Boyd v. Nebraska, 170

Braid of Feathers, 6
Brendale v. Confederated Tribes and Bands
    of Yakima Nation, 224, 378 n.
    120
Brosius, Samuel, 134
Brown v. Board of Education, 117
Buck Act, 59, 215
Buffalo, 15, 315 n. 31
Bureau of Indian Affairs, 31, 113, 127,
    204, 217, 241, 251, 267
Burke Act, 160
Burke, Charles, 188

California v. Cabazon Band of Mission
    Indians, 246–47
Canada, 37, 94, 100, 259, 268, 276,
    281, 284, 285–87, 288,
    290–93, 312
  Constitution, 285
  Doctrine of Discovery, 100–101
  Indian Act, 276
Capitalism, 14, 15, 149
Carr, E.H., 116
Casas, Bartolomë de las, 260
Chae Chan Ping v. United States, 69–70,
    144, 145
Chemerinsky, Erwin, 380 n. 131
Cherokee Nation Delegate Right, 83
Cherokee Nation v. Georgia, 61, 87, 101,
    261, 263, 268, 296
Cherokee Tobacco Case, 329 n. 190
Chinese Exclusion Case, see Chae Chan
    Ping v. United States
Chisholm v. Georgia, 49
Christianity, 10, 24–25, 90, 104, 184, 189,
    260, 262
  missionaries, 184–85, 189
Church of Jesus Christ of Latter Day Saints
    v. United States, 148
Citizenship, 129, 138, 142, 146–49, 155
  "citizenship ritual," 160–62
  federal, 155–71
    statutes, 159–64
  Indians, 155, 168, 172
  African-Americans, 170–71
  state, 171–81
    Idaho, 172
    Minnesota, 172
    New Mexico, 172
    North Dakota, 172
    right to fair representation, 177–81
    right to vote, 171–76
    Washington, 172
    treaties, 156–59
    tribal, 180–81
  Citizenship Act of 1924, 159, 163,
    168–70, 174–75
City of Boerne v. Flores, 199–200
City of Sherrill v. Oneida Indian Nation of
    New York, 231, 345 n. 166
Civil Rights Act of 1866, 166
"Civilization," 10, 21, 24, 83, 90, 104, 118,
    123, 126, 158–59, 172, 175–76,
    185, 262
Cleveland, President Grover, 129
Cleveland, Sarah, 145, 147, 150
Clinton, President William, 195, 199, 371
    n. 146
Clinton, Robert, 30, 46, 59, 83
Cohen, Felix, 92, 234–37, 298, 302–3
Collector v. Day, 47–48
Collier, John, 189, 235
Colonial governance, 22
Colonialism, 46, 112–13, 119, 142, 171,
    229, 266, 271–72, 284
Colony formation, 7, 21, 26, 27
Columbus, Christopher, 260, 314 n. 2,
    317 n. 67
Commerce, 3, 9, 11, 13, 17, 22, 24, 26
  land acquisition, 3, 9, 16–17, 21–22, 87,
    90, 93, 95–96, 140–41, 146
Compact, 82, 248, 303
Comparative law, 284, 291, 292
  Australia, 284–85, 289–91
  Canada, 285–87, 291–93
  New Zealand, 287–89
Conquest, 10, 22, 89, 91, 94, 100, 108–9,
    237, 262–64, 290
Constitution, 3–7, 9, 26, 30, 33–39,
    43–49, 51, 84, 87, 90, 95,
    103, 106, 109–15, 143–51, 155,
    160–65, 169, 170
  admission of new states, 356 n. 113
  African-Americans, 170, 310–11
  amendment process, 309–10
  amendment proposals, 304–8
  and Indian tribes, 38–39
  architecture, 34, 84, 303
  Article I, Section 2, 155
  Article I, Section 8, 104

Article III, 43, 49–50, 103–4, 107, 249
Article IV (Territory Clause), 51, 145–46
Article VI (Supremacy Clause), 216
Bill of Rights, 36, 49, 238
constitutional crisis, 110–11
Convention of 1787, 33
dignity and equity, 5
Dormant Commerce Clause, 41
due process, 256
Eleventh Amendment, 34, 48–50, 84, 249–50, 312
equal protection, 177, 203–4, 227, 240, 255–56
extra-constitutional, 4
Fifteenth Amendment, 164, 174, 176, 178
First Amendment, 6, 183, 184
  Establishment Clause, 186, 190, 195–96, 205
  free exercise
    18th–19th centuries, 184–86
    20th century, 184
    "incidental effects," 192–93
Foreign Commerce Clause, 143–44
Fourteenth Amendment, 148, 163–70, 174, 249, 299, 305, 307
Full Faith and Credit Clause, 34, 51
  foreign judgment, 52–53
  implementing statute, 28 USC § 1738, 54–55
  state approaches, 55–57
    Alaska, 55
    Arizona, 55
    New Mexico, 55
    North Dakota, 55
    South Dakota, 55
    Washington, 55
    Wyoming, 55
  tribal approaches, 56
  tribal court judgments, 54–55
Indian Commerce Clause, 3, 4, 30, 34, 39, 43, 46, 57–63, 84, 106, 112–13, 138–39, 212, 214, 217–18, 229, 243, 250, 252, 253, 299–300
"Indians not taxed," 155, 164–67, 172–74
Interstate Commerce Clause, 34, 39–43, 50, 57–59, 61–62, 84, 218, 249, 298–99

preemption, 44, 59, 63, 91, 95–96, 98, 215–18
reform and amendment, 6
"refounding," 405 n. 90
right to counsel, 256
roots of, 34–36
separation of powers, 34
Supremacy Clause, 34, 40–41, 43–46, 65–66, 84, 216
  Indian Tribes, 45–46
Tenth Amendment, 34, 41, 46–48
treatymaking, 46
women, 38, 160, 163, 311
Contact, 3, 5, 9, 12, 15, 23, 25, 77, 96, 122, 123, 183, 397 n. 133
Continental Congress, 39–40, 88, 99, 101
  Six Nations speech, 30
Corn Tassel, George, 111
Cornell, Stephen, 315 n. 19
Cotton Petroleum Corp. v. New Mexico, 218, 233
Court of Claims, 64, 116
Courts of Indian Offenses, 187
Cronon, William, 15, 18, 27
Crow Allotment Act, 220–21, 228, 297
Crown Charters, 19, 20, 21, 32
Cruz v. Beto, 206
Culture, 9, 15, 24–27
Cultural difference, 3, 271

Dann sisters, 281, 283–84
Darwish, Mahoud, 346 n. 188
Dawes Severalty Act, see Allotment
Dawes, Henry, 133
Declaration on the Rights of Indigenous Peoples, see United Nations
DeCoteau v. District County Court, 73
De Geofroy v. Riggs, 66
Delgamuukw v. British Columbia, 285–86
Delaware Tribal Business Committee v. Weeks, 70, 394 n. 49
Deloria, Ella, 344 n. 158
Deloria, Jr., Vine, 162
Dependence, 106, 107, 112, 141, 166
Devils Tower, 195–96
Diderot, Denis, 12
Diplomacy
  war, 3, 33, 106, 265
    multicultural frontier, 77

Discovery Doctrine, 90, 96, 263–64
Disease, 15–16
  mourning war, 16, 79
Domestic dependent nations, 61, 105,
    108, 264
Dred Scott (Scott v. Sandford) Case, 125,
    147, 148, 170, 347 n. 2
Duro override, 237, 251–52, 256, 300
Duro v. Reina, 229, 251
Dussias, Allison, 184, 364 n. 29

Eagle feathers, 183, 189, 201–5, 208
Ecology, 7
Economics, see Commerce
Ecosystem, 15, 317
Education, religious content, 186
Edye v. Robertson, 355 n. 102
Elk v. Wilkins, 155, 163–64
Ellesmere Island, 100
Employment Division v. Smith, 199
Endangered Species Act, 201
Epidemiology, 11, 14
Executive Order 13,007, "Indian Sacred
    Sites," 195

Federal courts, 6
Federal Maritime Comm'n v. S.C. Ports
    Authority, 403 n. 77
Federalism, 4, 38–39
  federal-state, 4
  federal-tribal, 4
Federalist Papers, 39, 46
Florida Prepaid Postsecondary Education
    Expense Board v. College Savings
    Bank, 50
Foreign Commerce Clause, see
    Constitution
Fort Laramie Treaty of 1868, 53, 68,
    73, 75, 115–16, 158–59, 221,
    343 n, 142
Fort Pitt Treaty (1778), 82, 333 n. 273
Franklin, Benjamin, 38, 88, 92, 401 n. 53
  draft of Articles of Confederation, 31
French and Indian War, 19, 20, 94
Frickey, Philip P., 347 n. 2, 354 n. 93,
    379 n. 126
Friedman, Benjamin, 11, 315 n. 7
Friel, Brian, 121, 346 n. 179

Gaddis, John Lewis, 345 n. 169
Gage, Matilda Joslyn, 38

Gallahan v. Hollyfield, 206
General Allotment Act, see Allotment
General Crimes Act, 211–12
Getches, David, 354 n. 92, 374 n. 15, 379
    n. 126, 380 n. 129, 400 n. 25
Ghost Dance, 188, 364 n. 25
Gibbons v. Ogden, 40–41, 43, 322 n. 25,
    322 n. 36
Gibson v. Babbitt, 204
Gilmen, George, 102
Give Away Ceremony, 365 n. 33
Givens, Joshua, 132
Gonzales v. O Centro Espirita Beneficente
    Uniao Do Vegetal, 200
Gonzales v. Raich, 42
Grant, President Ulysses S., 65, 117
Graves v. New York, 48
Great Law of Peace, 36–38
Guardian-ward relationship, see Trust
    Relationship

Handbook of Federal Indian Law, 235–36
Hans v. Louisiana, 49–50
Harper, Robert Goodloe, 99
Harrison v. Laveen, 175
Head Money Cases, 69, 144
Henderson v. New York, 143
Henderson, James Youngblood, 303–4,
    307
Hilton v. Guyot, 52, 56
History, 4–7, 100–101
  Indian law, 115–20
  Ireland, 121–23
  maps, 115–16
  Middle East, 24, 93, 121–22
Hobbes, 35–36
Huakina Development Trust v. Waikato
    Valley Authority, 289

Idaho v. Coeur d'Alene Tribe of Idaho, 50
Illinois and Piankeshaw Indians, 89, 98,
    338 n. 52
Illinois and Wabash Land Companies,
    98, 338 n. 52
Immigration, 137–38, 143–46, 353 n. 87
In re Heff, 168–69
In re Marriage of Red Fox, 55
Indian
  agency, 27
  definition of, 313 n. 1
  governance, 22–23

incarcerated, 167, 206–8,
nature, 11, 14–15
tribe, definition, 313 n. 1
Indian Child Welfare Act, 55, 237,
    242–51, 256
Indian Civil Rights Act of 1968, 184, 205,
    227, 237–42, 246, 251, 255–56,
    300
Duro override, 237, 251–52, 256
Indian Claims Commission, 64, 283
Indian Claims Commission Act, 64, 71,
    330 n. 224
Indian country
    definition, 376 n. 68
    poverty, 185, 243, 388 n. 270
Indian Gaming Regulatory Act of 1988,
    50, 237, 246–51, 256
*Indian Inmates of Nebraska Penitentiary
    v. Gunter*, 207
Indian law federalism, 39, 57
Indian Reorganization Act of 1934, 130,
    189, 235, 303
Indian Rights Association, 126, 133–34,
    186, 188
Indigenous Peoples, *see also* Indians,
    Native Americans
Indigenous Peoples, definition, 391 n. 1
Infringement test, 59, 214, 216–18
Insular Cases, 149–51, 357 n. 136
Inter-American Commission on Human
    Rights, 277, 281, 284
Inter-American Court of Human Rights,
    277, 280, 281
International Labor Organization (ILO)
    Conventions, 271, 282
International law, 5, 150
    self-determination, 274–80
    trusteeship, 266–69
Inuits, 100–101
Iowa Mutual Ins. v. LaPlante, 233
Ireland, *see* History
Iron Eyes v. Henry, 207
Iroquois Confederacy, 30, 37, 170, 301,
    321 n. 17, 401 n. 53

Jackson, President Andrew, 102–3, 111,
    340 n. 76
Jefferson, President Thomas, 93, 96,
    145–47, 319 n. 75, 336 n. 44
Jennings, Francis, 15, 23
Jerome Commission, 131, 133, 138

Johnson v. McIntosh, 17, 21, 87–89,
    93–101, 112–113, 149–50, 184,
    186, 261, 267, 276
Johnson, Senator Tim, 179
Judiciary Act of 1789, 43, 111

*Kassel v. Consolidated Freightways
    Corp.*, 59
Kiberd, Declan, 346 n. 179
King's Privy Council, 39
Kinship state, 23, 77
Knox, Henry, 101

Land acquisition, 3, 9, 16–22, 87, 93,
    95–96, 140
Le Gris, Chief, 81
Legal pluralism, 234–36, 382 n. 167
Legal realism, 234–35
Lemon v. Kurtzman, 371 n. 144
Lewis and Clark Expedition, 93, 96, 337
    n. 44
Locke, John, 25, 84, 333 n. 279
Lone Wolf v. Hitchcock, 4, 5, 59, 62, 69,
    70, 74, 112, 115, 125, 130, 131–15,
    150, 169, 238, 268–69, 298
Louisiana Purchase, 54, 93, 96, 146–47,
    150
Louisiana Territory, 146–48
Lovelace v. Canada, 276, 395 n. 82
Lumpkin, Wilson, 102, 111, 340 n. 73
Lynch v. Donnelly, 371 n. 145
*Lyng v. Northwest Indian Cemetery Protective
    Association*, 191, 195, 197–99,
    201, 203, 208, 367 n. 68

Mabo v. Queensland, 119, 289–90, 292
Madison, President James, 40, 43, 58, 355
    n. 98
Major Crimes Act, 61, 138, 144, 211, 253,
    352 n. 80, 373 n. 6, 400 n. 30
Manifest destiny, 10, 115–16, 126
Mann, Charles, 317 n. 66, 335 n. 20, 392
    n. 7
Maori, 287–89, 291
Marbury v. Madison, 108
*Mayagna (Sumo) Awas Tingni Community
    v. Nicaragua*, 277, 396 n. 86
*McClanahan v. Arizona State Tax
    Commission*, 59, 62–63, 214–16,
    232, 296, 334 n. 280, 343 n. 133,
    375 n. 41, 384 n. 210

McGrath, Melanie, 339 n. 62, 339 n. 63
McGrath, Thomas, 347 n. 190
Mexican v. Circle Bear, 56, 326 n. 134
Middle East, *see* History
Minnesota v. Mille Lacs Band of Chippewa Indians, 74, 232
Mississippi Band of Choctaw Indians v. Holyfield, 244, 256
Montana v. United States, 67–68, 142, 218–28, 230, 233, 296–97, 300, 353 n. 89, 353 n. 91, 376 n. 64, 376 n. 67
Montoya v. Bolack, 177
Morgan, Thomas, 185
Mormon Church, 148
Morison, Samuel Eliot, 117–18
Morton v. Mancari, 204
Mott, Lucretia, 38
Multicultural change, *see* Treaty

National Bank v. County of Yankton, 148
National Congress of American Indians, 300
National Farmers Union Insurance Companies v. Crow Tribe of Montana, 222–23, 230
National Historic Preservation Act of 1966, 195
National Park Service, 196, 344
Native American, *see* Indian
Native American Church, 197–99, 201, 207, 367 n. 82, 368 n. 85
Naturalization Oath, 160, 162
Navajo Treaty of 1868, 59, 73, 215
Nevada v. Hicks, 226, 228, 233, 300, 353 n. 89, 399 n. 154
New York v. United States, 48, 324 n. 76, 324 n. 86
New Zealand, 259, 284–85, 287–89, 290–93, 395 n. 76, 398 n. 144
New Zealand Maori Council v. Attorney General, 289
Non-Intercourse Act, 20, 59–60, 71, 87–88, 316 n. 49, 334 n. 4
Northwest Ordinance of 1787, 89, 147
Novak, Robert, 179
Nunavut Land Claims Agreement of 1993, 101

Oklahoma Indian Territory, 83, 167
Oliphant v. Suquamish Indian Tribe, 142, 212, 219, 222–23, 228, 230, 251–52, 297, 300
O'Lone v. Estate of Shabazz, 207
Osphal v. Johnson, 175, 360 n. 82

Paine, Thomas, 88, 92
Papal Bull, 25, 94
Parker, Quannah, 133
Pasqualucci, Jo, 280–81
Peace Policy, 185
Penn, William, 81
Pennsylvania v. Union Gas Company, 50, 249–50
People v. Woody, 197, 367 n. 79, 367 n. 80
Peyote, 183, 189, 197–201
Plains Commerce Bank v. Long Family Land and Cattle Co., Inc., 262, 421–22, 428, 569
Plenary power, 46, 137, 145, 148, 243, 250, 253, 297
  criticism of, 352 n. 84
  judicial, 297
Political question doctrine, 70–71, 138, 349 n. 65
Pope Alexander VI, 94
Porter v. Hall, 174
Powell, Father Peter John, 78, 333 n. 262
Preemption, 215–16
  in Indian law, 215
  in purchase of land, 91, 98
Prince v. Massachusetts, 194
Printz v. United States, 48
Proclamation of 1763, 20, 88, 97–99
Prohibition, alcohol, 199
Prucha, Francis Paul, 348 n. 14, 351 n. 75
Public Law 280, 214, 215, 247, 374 n. 24
Pueblo Indian dances, 188

Quakers, 185
Quick Bear v. Leupp, 186

Rakove, Jack, 319 n. 80
Randolph, William, 43
Red Cloud, 73
Reid v. Covert, 66
Religious Freedom Restoration Act, 199, 202, 368 n. 94
Removal Act, 102

Resnik, Judith, 312, 352 n. 84
Revolutionary War, 3, 9, 20–21, 27,
    30–31, 39, 49, 87–89, 95, 99,
    100
Richter, Daniel, 14, 318 n. 69
Robertson, Lindsay, 98–100, 338 n. 52,
    338 n. 57
Robertson, Pat, 179
Roosevelt, President Theodore, 131, 186
Roth, Philip, 347 n. 190
Rousseau, Jean-Jacques, 12
Royal Proclamation of 1763, see
    Proclamation of 1763

Sacred pipe, 78, 206
Sacred sites, 189–97
Sahlins, Marshall, 26
Said, Edward, 122
Santa Clara Pueblo v. Martinez, 239, 246,
    256
Sargeant, John, 103
Savagery, 24–25, 118, 186
    noble savage, 26
Scott v. Sandford, see Dred Scott Case
Self-determination, 5, 171, 222, 270, 272,
    274–80, 282–83, 291–92, 295,
    301–2, 350 n. 72
    domestic law, 261
    international law, 274–80
Seminole Tribe of Florida v. Florida, 50,
    249–50, 256
Sequoyah v. Tennessee Valley Authority,
    190–91
Seventh Day Adventists, 190
Sherbert v. Verner, 365 n. 42
Sitting Bull, 188
Six Nations speech (1775), 30
Skibine, Alex Tallchief, 302, 402 n. 54
Slavery, 113, 147–48, 165, 170, 185, 309
Smith, Adam, 11
Sosa v. Alvarez-Machain, 230
South Carolina v. Katzenbach, 178
South Dakota v. Bourland, 224, 233, 300
Sovereignty, see Tribal Sovereignty
Springer, William, 134
Stamp Act, 36
Standing Bear (Ponca), 167
Standing Deer v. Carlson, 207
Standing Bear, Luther, 344 n. 158
Stanton, Elizabeth Cady, 38

Strate v. A-1 Contractors, 223–25, 233, 300
Suk, Julie Chi-hye, 312
Sun Dance, 187–88, 364 n. 29
Sweat Lodge Ceremony, 207

Talton v. Mayes, 184, 238
Teller, Henry, 127, 186
Terra nullius, 94, 290
Teterud v. Gillman, 206
Trade and Intercourse Act, see Non-
    Intercourse Act
Trade, see Commerce
Treaty, 63
    abrogation, 66, 75–76, 137–39
    agreement substitute, 65
    Article II of Constitution, 63, 66, 68,
        253, 308
    canons of construction, 70–71, 73–74,
        330 n. 213
    cultural covenants, 77
    enumerated rights model,
        67–68
    multicultural change, 14
    protocol, 79, 81
    reserved rights model, 67–68
    supreme law of the land, 40, 43, 66,
        69
    treaty federalism, 82, 303
    treatymaking, 64–65, 308
    specific
        Treaty of Dancing Rabbit Creek, 157,
            159
        Treaty of Guadalupe Hidalgo, 125,
            159
        Treaty of Holston, 104, 109–10
        Treaty of Hopewell, 104, 106, 109,
            264
        Treaty of Medicine Lodge, 131
        Treaty of New Echota, 83
        Treaty of Paris, 19–21, 94
        Treaty of Waitangi, 287, 289
        Treaty with the Cherokees, 101, 156
        Treaty with the Choctaws, 358 n. 8
        Treaty with the Delawares, 158
        Treaty with the Sioux Indians, 358
            n. 14
        Treaty with the Wyandotts, 158
Tribal sovereignty, 4–6, 34, 36, 39, 46,
    50, 57
    models, 5

Tribal Sovereignty and Economic
    Enhancement Act, 300
Tribal Sovereignty Protection Initiative,
    300
Tribe, Laurence, 47, 313 n. 6, 323 n. 52,
    325 n. 109
Trujillo v. Garley, 174
Trust relationship, 112–13, 136, 139
    guardian-ward, 105
Trusteeship, 266–69
Tucker Act, 71
Turner v. Safley, 207

United Nations
    Charter, 270, 275, 282
    Declaration on the Rights of
        Indigenous Peoples, 274, 279,
        291, 395 n. 75, 395 n. 76
    Human Rights Committee, 276
United States ex rel. Mackey v. Coxe, 54
*United States v. Thirty Eight (38) Golden
    Eagles*, 201
United States v. Antoine, 201, 202
United States v. Celestine, 358 n. 20
United States v. Darby, 48
United States v. Dion, 69, 75–76, 202, 329
    n. 198, 349 n. 65
United States v. Hardman, 201–2, 204
United States v. Kagama, 61–63, 138–39,
    141, 144, 149, 211, 238, 253,
    296–97
United States v. Lara, 63, 150, 230, 251–56,
    296, 299–301, 391 n. 328
United States v. Lopez, 41–43, 63, 298–99,
    400 n. 30
United States v. Mitchell, 394 n. 49
United States v. Morrison, 42–43, 63,
    298–99
United States v. Nice, 169
United States v. Sioux Nation of Indians,
    70, 75, 116–19

United States v. Top Sky, 201
United States v. Washington, 23
United States v. Wheeler, 45, 230, 252, 324
    n. 71, 357 n. 140, 373 n. 6
United States v. Winans, 67, 74
United States v. Winters, 67

Vattel, Emmerich de, 260, 265
Violence Against Women Act, 42, 55,
    299
Vitoria, Francisco de, 94, 260
Voting Rights Act, 178, 180, 360 n. 97

*Washington v. Confederated Tribes of
    Colville Indian Reservation*, 217,
    233, 296
Washington, President George, 82, 88,
    92, 99, 101, 401 n. 53
Weaver v. Jago, 206
Weber, Max, 11
Weil, Simone, 115
White Buffalo Calf Woman, 78
White Mountain Apache Tribe v. Bracker,
    213–18, 233
White, G. Edward, 335 n. 25, 392 n. 23
Wilkinson, Charles, 213, 351 n. 77
Williams v. Lee, 59, 213–18, 225, 227, 232
Williams, Robert, 77, 81, 317 n. 67, 336
    n. 33
Williams, Roger, 18, 37
Wilson, James, 35, 43, 319 n. 80
Winthrop, John, 17
Wirt, William, 103
Wood, Gordon, 314 n. 9, 318 n. 75
Worcester v. Georgia, 29, 61, 87, 100,
    101, 108–12, 114, 214, 215, 261,
    263–66
Worthen, Kevin, 202–3
Wounded Knee, 188

Yava, Albert, 128